HOMOSEXUALITY RE-EXAMINED

HOMOSEXUALITY RE-EXAMINED

D.J. West

Duckworth

First published in 1977 by
Gerald Duckworth & Co. Ltd
The Old Piano Factory
43 Gloucester Crescent, London NW1
Original edition (as *Homosexuality*) 1955,
second edition 1960, reprinted 1962, 1963,
1965, third edition 1968
This fourth edition (as *Homosexuality
Re-examined*) revised, augmented and reset

ISBN 0 7156 0935 1

Filmset by Specialised Offset Services Ltd, Liverpool
and printed and bound in Great Britain by
REDWOOD BURN LIMITED
Trowbridge & Esher

Contents

PREFACE

Since I first wrote the book *Homosexuality* over twenty years ago an enormous amount has been published on the subject. In order to present an up-to-date review of current information and opinion I have had to write a different and much enlarged work. As before, my aim has been to describe the available observations, as well as the very varied opinions and interpretations, as fully and fairly as possible, but of course the book will reflect changes in my own judgments and thinking just as much as changes in the state of knowledge.

A generation ago the word homosexuality was best avoided in polite conversation, or referred to in muted terms appropriate to a dreaded and scarcely .mentionable disease. Even some well-educated people were hazy about exactly what it meant. Adults privately troubled by homosexual feelings might believe themselves to be rare freaks, while youngsters who indulged in erotic games with members of their own sex could do so blissfully unaware they might be considered deviants. The Kinsey reports, the parliamentary debates on homosexual legislation, the rise of permissiveness in books and films, and the advent of Gay Liberation, have forced public attention. Official attitudes have changed remarkably in twenty years. When my first book about homosexuality appeared copies were confiscated as obscene by Australian customs officials and the American distributor, finding the title *Homosexuality* too blatant, bowdlerised it to *The Other Man*. Since those days, wilful refusal to acknowledge the importance of the subject has become less common, but public discussion has not always produced enlightenment. The origins of homosexual orientation, and the problems to which it may give rise, remain matters of controversy. As readers will rapidly see for themselves, a great deal more research will have to be carried out before the main issues are solved.

I have tried to take into account modern surveys based upon ordinary homosexuals and lesbians recruited from the community rather than from populations of clinic patients, who may present a biassed picture. I have also taken note of the large body of literature produced by the homosexual community itself, as well as the many critical comments received as a result of my previous writings. Recent publications include some extensive bibliographies (Homosexual Information Center, 1972: Legg and Underwood, 1967; Parker, 1971;

Sharma and Rudy, 1970; Weinberg and Bell, 1972; American Library Ass., 1974) which it would be superfluous to duplicate. Interest among medical psychologists and other professionals has increased to such an extent that a specialist *Journal of Homosexuality* (New York: Haworth Press) has come into being. The list of references in this book has accordingly been selected, not for comprehensive coverage, but to help readers follow up specific points in the text. Increased freedom of expression on sexual matters has brought forth a spate of books written by self-declared homosexuals, as well as a number of magazines frankly aimed at a homosexual readership. These sources provide very detailed accounts of the homosexual way of life, and the subculture associated with it. A great deal that was formerly somewhat esoteric information, is now well-documented common knowledge; so this aspect can now be written about more didactically than before, without fear of contradiction.

D.J.W.

CHAPTER ONE

Definitions

1. *Homosexual behaviour and homosexual persons*

Both men and women are liable to homosexuality; the word has nothing to do with maleness. Homosexuality and heterosexuality, which mean literally 'same' and 'other' sex, are terms needed to distinguish between erotic attraction to one's own or to the opposite sex. The use of the word homosexual as a label for persons is ambiguous. Few people pass through life without at some stage experiencing homosexual feelings, even if only slight and fleeting. Among adolescents such feelings are so common that many authorities regard a homosexual phase as a normal part of development. Many adults with active heterosexual interests also have pronounced homosexual inclinations. Moreover, an individual's sexual preference may change considerably over time. A further complication arises because sexual preference and sexual behaviour do not always correspond. For instance, a homosexual wife may allow her husband intercourse from duty rather than pleasure, while a male prisoner may behave homosexually only when denied access to women. By imagining themselves in different and more exciting encounters, some people are able to respond sexually in situations that do not at all correspond to their true preferences. Others, especially young males, may be quickly aroused by simple genital manipulation, no matter what the age or gender of the stimulator. In short, each individual occupies a unique position in regard to the strength, direction and stability of his sexual behaviour and sexual fantasy. The attempt to categorize all humanity into two mutually exclusive and contrasting groups of homosexuals and heterosexuals, a form of 'them' and 'us', besides being ethically and politically dubious, produces misleading over-simplifications.

The term homosexual ought therefore to be applied with caution. In this book it is used to describe persons whose erotic concerns are quite persistently and predominantly directed towards members of their own sex. Among this minority there are many who can obtain no erotic stimulus whatever from the opposite sex, and may even experience a positive revulsion at the idea of heterosexual contact. Being thus forced to seek sexual satisfaction exclusively with their own kind, they are accurately described as 'obligatory' homosexuals. Many obligatory male homosexuals never dare to attempt sexual intercourse with women because they fear they would prove impotent. This fear is a common complaint among the male homosexuals who approach psychiatrists wanting help to achieve a change in their sexual orientation.

Persons who ordinarily prefer heterosexuality, and behave homosexually only occasionally, or only when debarred from access to the opposite sex, scarcely merit the term homosexual. They are sometimes called 'facultative' homosexuals, because they indulge only when it suits them, and not because they are incapable of enjoying heterosexual outlets. Persons who respond strongly to both sexes, choosing sometimes the one and sometimes the other, are best called bisexuals or ambisexuals. That does not mean they show no discrimination whatsoever. Often the quality or strength of the attraction differs according to whether they are with a male or female sex partner.

Overt homosexuals are individuals who are well aware of their sexual disposition. Usually they acknowledge it freely when among friends they can trust. Either from choice or, more often, from lack of opportunity, they can be chaste, that is non-practising, just as heterosexuals can be celibate. Some guilt-ridden homosexuals, however, struggle to be more than chaste. They feel their inclinations shameful, and so they try to suppress them altogether and to deny ever having experienced them. These repressed homosexuals are apt to condemn most violently in others the tendencies they feel so loath to admit in themselves. Even overt homosexuals, to avoid the condemnation of employers, workmates and relatives, often pretend to disapprove of other homosexuals while pursuing their own desires in secret. Men who never mix in homosexual groups for fear of being compromised, limiting their sexual outlets to brief, furtive contacts with anonymous strangers, are derisorily referred to as 'closet queens' in American homosexual slang.

Persons of predominantly homosexual orientation, being in a minority, are undeniably deviant in a statistical sense, like the left-handed. They also deviate in the sense that their conduct breaks an important rule of Western culture, a rule that has been hallowed by religious doctrine and institutionalised in the criminal law of many states. The belief that homosexuals in general are peculiar in other respects than their sexual orientation has not been established, and is in no way implied by the term sexual deviation as used in this book. It has been said that homosexuals are apt to be weak, immature or neurotic, to lack moral sense and to be unreliable and unhappy people. Evidence on these points, to be discussed later, does not favour any such sweeping generalisations.

Being in a minority is not the same as being inferior. Some Gentiles look upon Jews as their social inferiors, but really they have no more justification for that than have Jews to think themselves superior to the rest of humanity. The assumption that a heterosexual orientation is somehow superior to a homosexual orientation no longer passes unchallenged. Increasing numbers, especially among young social radicals, not only declare openly their allegiance to the homosexual way of life, but proclaim that they see nothing sick, or immoral, or inferior about their particular erotic preferences. They may be different, but in their own estimation they are at least equal to heterosexuals. They argue that the tradition and prejudice that causes them to be treated as second-class citizens has no more justification than the tradition that maintains the inferior status of women and blacks. This point of view rests upon a system of values which seems to conflict with notions about the key role of heterosexual mating and the nuclear family in the preservation of the species and the maintenance of valuable cultural standards. The moral and social significance of homosexuality, and the question whether it should be considered a serious personal defect, a harmless variant, or possibly even a social asset, cannot be resolved by abstract argument. The probable origins of heterosexual and homosexual orientation, the prospects of modifying or controlling orientation according to the wishes of the individual or the needs of the community, and the social effects of the existence of a non-conforming sexual minority, have all to be taken into account. It is the aim of this book to consider this factual background as far as possible on its merits before venturing upon global value judgments or advocating particular social policies.

Some of the more popular notions about homosexuals, for instance their supposed predilection for unusually disgusting methods of making love, are both unflattering and to some extent misconceived. Apart from the limitation that genital copulation is not available to them, homosexual couples differ little from heterosexual couples in the methods they employ to stimulate each other. Kissing, bodily fondling, manual masturbation, mouth-genital contact, and even anal intercourse are by no means the prerogative of homosexuals. After generations of disapproval of techniques of excitation considered 'perverse' or 'deviant', Western authorities are beginning to doubt that variety in sexual behaviour is either unhealthy or immoral. They now find virtue in the thinking of oriental philosophers, as exemplified in the Kama Sutra, who see no contradiction between the search for spiritual fulfilment and the search for erotic fulfilment. The artificial conflict between the two seems to have been largely generated and promulgated by Judaic traditions and their Christian and Islamic derivatives. The modern approach, exemplified by a recent treatise on oral sex (Legman, 1969), inclines towards the view that anything goes so long as it is done by heterosexuals. A recent guide to love making, edited by the well known British authority Dr Alex Comfort (1972), suggests that nearly every couple tries anal intercourse once, and some women find it gives them intenser feelings than the normal route. The man is advised that the quick, virile thrust effective for vaginal entry is unsuited to the anal route which, if pain is to be avoided, requires gentle, steady pressure with a well-lubricated penis and a slow initial penetration. The book warns that too much vigour on the man's part can cause injury, and that the presence of haemorrhoids will render the process painful even for experienced women.

Pleasurable sensation is a universal response to rhythmic friction of the penis or its feminine analogue, the clitoris. Otherwise, the bodily zones erotically sensitive to touch, or stimulating to vision, vary between individuals according to their social learning and traditions. Fashion in clothes plays a part. A reading of nineteenth-century novels suggests that the sight of ankles peeping from below long skirts was peculiarly exciting to the Victorian male. The American emphasis on large breasts in female sex idols suggests a different preoccupation. The stimuli capable of producing sexual climax are truly multifarious. This is because orgasm is largely a cerebral phenomenon, which may be inhibited or facilitated by all kinds of learned associations and situational stimuli. Orgasm involves far more than just a simple local reflex based on nerve paths to and from the genitals. Indeed, once the capacity for orgasm is well established, sexual climax may be achieved without any genital manipulation, for instance by watching pornographic displays, or by stimulation of the breasts. The variety and complexity of possible techniques of sexual stimulation is a human characteristic not peculiar to homosexuals. Among heterosexuals, however, cultural and biological pressures give vaginal copulation an obvious first place among all possible methods of sexual enjoyment. Lacking this clearly defined first choice, homosexuals have more reason to experiment with a wider range of sexual techniques.

The notion that most male homosexuals behave effeminately and most female homosexuals (lesbians) are aggressively masculine dies hard, but as a result of survey findings modern authorities now recognise this to be true only of a minority (Bancroft, 1972). Many male homosexuals have typically masculine interests, attitudes and mannerisms and like to assert their maleness with clothes that accentuate the masculine physique. They enjoy a firmly masculine self-image or 'gender identity', dislike being thought effeminate because of their homosexual inclinations, and would be horrified to be offered the possibility of surgical interference to alter the sex of their genitals. The converse holds true for many lesbians.

The subject of gender identity has come to the fore in recent years as a result of the pioneer work of Hampson and Money at Johns Hopkins medical research centre and the establishment of a gender identity research clinic at the University of California at Los Angeles (Green and Money, 1969). From the moment of birth a baby's anatomical sex determines the reactions and expectations of his parents and the style of upbringing. By the age of three a normal infant is well aware of his status as boy or girl, and acts accordingly. This sense of identity, or sexual self-image, is more basic, and certainly less alterable, than erotic preference, which becomes manifest only years later.

Disturbances of gender identity (gender dysphoria) are relatively rare. Sometimes they have an obvious basis in physical intersexuality (hermaphroditism). These are genital deformities or bodily maldevelopments which obscure genetic sex. Understandably, babies born with such deformities, whose parents are unsure about their true sex, may develop doubts or confusion about their sexual identity. Usually, however, if they are reared firmly and consistently as either boy or girl, they develop the corresponding gender identity and erotic preferences, regardless of their true genetic or anatomical sex.

Cross-sex gender identification, known as transsexuality, can also occur in individuals of apparently normal physical appearance and genetic endowment. In a typical case the affected person, usually a male, develops a firm conviction that he should have been born female. 'He' feels 'himself' to be a woman cruelly trapped inside an unsuitable male body, and 'his' dearest wish is to have 'his' female identity accepted. To this end 'he' will agitate for surgical removal of the unwanted genitals and for change of name and civil status. Most male transsexuals are much more interested in cross dressing and 'passing' as women than in having sexual relations with men. They particularly dislike being classified as male homosexuals because in their own estimation they are not men at all.

A minority of homosexuals do suffer to a certain degree from disturbance of gender identity. In some cases it amounts to no more than an inner feeling of dissatisfaction or incompetence when performing the social or occupation roles expected of a' man or woman. Sometimes the disturbance is more overt. The effeminate male homosexual (queen) who advertises himself with falsetto voice, make-up, and girlish mannerisms is only too well known. So also is the hearty, gruff-voiced 'butch' lesbian (bulldyke). Both types usually enjoy dressing up in clothes of the opposite sex. Male 'drag queens' will spend hours arranging coiffeur, make-up, perfume, bras, dress and accessories. Behaviour of this sort is not always due to gender role confusion. Male homosexuals may use 'drag' for motives other than feminine self-expression, for instance to attract sex partners or to win acceptance at 'gay' homosexual parties. Cross dressing (transvestism) may also be practiced by heterosexual males, who obtain a fetishistic sexual excitement from contact with garments that are associated with females. The male homosexual, however, is not excited by the clothes themselves, but by what the clothes may do for him in projecting a feminine image, or in attracting the attention of other males.

Noticeable gender confusion is sufficiently prevalent among homosexuals to have given rise to the slang terms 'butch' and 'queen'. which are used as labels for sub-groups with predominantly male and female identifications respectively. In the context of sexual behaviour, the 'butch' male homosexual is expected to want to be the dominant party in seduction and to make the active or insertor role in anal intercourse or fellatio (penis sucking). The butch lesbian may even want to use an artificial penis (dildo). Of course numerous factors other than gender role playing influence the choice of love-making techniques. Many homosexuals, regardless of their social stance, are happily 'versatile' in bed, switching from active to passive according to mood, or at least sufficiently pliant to change roles to suit the wishes of a favoured sexual partner. The passive role in anal intercourse requires practice in relaxation before it becomes easy and painless, so this technique is usually developed only by the more experienced. Ageing males of dwindling attractiveness may take to the passive role as a last resort in the search for a sexual partner, or alternatively they may be obliged to forgo anal pleasures on account of the various painful medical conditions that affect that part of the body.

Some bisexual men who enjoy homosexual practices hate to think of themselves as 'queer', so they try to preserve a self-image of aggressively masculine heterosexuality by insisting on always taking the insertor role. This enables them to maintain that they are merely using the male partner as a substitute for a woman, and hence to deny their homosexual tendencies. Since emotional involvement with a man seems unfitting in a lover of women only, they may further reassure themselves by treating their partner roughly, avoiding any show of affection towards him, and by reacting with violence should he try to reverse roles. This kind of approach to homosexual relationships is quite common among professional male prostitutes ('hustlers' or 'rent boys') and among some imprisoned criminals.

The boyish hero worship and girlish crushes so common at adolescence reveal a diametrically opposite attitude. Instead of sex without affection one finds affection without sex, intense or romantic attachments that stop short of overt love-making. In adult life platonic attachments to members of the same sex occur more obviously among women than among men, possibly because displays of affectionate intimacy between women attract less social disapproval than would similar conduct between men. Unless the individual concerned is actually aware of an underlying erotic attraction, emotional attachments without sexual expression scarcely deserve the label homosexual. Too liberal use of the concept of platonic homosexuality risks confusing ordinary friendships with homosexual love. Nevertheless, the fact that love life and sex life are not always congruent is relevant to an understanding of sexual attitudes. Psychoanalysts have often pointed this out in relation to the Madonna complex, which obliges some heterosexual men to pay for impersonal sex with women prostitutes because they can obtain no erotic satisfaction from women they love and admire. Some heterosexually erotic individuals seem incapable of loving the persons they desire sexually. They expend their time, interest and emotion exclusively with friends of their own sex, becoming concerned with their marriage partners only at bed time.

These introductory descriptions of varied patterns of sexual life, besides helping to define and illustrate some essential technical terms, are intended to emphasise the different factors in sexuality which must be taken into account if the deceptively simple concept of homosexuality is to be properly explored. Four aspects have to be considered, anatomical sex differentiation, which is evident from the genitals at birth, psychological gender identity, which develops in infancy, erotic preferences, which manifest later, and capacity to enjoy a love relationship with other persons of appropriate age and sex. In normal heterosexuals all four aspects of sexuality develop in harmony, but among sexual deviants one or more of these four aspects are out of tune with the rest. The essential criterion of homosexuality is an erotic preference for the same sex. In most homosexuals, gender identity and anatomical sexuality are in accord, but out of keeping with both erotic preference and love relationships.

2. *Theories of homosexuality*

Knowledge about homosexuality and its causes remains in an uncertain state, and a diversity of observations and opinions will need to be reviewed. In order not to lose sight of the important issues, and so that the relevance of the details to come will be apparent, one or two of the major conflicts of opinion will be summarised here. According to one school of thought, exclusive homosexuals (sometimes referred to as true inverts as opposed to casual indulgers in vice) form a sort of third sex possessed of an inborn physical predisposition that sets them apart from the rest of humanity. The anomaly may reside in their genes, their endocrine glands, or in some neurological peculiarity, but whatever the cause their sexual condition seems predestined from birth and unalterable by any known therapy. The only reasonable policy, both for the persons affected and for the community as a whole, would seem to be to accept the state of affairs as inevitable and to try to adjust to it without fuss.

This way of thinking was once very popular among homosexuals themselves, since it relieved them of all personal responsibility for their deviation, but it has fallen into temporary disrepute, owing to the failure to discover convincing evidence of any underlying physical anomaly in the majority of cases. Recent reports of abnormal hormone levels in homosexuals, and experiments suggesting that hormone disturbances soon after birth can induce permanent reversals of sex behaviour in rats, have led to renewed interest in these physical explanations of homosexual predisposition. Even so, the weight of contemporary scientific opinion is against such explanations, emphasising instead the great pliability of human sexual instinct and the diffuse, undifferentiated quality of early erotic feelings. Unlike Sleeping Beauty, real life children have no built-in mechanism ready to spring into full operation the moment the first Prince comes in sight. The use of the genitals for social interaction in the sexual sphere is a learned skill governed by social rules, just as much as the use of language for verbal communications (Gagnon and Simon, 1973). The development of acceptable sexual behaviour depends upon cultural indoctrination. The necessary learning processes begin in earliest infancy. According to psychoanalysts sexual deviations due to faulty learning arise early in life in the context of the intimate and emotionally charged interaction between infant and parents. Parents provide the child with a foretaste and a rehearsal of all subsequent personal relationships. Parents' confusions and guilt about their own sex lives are communicated to the infant, inspiring all kinds of fears, inhibitions and conflicts about sexual feelings. Psychoanalysts stress the symbolic meanings of sex to each individual, the fantasy links with power struggle, submission, castration and incest. These anxiety-provoking associations cause some children to turn against heterosexuality and take refuge in alternative forms of sexual expression, notably homosexuality.

The social learning theories favoured by academic psychologists run along somewhat different lines. They stress simpler, more direct processes of reward and punishment gradually conditioning young persons into sexual conformity. They agree that the early years are important, for these cover critical phases of development when conditioning occurs most readily and establishes itself most indelibly. They recognise, however, that sexual learning takes place not only in contacts with parents, but also during social intercourse among peers, and through general educative influences. They therefore give weight to conditioning experiences in later years, particularly at adolescence, which may either reinforce or counteract what has gone before. In contrast, the psychoanalysts tend to place almost exclusive emphasis on the early years in the parental home.

While both schools of thought agree that homosexuality is an acquired condition, the psychoanalytic standpoint has gloomier implications than that of other learning theories. If sexual disorientation arises from early and profound disturbances in the mother-child relationship, it is likely to be associated with all kinds of personality problems and to be difficult to alter. Many psychoanalysts believe that a homosexual orientation develops only in disturbed personalities. This view is contested not only by homophile writers, but also by psychologists, who have applied tests to samples of homosexuals without finding evidence of any great neurotic tendency. On the other hand, if sexual learning can occur later in life, in situations that do not have much bearing upon personality development, there is less reason to expect homosexuals to have other peculiarities in addition to their erotic preference.

If the crucial sexual learning processes take place in infancy, later influences playing a minor part, then overt sexual behaviour, commencing with the approach of puberty, merely unfolds pre-established dispositions. On this view, adolescent homosexual experience, and incidents of seduction, are unimportant as determinants of adult sexual orientation. Homosexual practices continue into adult life and become an exclusive sexual preoccupation only if the heterosexual channel has been blocked in infancy. On the other hand, if conditioning exerts a significant effect even in later years, then an exclusive homosexual has some prospect of learning to respond heterosexually (or a heterosexual to respond homosexually) if appropriate learning situations occur or can be provided. Exponents of 'behaviour therapy' firmly believe in the reality of the prospect of conversion to a different sexual orientation. Most psychoanalysts are less optimistic about the results of treatment to convert homosexuals into heterosexuals, since they believe that deep-rooted disturbances in the capacity to respond emotionally to others have to be sorted out before any change in sexual habits can be expected.

The professional training of psychologists and psychiatrists alerts them to the personal shortcomings of non-conformist individuals, but does less to urge them to examine the validity of the ideals which define social success and failure. Clinical authorities have tended to adopt the conventional wisdom that a homosexual orientation is 'unnatural' and socially undesirable and that homosexuals stand in need of treatment to rectify their unfortunate deficiency. Social anthropologists, who study the varying norms of different cultures, have every reason to question the reasons for labelling a substantial minority of the population psychologically, criminally or medically abnormal. The civilisations of ancient Greece and some of the civilisations of the Orient had a vastly different and generally more favourable attitude towards homosexual behaviour, at least among males. Times might change. Until recently, Western authorities denounced masturbators as sinful degenerates and potential madmen. Today masturbation is widely accepted as an ordinary, non-problematic, and often necessary sexual outlet. Might not a similar attitude develop in regard to homosexuality? Some sociologists believe that the present culture, by seeking to categorise individuals as either 'normal' or 'queer', forces those who behave homosexually into a class apart, thus exaggerating their deviance. In a truly permissive environment bisexuality might thrive but exclusive homosexuality would probably decrease.

The point of view that regards homosexual problems as a manifestation of cultural intolerance rather than of individual maladjustment receives warm support from 'homophile' societies and 'gay liberation' organisations. These are pressure groups set up to serve the interests of homosexual men and women. They try to combat legislative and social discrimination, and by educative propaganda to promote a favourable image of the homosexual way of life. They argue that a love mate of the same sex is the natural choice of a substantial minority of the population. Provided the heterosexual majority does not interfere or persecute, homosexuals can lead a full, healthy and happy existence. They deplore the idea that homosexuals are immoral or sick or in need of any cure.

Arguments about the 'naturalness' or 'desirability' of homosexual

behaviour are incomplete without some consideration of other forms
of sexual variation, the origins of which may well be similar to those of
homosexuality. Exhibitionism (a compulsion to expose the genitals to
strangers), fetishism (erotic arousal from objects rather than persons),
and paedophilia (a concentration of sexual interest upon small
children) are three of the commonest. All of these affect males rather
than females, but sado-masochism (a need to give or to receive pain to
obtain sexual satisfaction) affects both. On the face of it, these
deviations seem more anomalous than erotic attraction to the same
sex, and more obviously a product of faulty sexual learning.
Exhibitionism and fetishism occur almost exclusively in men of
heterosexual orientation, but paedophilia and sado-masochism occur
among both heterosexual and homosexuals. Indeed, a reputation for
child molestation is one of the least enviable features of the popular
stereotype of the male homosexual.

Understandably, the homophile organisation extend no official
welcome to these less acceptable forms of sexual unorthodoxy, since
homosexuality itself might so easily be classed among them as just one
more example of sexual maldevelopment. One medical writer,
however, has pointed out the injustice of toleration for one form of
deviation only, arguing that the other erotic minorities are also
relatively harmless and should be allowed facilities to satisfy their
respective needs (Ullerstam, 1966). Homosexuality, however, differs
in one essential respect from most other sexual deviations. Like
heterosexual relations, homosexual intercourse permits mutual
fulfilment and sometimes a positive love relationship between the
partners in a sexual union, whereas deviations which oblige men to
seek sexual release without benefit of a willing or fully responsive
partner inevitably leave important psychological and social needs
unsatisfied.

The first chapter has given a brief outline of the scope of the
phenomena under review and some of the issues to which they give
rise. Subsequent chapters provide more details, discuss tentative
theories as to causes, and lead up to an examination of social and
legal issues. Undue preoccupation with causes has been criticised as
an unprofitable academic exercise calculated to distract attention
from the need to deal with situations as they exist. Causal
considerations will not be neglected, however, because this author still
believes them to be important in the formulation of moral attitudes
and social policy.

CHAPTER TWO

The Development of Homosexual Behaviour

1. *Incidence of homosexual behaviour*

From the scientific standpoint, the origins of heterosexual attraction and of homosexual inclinations are equally mysterious and equally in need of investigation. The main source of information on the natural history of sexual preferences derives from adults' recollections of the onset and development of their own erotic interests and sexual habits from childhood onwards. Of course individual memories, especially on sensitive events dating back to early childhood, cannot be expected to be accurate, and the descriptions that are volunteered will not reveal the whole truth, but by judicious and confidential questioning of large numbers of persons of different ages and both sexes some useful information emerges. The two massive Kinsey reports (Kinsey *et al.*, 1948; 1953), the first dealing with males and the second with females, are still the best and most comprehensive inquiries of this kind available.

Kinsey and his collaborators studied a large and hopefully representative cross section of the white population of the United States. Elaborate precautions were taken to ensure confidentiality. Interviewers were specially trained to probe delicate topics and to detect inconsistency or evasion. Although they depended upon people volunteering to answer questions, they used such persuasive methods that in many situations few of those approached actually refused. They concentrated their attention upon relatively objective matters, actual behaviour rather than emotional feeling or subjective fantasy. They attempted a form of sexual accountancy. They wanted to find out the frequency of sexual outlets (orgasms) in their subjects, and the incidence of the various kinds of sexual behaviour by which people achieved their orgasms.

Kinsey and his colleages checked their incidence figures in a variety of ways. They were acutely aware of the danger of lies, suppressions and exaggerations. The interviewers were familiar with the slang terms and mode of life associated with different sexual habits. A deliberate cheat would be likely to give himself away with inconsistent answers to the many inter-related questions fired at him in the course of the interview. The Kinsey workers tackled the problem of bias in the selection of subjects for interview by approaching whole groups, such as college classes or all the occupants of a particular lodging house, and making a special effort to prevail upon every member of the group to cooperate. The statistics from these complete groups, and from near-complete groups, were much the same as the figures from the total sample. 'Retakes' of case histories from the same subjects after a lapse of years, and comparisons between the incidence figures obtained by different interviewers, confirmed the substantial reliability of the data collection methods. Where possible external checks on the subjects' truthfulness and accuracy were made, which confirmed the validity of the findings. For instance, recollections of the age at which pubertal changes occurred agreed with the results of direct observation and measurement. The statements of married couples were compared one with the other. Substantial agreement emerged between the versions given by men and women as to the incidence of activity involving both sexes. The incidence of homosexual practices was scrutinised with special care. When the incidences reported by subjects of different age, geographical location, religion and education were compared, the overall percentages were found to be surprisingly consistent throughout. Of course the Kinsey reports attracted many criticisms of detail (Cochran *et al.*, 1954; Hyam and Sheatsley, 1954), and the failure to explore subjective aspects clearly lessened their value (Bergler, 1948; Kubie, 1948), but the essential results concerning the incidence of different forms of behaviour, and especially of homosexuality, have never been seriously challenged.

Kinsey's incidence figures for homosexual behaviour are so important and relevant they will bear quoting yet again. '37 per cent of the total male population has at least some overt homosexual experience to the point of orgasm between adolescence and old age.' The orgasm experience of '13 per cent of the population has more of the homosexual than the heterosexual for at least three years between the ages 15 and 55', and '8 per cent of the males are exclusively homosexual for at least three years between 16 and 55'. Finally, '4 per cent of white males are exclusively homosexual throughout their lives after the onset of adolescence'.

The incidence figures for females were much smaller, and comparisons were complicated by the fact that women who were conscious of homoerotic arousal and engaged in overt sexual contact did not necessarily achieve orgasm by that means. Kinsey found that, by age forty-five, 13 per cent of women had had overt homosexual contacts leading to orgasm, although double that number had experienced erotic responses in homosexual situations. Homosexual 'contacts which had proceeded to orgasm had occurred in about a third as many females as males. Moreover, compared with the males, there were only a half to a third of the females who were, in any age period, primarily or exclusively homosexual.' Furthermore, the maintenance of exclusively homosexual contacts over a long period of years was far rarer among women than men. On the other hand, fidelity in homosexual contacts was a feminine characteristic, affairs with one or two women only being the general rule. In contrast, many of Kinsey's homosexual males had been highly promiscuous, some of them describing scores or hundreds of different sexual partners.

2. Onset of erotic feelings and preferences in males

Adolescence is a period of rapid skeletal growth, swift maturing of genital size and function (shown by the onset of ejaculation in the male and menstruation in the female), and the development of secondary sexual characteristics (female breasts, male voice, female pubic hair, and male pubic and facial hair). In males these physical changes come on rather abruptly, usually between the ages of 11 and 14, but take four years to reach full completion. The appearance of pubic hair may precede the onset of ejaculation, which in turn may precede the change of voice. In girls, the growth spurt and appearance of pubic hair begin a year or more before the average age of onset of male puberty. Adolescent female changes are usually completed some two years ahead of those of the average boy.

The bodily changes of adolescence herald an upsurge of physical excitability, but sexual curiosity, sexual fantasy and erotic sensations manifest very much earlier (Strain, 1948). The Kinsey research confirmed once and for all that the capacity for erotic experience and orgasm develops long before the physical changes of puberty. This point has been largely overlooked because the cultural conventions of Western society carefully shield young children from sexual stimulation. In his well-known study of sexual life among the natives of the Trobriand Islands, Malinowski (1929) observed that children in that society were left very much to their own devices as far as sex was concerned. In consequence, from an early age the children indulged in genital manipulation and a variety of erotic pastimes, which their parents looked upon as normal play. The younger children received practical example and direct instruction in sexual stimulation from slightly older companions. Girls were thought to be ready for sexual amusement from the time they first began to wear a fibre skirt at the age of 4 or 5. In some primitive communities adults fondle children sexually as casually as we might stroke their hair, and in some places actually masturbate children as a method of pacifying them (Davenport, 1965). In the opinion of some well known authorities (Money and Ehrhardt, 1972, p.144) the straightforward attitude towards nudity and copulatory play taken by such tribes as the Yolngu of Arnhem Land leaves the young with no confusion about their reproductive and sexual roles, and probably accounts for the low incidence of sexual deviation in these less inhibited cultures.

In the male sex, some degree of spontaneous penile erection occurs very frequently in infancy and can be seen even in small babies. The response occurs during fear, anger or excitement, and does not necessarily have sexual significance. However, an unmistakable sexual orgasm in response to genital stimulation has been observed in male infants a year old, and can be quite readily induced in many boys of five or six years. As described by Kinsey (1948, p.177): 'A fretful babe quiets down under initial sexual stimulation, is distracted from other activities, begins rhythmic pelvic thrusts, becomes tense as climax approaches, is thrown into convulsive action, often with violent arm and leg movements ... After climax the child loses erection quickly and subsides into the calm and peace that typically follows adult orgasm.' These particulars were obtained from '317 pre-adolescents who were either observed in self-masturbation, or who were observed in contacts with other boys or older adults'. Self-masturbation to orgasm in very young boys who have not been initiated into stimulatory techniques by older persons is rather rare. Kinsey found that not more than 13 per cent of boys masturbated in any real sense before the age of 10.

Spontaneous self-masturbation was observed more often in female infants, and 9 per cent of Kinsey's female sample were able to recall masturbating to orgasm by the age of 11. At later ages, however, masturbatory practices were much more common in males. By the age of twenty, 92 per cent of males compared with only 33 per cent of females reported the experience of having masturbated to orgasm.

With the approach of puberty, erotic thoughts, images and dreams become increasingly insistent, but in our sexually inhibited culture youngsters generally keep silent about them, and investigation is scarcely possible. In pubertal males, spontaneous ejaculations during sleep are often accompanied by vivid 'wet' dreams that may include all kinds of deviant sexual thoughts, which the boy cannot control and which in fact he may find quite disturbing. A little later adolescents of both sexes become prone to intense, romantic feelings, linked with sexual desire, and centred upon a particular individual. These first manifestations of the phenomenon of falling 'in love' are familiar to almost everyone, but like so much in the field of sexuality they have been strangely neglected by research psychologists.

Such data as are available concerning the early erotic history of normal persons add credibility to the accounts of the very early onset of homosexual feelings given to doctors by their homosexual patients. However, conclusions about age of onset, or about any other aspect of homosexuality, ought not to be drawn solely from samples of psychiatric patients, since these include many neurotic and criminal personalities whose development may not be typical of homosexuals in general. In recent years, usually with the aid of homophile organisations, it has been possible to carry out surveys on volunteer homosexuals who have never been either psychiatric clients or prison inmates. Collections of case histories gathered in this way (Liddicoat, 1961; Loney, 1972), whether from males or females, confirm that erotic interest centred upon the same sex usually develops long before adolescence, often between the ages of 6 to 10. Moreover, a definitely romantic feeling, which differs in quality from ordinary companionate friendships, characterises the same-sex attachments formed by children destined to become homosexual adults.

Saghir and Robins (1973), who studied volunteer samples of American homosexuals and heterosexuals, distinguished between emotional attachments, the psycho-sexual fantasies accompanying them (which they called cognitive rehearsals) and actual physical sex experiences with another person. A history of romantic attachments, usually beginning before or during early adolescence, was universal. All of the 35 heterosexual males and, surprisingly, a majority (53 out of 89) of the homosexual males, had also had romantic youthful attachments to the opposite sex.

In the case of heterosexuals, the fantasies which accompanied early romantic attachments were mostly platonic, a wish to be near the person, to do favours, or to give presents. The homosexuals' fantasies, however, often had a more physical content; 23 per cent of them said they used to feel they would like genital contact with the person of their desires. Incidents of youthful sexual arousal by another male were recalled by all of the homosexuals, most of them (76 per cent) saying that this had happened for the first time when they were less than fourteen years of age. Of the heterosexuals, 23 per cent recalled experiences of mutal masturbation with other males during early adolescence or before. The heterosexuals had all experienced arousal by a female, but most of them (77 per cent) said this did not happen until they were turned fourteen. Only 10 per cent of the heterosexual males reported having been aroused by another male, but nearly all those who had had such experiences said they first took place before 14. In contrast, 60 per cent of the homosexuals claimed past experiences of arousal by a female, but most said this did not happen until they were turned 14.

The following example, given to the author by a man aged 35, reflects many of the points revealed by collection of male homosexual case histories:

I was never anything but homosexual, even though I didn't realise it at first. I was a shy, timid boy and bullied a lot at school. Mother was strong-minded and puritanical. I was her only son and she doted on me and liked to keep me near her instead of mixing with other children. She quarrelled with father all the time, about his drinking and other things. He was a mild man and kept out of her way as much as he could, so I was definitely a mother's boy. I remember being very curious about sex, and interested in dirty stories at school, but embarrassed because so often I didn't understand the point. I knew I must never mention these things at home.

I can't remember just how or when it started, but I know that by the time I was 10 I delighted in the sex games boys used to play, jumping on top of each other and groping the privates of anyone at the bottom of the heap. This was the only sport I took part in, as I was a clumsy, puny type. I used to get a thrill from imagining boys touching me round the privates. When they actually did so I had to pretend so as not to let them know how much I was really enjoying it. When I was 13 or 14 I used to go for long walks into the country with one particular boy. We used to undress each other and play about, always ending up by masturbating, but we never spoke about it afterwards. He lost interest after a few months. He started going with girls and some years later I heard he had got married quite young.

When other boys were talking about their dates with girls I was very much out of it all. I must have been 15 when I forced myself to approach a girl. I managed to get her to come home with me when my parents were out, but mother came home early, before anything had happened, and there was a big scene. I don't think I tried very much again after that. Once, when I was about 18, I took a girl to my lodgings. ·I petted her and got an erection, but she wasn't very willing and I was too nervous to try to persuade her. So I gave up and have been a virgin as far as women go ever since.

I've always been sexually excitable with young men. When I left school I was a bit lost. I went around with some normal friends and fancied some of them like mad, but I daren't show it. Then I found out about the gay places and I've been pretty promiscuous since. I don't mind what I do in bed, I like to please the other fellow. I like to be free. I don't believe queers are made for marriage. I know several queer couples, but they are always having jealous scenes. I hardly ever think about women now, though I've nothing against them. I got quite a kick out of it recently when a bisexual friend brought a girl back and had sex with her with me in the same bed.

This example is in many ways typical, and will serve as starting point for a description of the natural history of male homosexuality (Krich, 1954; Henry, 1941, 1955). Homoerotic feelings usually commence long before adolescence, and by the time adolescence has passed, self-identity as a homosexual, or at least as a non-heterosexual, is well established. Feelings usually precede behaviour, so that early homosexual contacts are usually made by mutual consent. Overt seduction or persuasion by older and more experienced males certainly occurs, but most homosexuals do not refer to this as an important factor in their sexual development, and many admit to having made the initial advances leading to their first homosexual experience (Loney, 1972).

Among normally developing pubertal boys, verbal exchange of sexual experiences, curiosity about each other's genitals, mutual display, communal masturbation, and homosexual horseplay are exceedingly common. So long as the culture insists on modest separation of the sexes, and prescribes different pursuits for boys and girls, the likelihood will remain that the first sexual contact with another person will be with one of the same sex. Recall of homosexual episodes in childhood therefore has limited significance. The distinguishing characteristic of the recollections of adult homosexuals is the singular absence of any developing interest in the opposite sex, coupled with a persistence of homosexual interests beyond adolescence, reinforced by actual sexual encounters with others similarly inclined.

3. *The prospects of persistent homosexual orientation*

Overt homosexual activity at puberty is particularly common in boys, and most authorities agree that usually this has no great significance for future sexual orientation. Involvement in such incidents, or awakening awareness of homoerotic attraction, sometimes produces unjustified anxiety in the adolescent, who dreads being different or abnormal. Authoritative reassurance from a doctor is usually sufficient to restore confidence and permit heterosexual interest to develop naturally (Kirkendall, 1961). However, if other signs, such as effeminate mannerisms, avoidance of masculine activities, falling in love with another boy or unbalanced relationships with parents, accompany the homosexual conduct, a lasting homosexual orientation is more likely (Gadpaille, 1968).

Many males who ultimately become well-adjusted heterosexuals indulge in a great deal of homosexual play during boyhood. In his survey of a sample of normal adolescents, Schofield (1965b) found that over a fifth of boys said they knew of homosexual activities among their schoolfriends. Due to the embarrassment attaching to this topic among teen-age boys, this was probably an underestimate. Except for those who had attended boarding schools, 28 per cent of whom reported having themselves taken part in homosexual activities, relatively few admitted any personal involvement. Schofield considered that sexual play between boys, occurring between the ages of 13 to 15, was frequently not recognised or acknowledged as homosexuality by the boys themselves. In their late teens, when sexual self-consciousness and fear of being different is at its height, boys tend to abandon playful homosexuality. Even those destined to be homosexuals as adults often go through a phase of fighting against their inclinations and struggling to become 'normal'. Among pubertal girls, playful homosexuality is distinctly less common than among boys. In Schofield's sample, among those who had been boarders, only 12 per cent of girls, compared with 44 per cent of boys, reported that homosexual activities took place at their school.

Two American psychologists, Brady and Levitt (1965), using as subjects 68 male college students, carried out a systematic survey to demonstrate the influence of early sexual experience upon adult sexual preferences. Presented with a questionnaire about past adult sexual behaviour, including homosexual behaviour, 24 of the students reported that sometime in their lives they had experienced 'manual manipulation of your genitals by another male' while 5 admitted to 'penile penetration of another male'. In all, 28 admitted some overt homosexual activity. Since only 2 of the students reported any such activity 'during the last five years', their homosexual experiences must nearly all have taken place in childhood or adolescence.

The same sixty-eight students were shown photographs of sexual acts, and were asked to rate each picture on a six-point scale according to the degree they found it sexually stimulating. Among the nineteen different 'themes' depicted, pictures of face-to-face heterosexual intercourse received the highest ratings (average score 4.13), other types of heterosexual activity received lesser ratings (e.g. 'oral-genital contact, male or female' – 3.04) and various types of homosexual activity came lower still (e.g. 'anal intercourse, two males' – 0.42). Last of all in order of stimulatory power came pictures of a partially clad male (0.04).

The investigators were interested to see whether students who had experienced specific forms of homosexual activity found the photographs of corresponding acts particularly stimulating. No significant (point biserial) correlations emerged between admission or denial of any particular homosexual activity and preference scores for pictures of corresponding acts. The only evidence for a carry-over of early experience into adult preference was a tendency for students who had experienced homosexual activity to give relatively higher ratings to the pictures of a partially clad male. The investigators suggested that the frank homosexual pictures may have failed to stimulate because they were too blatant, whereas the partially clad male, being more subtly suggestive, could have elicited some response from homosexually sensitive subjects. However that may be, the main result was that reports of early homosexual experience were not in fact correlated with responsiveness to photographs of overt homosexual activity.

Assumptions about the long-term effects of early sexual experiences are rarely put to any practical test. The Brady and Levitt project was a commendable attempt to do so, but the outcome of that particular experiment cannot be taken too seriously. The researchers did not fully succeed in overcoming some of the serious technical difficulties involved. The versions of past experience and of present erotic preference depended upon the accuracy and truthfulness of the students. Perhaps because of the methods of recruitment, the sample apparently consisted entirely of heterosexuals, whose variations in sexual preference were necessarily limited. With relatively small differences between subjects, no great weight could be attached to the absence of significant correlations.

Believing in the likelihood of permanent damage from sex play between boys, some teachers feel justified in taking drastic action against the young participants when such incidents come unexpectedly to their notice. This policy, though perhaps well-intentioned, can be unnecessarily cruel. Here is an example, described in his own words by the person concerned, now a married heterosexual of 31 and the father of four children:

When I was eleven I was sent as a boarder to a grammar school. I felt afraid and eager. For months I had been reading boarding school stories in anticipation. The dormitory had about ten beds in it, and that first night something began there which led to disaster just over a year later. After lights out the boy who was head of the dormitory asked me if I'd like to get into bed with him. I went over to him. There were anonymous giggles in the dark. He guided my hand between his legs and then asked me to lie on my face while he rubbed himself off against my buttocks. As an only child I had never felt hot flesh before. I was appalled and thrilled.

There was a lot of sex in the dormitories at that time. It seemed quite natural. I didn't think of myself as a homosexual. I had fantasies of making love to the head's wife, but had no clear idea of female anatomy, so it was a sort of guesswork. The boys used to entertain each other with stories of exploits with girls during the holidays, but my tales were all fictitious, as I am sure were most of the others. I can hardly remember the boy with whom I was caught. He was a bit older and used to come to our dormitory to persuade whoever was willing to let him get into bed. He had a 'crush' on me, which I found rather funny and a bit flattering. It was my bed he was in when a torch flashed and he fled naked, while the head's voice called stop.

Red and angry, the head told me I was to be expelled. 'I regard this as a tragedy,' he said. He drove me home in his car. I was in a state of shock, and remember every detail of the journey. I was sent upstairs while he talked to my Grand-dad. For days after Grand-dad and I stared at each other. When he asked questions I never told him the truth. It didn't take long for the whole village to find out what happened. Soon almost every child in the village was forbidden to go near me. I felt dirty, evil, lost, and for months I spent my time wandering the woods alone. It took a long time to find another school that would have me. I never felt at ease at the new school. I told no one what had happened. Before I had been a happy, busy, bullying, rugby-playing cock of the junior school, but now I kept to myself and the others left me very much alone. I think I only had one fight at that school.

When I was 14 and branded a homosexual I believed it totally. For years the taunt went on in my head – you're a poof, a queer. Now I can look at those self-made male sex objects you see on the beach at St. Tropez (self-made isn't fair, I believe mothers make them) and realise I have different habits from them, a very different self-image, and different desires.

The outcome of this boy's experience was less devastating than it might have been. Early disgrace cut short his education, soured his attitudes towards accepted social values, and killed his aspirations to intellectual work and a conventional career, but did not divert his sexual development. For several years he continued solitary masturbatory rituals with fantasies of women. Then he accomplished in reality the heterosexual goal towards which his thoughts had been directed all along. In this instance, the homosexual label proved as inaccurate as it was cruel.

Opinions vary on the question of whether adult male homosexuals have been sexually precocious or sexually retarded as children. One headmaster, basing himself on extensive personal experience with delinquent boys, declares his belief that the 'true' deviants, those destined for a life of permanent, exclusive homosexuality, behave distinctively from an early age. They are given to extensive homosexual fantasies from infancy, and as early as 6 or 7 take the initiative in seducing their peers into homosexual play. They are not necessarily effeminate, but by the time they reach adolescence they are already set in their sexual habits and fear to change (McCleary, 1972). Kinsey and his collaborators recorded in their famous study (1948, p.315) that boys who come to sexual maturity earlier than usual are particularly likely to have homosexual experiences. The authors commented: 'As a factor in the development of the homosexual, age of onset of adolescence (which probably means the metabolic drive of the individual) may prove to be more significant than the much discussed Oedipus relation of Freudian psychology.' For social reasons a young child's contacts are more with his own than with the opposite sex. Those who mature at an early age incur an increased likelihood of pre-adolescent homosexual experience, and a consequently increased liability to permanent homosexual orientation, or so the argument runs. Gebhard *et al.* (1965), also from the Kinsey Institute, who later studied a large sample of sexual offenders, many of them homosexuals, reached similar conclusions.

They noted that social constraints against overt heterosexual contacts tend to be specially obtrusive at the time of puberty, when physiologically the sex drive reaches a peak. 'A young boy without a great backlog of homosexual conditioning can wait out this period when he is robbed of girls and still emerge primarily heterosexual; a male with much previous homosexual conditioning cannot.' A more recent questionnaire survey, comparing non-patient groups of homosexual and heterosexual adult males (Manosevitz, 1970), yielded some confirmatory findings. The homosexuals reported significantly more childhood sexual experience than the heterosexuals. Very often their contacts had been exclusively with other boys, but many of them had had experiences with both boys and girls, and continued to do so after adolescence.

These results appear to conflict with other surveys (Westwood, 1960; Hemphill *et al.*, 1958) which suggest that males who later become permanent homosexuals commence their overt sexual experiences relatively late, most often around 15 or 16, and sometimes not until 21 or later. It may be that the homosexual population includes two contrasting groups, those who, as youngsters, were highly sexed and uninhibited, and those who were too inhibited to indulge in any form of sex. The former group may have taken to homosexuality at an early age as the quickest and easiest outlet. The latter may take the same course later, when socio-sexual needs become imperative, but the prospect of delayed confrontation with the opposite sex seems to them too daunting. But all such speculations are premature until research can establish more clearly the basic facts of sexual development.

In the opinion of some medical authorities, homosexual experiences among juveniles are not only very common but potentially very damaging. Thus Ollendorff (1966, p.63) writes: 'As any rational methods of sex education in our society are practically non-existent, the mysteries of sexual urges in a world from which sex is banned are pondered over by the boy and his mates, and mutual masturbation of groups of boys is a basic common event which only the overprotected or over anxious child does not share.' Ollendorff argues further that the experience of achieving orgasm, especially for the first time, in a homosexual context, exerts a great influence in conditioning future sexual responses along similar lines. Then 'the whole weight of social disapproval, of legal restriction and religious taboo, has to be exerted to force the adolescent off this acquired habit'. In Ollendorff's view the homosexual inclinations so acquired are frequently never fully corrected, and their persistence in the face of contrary pressures constitutes a major cause of much emotional maladjustment and frank mental illness.

Some authorities have credited initiatory sexual experiences with a very special importance in the determination of subsequent masturbatory fantasies and sexual preferences. McGuire *et al.* (1965) cite two cases of compulsive exhibitionism in which the afflicted men believed that their deviant impulses developed following an experience of being unexpectedly surprised by a woman while they were innocently urinating in a semi-public place. The same authors also quote the example of a man of twenty-five who traced the origin of his homosexual orientation to an incident at the age of eleven when he was initiated into mutual masturbation by another boy. At about the same time he was punished for trying to touch a girl's genitals. Thereafter he masturbed exclusively to a fantasy of nude males.

These conflicting views as to the likely results of early homosexual indulgence cannot be resolved by collecting case histories, since examples can readily be found to support opposite viewpoints. Until more experimental research has been done, the effect of early conditioning must remain a matter for speculation.

As in the example quoted earlier, emotional neutrality and lack of interest, rather than positive disgust, characterises the conscious attitude of many male homosexuals towards women. In fact, many who later on settle to a life of exclusive homosexuality have had a certain amount of heterosexual experience in early adult life. Sometimes this spontaneous experimentation leads to a change of orientation. This can be seen in Kinsey's figures. He found that the incidence of exclusive permanent homosexuality in males was only 4 per cent, although double that proportion had had a period of exclusive homosexuality lasting at least three years. Furthermore, the incidence of currently active and exclusive homosexuality decreased with age, from 4.9 per cent of males at 20 to 2.9 per cent at 25 (Kinsey Table 147). These figures suggest a spontaneous drift towards heterosexuality during early adult life, even among those who start off exclusively homosexual.

These observations do not accord with the clinical experience of psychiatrists, who find that exclusive male homosexuals, especially those who have been for some time actively engaged in overt homosexual practices, rarely experience spontaneous conversions to heterosexuality after the age of 20. But clinical experience could be misleading, since homosexuals who have enough confidence to commence heterosexual activities on their own initiative are less likely to be seen by psychiatrists.

Although a drift towards heterosexuality preponderates, the changes in sexual behaviour which occur as age increases are not always in this direction. Some persons begin or revert to homosexual practices following marital disillusionment or boredom, the death of a marriage partner, or difficulty in securing heterosexual satisfaction due to advancing age. These reasons are often put forward to explain why men in their declining years take to molesting children, but they are equally valid explanations for a reorientation towards homosexuality on the part of elderly men who find it provides them with relatively easy, undemanding sexual contacts. According to one survey of men in their 60s, some 6 per cent were actively homosexual. Most of these were socially competent, normal-seeming married men who had had no homosexual experience between adolescence and age 60, but who found a need for male contacts as heterosexual satisfactions receded. They generally preferred masculine types of mature years rather than youths (Calleja, 1967). A regression towards adolescent homosexual practice has also been reported among males in an old people's home (Hader, 1966).

4. *The development of sexual techniques*

As has been remarked, sexual games involving genital and masturbatory displays are commonplace when young boys are left together. Only a small step separates such masculine fun and games from mutual masturbation, which is often the first introduction to homosexuality. For many homosexual men mutual masturbation remains the dominant form of sexual expression throughout life. It provides a convenient method for those wanting a quick, impersonal sexual exchange under circumstances of minimal privacy. If the participants are unbuttoned rather than unclothed, and sitting side by side in cinema or car seats or in the back row of school desks, or standing at adjacent stalls in a urinal, one man simply stretches out a hand to the other's genitals, and it is all over very soon. The absence of more affectionate gestures may serve to preserve the feeling of not being truly committed to the other person, and hence of not being homosexual at all. Rightly or wrongly, the popular notion that mutual masturbation represents a less serious sexual commitment than attempts at intercourse remains enshrined in the legal distinctions between buggery and indecency.

The introduction of kissing and nude petting to the masturbatory ritual adds another dimension of intimacy to the homosexual exchange. Beyond this, the use of mouth genital stimulation, or of anal penetration, and finally of mouth anal contact (rimming) require the overcoming of increasingly powerful taboos. Many male homosexuals, after experience with numerous partners of varying tastes, overcome all such taboos in time, indulging with enjoyment any or all of these practices. Others retain distinct preferences or distinct dislikes. The attitudes and customs of the wider society have as great an influence on homosexual practices as they do on heterosexual ones. Oral sex appears to be a commoner preference among American male homosexuals than among Europeans, whereas the reverse holds true of anal sex. Among Americans the passive role in anal intercourse may be adopted only after considerable experience of other techniques. In Arab countries, where tradition tolerates man-boy affaires, with the younger partner taking the feminine part, a passive role in anal intercourse is more acceptable to boys than to men. Europeans and Americans will often switch from active to passive role according to mood, physical convenience, or the desires of their homosexual partner. These switches have little to do with the adoption of a feminine or masculine stance in domestic or social life.

In countries where male and female roles are more rigidly defined such reversals of roles in love-making are less common. A survey of Mexican male homosexuals reported a much commoner preference for anal intercourse, and a sharper distinction between active and passive habits, than pertains in the United States (Carrier, 1971). In a recent questionnaire survey of 86 American male homosexuals, mostly college students, few of them had a partiality for any one form of sexual activity, and the majority had no particular preference between the insertor or insertee role during anal or oral intercourse (Greenberg, 1973).

In their physical contact with each other, women display more restraint and less venturesomeness than male homosexuals. Kinsey (1953, p.466) found that their relations often consisted of little more than simple lip kissing and generalised body contact. Even among those who had had extensive homosexual experience, some had not gone beyond this, although most of them, in time, progressed to manual manipulation of breasts and genitalia. The majority (78 per cent) of experienced lesbians employed cunnilingus (stimulation of the labia, clitoris or vaginal entrance with the tongue), and 56 per cent had practiced tribadism (rhythmic genital apposition with one woman lying on top of the other – 'a rub job'). Contrary to the salacious fantasies of heterosexual males, few lesbians had used an artificial phallus. Since stimulation of the clitoris and the entrance of the vagina are the most important elements in female sexual arousal, lesbians do not depend upon artificial penetration to obtain an orgasm.

Kinsey compared women married for five years with experienced lesbians in regard to ability to attain orgasms. Among the married women, 30 per cent reported that on most occasions they did not have an orgasm during sexual relations. The proportion of lesbians who reported absence of orgasm on most occasions was only 14 per cent. Among married women, only 40 per cent had an orgasm nearly every time, whereas among lesbians the figure was 68 per cent. Kinsey speculated from these results that lesbians may be more adept than the average husband at understanding and satisfying a woman's psychological and stimulatory requirements. However that may be, difficulty in attaining orgasm is a common feminine problem shared by homosexual and heterosexual women.

The belief that homosexuals, males in particular, enjoy a riotously free sex life is largely unfounded. Many homosexual youths yearn for a lover but are too shy, inexperienced or fearful to make contact and so remain unwillingly chaste for months or years. They may be frightened to be seen going into 'gay' bars, or live too far from any big city, or simply lack knowledge of where such meeting places are to be found. The commonest complaint of young homosexuals seeking counselling is loneliness and lack of contact with others of their kind. Some of them find the brash attitudes of 'gay' society intimidating and disillusioning to romantic aspirations. Women homosexuals are at an even greater disadvantage. They lack the bars and drinking clubs used by men, and have to rely upon finding other homosexuals among friends and acquaintances encountered in the ordinary course of social life. Their difficulties arise in part from their own feminine psychology. Women prefer sex to develop out of a close friendship, whereas men see no objection to sex first and love later. Lesbians would not think of trying to pick up strange women in public toilets or elsewhere in the way that male homosexuals so often do. As a consequence, some homosexual women go for very long periods without any sexual outlet.

Once they have 'come out', that is been introduced into gay circles, male homosexuals tend to have a rapid turnover of sexual partners. A succession of scores or hundreds of one night stands is nothing unusual. But as Kinsey pointed out, even promiscuous homosexuals fall way behind the average young married heterosexual in the number of times per week they have sexual relations. The opportunities open to promiscuous roamers, though varied, are limited in frequency by the need to go out to hunt.

5. *Feelings towards the opposite sex: positive, neutral or aversive*

Kinsey found that a large proportion of grown men behave homosexually on occasion, and many observers have noted the high frequency of homosexual behaviour in prisons and other uni-sex institutions. Such facts suggest that a substantial proportion of adults are, at least potentially, bisexual. A distinction must be drawn, however, between capacity for sexual arousal and true sexual preference. Given suitable circumstances, a man may find some sexual release with other men when opportunity presents, yet still retain a strong preference for women. Similarly, a predominantly homosexual male may discover himself capable of heterosexual intercourse, and may choose to go with women to fulfil social obligations, although this behaviour does not express his true erotic preference. Kurt Freund (1965a) points out that although many adult homosexuals recall mild heterosexual activities or fantasies, especially during their younger days, their descriptions suggest that the experiences were uninspiring and abortive. They discuss them in the same mildly deprecatory manner that an adult heterosexual might recall adolescent involvement in mutual masturbation. Their descriptions reveal a noteworthy absence of the emotional satisfaction and personal involvement with the sex partner that occurs in sexual relations with a member of the preferred sex. Such episodes do not provide real evidence for a bisexual orientation.

Freund has pioneered the use of the phallometer to determine a man's true erotic preference. This is a device resembling a finger stall which fits over the penis and measures slight changes in volume in response to erotic stimuli, such as pictures of male or female nudes (Freund et al., 1973). On comparing the reactions of heterosexual and homosexual males, the two were shown to be quite distinctive. The heterosexuals gave little or no reaction to pictures of males, the homosexuals gave little or no reaction to the pictures of females. In this sample, at least, true bisexuals, that is individuals displaying a strong erotic response to either sex, were conspicuously absent.

Psychoanalysts who support the theory of the innate bisexuality of man would say that the fact that most adults do not display bisexual responses when tested with the phallometer merely goes to show how effectively the unwanted components of sexuality are repressed. Homosexual men who deny early heterosexual experiences, or who try to play them down as uninteresting or unimportant, are concerned to preserve their adult self-image of exclusive homosexuality. In the course of treatment, however, many of these patients eventually recall vivid heterosexual dreams and childhood fantasies which they had previously suppressed. If correct, this observation lends support to the psychoanalytic contention that homosexuality arises from a positive rejection of heterosexuality rather than from mere lack of opportunity for early heterosexual experience. Psychoanalysts contend that the rejection of heterosexual intimacy expresses a deep-seated, early-acquired fear or dislike of the opposite sex. In support of this view they cite instances of patients who have expressed strong distaste, if not actual revulsion, at the physical appearance, and especially the genital appearance, of the opposite sex.

The researches of Freund *et al.* (1973) lent no support to these notions. Using the rapidity of subsidence of a previously aroused penile erection as a measure of aversion, the experimenters compared the aversive effectiveness of neutral pictures of landscapes, pictures of members of the non-preferred sex, and disgust-arousing pictures of skin diseases. The disease pictures were effective in rapidly extinguishing penile arousal in both homosexuals and heterosexuals. Pictures of the non-preferred sex were no more effective than landscapes in extinguishing arousal in either heterosexuals or homosexuals. Apparently homosexual men react to nude females like heterosexual men react to nude males, with a bland indifference similar to that evoked by emotionally and sexually neutral material.

Other researchers have investigated the same question by comparing the penile reaction of homosexual and heterosexual males to three cinematograph films depicting explicit sexual activity between two women, two men, and a mixed couple. Heterosexual males were aroused at least as much by the lesbian acitivity as by the spectacle of heterosexual coitus, but their reactions to the homosexual scene were minimal and they tended to rate the film 'unpleasant'. The homosexuals, however, rated the heterosexual stimuli 'mildly unpleasant'. They produced penile reactions to the film of heterosexual coitus almost as strongly as to the homosexual film, perhaps because of their interest in the male's sexual performance, regardless of the gender of his sexual partner. Certainly the presence of a woman in the scene did not inhibit their erotic response. Moreover, the homosexual group also gave some positive responses to the lesbian film, more than the heterosexuals gave when watching the male couple (Mavissakalian *et al.*, 1975).

This evidence suggests that male homosexuals are mildly attracted rather than completely ,repelled by observing females in sexual acts. They show less aversion towards heterosexuality than heterosexual males show towards homosexuality. However, the particular investigation described included only six homosexuals, all of them men seeking medical help to change their sexual patterns and only one of them exclusively homosexual (Kinsey rating 6), so it would be unwise to generalise. Different types of homosexual probably react differently. Mathews and Bancroft (1972), who compared 15 male homosexual clients of a psychiatric clinic with 60 presumptively heterosexual males from a variety of sources, found that both groups identified similar qualities in pictures of women they considered 'attractive'. Descriptions such as 'graceful', 'young', or 'slender' applied to the attractive pictures, whereas those rejected were described as 'old', 'vulgar', 'gross' etc. The homosexuals differed from other men, however, in rejecting rather than favouring the more overtly sexual pictures, the ones described as 'bedroom poses', 'large-breasted', 'sexy' etc. Homosexuals, it seems, appreciate prettiness in women much the same as other men, but do not find explicit sexual pose or gesture particularly attractive. Some of the investigators who have measured penile volume changes in homosexuals have reported significant decreases in volume in response to presentations of pictures of the non-preferred sex, which seems to indicate that some kind of inhibitory process is going on in at least some cases (Barr and McConaghy, 1971; Barr, 1973). As so often happens in these difficult issues concerning human sexuality, we must await patiently the outcome of further research.

Whatever answer ultimately emerges concerning the number of men with a strong erotic attraction to both sexes, or the numbers with a strong aversion to one or other sex, neither category seems likely to form a majority of the population. The typical homosexual, like the typical heterosexual, has a definite preference for one sex, and a relative indifference towards the other sex, but can still be aroused by members of the other sex given sufficiently favourable circumstances. This residual capacity for physical arousal by the non-preferred sex has to be taken into account in judging whether transient manifestations of heterosexual behaviour in a homosexual patient reflect any real change of sexual orientation.

Erotic indifference does not necessarily mean emotional neutrality. Physiological sex reactions are easier to measure than more subtle feelings, but psychotherapists experienced in listening to homosexuals ventilating their feelings have been struck by the hostility and suspicion which, in some cases, seems to colour their reactions to the opposite sex. It seems that temperamental distrust is sometimes more prominent than a specifically sexual aversion. Heterosexual friendships are avoided in anticipation of an eventual hurtful rejection, or from fear of becoming dependent or subordinate, or from reluctance to give up the psychological and social freedom of the emotionally unattached. These exaggerated suspicions usually stem from unfortunate experiences in early life. The boy who has suffered for years at the hands of a dominating mother, and been kept unhappily clinging and dependent, may acquire an image of the female dragon which he transfers unfairly on to the women he meets in later life. In this chicken-and-egg situation it can be difficult to tell which is the more basic, the emotional coldness or the sexual indifference.

6. *Identifying characteristics*

The most straightforward way to find out whether a person is homosexual is to ask him. The Kinsey rating scale, applied to reported sexual contacts over a period of time, provides a convenient method of recording the preferences of individuals who have had an active sex life in accord with their true desires. An alternative method, which records the subjective sexual preferences of the moment, has been developed by Feldman *et al.* (1966). It has been employed with some success to chart changes in sexual feelings in persons undergoing treatment to modify their sexual orientation. Known as the Sexual Orientation Method, it takes the form of a questionnaire with two open-ended statements 'Men are sexually to me ——————' and 'Women are sexually to me ——————', followed by an adjective such as 'attractive'. The subject is required to complete each statement with the adjective supplied, but qualified by an expression of degree according to their true feeling. Thus men might be said to be 'very attractive, 'quite attractive', 'neither attractive nor unattractive', 'quite unattractive' or 'very unattractive'. The total test included six adjectives (interesting, attractive, handsome, hot, pleasurable, exciting). Subjects had to place each adjective on a five-point scale showing how closely it applied, first to their sexual feelings towards men, and then to their sexual feeling towards women. More than one method of scoring the test has been tried (Sambrooks and MacCulloch, 1973; Woodward *et al.*, 1973), but whatever system is used the responses have been found to discriminate well and sensitively between groups of known homosexuals, heterosexuals and bisexuals.

Doctors and psychologists, especially those engaged in classifying prisoners, examining sex offenders, or helping to screen candidates for posts considered unsuitable for homosexuals, would like to find some indication of sexual orientation rather more trustworthy than unsubstantiated self-report. The search for tell-tale signs of homosexuality, difficult for the individual to conceal, has led to some amusing medical pronouncements. Older text books of forensic pathology suggested that examination of the anus might give the game away, habitually passive male homosexuals showing lax sphincters, scarring from repeated small tears, a funnel-shaped entry to the anal canal, and a suspiciously convenient stance when required to prepare for the insertion of a speculum. According to one modern authority (Paul, 1975), the funnel-shaped anus 'so loved by the authors of textbooks of forensic pathology' is an extreme condition rarely seen except on post-mortem examination. However, regular anal intercourse over a period of six months suffices to produce a detectable laxity of the anal sphincter and a positive response to the 'lateral buttock traction test'. On gently pressing apart the cheeks of the buttocks, instead of the normal response, which is a reflex contraction of the anal sphincter, the lax anus may gape slightly. Longer periods of regular exposure to anal penetration gradually induce a permanent laxity and dilation of the anus, a thickening of the skin around the margins, and a progressive smoothing out of the skin folds that normally surround the anal ring.

To detect those who practice fellatio rather than passive anal intercourse, one American psychiatrist (Gioscia, 1950) recommended stroking the inside of the throat as a useful method of screening. Normally subjects respond with what doctors call a gag reflex, an involuntary retching and choking, but a man who likes to have a penis thrust deep into his mouth learns to suppress this response. Hence, absence of a gag reflex indicates homosexual experience.

Small, covert and sometimes unconscious psychological responses may betray to the astute observer an individual's sexual preferences. Glances tend to stray towards and to linger longer upon persons found sexually attractive. Zamansky (1956) tried to make use of the principle in an experiment using a tachistoscope, an instrument for viewing pictures under controlled conditions of illumination and for measured intervals of time. He recorded the eye movements and viewing time of homosexual and heterosexual males in response to pictures of men, women and neutral subjects, and found that the homosexuals tended to linger longer over the male pictures and to avoid the female ones.

In theory at least, involuntary eye movements and reflexes can be used to detect sexual interest without the subject realising what the investigator is trying to do (Hain and Linton, 1969). In tests making use of an instrument for measuring the dilatation of the pupil which occurs when a subject looks at something he finds of particular interest, it has been claimed that homosexuals dilate their pupils while looking at pictures of persons of their own sex to a greater extent than heterosexuals (Hess *et al.*, 1965). More recent evidence, however, suggests that the technique is so unreliable, and individual variations in reponse so great, that the method has little practical value (Scott *et al.*, 1967; Schnelle *et al.*, 1974).

With a subject wired up to lie-detector-type apparatus, capable of registering the small changes in blood pressure, sweat secretion or breathing that accompany emotional excitement, it is possible to detect the arousal of sexual interest even when the subject tries to conceal it. The most direct and efficient measure, namely volume changes in the penis or clitoris, is to some extent proof against attempts at deception. If a man tries to cheat by conjuring up sexual images of his own, contrary to the stimuli provided by the investigator, he is liable to produce a detectably anomalous record. Of course, unlike other instruments, the phallometer cannot be applied without a man realising its purpose, so if he wishes to conceal his sexual preferences he has only to decline the test.

Koegler and Kline (1965) successfully used less obtrusive instrumental recording of emotional responses to investigate the sexual concerns of a group of patients with paranoid symptoms. They found that the patients evinced considerably more than average signs of anxiety when confronted with pictures suggestive of homosexuality. This result fitted in very well with the Freudian theory that paranoid patients suffer from repressed homosexual conflicts. Unfortunately for the theory, however, the paranoid patients also showed increased anxiety reactions to heterosexual situations. Solyom and Beck (1967) applied a similar technique to non-psychotic patients with sexual problems. They found a significantly increased galvanic skin response among homosexually oriented patients whenever a homosexually stimulating picture was inserted among a series of neutral or heterosexual pictures.

A number of tests take advantage of the contrasting experiences, interests and attitudes of homosexual and heterosexual groups. One of the most elementary of tests asks the subject to draw a person. Most heterosexuals, especially males, choose to draw first a person of their own sex (Frank, 1955; Mainord, 1953). According to some surveys, many male homosexuals, when specifically asked to draw a man, produced figures with effeminate characteristics (Whitaker, 1961; Geil, 1948), but other workers (Grams and Rinder, 1958) have not found this to be the case. A number of tests make use of the different vocabulary or use of words current among homosexual and heterosexual groups. Slater's Selective Vocabulary Test was based upon the idea that homosexual males would be familiar with more of the words commonly used by women and less of those commonly used by men. Clarke (1965) who compared homosexual male patients with a control group, and Berdie (1959), who compared non-patient homosexuals and heterosexuals, both found that on average male homosexuals knew less 'masculine' words than male heterosexuals, but differences between the scores of individuals outweighed the general trend.

The Word Association Test could be used to detect homosexuals. A list of stimulus words is put to the subject one by one, and he is required to respond as quickly as he can with the first word that comes into his head. A delayed reaction time to a particular word, or sudden lowering of skin resistance, due to momentary anxiety and sweating, which can be registered on a galvanometer, indicates that the word in question has special emotional significance to the subject. By inserting words with an aggressive or sadistic sexual connotation in an otherwise neutral series, Tong (1960) was able to show that a group of sex criminals were more sensitively reactive to such stimuli than were normal males. It would be just as easy to compile a list containing some slang words or local place names, notorious among homosexuals, but less familiar to heterosexuals, in order to detect, by their more sensitive responses to these particular items, who were the homosexuals among a group of men of unknown sexual orientation.

Kuethe and Weingartner (1964) tried to distinguish male prisoners who were homosexual by their responses to a test which required them to arrange cut-out figures of men, women and neutral objects on a felt background. In their efforts to reproduce from memory a display shown to them previously, the homosexual prisoners tended to err by placing the male figures too close to each other and too far from the female figures, whereas the heterosexual prisoners were said to err in the opposite direction, placing the males and females closer to each other than had been the case in the original display.

A word or picture, even though it has nothing directly to do with sex, may have different emotional overtones and mental associations for homosexuals and heterosexuals. One well-known technique for exploring personality, the Thematic Apperception Test (TAT) works on the principle that an individual's imaginative fantasies, stimulated by gazing at ambiguous pictures, will reveal a great deal about his intimate thoughts, interests and emotional preoccupations, and will furnish clues to his probable sexual orientation (Davids *et al.* 1956). The test material consists of a series of pictures of persons portrayed in surroundings and contexts that permit a variety of interpretations. The test psychologist asks the subjects to use their imaginations to describe what the characters shown are doing and thinking. The stories so obtained are analysed for the presence or absence of key themes or associations. In investigations with males, homosexuals reveal themselves in themes of aggression towards women, expressions of uncertainty about the sexual identity of the pictorial characters, in the use of symbolism suggestive of homosexuality, and in the production of stories indicative of castration anxiety (Schwartz, 1956). These and other similar clues are said to have enabled independent judges to identify, with surprising accuracy, which sets of stories came from homosexual subjects (Lindzey *et al.*, 1958; Lindzey, 1965).

An even more widely used method, the Rorschach (inkblot) test, in which subjects have to voice their mental associations to a series of irregularly shaped patches, has also been claimed to elicit 'signs' enabling the psychologist to diagnose homosexuality (Wheeler, 1949). The sort of responses allegedly produced by male homosexuals included frank, undisguised references to genital shapes, indicative of a preoccupation with sex in general, perceptions of feminine clothes and feminine objects, and associations suggestive of anal preoccupations. Some careful investigations by Evelyn Hooker (1958), using non-patient male homosexuals as subjects, confirmed that, in a small minority of cases with pronounced feminine traits, the homosexual orientation was fairly obvious; but in most cases it was not, and the Rorschach could not be used as a reliable method of identification in the absence of other sources of information. Most present-day authorities seem to agree with this view, not only in regard to the Rorschach, but also in regard to the TAT and other similar projective tests of personality (Coates, 1964). One investigator (De Luca, 1966) believed that homosexuals with a preference for sodomy rather than fellatio, or those who liked the active rather than the passive role, produced detectably different Rorschach responses. He admitted, however, that these trends, although sufficient to produce significant differences between groups, were insuffiicient to permit confident diagnosis of an individual case.

Subjects who are anxious to conceal or to suppress homosexual inclinations may avoid any display of overt interest in psychological test items designed to elicit homosexual associations. Goldberg and Milstein (1965) who used a tachistoscope to flash pictures on a screen for brief, measured periods of time, found that some persons gave themselves away by taking a longer than average time to perceive accurately any pictures which had a homosexually suggestive content.

Among the many questionnaires in current use by clinical psychologists one of the best known, the Minnesota Multiphasic Personality Inventory (MMPI), purports to measure a wide range of personality attributes, some of them of relevance to homosexuality. Panton (1960) devised a special method of scoring this questionnaire, taking into account twenty-two items to which heterosexuals and homosexuals responded differently. The resulting scale produced a measure, uncorrelated with assessments of 'femininity', that significantly discriminated between groups of homosexual and heterosexual inmates of a prison for men. As with so many such measures, however, the homosexuals' scores were not sufficiently distinctive to permit the psychologist to diagnose an individual's sexual orientation from the test result alone. According to a later piece of prison research (Pierce, 1972) the method proved more efficient than originally reported. Among 36 prisoners who underwent the test, of whom 12 were known as fully committed homosexuals, the homosexuality scale successfully picked out 10, without making any false identifications among the 24 non-deviant prisoners.

7. Testing for personality defects

Apart from these dubious attempts to determine the sexual orientation of persons whose self reports cannot be taken on trust, psychological tests have also been used in efforts to demonstrate that known homosexuals differ in personality characteristics from the average, heterosexual population. Some of the tests, concerned with masculine and feminine personality traits, purport to show that many homosexuals deviate from the norm in having interests, attitudes and personality characteristics more typical of members of the opposite sex than of their own. This topic is taken up more fully in the next chapter. Other tests, meant to measure more general attributes of personality, have been used to try to show that groups of known homosexuals are more often neurotic, anxiety-prone, suspicious, socially maladjusted, and emotionally conflicted than heterosexuals. Naturally homosexuals contest, often with good reason, both the motives and the methods of psychologists who try to demonstrate these alleged inferiorities.

The results of personality tests applied to lesbians are discussed in a later chapter. In the past, the results of psychological assessments of male homosexuals have been in large part vitiated by the abnormal, and almost certainly untypical, samples of men investigated, who have usually been inmates of prisons or clients of psychiatric clinics. A typical example of the questionable conclusions likely to be reached by the use of atypical samples was a survey of 100 homosexual males in federal prisons in the United States, 85 of whom were serving sentences for offences unconnected with homosexuality (Smith, 1954). It was found that, compared with the general prison population, the homosexual group had a higher incidence of diagnosed mental disorder, and a higher incidence of arrests for impulsive and poorly planned crimes such as car theft, mail theft and forgery. Their frequent unjustified complaints about unfairly discriminatory treatment in prison led the investigator to agree with Bergler that homosexuals tend to be 'injustice collectors', men with an ineradicable chip on the shoulder. The abnormality of the homosexual group in this survey, however, was not a fair indication of the mental instability of the generality of male homosexuals. Apart from the minority who are convicted for sex offences, the sexual orientation of prisoners only comes to the notice of the authorities if they behave in ostentatiously effeminate ways, flaunt their sexual interests, or become involved in imbroglios with other inmates. In Smith's sample, only 30 per cent were said to be effeminate, but many others were men who had proved 'not at all reticent' in bringing their homosexuality to the attention of the authorities. More stable homosexual prisoners, who behave with reasonable discretion, would not have been included in the survey. The same criticism applies to another prison survey by Oliver and Mosher (1968) in which homosexual inmates, especially those who were aggressive and who took the active role in anal intercourse, were said to have 'psychotic' features.

In an attempt to overcome these criticisms Cattell and Morony (1962) used the 16 Personality Factor Questionnaire with four groups of Australian males, prisoners convicted for homosexuality, prisoners convicted of other crimes, working class males of similar age, and unconvicted male homosexual patients. The two homosexual groups resembled each other and differed from the others. They presented a profile characteristic of neurotics with 'an unusual degree of extraversion' and 'a weak ego'. These results still fail to establish that homosexuals who are neither prisoners nor patients have abnormal personality profiles. Turner *et al.* (1974), working in England, studied two groups of male homosexuals, one referred for aversion therapy, and the other consisting of volunteers from a homophile organisation. On the Eysenck Personality Inventory the prospective patients produced scores indicative of a markedly neurotic tendency, whereas homosexual volunteers who had never sought treatment did not. On the Cattell 16 PF Test, the patients were significantly more 'apprehensive', 'group dependent' and 'tense' (factors Q1, Q2 and Q4) than the non-patient homosexuals. The authors concluded that candidates for therapy are untypical of non-patient homosexuals and ought not to be used for making generalisations about the personality of homosexuals at large.

In another prison research, Pascal and Herzberg (1952), using the Rorschach Test, reported that homosexuals and paedophiliacs gave significantly more 'deviant' responses than either rapists or prisoners in general. A more convincing account of Rorschach protocols obtained from male homosexuals was given in reports by Evelyn Hooker (1957, 1958) who studied men living in the community rather than patients or prisoners. Independent judges scored the Rorschach and TAT responses of 30 male homosexuals and the same number of heterosexuals, without knowing which was which. The ratings of 'adjustment' awarded did not distinguish between the heterosexuals and homosexuals. In short, whatever the peculiarities of individual homosexuals, there was no evidence of any consistent trend, or any general inferiority in personal adjustment, among the homosexual group. Sexual orientation appeared to be substantially independent of other aspects of personality and social adjustment, a conclusion entirely in accord with clinical observation.

One of the larger and more interesting personality test surveys of a non-patient group of male homosexuals was reported by Siegelman (1972a). The sample consisted of 307 males who described themselves as either exclusively (202 cases) or predominantly homosexual. They were recruited from lecture audiences, homophile organisations and the clients of a homophile bookstore. They were compared with a group of heterosexual students who were rather younger than the homosexuals, but from families of similar educational and social status. The respondents were asked to complete the Neuroticism Scale Questionnaire of Scheier and Cattell and the Gough Femininity Scale, as well as selected items from a number of other personality tests. The NSQ results revealed that, as a group, the homosexuals were less depressed but more neurotic than the heterosexuals. Among other traits tested, the two groups did not differ significantly on Alienation, Trust, Self-Acceptance or Dependency, but the homosexuals appeared more 'goal-directed' and 'nurturant' than the heterosexuals. The differences were clearly complex, and in some respects the heterosexuals were at a disadvantage compared with the homosexuals. The finding that the homosexual group were distinctly more 'neurotic' had to be qualified when allowance was made for traits of 'femininity' measured by the Gough questionnaire scores. The least 'feminine' half of the homosexual sample were not in fact more neurotic than the heterosexuals. It would seem that male homosexuals who identify with a conventionally masculine style do not show up as neurotic on questionnaires. Whether the feminine type have a genuinely unusual and neurotic psychological make-up, or whether their manifest anxiety results from dissonance between their own attitudes and preferences and the social demands placed upon them remains an open question.

CHAPTER THREE

Learning to be Male or Female

1. *Psychological contrasts between the sexes*

Apart from their contrasting genital anatomy and erotic preferences, men and women differ in a thousand ways. Physical differences in height, body contour, bone structure and muscular development are all too obvious, and must be a consequence of inborn genetic differences between the two sexes. The growth and development of boys and girls are programmed differently from the moment of conception. Even so, environmental influences may interfere with or modify the programme. If society encourages sport and manual pursuits only for men, this will tend to increase the innate muscular advantage of the male sex. Acquired diseases affecting growth, especially diseases of the endocrine glands, may prevent particular individuals, despite a normal genetic potential, from attaining the physique appropriate to their sex.

In the psychological sphere also men and women differ in important respects. Men tend to be more aggressive, adventurous, competitive and inclined to abstract intellectuality; women tend to be more concerned with interpersonal feelings, less assertive and more responsive to small children. Notwithstanding these considerable differences between the average man and woman, individual variability often transcends general trends. Some women are more athletic than most men, and a minority of men are even less aggressive and more affectionate than most women. On the whole, the temperamental differences between the sexes are more subtle, less consistent, and more dependent upon upbringing and environment than the physical differences between them. In fact, some authorities believe that the typical masculine or feminine personality develops entirely through social learning, and that the new-born babe, though physically differentiated, is quite neutral as regards potentiality for male or female personality development. Other authorities consider that most of the observed differences between male and female behaviour arise inevitably from inborn aggressive and maternal instincts, and do not depend upon the kinds of conduct contemporary society happens to applaud or parents try to instil. While the truth must lie somewhere between these two extremes, there is no doubt that in the human species environment exerts a tremendously powerful effect upon the attitude and behaviour of the sexes. In the days when relatively minor deformities of the genitals might lead to a baby being assigned to the wrong sex, it was evident that social behaviour and erotic preferences followed the direction of early parental training rather than that expected from the child's genetic sex.

Corinne Hutt (1972), who believes firmly in the biological basis of male and female temperament, has produced a succinct and scholarly review of the evidence that the physical performance and general behaviour of males and females differ in fundamental ways from the moment of birth. Male babies are heftier, their hearts stronger, their chemical consumption (basal metabolism) greater, their hand clasp stronger, their activity more marked and their movements more vigorous, but they are more susceptible to lethal diseases. Males predominate among the still-born, females predominate among the aged. Direct measurements prove that, from infancy onwards, females detect touch and sound more readily, whereas males have more acute vision and excel in the perception of size, position and relationships between objects (visio-spatial skills). New-born females are more responsive than males to sweet tastes, and increase their consumption of feed when a sweetener is added (Nisbett and Gurwitz, 1970). Girls develop superior verbal abilities, they learn to talk at an earlier age than boys, and at every stage of development they have a larger vocabulary and a greater verbal fluency. Boys are better at the comprehension of mechanical relationships, but girls are more deft with their hands, which may account for women's superiority in typing, sewing and assembling small components. From a very young age boys are noticeably more physically aggressive, they destroy toys and attack other children more readily than girls do. In later life, males tend to become more ambitious and competitive than females. Even in the nursery, girls seem to be more friendly, attentive and protective towards newcomers than boys, a difference which heralds the adult female's special facility for maternal responsibility and for succouring and nurturing roles (McGrew, 1972). On tests of creativity, which give credit to originality in response to such questions as 'How many uses can you think of for a tyre?' males usually do better than females, being more inventive and more willing to explore unconventional ideas. In personality, as well as in height and weight, males are more variable than females, and apt to run to extremes. The male sex has more than a fair share of geniuses and mental defectives, of artistic and intellectual innovators, of social reformers and revolutionaries, as well as criminals, sex deviants, drug addicts and suicides. In contrast, females more often cluster round the average, a phenomenon that has been dubbed the 'mediocrity of women' (Heim, 1970).

2. *Masculinity and femininity among homosexuals*

The normal variations between males and females are of relevance in connection with the theory that homoerotic inclinations represent just one aspect of a general tendency for certain individuals to develop psychological characteristics typical of the opposite sex. The theory reflects a popular belief that homosexual men resemble women while lesbians resemble men. Any such tendency cannot be too extreme; otherwise concealment of the homosexual condition would be socially impossible. Some people think they can pick out homosexuals by anomalous physical characteristics, such as wide hips in men or large bones and deep voices in women, but this is mistaken. Save for a few exceptional individuals, homosexuals conform in outward appearance and performance to the usual physical standards·of their biological sex. Erections and ejaculations in the male, and menstruation in the female, occur at.the normally expected ages. The only reason for infertility among homosexuals would seem to be avoidance of heterosexual intercourse (but see p. 69).

The position is less simple in regard to psychological characteristics. Save for their unconventional erotic interests, many male and female homosexuals come close to society's ideal of masculinity or femininity. An important minority, however, display to a pronounced degree social mannerisms and attitudes generally considered more appropriate to members of the opposite biological sex. Clinical psychologists have developed attitude and interest questionnaires which discriminate between men and women. Many homosexuals, if asked to complete such questionnaires, give a high proportion of responses typical of members of the opposite sex.

One of the earliest and most ambitious researches of this kind was carried out by the American investigators Terman and Miles (1936). They developed an extensive, 910-item test which called upon subjects to choose between various statements of opinion, attitude and interest according to which fitted themselves most closely. The subjects' associations to lists of words and to the ink-blot shapes were also analysed. The average scores of men and women on this test differed radically. In interests, women liked indoor, artistic and decorative occupations, while men liked adventure and pursuits involving muscle power. Women expressed emotions of disgust, pity and fear more often than men, and in moral attitudes they were more censorious. Men more often gave outdoor and·mechanical associations to the ink-blot shapes, while women gave more domestic and aesthetic associations.

Responses to such tests are greatly influenced by individual experience and training. Terman and Miles found that the more intelligent and better educated among women scored closer to the masculine norm. Male musicians and artists gave score averages that were almost female, whereas women athletes, doctors and scientists gave scores that were almost male. They administered the test to two groups of male homosexuals. The first group of twenty-seven 'passive' homosexuals produced scores more typical of female than of males. The second group of forty-six 'active' homosexuals gave scores more

masculine than those of the average soldier. These contrasts were
meant to show the differences in temperament between homosexual
males of contrasting sexual habits, but they were probably a more
faithful reflection of the way the two samples were collected. The so-
called 'active' cases were recruited from the U.S. Disciplinary
Barracks at Alcatraz, and were presumably aggressive criminal types
with exaggerated masculine attitudes. The 'passive' group consisted
of the friends of an effeminate male prostitute located in a gaol. Most
of them were also prostitutes, and might therefore be suspected of
having some professional interest in the projection of a female image.

Over the years many different tests of personality have been applied
in an effort to demonstrate that homosexuals produce responses
untypical of their own sex and more like those of the opposite sex.
Results have been variable, and not particularly dependable.
Although a certain tendency to deviate from the norm in the direction
predicted has been reported frequently, many individuals fail to
conform to the general trend. The homosexual population seems quite
mixed in this respect, some groups giving responses emphatically in
keeping with their biological sex, and only a minority responding like
the opposite sex.

Among the better-known personality questionnaires the MMPI,
which includes a masculinity-femininity scale, has been the one most
widely used in surveys of homosexuals (Dean and Richardson, 1964,
1966; Singer, 1970). This test has been claimed to identify the
majority of male homosexuals successfully (Krippner, 1964), and it
has been extensively employed in America by organisations wishing to
reject job applicants who might be homosexuals, but obviously it will
not detect the sub-group of male homosexuals who have distinctively
masculine personality profiles (Aaronson and Grumpelt, 1961). A still
more serious drawback to the use of such tests for social purposes is
that they are liable to misidentify as probable homosexuals some
heterosexual men who happen to have untypical intellectual or
occupational interests.

Evidence suggests that male homosexuals who are habitually
'passive' in their sexual relations, and female homosexuals who are
'active', are particularly likely to produce anomalous scores on
masculinity-femininity tests. The relationship is far from being
invariable. Evelyn Hooker (1965b) who interviewed volunteers from
the homosexual community, confirmed that some males insisted on
taking the passive role in sex because to do otherwise was unlady-like
and in conflict with their concepts of themselves as feminine. On the
other hand, many others felt themselves to be perfectly masculine, and
considered masculinity to have no connection with homosexual
inclinations or with erotic preference for an active or passive role in
sex. Certainly, in clinical experience one finds men of indisputably
masculine physique and attitude who derive immense erotic
satisfaction from the experience of penetration *per anum*.

Temperamental unfitness for the role expected of one's sex has been

cited as a possible cause for becoming homosexual. The boy who will
not or cannot become proficient at fighting, at physical games and
sports, or at self-assertion, may lose confidence in his ability to
perform any kind of masculine role, and so turn away from
heterosexual contacts. A wide variety of early conflicts or discouraging
experiences may help to instil in a boy the idea that masculine
attitudes are dangerous, reprehensible or unrewarding, and thus
engender a character who is a passive, compliant and compulsively
self-effacing (Hewitt, 1961). In a survey of the families of Danish
sailors Tiller (1967) observed that father's absence from home caused
many mothers to overprotect their sons and thereby to encourage the
development of feminine traits. Boys subjected to these kinds of
pressure, in an effort to compensate for a sense of masculine
inadequacy, may react on occasion with excessive, violent or
inappropriate displays of toughness or self-assertion. The results of
psychological tests applied to male homosexuals support the idea that
the condition is sometimes associated with a feminine identification,
but the tests cannot show whether cross-sex traits develop before or
after the establishment of a homosexual orientation. Some young male
homosexuals begin to develop effeminate mannerisms for the first time
after being introduced into 'gay' circles. One doubts in such cases
whether the mannerisms indicate a truly feminine disposition, or
whether they are cultivated in order to win acceptance and attract the
notice of potential sex partners. Similarly, the choice of supposedly
'feminine' occupations, such as hairdressing, shop display or
theatrical work, may be the result of natural aptitude and interest, but
may also be governed by the need to secure a position where colleagues
and superiors will be unlikely to show active hostility towards a
homosexual employee.

Thompson *et al.* (1973), in a survey comparing non-patient
homosexuals with a control group, found that the homosexuals
differed not only in giving more feminine scores on masculinity-
femininity tests, but also in describing less masculine interests and
attitudes in childhood. For example, they played less baseball and less
competitive games, felt themselves to have been clumsy and not
athletic, were more fearful of physical injury and more likely to avoid
fights. They were also likely to categorise themselves as 'lone wolves'.
The investigators concluded that alienation from peers, who normally
provide boys with male role models and stimulate heterosexual
identification, probably reinforced parental influences in turning
them into homosexuals.

In the important research of Saghir and Robins (1973) male
homosexual and heterosexual volunteers (who had never been
psychiatric hospital patients) differed most strikingly in the high
frequency (67 per cent) with which the homosexuals reported girlish
or sissy tendencies in childhood, and the low frequency (3 per cent)
with which the heterosexuals recalled such tendencies. Strong wishes
to change sex, indicative of a clear feminine identification, were rare,

but a .constellation of small peculiarities, amounting to a definite
effeminate trend, was noticeable in the histories of the majority of the
homosexuals. The features described included odd appearance,
timidity, ineptness at sports, occasional interest in putting on girls'
clothes, attraction to girls' toys and girls' company, social isolation in
boys' groups and a tendency to be teased and called 'sissy' by school
fellows. The childhood 'sissyness', which these investigators found so
frequently, did not necessarily develop into adult effeminacy, but it
was associated with a particular type of deeply committed
homosexual male. For example, the childhood sissies were
particularly likely to be closer to their mothers than their fathers, to be
oldest or youngest sons, and to deny having ever had heterosexual
fantasy or arousal in adolescence. As adults, all of the sissies were
exclusively or almost exclusively homosexual, but three out of 24 non-
sissies were to some extent bisexual in behaviour (Kinsey rating 1-4).
More of the sissies expressed in adulthood some feeling of feminine
identification. The majority of the homosexual sample practised
mixed or alternating roles in their sexual relations with other men,
being sometimes the 'insertor' sometimes the 'receiver'. Among the
minority who maintained for any length of time a consistent 'receiver'
or female role the childhood sissies predominated.

The psychological tests of masculinity – femininity commonly used
in researches on homosexuals have contributed comparatively little to
an understanding of the nature and origins of the cross-sex deviations
observed. Test scores are largely determined by attributes of a
somewhat superficial kind, which could be a by-product of the
homosexual life style rather than a cause of the homoerotic
orientations. The more basic psychological factors which distinguish
males and females, such as their perceptual habits and abilities, have
hardly ever been investigated in connection with homosexuality. One
suspects that a much larger proportion of homosexuals would be
found to conform to the norms for their true sex on these basic
qualities than on attitudes and interests, which are greatly influenced
by the individual's social situation and experience. In the manner in
which erotic arousal occurs, for example, males and females differ in
the same way irrespective of whether they are homosexuals or
heterosexuals. Males are more readily aroused by visual stimuli, by
the sight of an attractive person, or by the contemplation of pictorial
pornography. Females, whether lesbian or heterosexual, prefer lasting
relationships developing out of romantic attachments to the
promiscuous dalliance, or quick impersonal sex, that appeals to many
males.

Only a small minority of homosexuals display obvious cross-sex
interest and behaviour from an early age, but in such cases it could
well be that peculiarities of temperament, with consequent difficulty
in establishing gender identity, have favoured homoerotic
development. The small group of extreme cases, known as
transsexuals, provide particularly instructive examples. They are

quite rare. It has been estimated that only about one in a hundred thousand males and one in four hundred thousand females are so afflicted. Usually they are of normal physique, but dissatisfaction with their sexual identities, and attempts to play the role of the opposite sex, commence in childhood. By the time they reach adulthood, psychological gender identity overcomes physical reality. A male transsexual will assert with complete conviction that his body and genitals have developed wrongly and that in mind and soul he is truly a woman.

3. *The acquisition of gender identity*

As was mentioned earlier, males and females behave differently from the moment they are born. Studies of normal infants show that self-awareness of gender identity manifests remarkably early. By the age of 3, most children are able to identify the sex of dolls correctly, and begin to show greater interest in the toys and activities considered appropriate to their sex. They also begin to evince clear preferences for playmates of their own sex, and for imitating the behaviour of older persons of the same sex. This developing sense of gender identity becomes firmly and possibly irrevocably established by the age of 6 or 7.

Appreciation of gender is a more fundamental and earlier acquired attribute than appreciation of adult concepts of sex. Even though they may have been freely exposed to and fully aware of anatomical differences between the sexes, children do not learn that the dominant criterion of sex is genital, rather than clothing or hair style or behaviour, until they are about ten years of age (Levin *et al.*, 1972). Furthermore, the curiosity infants show about their own and other peoples' bodies and genitals, although it may contribute to the child's ideas of gender differences, does not necessarily have sexual significance in an adult sense. Infants may exhibit jealousy when their parents kiss and cuddle in their presence, while remaining apparently indifferent to the spectacle of actual intercourse.

Kohlberg (1967) argues that a child's appreciation of gender develops in conformity with, and at the same stage of life as, other comparable concepts. For instance, at the age when first aware of boy-girl distinctions, the infant cannot yet conceive the constancy and unalterability of gender any more than he can grasp the notion of constancy in other situations, such as the size of a figure seen retreating into the distance. Kohlberg believes that young children's ideas of gender become linked very early in life with stereotypes of male and female conduct. Males are perceived as bigger, stronger, and more aggressive than females. By the age of 6, children consistently attribute greater social powers to males. These childish notions exhibit a curious constancy, even in the absence of a father figure in the home, and despite recent modifications of the status of men and women in society. Kohlberg argues that the child's sex-role attitudes, interests and identifications develop partly in response to parental training and cultural expectations, but more particularly as a result of relatively universal experiences of body differences and gender roles inside and outside the family. All authorities seem agreed that once a young child's gender role has been firmly established, attempts to encourage contrary interests or behaviour by reward or punishment meet with a singularly poor response.

Most modern psychologists reject the Freudian psychoanalytical theory that gender development consists of an unfolding of instinctual tendencies, aided, but not determined by, parental training. Instead, learning theorists assume that gender differences are acquired by conditioning, by a subtle programme of rewards and deterrents to which all children in our culture are exposed. Careful observation has shown that parents, to a far greater extent than they themselves realise, adopt different attitudes and strategies in the rearing of boys and girls (Sears *et al.*, 1957). For instance, they are far more tolerant of boisterous, aggressive and cheeky behaviour in boys, and positively encourage boys to stand up for themselves and fight back when attacked. Dependency behaviour, and demonstratively affectionate gestures which are expected of girls, are discouraged as 'sissy' in boys. Consequently parents differ in their own expressions and gestures when dealing with boys or girls. Noisy tantrums are thought unfeminine, whining and crying unmanly. Physical punishments are more frequently used for boys. Masculine play preferences are thought to arise because boys receive different toys from girls, building bricks and model cars rather than dress materials or make-up.

Direct training by parents is only one of many ways in which sex roles are communicated to children. The behaviour of males and females in the home and on television provide models which children can imitate. Once gender distinctions have been learned, infants can see that certain activities, for instance boxing and wrestling, are exclusively masculine, whereas others, such as looking after babies, are predominantly feminine. The next step is to learn that imitations of their own sex lead to more favourable consequence than imitations of the opposite sex.

From their earliest years infants receive encouragement to behave in the style expected of their sex by a continuous feed-back from their parents. Goldberg and Lewis (1969), who demonstrated significant differences between the behaviour of girls and boys at age thirteen months, showed that the differences correlated with the way they had been handled by their mothers at six months. At this age mothers touch infants girls more often than they touch boys. At thirteen months, boys who had earlier been treated in a particularly masculine way, being touched less often than average, behaved in a more masculine way themselves, by less often trying to touch their mothers than did boys who had earlier experienced more maternal contact.

Some psychologists believe that an additional process, known as 'identification', intervenes and greatly facilitates social learning, particularly in the spheres of moral and sexual conformity. In modelling himself on parents, with whom the child has a close relationship, the child is strongly motivated to win their approval, since they are the sources of fulfilment of all his most basic needs. He not only imitates, but also admires and emulates them, and strives to become like them. In time he develops an image of himself as the same sort of person as his parents. If at any time he gives way to impulse or temptations to behave in ways that do not fit this image, he feels anxious and guilty, in other words he develops a conscience. By virtue of 'identification' he takes up as his own, in psychological jargon 'internalises', values and standards of conduct originally observed in the parents. Since the child's earliest perceptions are fairly crude, his internalised standards are likely to consist of somewhat primitive black and white distinctions. According to psychoanalysts, these early-acquired feelings of right and wrong (referred to as the 'super-ego'), in spite of their crudity, influence the individual throughout his life, although he may no longer be consciously aware of their origin.

In the earliest stages of development boys and girls alike identify most strongly with their mother, since she is the person closest to them, upon whose affection and approval they depend completely. At a later stage boys learn to identify with their fathers in the matter of gender roles. This need to transfer identification from one parent to the other could be one reason why gender confusion occurs more commonly in males than in females. Since the child's concepts of gender roles appear to be internalised at the same time, and by similar processes, as his earliest notions of right and wrong, this may account both for the surprising firmness with which children adhere to their gender roles, and for the surprising rigidity of many adults in condemning any deviation from what they consider to be right conduct for males and females.

Another possible learning mechanism, the implantation of gender identity by 'imprinting', although cited by no less authorities than Hampson and Hampson (1961), is probably not very relevant. Imprinting is a mechanism which occurs most prominently in lower animals. If presented with suitable stimuli at a very early, critical stage of their development, birds are liable to attach themselves to and respond to thoroughly inappropriate objects. Many such examples were described by Lorenz (1958). He found that, by substituting himself for the mother bird at the critical moment, he could cause new-born geese to follow him about instead of following their mothers. Under ordinary circumstances the social responses of baby birds are 'imprinted' upon members of their own species, but if this is prevented artificially, birds may become permanently attached instead to their human keepers. As a result, when they grow up they start to show courtship behaviour and to make copulatory gestures towards humans. Similarly, if young male mallard ducks are allowed contact only with male ducks during the imprinting period, they will respond only to males when they grow up and so become exclusive homosexuals.

Nothing like these dramatic imprinting phenomena have been observed in human beings, but there is considerable evidence that both humans and higher mammals pass through developmental phases when they are very responsive to particular learning tasks. The acquisition of a second language, for instance, is far easier in infancy than at later ages. It is said that babies separated from their mothers and placed in impersonal orphanage surroundings, where they are denied the experience of maternal affection during a critical stage of development, are never able to learn to respond properly in personal relationships, and are doomed to become what Bowlby (1953) called 'affectionless' characters. More extreme deprivations inflicted upon experimental animals produce correspondingly severe disabilities. Baby monkeys separated from mother and siblings during early life never catch up in social learning later on. As adults they are quarrelsome and unsociable and inept at courtship and mating. In the case of females, maternal skills fail to develop, and offspring are neglected or maltreated (Harlow and Harlow, 1962). Empirical research on the matter is so far lacking, but it seems likely that the years from 3 to 5 are rather critical for the acquisition of gender identity in humans, and that hindrance to learning during this period may have a lasting effect on the performance of socio-sexual roles.

One of the strongest pieces of evidence for the crucial importance of parental behaviour in promoting an infant's gender identity comes from the study of cases of physical hermaphrodism in which infants with ambiguous genital appearance are sometimes reared as male or female according to an early parental decision that may not correspond to their genetic sex. Even when subsequent anatomical developments show that the original sex of assignment was mistaken, they still cling to the sexual identity they learned in infancy. Money and Ehrhardt (1972) illustrate the point with a number of telling case histories. Girls who have been reared as boys, when they begin to experience at puberty breast development or other signs out of keeping with their concept of themselves as boys, are only too pleased to undergo any surgical procedure to make them more like the normal males they believe themselves to be. Likewise, individuals reared as girls want to remain girls, and if they seek surgery it is in the interest of preserving their feminine self-image. The erotic preferences and sexual fantasies of these individuals generally accord with the gender identity they have learned. The minority who become 'homosexual', or who seek to change their sexual status, have usually been reared by parents who were doubtful about their offspring's sex. Such confused parents fail to reinforce sex-appropriate behaviour with that automatic and consistent feed-back which enables infants to establish a firm gender identity. In situations in which parents and offspring are both confident as to gender, the usual outcome is a firm sense of sexual identity, with erotic and romantic attachments clearly directed towards members of what is conceived as the opposite sex, and sometimes pursued in practice with considerable determination, notwithstanding serious and embarrassing physical impediments.

4. *Cultural pressures towards distinctive sex roles*

Even without external encouragement, some psychological differences between the sexes would surely emerge on the basis of innate, biological factors. The intervention of cultural pressures profoundly modifies behaviour and usually sharpens the contrasts between male and female. For example, many of the distinctive responses to conventional tests of masculinity – femininity evidently depend upon social expectations. On these tests men show more knowledge of outside activities while women know more about children and domestic affairs, but the contrasts between them are much less in the better-educated classes than among the labouring classes. Moreover, in all classes, contrasts between the sexes in these respects are decreasing. as more men and women follow the modern trend of sharing their interests and activities both inside and outside the home. Some items are ludicrously culture-bound. As women take to driving cars and using complicated domestic appliances, their traditional ignorance of mechanical contrivances cannot fail to diminish.

Anthropological evidence suggests that cultural pressures serve to amplify the basic differences between the sexes. A wide range of primitive cultures emphasise the same characteristic differences in sex roles. In addition to their insistence upon firm divisions of occupation and social role, they ascribe to women a lower status and impose particularly heavy restrictions on female sexual freedom. In a survey of 110 societies, Barry *et al.* (1957) noted a striking consistency in the different child-rearing methods applied to boys and girls, boys being brought up to be self-reliant and achieving, girls being trained to be obedient, nurturant and dependable. They attributed these trends to more or less universally accepted stereotypes of adult sex roles, males being required to develop skills in hunting, warfare, and other activites essential to the tribal economy, females being expected to look after home and children and prepare meals.

The dominance of males is an almost constant feature in primitive societies. In the World Ethnographic Sample summarised by Murdock (1957), 427 societies permitted a man to have more than one wife, but only 4 allowed a woman more than one husband. In most societies married couples must reside near the husband's relatives rather than near the wife's family. Within the marital home the husband has more authority than the wife. In the sexual sphere, women are generally expected to leave the initiative to the menfolk. Extra-marital affairs are condemned much more severely if the wife strays rather than the husband. Male nudity is quite commonly allowed, but most societies make women wear some genital covering.

These common features in the cultural definitions of sex roles reflect essential physical differences between the sexes. Since women become pregnant and have to suckle babies, they are less mobile than men and better suited to staying at home and looking after children. Since men are swifter and more muscular they become better hunters and providers. These needs are more pressing in hunting communities than in farming societies, where much of the essential labour can be done effectively by either sex. One might therefore expect hunting communities to develop particularly rigid sex roles and sex hierarchies, and anthropological evidence confirms this (D'Andrade, 1967). The amalgamation of tribes into larger units, governed by an autocratic ruler or king, also encourages a big status gap between the sexes. The economic exploitation of commoners by autocratic rulers is paralleled in the home, with husbands lording it over wives (Stephens, 1963). The more radical exponents of present-day women's liberation claim to discern a similar connection between the exploitative capitalist economic system and the subjugation of the female sex.

Once embedded in the culture, sex-role stereotypes become self-perpetuating, and efforts to modify them to take into account changing social needs meet with great resistance. Under modern conditions a wide range of professional jobs can be performed by women, but tradition still ensures that they gravitate to teaching, nursing and social work rather than to law, politics or science. Marriages in which the woman acts as breadwinner while the man looks after the children have become viable, but are not approved. One couple who had done this from choice described their arrangement in a television programme recently broadcast from London, and members of the public were brought to the studio to comment. Some of them criticised the couple so fiercely and contemptuously it was evident that they found the reversal of traditional sex roles too unpleasantly shocking to consider dispassionately.

In the matter of sexual behaviour human nature is extraordinarily compliant to cultural demands. Societies have existed in which approved sex-role behaviour runs contrary to the trends accepted as 'natural' in most places. Margaret Mead (1935), in her vivid descriptions of sex and temperament in three primitive tribal societies in New Guinea, has provided the best-known examples. In one community, the Tchambuli, sex roles were the opposite of contemporary expectations. The women did the productive labour, dominated the social organisation and took the initiative in sexual relations. The men had a more decorative function. Supported by female labour, they spent their time on art and ceremonial dances. The ideal Tchambuli woman was efficient, businesslike, loyal and comradely. Tchambuli men were temperamentally less responsible and more emotionally dependent. It was normal for them to engage in catty gossip and jealous squabbles and to affect precious manners. In another tribe, the Mungudumors, both men and women exceeded in aggressiveness the ideal 'he-man' of most ordinary societies. The Mungudumors placed no value on tolerance and affectionate relationships. The men were in a perpetual state of jealous hostility, fighting and insulting each other in ceaseless conflict over the possession of the best women. The male ideal was a life of splendid isolation within a stockade housing many wives to look after him and only a few puny male relations unable to challenge his supremacy. The women were only a degree less hostile, quarrelling among themselves and refusing to help each other's children. In their brief passionate sexual contacts both men and women enjoyed sadistic foreplay, biting, scratching, ripping clothes and tearing ornaments. In absolute contrast to this, a third tribe, the Arapesh, maintained the ideal of a mild, responsive man married to a mild responsive woman. Both sexes were trained to be cooperative, unaggressive and sensitive to the needs of others. There was no conception of sexual demands constituting a powerful or competitive driving force among either men or women. Both sexes displayed parental behaviour which we should call maternal and sexual attitudes which we should call feminine.

It may be possible to identify accidental climatic, economic or historic factors to account for the origins of these peculiar cultures. No tribe in competition with aggressive neighbours for limited natural sources could have survived and at the same time maintained ·the peaceful cultural traditions of the Arapesh. However that may be, the lessons for present purposes are the relativity of ideals of masculinity and femininity to cultural expectations, and the plasticity of the temperament of both sexes in the face of cultural demands. Traits of dominance or submissiveness are not inevitably sex-linked characteristics. To a large extent they are developed by social training, and most members of either sex are potentially capable of fulfilling either stereotype. Furthermore, the nature of the socio-sexual role men and women are required to perform bears no direct relation to the prevalence of homosexual deviants. Mead found no evidence that the effeminate male Arapesh or Tchambuli, or the aggressive female Mungudumors, were prone to homosexuality. Certainly a cultural preference for decorative adornment among males, as in the painted and bejewelled warriors of primitive tribes, or the wigged and powdered eighteenth-century beaux, or the long hair styles of recent decades, is no indication of homosexual tendency. On the other hand, it may be that cultures which exaggerate sex differences, put restrictions on what is permitted to each sex, and place special emphasis on male supremacy, are likely to produce temperamental misfits who cannot meet the heavy demands attached to their sex role.

Anthropologists have noted that some societies have institutionalised arrangements which allow exceptional individuals to change their official gender identity. Usually they are men, variously called *berdaches*, *alyhas* and *shamans*, who dress as women, assume female social roles, and even marry other men. George Devereux (1937) made a study of this system among the Mohave Indians, a warrior race who inhabited the south-west of North America. Youths of effeminate manners and interests who did not fit in with the usual pursuits of the male members of the tribe went through a testing ceremony which might change their status. Spectators gathered and special songs were sung. If the boy responded by dancing enthusiastically in the manner of a woman he was proclaimed an *alyha*, led away by the women, and dressed in skirt and female adornments. After that, he lived as a woman, was permitted to go to feasts as a woman, to be courted by men and to take a husband. *Alyhas* were said to make good wives, being more efficient, industrious and powerful than an ordinary young woman. Sexual relations took the form of anal and oral intercourse, but the Mohaves were sexually uninhibited and permissive and these were common practices among heterosexual couples, so they generally proved acceptable to the alyha's husband. Once established in the role, the *alyha* was always referred to as a woman. He would even scratch his thighs to produce blood stains in imitation of menstruation, and insist that his husband observe the appropriate taboos at these times. Sometimes the *alyha* would go further, stuffing his skirt with rags, proclaiming a pregnancy and forcing his husband to go through appropriate rituals. By imbibing constipating concoctions he would produce abdominal pains, said to be labour pains. He would then retire to the woods to defecate and bury the product, saying on return that a still birth had taken place, and putting on mourning. On the whole the *alyha* was a fairly respected figure, his eccentricities being overlooked because destiny had singled him out for the role. In all his doings the *alyha* would preserve a facade of femininity, referring to his anatomy in feminine terminology, the penis as a clitoris and the rectum as a vagina. To be reminded of the continued presence of testes and penis was the worst insult an alyha could receive. The *alyha*'s husband, on the other hand, had to suffer a certain amount of teasing about his anomalous position.

Although of sunny disposition and sexually highly permissive, the Mohaves were warriors who greatly admired physical courage. This may have been a factor in persuading some timorous youths to abandon the masculine role. Opler (1965) points to the coexistence of cross-sex institutions with the presence of particular difficulties in a society's expected role for men. He cites the example of the Chukchee shamans of Siberia, a class of male transvestites accorded special status as religious figures. The Chukchee insisted on an exorbitant price for brides, which men might spend years trying to amass. This led to the accumulation of a floating population of frustrated, unmarried labourers of low status. The institution of shamanism provided a means of escape for those wanting to give up the struggle and contract out of the system without losing too much face.

In addition to the *alyhas*, the Mohaves also had a small class of women who changed sex role, but this is relatively unusual. However, Marise Querlin (1965, p. 113) quotes a description by Dominque Troare, a Sudanese schoolmaster, of institutionalised marriages between women of the Bobo-Nienegués. These usually took place between older childless widows and young girls, the older woman contributing a substantial bride-price in order to improve her status from that of a despised sterile woman to that of titular husband. Male lovers were allowed to visit surreptitiously in order to produce children for the marriage. In general, however, the occurrence of extensive lesbianism, institutionalised or otherwise, has rarely been noted by anthropologists.

A slightly disguised form of identification with the opposite sex role occurs in the ceremonies known as the couvade. These are customs which enable husbands to enjoy a vicarious participation in the birth of their children by adopting, as a ritual, the behaviour and taboos of a pregnant wife. They may even experience labour pains and other symptoms connected with childbirth. These customs involve only a temporary disruption of the usual male role, and seem to express envy of one particular aspect of femininity, the ability to give birth. The Islamic tradition which predicts that the Messiah will be born to a man appears to reflect a similar preoccupation.

Theoretically, because of the generally inferior status ascribed to the female role, there should be more women than men wanting to change places. In primitive societies, however, one finds relatively few examples of institutional expression given to women wanting to become men. This may be due to the tight control of social institutions exercised by men in male-dominated cultures. Dominant males may feel threatened by women who want to raise their sexual status, but they have nothing to fear from men who want to go down into the ranks of women. In modern society the situation is reversed. A change towards masculine habits on the part of females receives widespread support, but a drift towards effeminacy in males seems obnoxious. This difference possibly reflects a lessening of the males' confidence in their natural superiority. Any man who publicly rejects his sexual heritage inspires the resentment of other males because his behaviour casts further doubt upon the image of masculine superiority.

5. *Gender learning gone wrong*

Considering the complexity of learning processes, the different standards of gender behaviour adhered to by different social groups, and the varying capacities of individual parents to communicate gender concepts, it is surprising that things go seriously wrong so infrequently. Minor anxieties about gender performance are of course quite common. Women ponder about their appearance, demeanour and attractiveness and about the adequacy of their maternal and sexual feelings. Men are apt to wonder if their performance in sexual intercourse comes up to standard, to wish they were more powerfully built, and to envy those bolder and more successfully dominant than themselves. Extreme instances of gender anxiety or confusion, although rare, are particularly instructive for the light they throw upon how gender learning may go wrong. The following history of a male transsexual is a case in point:

Sidney was already in his forties when he came for consultation, dressed as a woman and calling himself Sylvia. He worked in a professional job, and had persuaded his employers to accept his female identity. He even belonged to a women's organisation, and was allowed to participate fully in their social activities, in spite of some of the leaders knowing he was genetically a man. The only embarrassing incident that had occurred was when someone who knew his secret objected when he was selected to nursemaid a group of young children at a garden party.

Sylvia's chief concern was with her acceptability as a woman. She was shy of her appearance and kept trying to hide her face. At first glance most people would not have queried her sex. She had been taking female hormones, and had developed some feminine contours of fat and a certain smoothness of complexion. She also spoke in a half-falsetto voice that could be taken as female. But she was tall, large-boned, with correspondingly big hands and feet, and the beard area of her face showed signs of plucking. She had only recently commenced 'passing' as a woman. Later on she was accepted by a specialist surgeon, who removed her unwanted testicles and altered her external genital appearance to resemble that of a woman. After that she became much less anxious and more adroit and confident in dress and manner. The operation removed one of her greatest fears, that of being put into a position of having to undress and be revealed as a man, and perhaps sent into a male ward in hospital.

Sidney gave the following recollection of his development. His father was a timid, shadowy, indecisive creature who took little interest in home or children. His mother was a strong character who coped well with making all the family decisions, but she enjoyed poor health and became an invalid. Sidney was very close to her and admired her bright mind and cultural interests, which his father did not share at all.

He explained: 'I always wanted to be a girl. I never told my mother, but I think she knew and I think she also wanted me to be a girl. Things would slip out like, "If you were a girl you could do so and so". Even before I went to school I was upset about being a boy. When I was three I was already admiring girls' clothes in the shops. Mother was amused by it, but father was angry. I didn't care, because mother meant everything to me and father was just a drip who made her cry. Mother taught me to sew and cook. My only playmates were girl cousins.

'At school I tried to do what I was supposed to as a boy, but I was no good at it. I had one brother two years my elder. He thought me very odd and cut me dead all through school. He thought me sissy because I wouldn't fight. He was always father's favourite. I was kicked around a lot at secondary school. I wasn't tough enough for cadets or teams, and very clumsy at physical training. Then a sympathetic doctor got me off games because I wasn't strong, even though I was quite tall.

'As an adolescent I was intensely upset about being a boy. At thirteen or fourteen I went down sick with it. I used to pray to die.

'I became a lone wolf, spending all my time studying. I got on at work, but was awkward socially. The people I mixed with for work were mostly girls. I was late developing physically, I didn't have to shave till quite old. I've never really had a sexual interest in anyone, only emotional attachments. I don't want to have sexual intercourse with anyone, male or female. I used to go around with an older man who was affectionate, but we were accused of being queer, though the relationship was quite platonic.'

Sidney became friendly with a girl colleague, and they shared house for some time. Their relationship was sociable and sisterly rather than romantic. The girl had serious emotional problems herself, and didn't want to have anything to do with normal men. Eventually, under pressure from relatives, and in order to keep up external appearances, they got married. But Sidney became increasingly unhappy. 'Life was quite intolerable. Outwardly my wife wasn't interested in men, but actually she wanted me to act more manly, but I just couldn't face up to people as a man. In a quarrel someone had only got to say disapproving things and I would lose my head and go off and dissolve into tears. I just couldn't be assertive. I could handle tools, but something in my manner told people I was odd. I could never be a man however much I tried and felt guilty when I failed. I expect men to be dirty and brutal and ugly in their bodies, and I can't identify with them.'

So Sydney decided to take the step of changing identity and passing as Sylvia. She obtained a divorce, secured a new job, and then felt much better. The process was painful. 'I kept going on tranquillisers. Several times I tried over-dosing. Since my change I've climbed out of all that. I've left off the drugs and am eating again. Everyone accepts me now and I can mix more easily.'

The first point to notice in this typical history of a male transsexual is the strong sense of being a female, and the intense preoccupation with gender, which began in infancy. Sidney was more interested in having his feminine identity accepted than in having actual sexual relations. The need was so compulsive that, in spite of being timid, conventional and hypersensitive to criticism, he went through harrowing confrontations with outraged relatives and astonished officials, to say nothing of protracted and painful surgery, all for the sake of changing his status. Until his need to be a woman reached fulfilment he remained ineffectual, recurrently depressed and even at times actively suicidal. Like most male transsexuals, he had experienced sexual feeling towards other men but did not class this feeling as homosexual, since he thought of himself as truly a woman. In fact he was not very sympathetic towards homosexuals. On one occasion he met some male transvestites and was revolted by their ugly and falsely feminine appearance.

Two further points in Sidney's history deserve note. The parental background was typical. Father was a weak man who exerted little influence, while mother was a dominant woman, closely attached to the son, who seemed positively to encourage his wish to be a girl. The delay in overt declaration of feminine gender until social circumstances and surgical intervention made it possible is also not unusual. Under pressure of family and social demands Sidney kept up appearances as best he could, and lived as a man for the better part of a life-time, even though all the time he felt his role a miserable pretence. The story has much in common with the various autobiographical accounts recently published by male transsexuals who have succeeded in changing their sexual identity and passing for a woman (Morris, 1974).

Case histories such as Sidney's are open to suspicion since recollections of childhood may be coloured by desire to shift responsibility for deviant conduct on to parents. Ideally, one needs continuous observation of the natural history of transsexuality from infancy to adulthood, but this is scarcely feasible, if only because no medical man who recognises severe gender disturbance in a small child could refrain from attempts to avert a tragic outcome. One must therefore try to piece together the probable course of events by checking the statements of adult patients, and by comparing their versions of transsexual development with observations of children who already display transsexual symptoms at an early age. Such inquiries cannot reveal how many cases of childhood gender-disturbance work themselves out without leading to permanent adult transsexuality, but at least they give an indication of the backgrounds associated with the more malignant and unremitting forms of gender disturbance.

Stoller (1968) has published some vivid case descriptions of small boys whose identification with femininity was apparent when they were only two or three years of age. Such boys watch and imitate their mothers dressing, making up, and arranging their hair. They pick up feminine gestures, intonations, posture and movement. They choose girls' parts in games. They follow their mothers around very closely, identifying themselves all the time with her interests and activities. The mothers themselves are equally unusual, in that they discourage the child from developing separate and independent activities and seem not at all displeased by the son's charmingly feminine ways. The fathers tend to absent themselves a great deal and to show no concern about the situation. The mothers tend to have problems of gender dissatisfaction themselves and to take little or no pleasure in sexual relations within marriage. Such parents have to be persuaded by outsiders that something is wrong; otherwise they seem content to let the situation drift.

If these cases are, as they seem, transsexuals in the making, they serve to confirm the family pattern as described by adult deviants. On occasion it proves possible to obtain some confirmation of adult recollections in another way, by questioning a surviving parent. Stoller (1968) quotes one particularly interesting example. This was a male transsexual who received surgical treatment for the removal of penis and testes and the construction of an artificial vagina, utilising skin from the penis. Even before this intervention, he had been living as a woman and, as a result of having taken female hormones secretly ever since the onset of puberty, he had developed breasts and other female characteristics. After the operation he became still more convincing in his role as a woman, since the genitals were now unequivocally female and it was possible to have sexual intercourse successfully with male lovers.

Interviews with this transsexual's mother confirmed the essential features of his background. He was the youngest in the family, and as a baby looked pretty and like a girl. The mother dressed him as a girl and let his hair grow long. Until he was 8, she took him to bed with her, sleeping nestled close together with her body curled round him. The father, a sick man who died when the boy was about 8, showed no concern.

From an examination of many similar histories Stoller concludes that the parental factors of particular importance in the genesis of male transsexualism are as follows: (1) Blissful physical and emotional closeness between mother and infant extended over years and uninterrupted by other siblings. (2) Problems of sexual adjustment and of gender identity in the mothers themselves. (3) Passive fathers who take little interest in the infant and absent themselves from the domestic scene as much as possible. (4) An empty, angry marriage between mother and father (Stoller, 1969).

Further studies by Green (1974) confirmed some of the main

features of the families of effeminate boys that had been described by Stoller, but found that the peculiarities of parental behaviour were not always so extreme as Stoller had suggested. The tendency of a mother to dote on her effeminate son to the exclusion of other members of the family was particularly noticeable. In admiring everything he did she would do nothing to discourage him from identifying with her and copying her feminine ways. The father would usually ignore the situation, thinking it a passing phase, but later, finding the boy had become an incorrigible sissy incapable of sharing male interests, father would adopt an aloof, rejecting attitude. The boy himself was usually of conspicuously non-aggressive temperament, the result, possibly, of some innate physical peculiarity. On this account he could fit into the company of girls more easily than he could hold his own among boys. His alienation from the male world was liable to be still further increased by teasing at school and by paternal rejection.

Case studies of boys with gender disturbances do not always fall so neatly into the categories of anomalous child-rearing described by Stoller. One New York psychiatrist, Bernard Zuger (1970), arrived at very different conclusions after studying 25 boys with persistent effeminate behaviour seen in his private practice or at a hospital psychiatric clinic. The boys' effeminancy revealed itself in such behaviour as girlish posture and gestures, putting on female clothes, voicing a wish to be a girl, liking dolls and girls' company or avoiding boys' games. In most cases the peculiarity became noticeable by two or three years of age. Of the boys followed up till adolescence or later, nearly all became definitely or probably homosexual, though not necessarily fully transsexual. In regard to parental relationships, Zuger could find no significant difference between the group of effeminate boys and a group of non-effeminate boys taken from the same psychiatric practice. The effeminate boys' parents conformed hardly at all to the expected pattern. For instance, no predominant preference for girls was expressed by either their mothers or their fathers. The boys received little maternal encouragement for their girlish habits, in fact more mothers than fathers stook a stand against such behaviour, but the boys persisted in spite of prohibitions. The fathers were not alienated, in fact some were dominant in the home, and in a majority of cases the parents' marital relationship seemed satisfactory. In most families the father was initially affectionate towards the boy, and any subsequent deterioration resulted from the effeminate boy's own spontaneous withdrawal. Zuger concluded that the causes of effeminancy in boys do not lie in parental influences, but in factors inherent in the boys themselves.

Granting that Zuger may have overlooked some of the more subtle or covert parental attitudes, and granting that his cases fall short of true transsexuality, it remains difficult to reconcile his data with the theory that parental mishandling is the sole cause of gender disturbance. Pending such time as the experts reach closer agreement as to the facts, the most plausible assumption is that gender disturbance has multiple roots. In cases where children with a cross-sex identification have been exposed to obvious and gross family pressures, this is probably the main determinant, but in other cases different causes may predominate.

Adolescent experiences of sexual seduction can scarcely play much part in bringing about the homosexual orientation of men who take to that path by a simple continuation of their childhood rejection of the male role (Holeman and Winokur, 1965). In these cases the process is firmly under way, and the effeminate tendency very apparent, long before adolescence. If seduction experiences occur, they are likely to have been deliberately sought out as a means of confirming and satisfying a previously acquired feminine identification.

The backgrounds of female transsexuals have been less often studied than those of males, since fewer females present themselves to doctors wanting sex change operations. Estimates of the prevalence of well-established cases (Hoenig and Kenna, 1974; Wälinder, 1971) suggest that about one in thirty-five or thirty-six thousand adult males are transsexuals, compared with about only one in a hundred thousand females. The greater publicity given to male-female transformations, and the relatively more straightforward surgery involved, encourage male transsexuals to come forward, but the apparent difference in incidence between the sexes is unlikely to be due solely to this factor. The rarity of female transsexuality seems curious in view of the fact that tomboyish behaviour in girls is both commoner and culturally more acceptable than effeminate behaviour in boys. Psychoanalysts have suggested that sexual orientation in girls develops more tortuously than in boys. In both sexes the first attachment is to the mother, but girls must learn to transfer their affection to father in order to become heterosexual. While that may be true in regard to choice of love object, it is not so in regard to the earlier process of gender identification. In this girls seem to have the easier task since they can identify with the adult closest to them, whereas boys have sometimes to reach out to find a male figure. Social permissiveness towards tomboys may encourage girls to experiment with the male role and male pursuits, and even to gain status thereby, while still maintaining a firm hold on their basic gender identity.

When a true cross-sex identification does occur in a girl, it tends to become, if anything, even more total and uncompromising than male transsexuality. Some male transsexuals go through periods of ambivalence about their gender, and may even establish heterosexual relationships and marriages, but this seems to happen less often with female transsexuals. In a survey by Hamburger (1953) no heterosexual female transsexuals were found, but a fifth of the males were actively heterosexual. If a female transsexual marries, or becomes pregnant, in the hope of overcoming her problem, the result is likely to be disastrous (Wälinder, 1967; Simon, 1967). Some female transsexuals have quite astonishing success in deceiving everyone, even on occasions their sexual partners, as to their true gender. Pauly

(1968) records one example of a 'husband' charged with assault and battery following a marital dispute who proved, on examination, to be a female transsexual wearing a false penis. Because 'he' never undressed in front of his wife, never allowed her to touch 'his' genitals, and made love by caressing without intercourse, it was some time before the wife discovered she had 'married' a woman. Female transsexuals often report that as children they found mother dull or unsympathetic, but that they liked taking part with father in interesting masculine activity. Stoller (1972), from direct contact with a number of such cases, considers that the low status of mother in the child's mind, which may be caused by the mother having a depressive illness, encourages the child to adopt a protective manly role towards her. This is further encouraged if the father likes the child to be a tomboy and share his interests, and permits the child to take over some of the tasks of looking after mother. Of course these observations are quite speculative. Usually the family situations seem less extreme than, and not so dramatically deviant as, the backgrounds described by male transsexuals, but this could be an illusion, since few such cases have been thoroughly explored (Green, 1974).

The striking peculiarities of upbringing found among male transsexuals suggest an explanation in terms of faulty learning, although there may well be, in addition, underlying genetic factors which render certain infants particularly susceptible to unfavourable parental influences. The backgrounds of male transsexuals are of special interest because they reveal, in exaggerated form, features commonly found in the histories of male homosexuals in general. An American survey, using a life history questionnaire to compare non-patient male homosexuals with heterosexuals of similar age and occupation, brought this point out particularly well (Stephan, 1973). The homosexuals' family backgrounds were often lacking in satisfactory male role models, and many of them had received no encouragement in masculine pursuits or attitudes from either parent. It seems likely that the relatively mild forms of parental mishandling revealed in this survey suffice to hinder learning of the heterosexual role and to promote homosexual orientation, whereas only the extreme forms of mismanagement result in complete reversal of gender identity. A recent survey (Freund, Zajac *et al.*, 1974) compared the responses of male homosexuals and male transsexuals on a questionnaire designed to elicit information about family background. It was anticipated that an unreplaced loss of father before the age of 13, or a recollection of feeling closer to mother than to father, both of which might be taken as factors predisposing to femininity, would be reported significantly more frequently by the transsexuals, all of whom had solicited a sex change operation, than by the ordinary homosexuals. No such difference emerged, although the frequency of absent fathers, close relationships with mother and poor relationships with father, were all greater among both the transsexuals and the homosexuals than among a control group of heterosexual males. As a means of exploring family dynamics, questionnaires have serious limitations, but so far as it went this research pointed to the presence of essentially similar parental influences in both male homosexuality and male transsexualism.

For convenience in description, and in accord with their own self-estimation, transsexuals have been discussed as a category apart from ordinary homosexuals. Nevertheless, it could well be that they are really nothing more than particularly extreme examples of the gender discontent which, in varying degrees, afflicts many homosexuals. At one extreme one has the woman who knows she is a man and adheres to this conviction with all the strength of a deluded psychotic. A stage less extreme comes the 'butch dyke' who feels happy in dirty overalls doing a man's job and eyeing the girls. At the opposite extreme one has the discreet lesbian who displays no more outward sign than a fashionably mannish style of dress. These examples point to the many grades and varieties of gender discontent which shade one into another and defy categorical definition.

The intensity of an individual's gender disturbance cannot be gauged by the frequency of cross-dressing. Some men take a fetishistic delight in female attire and are aroused by the touch and sight of female clothes, especially female undergarments. They put them on for the sake of increasing the pleasure of sexual foreplay, but their erotic interest remains heterosexual, and the transvestite ritual culminates in intercourse. On the other hand, some transvestites come nearer to the condition of transsexuality, and are preoccupied with the joy of being mistaken for a woman. Even though they may not be attracted to other males sexually, they love to walk the streets in 'drag' and to know that the passers-by think they are women. At the same time they don't look upon themselves as female, and they often take equal pleasure in undeceiving persons who have mistaken them for women. Typically, the male transvestite preserves a predominantly heterosexual life (he is often married with children) and a capacity for performing a normal male role, in spite of occasional lapses into 'drag queen' homosexuality during his transvestite episodes. Some transvestites take matters further and become deeply committed to passive homosexuality. They tend to be exhibitionists, and to be attracted to jobs as female impersonators. A few of them take hormones, and even contemplate surgery, for the sake of improving their feminine appearance and increasing their prospects of homosexual contacts. Only one important difference still separates these extreme transvestites from classic transsexuals: they know they are not true women and do not claim to be other than male homosexuals who like to play the female role. In practice, therefore, male transvestites range from the predominantly masculine and heterosexual at one extreme to those at the other extreme who are scarcely distinguishable from transsexuals (Benjamin, 1966). The varying behaviour of transvestites makes it evident that a deviant preference for a love mate of the same sex, and a deviant preference for the social role of a member of the opposite sex, are both matters of degree. In any given individual, the two deviations do not necessarily occur together, or to the same extent.

Childhood difficulties with gender role must be taken seriously, for not only have follow up studies shown that they frequently lead to adult homosexuality, or even to transsexuality (Lebovitz, 1972), but they may also have other undesirable psychological consequences. Earlier reports, based upon observations of hermaphrodites who had been consistently reared as either boy or girl, suggested that attempts to change a well-established gender identity often prove ill-advised or futile. An externally imposed change may merely result in the child, on reaching adolescence, demanding reversal to the sex to which he or she was originally assigned. On the other hand, anatomically normal children who display cross-gender preferences or gender confusion, apparently in response to injudicious parental handling, can be helped towards a more appropriate adjustment. Green *et al.* (1972) reported promising results from attempts to help prepubertal boys who had shown strong feminine tendencies since early childhood. The treatment, which continued over a period of four years, involved counselling the parents, in an effort to break the abnormally close maternal tie and to promote bonds of interest between father and son. At the same time the boy was encouraged to establish a constructive relationship with a male therapist.

Insecurity in regard to gender performance, and attempts to over-compensate for it, can lead to disturbance in other spheres of behaviour than the specifically sexual. Criminologists have been struck by the exaggeratedly masculine stance of many male delinquents, who seem to be apeing a crude image of the tough 'cowboy'. The parental background of some of these boys bears a fair resemblance to that of boys with overt problems of gender identity. The relationship with father is decidedly cool, mother dominates the scene, and even in the face of obvious neglect and rejection, the young delinquent shows strong feelings towards her and tries to find excuses for her. Instead of yielding to a feminine identification, however, the delinquent boy fights against it and desperately asserts his maleness by rebellious clamour. Since the feminine image in our culture is one of goodness, gentleness, obedience and helpfulness the delinquent must seek the opposite, that is wrongdoing, violence, rebellion and destructiveness.

This element in the psychology of certain delinquents was long ago noted by Martha MacDonald (1938). She described some violently antisocial young boys, in constant trouble for fighting, stealing, truancy, sex assaults, lying and obscenity, who also had gender problems. On occasions they would display preferences for girls' clothes and play activities. When alone with an older woman they would behave impeccably and show obvious interest in her activities, all of which was utterly out of keeping with their aggressive and destructive behaviour when among other boys. None of these boys had a satisfactory relationship with his father. Instead, their lives had been governed by dominating mothers who permitted their submissive husbands no say in matters of child-rearing. MacDonald interpreted the boys' aggressiveness towards other males as a panic defence against their own feminine tendencies. According to which side ultimately gains the upper hand in a conflict of this kind, the boy may develop into either a raging 'queen' or a raging psychopath.

CHAPTER FOUR

Physical Determinants of Sexual Behaviour

1. *The development of physical sexual characteristics*

The contrasting behaviour of men and women, and the peculiarities of individuals with cross-sex inclinations, have been discussed so far in terms of differential learning, but other important factors have to be taken into account. However great the influence of learning, culture and personal choice, human sexual behaviour ultimately depends upon the individual's reproductive equipment and bodily responses, and these are inexorably determined by hereditary endowment and glandular development. Every cell in the body bears the stamp of male or female, distinguishable in the composition of the nucleus, which contains the chromosomes. These tiny structures, which can be rendered visible by modern microscopic techniques, carry the spiral chains of DNA molecules which are the genes, the units of heredity. They provide the chemical template for development from a single cell to a human adult. They serve to transmit virtually everything that is physically passed on from one generation to the next, including the selection of a male or a female growth pattern.

The eggs which grow in the woman's ovary and the spermatozoa that form in the man's testes, are each a kind of half cell. Their nuclei contain a random selection of either one or the other member of each pair of chromosomes. When they unite at the moment of conception they reform a cell with a full set of paired chromosomes. This cell, implanted into the womb, by continual reduplication grows into a baby. Since the baby's cells include half of the father's chromosomes and half of the mother's chromosomes, its hereditary endowment consists of a mixture from both parents.

Human cells contain twenty-three pairs of chromosomes. The chromosomes have different sizes and shapes, but the two members of each pair look alike, save for the twenty-third pair, which are the sex chromosomes. In females both sex chromosomes are large (the XX combination) but in the male one looks smaller (the XY combination). In the process of reproduction the female ovary produces eggs with just one X chromosome. The male sperm cells have either an X or a Y chromosome according to the random splitting of the chromosome pairs ·which occurs as the sperm cells form in the testis. The offspring's sex is decided at the moment of fertilisation according to whether one of the father's X carrying or Y carrying spermatozoa unites with the egg to form an XX (female) or XY (male) combination.

Occasionally something goes wrong with this process. If the splitting and reuniting of the chromosome pairs occurs irregularly a baby may be produced with only one chromosome from a given pair, or with three or more from the same set of chromosomes instead of just two. Since each chromosome contains a massive sequence of genetic material governing a great many developmental processes, the loss of an entire chromosome, or the presence of an additional chromosome, constitutes a serious defect. Babies afflicted in this way are usually either stillborn or so gravely deformed at birth that they cannot survive. An exception is the condition known as mongolism, due to an extra chromosome on the twenty-first pair. Such babies often survive to become adults, but they are mentally subnormal, and have characteristic deformities of the face which gave rise to the name mongolism.

The small Y chromosome is not essential to life, but at least one X chromosome is needed for survival. A solitary X chromosome unaccompanied by a Y or a second X, the XO combination, usually causes abortion, but babies who survive suffer from Turner's syndrome. They are female in body and genitals, but their ovaries are rudimentary and sterile. At puberty they fail to menstruate or to develop adult breasts and other secondary sexual characteristics. In addition, they frequently suffer from other constitutional deformities, such as stunted stature, webbed neck, hole-in-the-heart defects, receding chin and kidney troubles.

Another well known medical condition, Klinefelter's syndrome, results from an XXY combination. The extra female chromosome does not cause sex reversal, but the affected male is of peculiar build with poor muscle development, a tendency to inappropriate distribution of body fat, and testes which fail to develop at puberty and remain small and infertile. In addition, some Klinefelter patients suffer from intellectual retardation, personality eccentricities, or serious psychiatric disorder.

The possession of an extra female chromosome does not necessarily impel a man towards homosexuality. Notwithstanding their poor genital development, most XXY males are heterosexually inclined (Raboch and Nedoma, 1958). They may sometimes lack sexual drive or confidence, and perhaps be rather more susceptible than the normally constituted male to pressures towards sexual deviations, but their extra chromosome does not predetermine their sexual orientation. Orwin *et al.* (1974) report a case of a predominantly homosexual XXY male aged thirty-five. He came to psychiatric attention following a complaint about sexual approaches to a youth at his place of work. He had had some heterosexual experiences in earlier years, but suffering from premature ejaculation, and being teased about his small testicles, he felt he would never be able to satisfy women, and settled into a pattern of more or less exclusive homosexuality. Following treatment by encouragement and aversive conditioning (see p. 260) he resumed heterosexual activities, this time more successfully, and when seen two years later he denied being troubled any further by homosexual thoughts. This relatively easy conversion suggested that even if the extra female chromosome had exerted some influence upon his sexual development, it could be readily counteracted by environmental experience.

The XYY combination, a more recently discovered chromosome abnormality, produces men who often grow unusually tall, but have a superficially normal physique, and may go through life happily unaware of any abnormality. Although endowed with a double dose of male chromosome, they are far from being supermen in practice. They are vulnerable to a variety of psychiatric disturbances, including mental retardation and psychopathic personality, and are said to be prone to sexual deviations. An unduly high incidence of this rare condition has been discovered among the inmates of the special hospitals for mentally abnormal criminals, and the presence of the anomaly has been used in legal pleas for mitigation in the case of some notorious murders (West, 1970).

Only a fraction of one per cent of the population suffer from any of these gross chromosome anomalies. Save for the exceptional few with manifest physical anomalies, homosexual men and women have been found to possess the normal chromosomal constitution appropriate to their sex, XY or XX respectively (Pare, 1956; Pritchard, 1962; Raboch and Nedoma, 1958). Although genetic factors may enter into the causation of homosexuality, a simple explanation in terms of abnormal chromosome counts will not work.

The basic body structure of human beings is feminine, but the presence of a Y chromosome, which occurs in half the race, modifies the course of development to produce masculinity. In the earliest stages of growth the foetus possesses both Wolffian and Mullerian ducts, the structures which are the precursors of male and female sex organs respectively. The foetal gonads, later to become the egg- or sperm-producing organs, are sexually undifferentiated until about the seventh week of uterine life. Thereafter, the presence of a Y chromosome induces rapid development of the gonads into male testes. Some of the cells take on the appearance of the sperm producing cells (although, of course, they do not come to functional maturity until puberty) while others start to secrete androgen, the characteristic male hormone. Once the sex hormones, which are chemical steroids, make their appearance, the sex chromosomes have completed their most essential task. From then on it is the level and composition of the circulating hormones which mainly governs further sexual growth and differentiation. The presence of androgens secreted by the developing male testes ensures that the Mullerian ducts regress while the Wolffian ducts grow into the characteristic male reproductive organs. In the absence of male type gonads producing androgens, the Mullerian ducts always grow into a female womb and vagina, even if, for some reason, active female gonads (ovaries) fail to develop (for instance in the XO or Turner Syndrome).

Interference with the balance of circulating hormones during the early months of pregnancy is likely to have profound effects upon the physical sex development of the foetus. Deliberate interference with human pregnancies for the sake of research is ethically impossible, but some of the effects of foetal hormone disturbance are known from experiments with animals and from observations of what happens to babies when accident or disease supervenes. The action of sex hormones upon developing cells is facilitated by the presence of other substances, the enzymes. In one rare hereditary disease, known as testicular feminisation, certain enzymes which aid the action of androgens are missing. A genetic male (XY) suffering from this anomaly develops foetal testes, which produce androgens, but their secretions are ineffectual, and the baby grows into an anatomic female, with female external genitals. Having no scrotal sac into which to descend, as they would in a normal anatomic male, the testes remain in their primitive developmental position in the lower abdomen, where they are detectable as lumps in the groin. Being genetic males without ovaries, sufferers from testicular feminisation cannot produce eggs or bear children, but they look like females, are reared as females, and they think and behave as females. They come to the doctor's attention only at puberty, when menstruation fails to occur, and their vaginas may be found to be too short for comfortable sexual intercourse. This condition provides a perfect example of how a hormone anomaly occurring early in the course of development in the womb can override the chromosomes to produce an almost complete reversal of sexual anatomy and sexual behaviour.

One result that hormone anomalies, or hormone treatment, cannot bring about is the development of functional egg-producing ovaries or sperm-producing testes in an individual of contrary chromosomal sex. Even this limitation does not apply in the case of animals low in the evolutionary scale, such as the killfish. Male larvae given female hormone develop into creatures that not only look and behave as female fish but also breed and reproduce as females (Yamamoto, 1962). Their male Y chromosome might as well not exist for all the effect it has during the lifetime of the treated fish.

Another well-known hormone anomaly, the adreno-genital syndrome, also produces a degree of sex reversal in humans. The trouble arises from a malfunctioning of the adrenal gland, situated near the kidney, which produces an excess of androgens from sources outside the gonads. In a genetic male, this causes precocious sexual development, but in a genetic female it has the effect of masculinising the anatomy, and producing the syndrome of female pseudo-hermaphroditism. The condition is a matter of degree, but in extreme cases a chromosomal female can be born with a fully developed penis, but since there are no testes, the scrotum remains an empty sac. At puberty, the continuing influence of circulating androgenic hormones causes male voice and beard to develop. The individual becomes sexually responsive and virile, and capable of what appears to be normal male heterosexual intercourse. In spite of having no testes, and in spite of having hidden within the abdomen rudimentary ovaries, fallopian tubes and a womb appropriate to female chromosomal sex, the individual behaves as a male. The condition demonstrates how a continuing and abnormally high level of androgen can result in both anatomic and behavioural masculinisation of a genetic female.

These observations support the view that learning is the crucial factor in the determination of psychological gender identity. Females with adreno-genital syndrome, so long as they are firmly and consistently assigned to the male sex as babies, usually accept a male identity without question, in spite of a certain ambiguity in their genital appearance, and in spite of any difficulties they may experience in heterosexual intercourse as a result of their genital peculiarities. In recent years, since diagnosis has become easier, and corrective hormone treatment and surgery to restore female appearance and function has become possible, these people are likely to be brought up as girls and to be given appropriate treatments during childhood. In this event they seem equally ready to accept a female identity. Even though the excess of androgens to which they have been exposed may have caused physical changes in the direction of masculinity, they do not usually behave homosexually, but they are apt to act like tomboys. They show predilection for outdoor and sporting activities, they are easily and quickly aroused sexually, and they are likely to put career before marriage (Lewis *et al.*, 1970). These results suggest that in human beings androgens stimulate physical vigour, swift sexual response, and the development of masculine qualities of temperament, but do not determine the direction of sexual desire or the choice of gender identity (Money and Ehrhardt, 1972).

The most spectacular effects upon sex development come about when sex hormone imbalance takes place early in foetal development, before anatomic differentiation into male or female has been completed. Less extreme, but still very pronounced, physical changes result from hormone disturbance in childhood, before the onset of puberty. Pubertal changes in boys, noticeable in the enlargement of the larynx (Adam's apple and male voice), the appearance of facial and body hair, the enlargement of the genitals, and the onset of ejaculations containing fertile sperm, depend upon a selective growth spurt stimulated by an upsurge of androgen secretion from the hormonal cells of the testes. If the testes are removed by castration, or destroyed by injury, or if the pituitary gland fails to stimulate the testes to increased secretion at adolescence, then normal pubertal changes will not take place. The youth retains a slender, childish build, smooth hairless skin, high-pitched voice, and small-sized penis.

Usually he lacks sex drive, cannot obtain satisfactory penile erections, and is incapable of producing fertile sperm. Castration after puberty has less extreme effects. Potency and sex drive are diminished, but not necessarily abolished, and although body fat distribution and pitch of voice may alter, these changes take time and are not always very dramatic.

The female ovaries have egg producing cells and hormone producing cells, just like the sperm cells and internal secretion cells of the testes. The hormones of the female ovaries, of which oestradiol is the most important, increase at puberty and stimulate the maturation of the genitals, the growth of the breasts and the onset of menstruation. All of this can be prevented by inactivation of the ovaries before puberty, but because the female organs are situated inside the abdomen they are subject to less risk of destruction than the male testes.

Unlike the male testes, which produce a more or less continuous supply of androgens, the ovaries are subject to rhythmic variations of hormone production. Secretion of progesterone, one of the ovarian hormones, is greatest at the beginning of a menstrual cycle. The effect is to induce a thickening of the lining of the uterus in readiness for the implantation of a fertilised egg. If the egg, which is normally released about the middle of the cycle, is not fertilised progesterone secretion diminishes, and the lining of the uterus regresses and comes away as the woman menstruates. Then progesterone levels increase again and the feminine cycle repeats itself. This cyclic activity is governed by the pituitary gland at the base of the brain. Both sexes possess a pituitary gland the secretions of which stimulate ovarian or testicular activities, but only in the female does the pituitary release its secretions in this rhythmic fashion. The rhythmic variation is controlled by a nerve centre in the hypothalamic region of the brain, which must therefore function differently in males and females.

In the long term hormones influence behaviour through their effects upon the growth and structure of the physical apparatus of sex. They also have a more immediate impact by stimulating or suppressing areas of the nervous system which regulate sex behaviour. In lower animals, whose behaviour is predominantly instinctive, that is rigidly programmed by their neurological constitution, either male- or female-type behaviour can be elicited in the same animal by manipulating the level of androgens and oestrogens, thereby activating male and female responses alternatively. For example, the domestic hen, given androgens, not only develops a male-looking comb, but starts behaving like a cock. She becomes extremely assertive, rises quickly in the pecking order until, like a natural cock, she bosses all the other hens in the roost. She also assumes male postures and makes attempts to mate with other hens. When androgens are withdrawn, she reverts to her former submissive ways and lowly hen-like status.

In higher animals, and particularly in human beings, sexual

behaviour ceases to be so directly and immediately dependent upon the hormone concentration at any given moment. For instance, unlike many female mammals, which only mate at certain phases of the menstrual cycle when oestrogen levels are at a maximum, human females vary only slightly in their sexual urges at different stages of the cycle, and such variations as do occur bear no direct relation to oestrogen concentration. At the menopause, when oestrogen levels fall off, women do not necessarily lose sexual feeling, indeed many experience increasing desire for coitus, perhaps because they no longer fear unwanted pregnancy. When androgens are taken by sexually normal females (for instance as a treatment for certain cancers) they may experience some masculinising physical changes, such as growth of facial hair and deepening voice, and enlarged clitoris, but they do not change the direction of their sexual interests. In both sexes androgens are likely to enhance sexual desire. They induce increased vascularity and sensitivity of the penis and its female analogue of the clitoris, but they do not change the direction of the individual's established sexual interests (Perloff, 1965). The belief that taking sex hormones will cure human homosexuality has long been exploded.

2. *Hormone imbalance and human homosexuality*

The possibility that homosexual behaviour in humans is caused by some glandular deficiency cannot be dismissed out of hand. The fact that upbringing and early experience have a powerful effect upon gender identity and sexual preference by no means rules out the simultaneous operation of physical causes. Variations in physical constitution may render some individuals particularly vulnerable to environmental pressures. For example, the readiness of persons with hermaphroditic bodily configuration and genital ambiguities to adopt whichever sex their parents assign to them could be due to their sexual potentialities being weaker or less distinctive than those of a biologically normal male or female.

As mentioned previously, physical causes, in the shape of an excess of androgens in the female or a deficit in the male, can be shown to induce homosexual behaviour among adult animals of some lower species. Humans do not respond to hormones in this simple fashion. Like many other physical factors, such as fatigue, febrile illness or a recent orgasm, androgen levels influence the strength of sexual desire, but they do not affect the individual's sexual preferences. A deficit of androgens in adult men diminishes the sensitivity and reactivity of the sexual apparatus, reduces lust and eventually produces physical impotence, but does not abolish heterosexual orientation. Artificially induced androgen deficiency has been used as a means of control of unwanted impulses. Sex offenders whose interests centre upon small children, who constantly risk social disgrace and long imprisonment, are given substances which inhibit the action of their circulating androgen, so that their sexual temptations become less dangerously compelling (Field, 1973). The psychological effects of loss of androgen are variable. As some old men discover to their chagrin, impaired sexual performance, and absence of urgent lust, do not kill the imagination or necessarily abolish all interest in familiar sexual situations.

In adult males, large injections of androgen, in the form of testosterone, can provoke an immediate but temporary sexual excitability. Continued administration of moderate doses helps to maintain an optimal libido in men whose sexual activity is reduced through androgen lack, but has little effect upon the normal male, since any excess is excreted (Heller and Maddoch, 1947). Maintenance doses of testosterone were once popular as a means of rejuvenation for ageing males, but continued over-stimulation with androgens is considered unwise by medical authorities. The feed-back, self-regulating mechanisms of the hormone system combat artificially high rises in androgens by a compensatory diminution of natural androgen secretion. Continued over-dosage can put the testes out of action, as well as having undesirable side effects upon other glands and tissues. Testosterone given to male homosexuals of normal physique has little effect. Any increase in sexual desire which may occur is likely merely to exaggerate their established behaviour pattern.

One circumstance in which hormone levels might be expected to influence sexual orientation is when androgen deficiency occurs in a boy before puberty, so that at adolescence the genitals remain small, and the characteristically sturdy male physique fails to develop. If replacement treatment with androgens commences before it is too late, these deficiencies can be rectified. If there is delay in recognising the problem and obtaining medical help, psychological complications may arise. Anxiety about sexual development and performance can deter heterosexual contacts at adolescence, and thus favour the development of sexual deviations, including homosexuality. The immature, girlish appearance associated with hormone deficiency, by arousing expectations of homosexuality, and by attracting sexual interest from other males, could increase the likelihood of exposure to homosexual situations. Finally, since physical vigour and aggressiveness appear to depend in part upon androgens, the affected boy might find himself cast in the role of a 'sissy', unacceptable in normal masculine society. In spite of these social pressures, boys whose development has been retarded by lack of androgen do not usually present as homosexuals. In their early years, when gender identity becomes established and sexual expectations are formed, they were effectively normal boys with a physique appropriate to their age. On reaching adolescence they usually have heterosexual interests and ambitions, in spite of their disappointing physical retardation. Their deficiency commonly results from a failure of the pituitary to stimulate increased androgen secretion when they reach the age of puberty. Their problem begins when their friends start to mature sexually while they remain comparatively infantile. At this stage they commonly come for medical help seeking support for heterosexual endeavours and wanting something to improve their masculine physique.

An equally acute problem besets the girl with hormone deficiencies whose breast development lags behind and who fails to menstruate at the expected age. Even a total lack of oestrogen does not usually alter the sense of being a woman or prevent heterosexual interests from developing. Girls with Turner's syndrome, in spite of the absence of ovaries and the consequent oestrogen deficiency, often have strong heterosexual urges.

A different situation confronts the female with physical changes caused by excess of androgens. As was mentioned before, even in extreme cases of adreno-genital syndrome, in which abnormality manifests from birth and includes partial masculinisation of the genitals, persons reared as girls usually preserve their feminine identity and develop a heterosexual orientation, but they tend to become tomboys. It seems that an excess of prepubertal androgen in girls does not masculinise their sexual preferences but may masculinise certain aspects of their social attitude and temperament. In animals, it is easy to demonstrate that many aspects of behaviour besides mating can be affected by androgens. Goy (1968), who produced an adreno-genital condition in rhesus monkeys by giving androgens prenatally, found that as they grew up the animals behaved in distinctly masculine ways in regard to chasing and play activity as well as in their tendency to mount other animals in male fashion. Similarly, the administration of androgens will induce in bitches a leg-lifting stance during urination normally seen only in male dogs (Martins and Valle, 1948).

It seems unlikely that human homosexuality is due to abnormal hormone levels. Even gross disturbances, sufficient to produce anomalous physical sexual characteristics, do not as a rule alter sexual orientation, although they may affect sexual performance and libido and possibly also affect sex-linked temperamental attributes. The vast majority of homosexuals have a normal appearance with none of the physical peculiarities found in individuals with gross hormone deficiencies. Nevertheless, if it could be shown that, in spite of the absence of external physical signs, individuals of homosexual orientation differ from the norm in their hormone levels, this would add plausibility to the theory that their condition results from some subtle glandular disturbance.

Most of the older investigations of androgen levels in males yielded no convincing differences between homosexuals and heterosexuals (Severinghaus and Chornak, 1945; Appel, 1937; Hemphill *et al.*, 1958; Dewhurst, 1969). However, in recent years, with the advent of more accurate methods of estimation, a number of workers have reported finding significant differences. The male hormone testosterone, secreted primarily in the testes, is broken down by the liver into androsterone and etiocholanolone, which are excreted in the urine, where they form part of the complex of substances called 17-ketosteroids. The remainder of the 17-ketosteroids derive from the secretions of the adrenal cortex. Some indication of testosterone secretion can be obtained from the total of 17-ketosteroids in twenty-four-hour samples of urine, but separate analysis of the androsterone and etiocholanolone components is now possible and more revealing. In an investigation by Loraine *et al.* (1970), in which very careful serial estimations of sex hormones and their breakdown products were carried out, they found abnormally low urinary testosterone levels in two men who were exclusively homosexual, but a normal level in a third man who had both heterosexual and homosexual experience. They also examined four lesbians, and found that their testosterone levels were unusually high while their oestrogen levels were lowered. Further support for the notion of androgen disturbance in homosexuals came from a research by Margolese (1970). He compared fifteen healthy homosexual males with ten healthy heterosexuals. Using 24-hour urine samples, he estimated the 17-ketosteroids by a modification of the method of Drekter, and then determined the ratio of androsterone to etiocholanolone, which is characteristically much lower in women than in men. The investigation showed that the homosexuals had consistently lowered ratios. Low ratios were also found in heterosexual males suffering from a variety of abnormal conditions, including psychiatric depression and diabetes. He concluded that low androgen ratios in healthy males is associated with a homosexual orientation. In a more extended confirmatory study, Margolese and Janiger (1973) compared 24 physically healthy heterosexual students with 32 healthy homosexuals in regard to levels of androsterone and etiocholanolone in their urine. They successfully reproduced the earlier finding that, compared with heterosexual males, the homosexuals had significantly lower androsterone to etiocholanolone ratios. The tendency was especially marked among those who were exclusively homosexual. The difference was not associated with lack of sexual activity on the part of the homosexual group since their reported frequency of sexual activity was similar to that of the heterosexual controls. Although the mean ratios differed significantly, the range of individual variation was considerable, and the amount of overlap between the two populations was too great to enable a confident identification of homosexuality or heterosexuality in a particular individual from his A/E ratio alone. Investigation of individuals with metabolic disorders, such as thyroid deficiency, or psychiatric depression, showed that these conditions also caused a lowering of the A/E ratio, but without producing homosexuality. The lowered A/E ratio of male homosexuals was insufficient to cause any external physical signs. Margolese and Janiger found no significant difference in pubic hair distribution, size of genitals, or skeletal measurements, between the homosexual and heterosexual groups. Margolese's finding of a decreased A/E ratio in homosexuals has been repeated in an independent survey by Evans (1972) but not in one by Tourney and Hatfield (1973).

Additional evidence of lowered androgen secretion in male homosexuals has been produced by some American workers (Kolodny, Masters *et al.*, 1971) who examined a group of 30 male homosexual students, using a method of estimating testosterone in blood plasma, which gives a more direct indication of the true level of activity of circulating androgens. They examined another group of 50 heterosexual students for comparison. Both groups were physically fit, healthy young men. Measurement of the size of the genitals and the appearance of secondary sexual characteristics were within the normal range for all the homosexual subjects, but their plasma testosterone levels were on average lower than those of the heterosexual men. The difference was entirely due to the men who were more or less exclusively homosexual in their practices (Kinsey rating 5 or 6). They had average testosterone levels of 372 ± 22 and 264 ± 15 mg per 100 ml respectively, compared with levels of 689 ± 26 among the heterosexuals. Men with considerable heterosexual as well as homosexual experience (Kinsey rating 1 or 2) had about the same plasma testosterone levels as the heterosexual group. The technician who carried out the analyses was kept in ignorance of which plasma samples came from the homosexuals. They found a significant lowering of sperm count, and a significant reduction in sperm motility, in nine of the homosexual students. These indications of relative infertility were found only among the half of the sample with Kinsey ratings 5 or 6.

The findings do strongly suggest that exclusive male homosexuals, at least, have some deficiency of hormone function, even though they appear physically normal and seem healthily virile. All of the homosexual subjects reported masturbatory activity during the month before interview (an indication of active sexual libido) and all of them had experienced both active and passive roles in sex activity with other males, and none of them admitted to any difficulty in obtaining erections or ejaculations during their sexual encounters. The results cannot therefore be accounted for on the grounds that the men were untypical, having been driven to homosexuality by poor sexual performance or passive tendencies. On the other hand, one cannot assume that the testosterone deficiency caused the homosexuality. The amount of sexual activity an individual undertakes alters androgen levels and may indirectly affect sperm production. If the frequency or quality of sexual activity (including masturbation) among the exclusive homosexuals differed from that among other subjects, the observed effects might be a consequence rather than a cause of homosexual behaviour. Whatever the explanation, the results are interesting and point to the need for more research along these lines. Unfortunately, the estimation of blood hormone levels still presents technical problems. More recently published investigations by Tourney and Hatfield (1973), which included testosterone estimations from blood plasma, as well as urinary estimations of 17-ketosteroids and etiocholanolone, have not confirmed the claims that homosexuals show disturbances in androgen metabolism. In another investigation (Brodie *et al.*, 1974) plasma testosterone levels actually proved higher in a sample of 19 young male homosexuals than in heterosexual males of similar age, while in another attempted repetition of the Kolodny study (Birk *et al.*, 1973) male homosexuals undergoing psychotherapy were found to have normal serum testosterone levels. In another study, based on a sample of 15 predominantly or exclusively homosexual males, Barlow *et al.* (1974) found plasma testosterone levels comparable with those attributed by Kolodny to heterosexuals and much higher than had been claimed as typical of homosexuals. The work of Doerr *et al.* (1973), however, supported the Kolodny results to some extent. In an investigation of 32 male homosexuals of average age twenty-six, semen count and plasma testosterone were not significantly different from those of a control group of 46 heterosexual males of similar age range, but plasma oestradiol was significantly higher in the homosexual group. An investigation by Pillard and Rose (1974) showed that the average plasma testosterone level was slightly lower among male homosexuals than among heterosexual control group, but the overlap was very considerable. The testosterone level was unrelated to psychological masculinity or femininity, but it did appear to be lowered to a greater degree in those who were exclusively homosexual. In view of all these conflicting reports, the presence of a hormone imbalance in male homosexuals remains open to question and its significance unclear.

3. *A possible physical explanation of human homosexuality*

It was mentioned earlier that the hypothalamic region of the brains of males and females function differently. The male hypothalamus lacks the characteristic rhythmic activity which, through its influence upon the release of pituitary hormones, sets the pace for the female menstrual cycle. Since this part of the brain is also concerned with the regulation of emotional reactions and aggressive responses, the areas of conduct in which the sexes differ most, it seems after all possible that male and female styles of behaviour, as well as male and female hormone patterns, are differently programmed from birth by the distinctive neurological constitution of the male and female hypothalamus. Studies of how and when these brain centres become functionally differentiated into male or female patterns, and the effect of these differences upon adult behaviour, have become a rapidly growing area of research.

The state of knowledge on this topic, which so far rests largely on experiments with animals, has been reviewed by Money and Ehrhardt (1972). It appears that animals such as rats and hamsters pass through a quite short, but critical phase of development, when the hypothalamus becomes temporarily very sensitive to the level of circulating androgens. During this phase a quite brief exposure to androgen suppresses the rhythmic activity upon which the female hormone cycle depends, so that even though an animal has the genetic endowment of a female, she will not as an adult display the periodic sexual receptivity of a normal female. Similarly, lack of androgen at this time ensures that the rhythmic feminine brain characteristics develop in spite of an animal being genetically male.

In animals that are born relatively mature, the critical phase for the sexual differentiation of brain centres occurs while they are still in the womb, but in the rat it occurs in the first few days of life. At this point, the influence of the circulating ovarian and testicular secretions becomes particularly critical, bringing about effects in the brain that cannot be reversed by manipulation of hormone levels later in life. The sensitivity of the brain, in regard to the type of hormone and the concentration of hormone to which it will respond subsequently, is permanently established at this time. Artificial manipulation of hormone levels during this critical phase can have far-reaching effects upon adult behaviour. For example, small doses of androgens given to female rats in the first few days of life will permanently abolish the cyclical variation of hormone levels characteristic of the normal female. When she reaches maturity the rat's sexual behaviour is affected. She fails to display the usual receptive position in the presence of males, and will not do so even when given artificially large doses of female hormones. Moreover, when given doses of androgens as an adult, in spite of the absence of male genitalia, she can be induced to perform mounting and male copulatory motions. This does not occur in normal female rats whose brains have not been sensitised to androgens (Levine, 1966).

If a new-born male rat is castrated, and then given doses of female hormones, a complete reversal of sexual behaviour can be produced, so that the animal attempts to mate by presenting itself to other males instead of mounting females. The administration of oestrogens will not produce anything like the same behavioural changes in normal rats or in rats castrated at a later stage in their development. It seems that a temporary lack of androgen at a critical point in development causes the male rat's brain to mature in a feminine way, that is, to become responsive to female hormones like a normal female brain (Levine and Mullins, 1968). The experiments of Dörner (1968) and Dörner and Hinz (1968) using rats are especially relevant because they succeeded in inducing homosexual behaviour in animals notwithstanding normal appearance and normal androgen levels. Male rats were castrated on the first day after birth. The resulting lack of androgens prevented the masculinisation of the hypothalamic mating centres that should occur at this particular period. On the third day, and subsequently, the rats were given injections of testosterone to compensate for their androgen deficiency and to induce normal sexual growth. When they reached maturity they were of normal appearance but showed strong tendencies to react like females. In the presence of sexually vigorous male rats most of them responded by arching up the hindquarters (lordosis), which is the normal response of the sexually receptive female ready to be mounted by a male. Among these experimentally treated males, female type responses were much more frequent than attempts to mate with receptive females. In fact, some of the rats showed feminine sexual behaviour exclusively.

In analogous manipulations of new-born female rats, homosexual behaviour was induced among adults of normal appearance by administering androgens briefly during the post-natal period, and then giving further doses at puberty to activate the masculinised brain centres. Normal female rats, whose brain centres have not been masculinised, on reaching maturity respond to androgens as do normal mature women, that is with an increase of sexual behaviour of the feminine type. In the experimental rats, however, female activity was completely abolished and the animals mounted other females and made copulatory movements just as often as did normal male rats of similar age. Dörner argues from these results that the direction of the sex instinct can be completely determined regardless of chromosomal sex, by the androgen level during the critical hypothalamic differentiation period, and that once having been fixed it remains unaffected by subsequent hormone fluctuations.

That may be true of the rat, but it has yet to be demonstrated in humans. In view of the long period human babies stay in the womb, and the difference in responsiveness of new-born males and females, the critical period of sexual differentiation of the human brain probably occurs before birth. If so, this opens up the theoretical possibility that hormone disturbances in pregnant women, or drugs taken during pregnancy, could influence the future sexual orientation of the unborn child. It could be, for example, that disturbances in the mother provoked by severe stress, if they occur at the critical time, may disturb the endocrine balance in the foetus sufficiently to affect sexual maturation of the brain. An effect, seemingly of this kind, has actually been produced experimentally by subjecting pregnant female rats to the stress of immobilisation under a bright light. When their male offspring grew up they proved defective in male copulatory performance. Their deficiency was evidently due to some degree of feminisation of the brain, because, when given female hormones, they started to present themselves with arched back in the manner of a sexually receptive female. Normal male rats do not do this even when given female hormones (Ward, 1972). Drugs taken during pregnancy might produce similar consequences. It has been found in animal experiments that barbiturates (commonly used as sleeping pills by women) and certain antibiotics (e.g. actinomycin-D) will prevent the masculinising effect which otherwise occurs when androgen is injected into the female rat foetus (Money and Ehrhardt, 1972, p.232). If these drugs have a similarly inhibiting effect upon the naturally circulating androgens of maturing male babies in the womb, they might prevent the normal masculinisation of the hypothalamus, and so produce a male person who, despite normal physique and a normal level of androgen production, has a 'feminine' type brain and a predisposition towards feminine type behaviour and a homosexual orientation.

One piece of positive evidence that feminising endocrine effects, similar to those that can be induced in the rat, may occur in human males has been published in a recent report by Dörner *et al.* (1975). They found that male rats, whose brains had been feminised by neonatal hormone manipulation, showed a characteristic feedback effect in response to oestrogen administration. A similar effect (in the shape of a preliminary decrease followed by a steeper increase in levels of serum progesterone) was found to occur in 21 homosexual men after an injection of oestrogen, but it did not occur in 20 heterosexual controls. The difference was not accounted for by lack of androgen in the homosexual group, since their plasma testosterone levels were within the normal range for heterosexual males.

So far all this is no more than a speculative possibility. Supposing such a chain of events does sometimes occur in humans, the effects would be unlikely to be anything like so clear cut as in the rat, since human sex behaviour is so strongly influenced by individual learning. Moreover, although it may sometimes be possible, by timing the moment of intervention precisely, to induce behavioural changes without altering sexual appearance, perinatal hormone manipulations usually do produce some noticeable hermaphroditic physical effects (Ward and Renz, 1972). Naturally occurring hormone disturbance of less limited duration would be more likely to leave behind some obvious physical anomalies, whereas, as has been repeatedly remarked, human homosexuals do not as a rule show any physical peculiarities. Money and Erhardt (1972), who find many reasons for treating the theory of a prenatal hormonal factor in homosexuality with some scepticism, do point to one feature in the personality development of exclusive, obligatory homosexual males that suggests a physical component. In boyhood relatively few of those destined to become homosexual are active fighters or strong competitors in the struggle for social dominance, whereas future lesbians are often tomboys as children. Insofar as hormonal factors may be responsible for an absence of aggression in certain males, or an excess of aggression in certain females, they may indirectly facilitate the development of a homosexual orientation.

The simplified account of the hormone research given in this chapter hardly does justice either to the complexities of the mechanisms revealed in recent investigations or to the large areas of continuing scientific ignorance. Plenty of scope remains for the discovery of previously unsuspected connections between sexual behaviour and endocrine function. In this expanding field of investigation, conclusions can be no more than tentative. The contribution of hormone factors to the development of human homosexuality remains uncertain, but in the light of recent research the possibility that such factors have practical importance seems more likely that it did some years ago.

4. *Physical peculiarities of homosexuals*

Apart from hormone estimations, which present many technical problems and complexities, simpler measures of body size and shape are relevant to the theory that a homosexual orientation arises from some peculiarity of physical constitution rather than from environmental influences. If it could be shown that homosexuals in general, or some particular sub-group of homosexuals, such as those with cross-gender leanings, deviate in their physique from the average heterosexual male or female, this would add weight to the theory of physical causation. In popular beliefs and writings a wide variety of physical traits have been cited as characteristic of male homosexuals, including small stature, excess fat, wide hips, smooth skin, a short stride, a feminine distribution of pubic hair, narrow shoulders, boyish face, graceful movements, lisping speech, luxuriant hair, an inability to whistle and a 'too good-looking appearance'. Such ideas owe more to prejudice than to reality. A homosexual who happens to fit the stereotype draws attention and will be remembered, while those who do not pass unnoticed. Anyone who has visited the special beaches or steam baths where male homosexuals congregate will be aware of the wide range of physiques represented and the impossibility of a homosexual being identified at a glance on this basis.

Surveys of samples of homosexuals have often failed to detect any systematic difference between their physical measurements and similar data taken from heterosexuals (Barahal, 1939; Wortis, 1937; Hemphill *et al.*, 1958). In one German investigation by Weil, based on a sample of 380 mature male homosexuals, the subjects were reported to have significantly greater height, longer legs and wider hips than a control group. The findings were subsequently severely criticised by Wortis (1940) who maintained that the results were invalid because the homosexual and the control groups came from different districts where average heights differed. Weil's measurements of height, hip width and shoulder width of homosexuals did not differ significantly from published data taken from other groups of German males. Henry (1941), quoting work done with Galbraith, reported that the ratio of shoulder width to pelvis width was further from the feminine average (that is more 'masculine') among a group of homosexuals than among a corresponding group of normal men. All such findings have to be viewed with some scepticism on account of the great difficulty of obtaining comparable groups of homosexuals and heterosexuals. Physical measurements vary according to social class, nutritional habits, racial affiliation, place of birth and many other factors. Owing to the fact that samples of homosexuals are usually drawn from either medical patients or members of homophile groups they are liable to differ in education and social background from the average person of their age, class and neighbourhood. Unless they are matched most carefully with a series of comparable heterosexuals, any differences in physical measures which emerge might well be due to extraneous factors that have nothing to do with homosexuality.

Such cautionary considerations should not prevent one looking at the evidence, such as it is. Some quite sophisticated techniques have been developed which measure and classify human physique, and show in what particular respects males and females differ most. W.H. Sheldon (1949) devised a method of typing body-build by taking standardised photographs of the nude figure, so as to project the contours on to a flat surface on which measurements of body ratios, such as height to girth, could be made with ease. One of the common physical types he identified, the sturdy, muscular, athletic 'mesomorphic' build, the kind of person who tends to be heavy for his height without being fat, was correlated with a vigorous outgoing temperament, and might therefore be regarded as relatively uncommon among male homosexuals. He applied the technique to samples of young male criminals. He found that criminals were more likely than non-criminals to have mesomorphic physique, but the homosexuals among them had no distinctive contours that he could demonstrate, and were just as likely to be mesomorphic as their heterosexual companions. He believed that the homosexuals could be picked out by their soft skin, feminine hands and tone of voice, but these were features difficult to demonstrate by objective measurements.

Since the days of Sheldon's pioneer work, Parnell (1958) and Tanner (1961) have developed improved methods of categorising physique, using simpler and more easily measured indices. Women tend to have relatively wide hips, men to have broad shoulders. The ratio of hip width to shoulder width, measured with calipers extended across the appropriate bony protruberances (i.e. bi-iliac: bi-acromial), has been used as a measure of the masculinity or femininity of a man's physique. Using this index, and the methods of measurement developed by Tanner, the psychiatrist A.J. Coppen (1959) investigated the physique of three groups of men, male psychiatric patients who were homosexual, male neurotic patients who were heterosexual, and a control group of unselected males who were members of a large business concern being screened for chest disease by mass radiography. Compared with the average from the normal controls, the hip-shoulder ratios deviated significantly in the feminine direction in the homosexual group, but the neurotic heterosexuals also deviated in the same way and to much the same extent. Femininity of physique was seemingly a characteristic of male psychiatric patients in general rather than of male homosexuals in particular.

Some later findings reported by Evans (1972) were more interesting because he examined homosexual men drawn from the community. He used 44 volunteers supplied by a homophile organisation, One Inc. of Los Angeles. These men all said that their sexual experiences had been exclusively or predominantly homosexual. They were healthy American-born Caucasian males with no history of psychiatric complaints or treatment. Evans compared this group with 111 healthy volunteers, presumed to be predominantly heterosexual, who were acting as controls for medical research into cardiac disease. The measures applied included, in addition to the shoulder-hip ratio, an assessment of muscle strength by means of a dynamometer registering the force of hand grip, and a categorisation of physical type using Parnell's technique. This system divides individuals into fat, muscular, linear or balanced body types, and is based upon skinfold caliper measurements of subcutaneous fat, estimates of muscularity based on the relation of limb girth to bone size, and height-weight ratio.

Evans found significant differences between the homosexuals and the controls. The former were significantly less often of muscular or of fat physique and more often of linear physique. Their muscle strength was significantly less, and their shoulder-hip ratios deviated towards femininity. He also found significant differences in certain biochemical tests, notably lower blood cholesterol levels and lower cholesterol-phospholipid levels. These peculiarities may have been linked with hormone imbalance, in the shape of lowered androgen-oestrogen ratio, which was another feature of the homosexual group. Altogether, this research provides considerable grounds for belief in the existence of a physical factor in male homosexuality. In spite of the apparent normality of the physique of most homosexuals, objective measures yielded evidence of minor but detectable deviations in the direction of femininity. Since the deviations were of a kind likely to be associated with disturbances of the sex hormone balance, the findings were entirely in keeping with the theory that subtle glandular dysfunctions may influence human sexual orientation.

Until further research on these lines has been reported it would be wise to suspend judgment. The numbers involved in the investigations were small, and the investigation needs to be repeated to establish the consistency of the trends observed. Physique varies in different social classes and occupational groups. As Parnell showed, male prisoners and male students differ very considerably in this respect. The selection of the sample is crucial. As Evans himself points out, his volunteer homosexuals were a selected group, notable for their good educational background and serious attitude to social issues. It is conceivable that such factors may have had more to do with the physical characteristics of this particular group than their sexual orientation.

5. An inherited factor?

Since many physical characteristics, such as blood groups and eye colour, are hereditary, it would lend weight to the theory that sexual orientation has a physical basis if it could be shown that homosexuality is to some extent an hereditary condition. Many difficulties hinder the collection of evidence on the point. The secrecy that surrounds sexual habits, especially within the family circle, prevents the investigator obtaining reliable estimates of how many of the relatives of a known homosexual may be similarly inclined. The fact that homosexuality is a relatively common condition means that two or more cases could occur in the same family by mere coincidence. It requires a fairly large sample to demonstrate that the prevalence of homosexuality among the relatives of known homosexuals is significantly greater than among the population at large. The criteria for classifying a relative as homosexual need careful consideration. If they are so stringent as to debar all save the exclusive homosexual, then by definition fathers of homosexuals can never be counted as homosexuals themselves. This point alone suffices to rule out an explanation of exclusive homosexuality in terms of a simple dominant characteristic passed directly from parent to children. Even if it were possible to show that homosexuality runs in the family this would not prove the heredity theory. Homosexual orientation might be passed from one generation to the next by faulty upbringing, or transmitted from one family member to another by bad example or frank seduction.

A good illustration of the problems of this type of investigation is provided by some early German research (Lang, 1941, cited by Rosenthal, 1970). The subjects were 33 male homosexuals located among inmates of prisons in the Munich area. Lang visited their homes and personally interviewed the families. In spite of their homosexuality, 6 of the prisoners were or had been married, and had produced between them 7 male children of whom two had themselves become predominantly homosexual, while a third had had an incestuous relationship with his own father, although he was believed to be predominantly heterosexual. More striking than the incidence of homosexuality among these families, however, was the high proportion of relatives with various forms of serious mental disorder. Among the siblings of the prisoners, 7 were psychotic, 3 were severely subnormal, and 5 were psychopaths. This suggests that a familial tendency towards homosexuality is linked with a tendency to serious psychiatric disorder. On the other hand, the disorders may have had nothing to do with homosexuality, but simply reflected the fact that prisoners' families are notorious for their high incidence of social pathology.

Homosexuals frequently report the existence of other homosexuals among their close relatives. Margolese and Janiger (1973) documented this point systematically in a comparison of 24 male heterosexuals (Kinsey rating 0–2) and 28 male homosexuals (Kinsey rating 4–6), all of whom were undergoing physical examinations in connection with research into biological factors in homosexuality. Of the homosexual group, 17 said they had a blood relative who was homosexual, and 5 of the 17 said that had two such relatives. Only 2 of the heterosexuals said they had a homosexual relative. A difference of this magnitude points to the existence of a pronounced familial predisposition to homosexuality. Unfortunately, the investigators had to rely on their subjects' reports, and this may have introduced bias. Those who are themselves homosexual may be in a better position to detect similar tendencies in others, whereas heterosexuals might not notice, or might not like to admit, a relative's homosexuality even when there are grounds for suspicion.

One of the best methods of proving hereditary transmission is by the study of twins, of whom there are two types. Dizygotic, non-identical twins, produced by the fertilisation of two different eggs by two separate sperm cells, are no more alike than ordinary brothers and sisters, except that they are conceived at the same time, share the womb together, and are born one after the other only minutes apart. Monozygotic or identical twins, supposedly produced by the splitting of a single egg into two shortly after fertilisation, have virtually the same hereditary endowment, since they both descend from the same pair of egg and sperm cells. They bear an uncanny resemblance to each other, both in outward appearances and in more subtle identifying characteristics, such as finger prints and blood groups. Both types of twins, so long as they are reared together, experience much the same social environment, but only the identical twins have the additional factor of precisely similar inheritance. Investigation commences with the recruitment of a sample of individuals affected by a supposedly hereditary condition who are twins. The twin siblings, some of whom will be identical twins and others non-identical twins, have then to be traced. If the condition is hereditary, it will be found to occur in both members of identical twin pairs more often than in both members of non-identical twin pairs, in other words the 'concordance rate' will be higher for identical than for non-identical twins. Sex provides a good example. Non-identical twins are of the same sex in about 50 per cent of cases, whereas identical twins are always of the same sex. This 100 per cent concordance rate occurs because physical sex differentiation, in all but a negligible minority of pathological cases, is a feature manifest in every living person which is completely determined by heredity.

One American authority (Kallmann, 1952a; 1952b) has reported a concordance rate for homosexuality in identical twins of 100 per cent. He identified a series of 40 men who were known homosexuals and who had identical twin brothers. He managed to trace 37 of the brothers, all of whom proved to be homosexually inclined (Kinsey rating at least 3) and 28 of whom were more or less exclusively homosexual (Kinsey rating 5 or 6). Kallmann also investigated 45 homosexual men all of whom had a non-identical twin brother. Twenty-six of their twin brothers were traced, but only 3 had a Kinsey rating of 3 or more, a concordance rate of 11.5 per cent, no greater than might be expected among a random sample of pairs of males from the general population.

Findings suggestive of an extreme degree of hereditary determination are difficult to explain theoretically. As Rosenthal (1970) comments, in reviewing studies of homosexual twins, it is difficult to see, from an evolutionary standpoint, 'why, if homosexuality is transmitted genetically, the disorder has become so prevalent at all. Moreover the fertility of homosexuals is probably far lower than that of persons with any of the other behavioral disorders.' The claim that a particular hereditary endowment makes the development of a homosexual orientation virtually certain is contradicted by reports of identical twin pairs with one member heterosexual and the other homosexual.

Experts have been justifiably sceptical of the exaggerated claims sometimes put forward on the basis of twin studies. Kallmann (1960) himself came to regard the figure of 100 per cent concordance as 'a statistical artefact'. Kallmann's studies of schizophrenic twins yielded results nowadays considered too extreme. At the time they were criticised on methodological grounds, such as use of unrepresentative samples and dependence upon uncorroborated personal opinion as to diagnosis (Pastore, 1949). Perhaps the greatest weakness in his study of homosexual twins was that the subjects he started with were seriously abnormal apart from their homosexuality. Of his 40 identical twins, one was actually schizophrenic, and at least 22 were 'definitely schizoid', 'severely unstable with obsessive compulsive features' or else alcoholic. The nature of the sample was dictated by the methods of recruitment, which relied upon the help of psychiatric, penal and charitable agencies. Sexual maladjustment is a frequent concomitant of severe personality disorder. Kallmann's subjects may have become homosexual as a consequence of other more serious and possibly hereditary abnormalities. A sample of homosexuals drawn from the normal community might have yielded quite different results.

Well over a hundred cases of pairs of identical homosexual twins have been studied and published (Klimmer, 1965, p. 283-5; Heston and Shields, 1968;). Although the concordance rate falls short of 100 per cent, it is certainly very high, and much greater than the concordance rate for non-identical twins. The major weakness in nearly all this work, however, is the same as in Kallmann's study, namely dependence upon subjects drawn from psychiatric hospital or prison sources. Homosexuality occurring as an isolated feature in a healthy individual need not necessarily have the same basis, hereditary or otherwise, as homosexuality in association with mental illness or severe personality disorder.

Another, but rather less serious, objection to the hereditary explanation of identical twin resemblances runs as follows. Because they look so alike, identical twins are treated the same by everyone with whom they come into contact, including their parents. They develop along similar lines because their life experiences are so similar, much more so than in the case of non-identical twins. The only sure way to counter this argument would be to study twins reared apart, but this would scarcely be practicable in view of the rarity of a combination of events of twin birth, early separation and homosexual development.

If the consequences of being born identical predispose both members of the twin pair to becoming homosexual, this would provide another way to explain the high concordance rate of identical twins without invoking the hereditary theory. It has indeed been suggested that having a twin double creates problems of sexual identity which may lead to homosexuality (Money, 1963). This explanation has been fairly conclusively disproved by the observation that the incidence of homosexuality is no greater among identical twins than among non-identical twins. Since 1948 the Maudsley Hospital in London has kept a register of all known twins among the psychiatric patients. Among 82 identical male twins, 6.1 per cent were homosexual, compared with 7.2 per cent among 97 non-identical twins (Heston and Shields, 1968).

Examples of identical twins where only one member of the pair is homosexual have been reported by Davison *et al.* (1971), Green and Stoller (1971), Heston and Shields (1968), Kallmann (1953, pp.116-19), Klintworth (1962), Koch (1965), Parker (1964), Rainer *et al.* (1960) and Sanders (1934). Such cases are of interest, not only because they show that the homosexual condition cannot be completely and inevitably predetermined by heredity, but also because the life histories of discordant twins provide clues to the kind of environmental experience that may be responsible for two persons of similar hereditary endowment developing dissimilar sexual orientations. For example, a number of these case histories suggest that a difference in sexual outlook was produced by a difference in the attitudes of the mother towards each of her twins.

Among the examples reported by Parker was a pair of identical male twins, one married happily with two children and no homosexual inclinations, the other single, actively homosexual and completely lacking in heterosexual interest or experience. Both twins were intelligent, free from neurotic symptoms and of normal masculine physique. The one great difference in their environments was the way they had been mothered. Their mother had wanted a girl. When the two boys were born, although they were physically virtually indistinguishable, she fastened upon the first-born, because a nurse had commented that he was pretty enough to be a girl, put a bracelet round his wrist and treated him like a girl. The father was ageing and inactive in family life and did nothing to counteract the mother.'s influence. Both the brothers and the mother herself were aware of her special relationship with the first-born twin. He became a sensitive, home-loving, mother-attached boy while his brother liked football, swimming and other outdoor pursuits. At adolescence, the affected twin had promiscuous sexual experiences with males of his own age group and also with older men, but eventually he settled down to a steady relationship with one male friend of similar age. His twin brother had shown no homosexual interest since the usual masturbatory experiences of early adolescence.

Mesnikoff *et al.* (1963), reported divergent sexual behaviour between the members of four pairs of identical twins. They found that the mother's fantasies during pregnancy regarding the sex of her unborn child, coupled with difficulties during delivery leading to the rejection of one of the twins, reinforced by minimal differences in anatomy between the twins, set in motion psychological processes whereby one twin came to be preferred by the parent of the same sex while the other was preferred by the parent of the opposite sex. As a consequence, each member of a twin pair experienced different child-rearing approaches and different systems of approval or disapproval of his social and sexual interests. For example, in one case a mother encouraged one of her twins to play with dolls and to learn the piano and dance, while his twin brother, who was given the same christian name as the father, was encouraged in sports and boys' pursuits. By the time the twins were six, the father felt that the first was just like a girl and the other like a boy, and he subsequently treated them accordingly. The one who was treated like a girl became homosexual while his twin became heterosexual.

The importance of identification with the parent of the same sex is stressed in another case of divergent identical twins reported by Rainer *et al.* (1960) under the pseudonyms Tom and Dick. Their mother, described as a cold, inhibited personality, was particularly rejecting towards Tom, whose difficult birth she blamed for causing her numerous subsequent disabilities. Tom was named after his father, and as a result of his mother's rejecting attitude his affections became centred upon his maternal grandmother. Both Tom and Dick had homosexual experiences as schoolboys, and both were discouraged by their parents from contact with girls, but whereas Dick developed into a confirmed homosexual, and rejected the idea of changing his sexual orientation when treatment was offered, Tom had affairs with older women and eventually married happily.

A striking case story reported by Davison, Brierly and Smith (1971) bears out the importance of maternal over-solicitude in the development of homosexuality in sons. An eighteen-year-old youth of effeminate appearance and sibilant voice, convicted for importuning an off-duty policeman in a public toilet, was found to have an identical twin brother who was normally mannish in bearing and interests, and completely heterosexual. The difference between them apparently dated from early infancy when Paul, who was destined to become homosexual, developed an almost fatal gastro-intestinal infection. His mother referred to his survival as a 'miracle' and admitted that she over-protected him as a child because she felt he was less strong than his twin brother Michael who was 'able to fend for himself'. At school Paul disliked sports, avoided rough play and was often protected by his more pugnacious and active brother Michael. Paul developed into a somewhat shy, fastidious nervous personality and became a trainee cook, while Michael took up car mechanics and was not at all put off by dirty jobs. Paul had a much closer relationship with his mother, who was an anxious personality like himself. His father, who gave the impression of a mild, submissive character dominated by his wife, admitted he found difficulty in getting on close terms with Paul, whereas he had no such difficulty with Michael.

In a pair of female identical twins described by Green and Stoller (1971), both were of slim boyish build, but one was born with a minor foot deformity. She experienced more physical illnesses than her sister and was regarded as less strong. In early life both attempted competitive sports, but the stronger twin was more successful and better motivated. She came to be treated by all the family with amused pleasure as the 'boy'. The weaker sister grew up with entirely feminine manners and interests, wanting nothing better than to marry and have several children. The stronger of the two day dreamed of becoming a man, dressed and behaved in mannish ways, fell in love with another young woman, and came to notice when she sought a sex-change operation. In this example, besides more parental encouragement of cross-sex behaviour in the homosexual twin during childhood, there was the additional factor of a difference in physical strength and athletic aptitude, which favoured the development of feminine and heterosexual ways in one sister and masculine and homosexual attitudes in the other.

A number of reports of identical twins of discordant sexual orientation suggest that some nervous weakness or physical damage may be the essential factor distinguishing the homosexual member of the pair from the heterosexual twin. Lange (1931), in an early study of criminal twins, discovered one identical pair, called Otto and Erich, of whom the former had been imprisoned as a result of homosexual activities while the latter denied any homosexual inclinations and regarded such behaviour with disgust and contempt. Otto had apparently sustained some damage during the process of birth, because he had a partial facial paralysis and a facial tic. Lange felt convinced of 'some connection between this brain lesion and his sexual abnormality'. In another pair of identical male twins described by Sanders (1934) the homosexual member of the pair suffered from epilepsy. In a more recent case study by Klintworth (1962) a young male came to notice as a result of a suicidal attempt due to guilt feelings about his homosexual inclinations and experience. His identical-twin brother was examined. He strongly denied having ever had the slightest homosexual desire, and reported having regular sexual intercourse with girl friends. Analysis of this twin's responses to a psychological projection test (the TAT, see p. 30) revealed some difficulties in attempts to suppress aggressive feelings, but no indication of homosexual tendencies. The twins looked extremely alike, attended the same school, had many friends in common, and had very similar life histories. Both had considerable interest in sports, especially tennis, but later their interests diverged and they grew apart. George, the heterosexual twin, took to motor cycling and dart playing with drinking companions, whereas John, the homosexual twin, preferred serious music and was interested in sewing and cooking. Ever since adolescence, when his twin brother started to go out with girls, John had masturbated to the accompaniment of homosexual fantasies and had experienced no erotic stimulation from girls. He felt he would like to be a girl and had to resist temptations to dress in girl's clothes. He had read of sex-change operations and secretly hoped he could one day become female. At birth, John was not quite so heavy as George, and as an infant was, according to his mother, 'a good child' and not naughty like most boys. Unlike his twin George, John displayed neurotic symptoms as a child, namely sleep-walking, thumb-sucking until age nine, and fear of being left alone in a room. Both twins had difficulty in relating to their father and strongly preferred their mother. George, however, thought that John was mother's favourite 'because he can't stand on his own'. The only notable contrast between these twins, other than their sexual interests, was the slightly neurotic disposition of the homosexual twin, a feature which could well have been the result of a different course of development in the womb. Because they are in a sense in competition with each other in the womb it sometimes happens that one member of a twin pair has less than a fair share of maternal blood supply and is consequently born relatively underweight and underdeveloped.

While the case histories of divergent twins highlight the importance of environmental factors in deciding sexual orientation, the life stories of concordant twins are equally revealing of the powerful force of heredity in predisposing the individual to particular life styles and sexual habits. In one case, reported by Holden (1965) a pair of identical male twins both developed, apparently unbeknown to each other, the unusual pattern of a strong and exclusive sexual attraction to elderly men. However, in this instance, as Holden himself pointed out, both men had been brought up by the same dominating, possessive mother and weak father. Moreover, they were closely identified with each other, had lived together, worked together, and in many respects acted as one person. Their similar sexual tastes could have been acquired as a result of the upbringing and experience they had in common.

Examples of identical twins who have developed independently, but along similar lines, are particularly interesting. Heston and Shields (1968) report two sets of male twins in which the brothers, independently and unknown to each other, developed homosexual interests during periods of life when they were living apart. These two sets of twins were born to the same mother and belonged to a large poor family remarkable for the number of members with social and psychiatric problems. The first pair of twins were aged 40 when interviewed. They had both set up a long standing homosexual cohabitation with another man, but during the period when this development took place one of them was away serving in the navy. He did not return home during this time or correspond with his twin. Each remained ignorant of the other's homosexuality until over ten years later when they confided in each other. The second set of twins began their homosexual experiences independently, after being evacuated during the last war to different foster homes when they were aged 10. One was seduced into homosexual acts by an older 'father figure' who lived in the home, while his twin was seduced by older boys living in the other foster home. Neither knew of the other's experiences. At age 17 they went to different places in military service, but began similar patterns of sexual conduct, namely frequent homosexual relations with a variety of partners, interspersed with sporadic and not very satisfying experiences of heterosexual intercourse. Both preferred heterosexual males as partners, and neither would consider living with another man. Both experienced periods of anxiety and depression attributed to fear of exposure of their homosexuality and inability to found a family.

The current state of research into homosexual twins scarcely permits firm conclusions to be drawn. However, both the statistical findings and the descriptive studies suggest that hereditary factors may have considerably more importance than is generally acknowledged. At the same time, it seems clear that the final outcome as regards sexual orientation, as in most aspects of human personality, depends upon an interaction between environmental circumstances and constitutional predisposition. Usually the two sets of influences reinforce each other, but when they happen to conflict environmental pressures are likely to be the more decisive as determinants of an individual's sexual orientation. The hereditary factor may be of relatively less importance among homosexuals who are at ease with their gender role than among those whose erotic interests are linked with cross sex temperamental and personality characteristics.

CHAPTER FIVE

Some Psychological Theories

1. *Preliminary thoughts*

Being reared in ways more suited to a girl, being frightened off sex by puritanical parents, being seduced by older boys or men, being the youngest or only son of a possessive mother, being segregated from women, being shy or ineffectual in making contact with the opposite sex, or being rejected by girls, are just a few of the countless reasons put forward to account for some boys becoming homosexuals. One point is certain. If any one of these simple factors, or any other easily identified circumstance, adequately accounted for most instances of homosexuality, the fact would have become apparent long since and there would be no need to write this book. Homosexuality, like any other pattern of human behaviour, is the outcome of a complex interaction between individual needs and dispositions on the one hand, and environmental pressures, constraints and opportunities on the other. No single causal explanation will ever suffice. Moreover, the key influences need not be the same in every case; different people may reach a similar sexual orientation by very different routes. Generalisations true for many cases will not apply to all. The scientific inquirer needs to discover which are the most important, that is to say the most ubiquitous and the most powerful, among the various possible factors which may combine to tip the scales towards a homosexual orientation.

Research in this field has to begin with painstaking searches for the features of individual upbringing and experience that distinguish persons of similar social and cultural backgrounds who have developed contrasting sexual orientations. As has been pointed out already, considerable difficulties stand in the way of assembling and investigating representative samples of homosexuals. Surveys based upon whole communities would give a clearer picture of the distinctive characteristics of the homosexual minority than surveys dependent upon the investigation of selected groups. Unfortunately community surveys have to contend with much resistance, not only from potential subjects, who find the questions embarrassing, but from research organisations, who have difficulty in obtaining funds for inquiries into such sensitive topics, and who may fear the effect of adverse publicity. The resources of a Kinsey type team of investigators, though much needed, are rarely available.

A great deal of psychiatric writing on the subject, although prolific in suggested explanations, has little scientific value because the opinions advanced are so often based upon the observation of limited numbers of cases taken from sources liable to produce untypical examples. For instance, a psychiatrist may notice that several homosexual men in his clinical practice are only sons. Another finds several instances of homosexual patients with many brothers. The first psychiatrist suggests that the absence of male peers hinders the development of masculinity. The second psychiatrist suggests that the presence of many brothers increases the risk of early homosexual experiences. A meticulous review of the contradictory opinions enshrined in psychiatric literature, appropriately labelled with the date and author's name, might impress the reader with the compiler's academic proficiency, but would be an unprofitable exercise. Few psychiatrists have the opportunity to check their impressions by prolonged statistical inquiry, or to obtain access to cases uncomplicated by mental disturbance. In the example just cited, even if statistically valid, the observation that only children among neurotic patients are often homosexual would not necessarily mean that non-neurotic only children share the same tendency to become homosexual. Limited experience and personal bias afflict many of the pronoucements of medical men on this topic, and hinder the dissemination of more accurate information.

2. *Parental influences and male homosexuality*

Most experts agree with the layman's view that male homosexuals tend to have dominating, possessive mothers who, from infancy onwards, smother their sons with maternal over-solicitude, keep them tied to the proverbial apron strings, and crush their early attempts to assert masculine independence (Hamilton, 1939). In contrast, the fathers of male homosexuals are described as either weak, ineffectual men who let their wives rule the home, or else cold, remote, unsympathetic personalities who shirk family responsibilities and take little interest in their sons, except perhaps to criticise and complain. In either case, the father fails conspicuously to shield the boy from maternal domination. The classic picture of a male homosexual's upbringing consists of an over-intense relationship with mother and inability to communicate with father (Neodoma, 1951; Bender and Paster, 1941; Shearer, 1966).

The surveys cited in this chapter represent only a small selection from a great many published reports by clinicians and research workers, nearly all of which point to the importance of this particular family constellation in turning sons into homosexuals. The presence of this classic background is not always decisive; it increases the likelihood of homosexuality, but does not guarantee that all or any of the boys from such a family will actually become homosexuals. In some cases quite different influences predominate, for parents who do not in the least fit the classic stereotype may have homosexual sons. Although psychoanalysts sometimes emphasise parental behaviour to the exclusion of all other causes, this is not the key to every case.

The American psychoanalyst Irving Bieber carried out one of the best-known investigations into this topic. He circulated among his colleagues a detailed questionnaire about the backgrounds of their male patients. From the replies received, supplemented by extensive further inquiries, he compared the backgrounds of 106 homosexuals and 100 heterosexual patients. The parents of the homosexuals emerged as odder than the parents of the heterosexuals. In 69 per cent of the homosexual cases (compared with only 32 per cent of the heterosexuals) the mother could be categorised as having a 'close, binding, intimate' relationship with the deviant son. These mothers exerted their binding influence by preferential treatment and seductiveness on the one hand, coupled with restrictive, over-protecting, over-controlling attitudes on the other. 'In many instances, the son was the most significant individual in her life and the husband was usually replaced by the son as her love object.' This kind of mother tended to favour the homosexual son over her other children, to spend a great deal of time with him, and to confide her most intimate feelings to him. In Bieber's evaluation, four-fifths of the mothers of homosexuals were dominating, three-fifths were over-protective, three-fifths openly preferred her son to her husband, and three-fifths tried to get her son to take sides with her against her husband. Over three-quarters were either sexually frigid or puritanical in their sexual attitudes or both. (See Bieber *et. al.*, 1962 Table III 3). In the more extreme cases the picture approximated to that of the overwhelmingly possessive mothers of male transsexuals described by Stoller (see page 52).

Bieber noted also that very few homosexual patients had enjoyed a warm relationship with their father. Over four-fifths of the homosexuals' fathers were either absent altogether from the home or spent very little time with their son. Detachment and hostility were the most frequently reported paternal traits. A majority of the homosexual sons both hated and feared their fathers, and many recalled being exposed to ridicule, contempt and humiliation as a result of their fathers' attitude. Struck by the consistency of this pattern, Bieber came to believe that a warm, supportive, masculine father figure practically precluded the possibility of a son growing up homosexual. He concluded that a close-binding-intimate mother who ruled her home and denigrated her husband, combined with a detached hostile father, who gave the son no masculine support, was the parental constellation which incurred the greatest risk of developing homosexuality in sons.

Challenging and important as they are, Bieber's findings are open to obvious criticism. The categorisation of parents depended upon the testimony of patients whose recollections were far from objective or dispassionate, and the decisions as to classification were made by analysts with strong theoretical preconceptions. The sample consisted of patients undergoing analysis, so that their disturbed relationships with their parents could have been due to their neurotic problems rather than to their homosexual orientation. Even Bieber did not go so far as to claim that a particular parental pattern invariably resulted in homosexuality. Indeed, in his study, some of the heterosexual patients had equally anomalous parental relationships. For example, as many as a third of the heterosexuals' mothers were classed as close-binding-intimate, and half of their fathers were hostile, indifferent or absent from home.

The contention that over-positive mothers and negative fathers encourage homosexuality in sons receives support from surveys of male psychiatric patients, and from the opinions of many experienced psychotherapists (Allen, 1958; Freeman, 1955; Lorand, 1951: Whitener *et al.*, 1964). Scrutiny of published collections of case histories of homosexuals produces a similar impression (Krafft-Ebing, 1934; Ellis, 1915; Moll, 1931; Wade, 1965). For instance, among the cases quoted by the psychiatrist G.W. Henry (1941) in *Sex Variants* about every other one runs true to form. Nathan B, the second case in Henry's book, had a father who was extremely puritanical, rigid and a slave to discipline, who used to strap the children frequently. His mother, a highly strung and energetic woman, and his elder sister, used to pet him outrageously. He grew up timid, terrified of his father, afraid of rough boys, an obvious 'sissy', and completely homosexual. The fourth case in the book, Michael D, was the only son of a family dominated by women. His mother, a competent business executive, bossed the home, while his father was a submissive man, often in disgrace in the eyes of his womenfolk, for whom the boy and his mother showed scant respect. Michael grew up a lonely, nervous 'sissy', and, after a few discouraging experiences with women prostitutes, became exclusively homosexual.

Systematic comparisons of groups of homosexual and heterosexual patients have regularly yielded massive differences in regard to parental backgrounds. O'Connor (1964) compared 50 neurotic males seen in the course of psychiatric work in the Royal Air Force with 50 male homosexuals who consulted him on account of anxiety, depression or other problems. The homosexuals had as many psychiatric symptoms as the heterosexual patients, but they differed in their family background, having a much higher incidence of preferential attachment to mother rather than to father (62 per cent as against 8 per cent) poor relationship with father (28 per cent as compared with 6 per cent) and a history of paternal absences during childhood and adolescence (24 per cent compared with 2 per cent). They also differed in more often choosing artistic hobbies and disliking robust sports. O'Connor concluded that the typical male homosexual was an artistic, unaggressive person devoted to his mother. In a somewhat similar study, with a sample of 40 American airmen, Brown (1963) reported that in 30 cases the family background conformed to the usual pattern of abnormally close mother-son attachment and negative paternal relationship. In fact, not one of the homosexual airmen had a warm, affectionate attachment to his father.

Similar trends were reported by Jonas (1944) who put a series of set questions to 60 overtly homosexual male patients and to a corresponding number of presumptively heterosexual controls. Forty-three of the homosexuals, compared with only 18 of the controls, stated their unqualified favouring of mother over father. Only one of the controls, compared with 9 of the homosexuals, admitted hating his father. West (1959) compared two groups of male psychiatric case histories from the files of the Maudsley Hospital, London, 50 with a diagnosis of overt homosexuality, and 50 with a diagnosis of neurotic disorder uncomplicated by homosexuality. Descriptions of each parent were copied from the notes and given to an independent judge, who rated them without knowing the diagnosis. A characteristic combination of intense relationship with mother and unsatisfactory relationship with father occurred very significantly more often in the homosexual than in the heterosexual group. A wide range of defects were reported in the fathers of the homosexuals, including dislike or contempt of their son, aloofness, ineptitude, absence from home, and subjugation to a dominant wife. Some of the homosexuals' mothers were soft and indulgent, others strong and domineering, but in either case they tended to have unusually intense relationships with their homosexual son.

Years later, Robertson (1972) carried out another retrospective study based upon the Maudsley Hospital files. He identified a group of 20 homosexual male patients who were not considered neurotic, and another who were both homosexual and neurotic. These two groups of homosexuals were compared, in regard to reported relationships with parents, with two other groups, both heterosexuals, one classed as sexual deviants and the other as neurotics. The heterosexual deviants had better relationships with father than any of the other groups. The non-neurotic homosexual men had good relationships with their mothers, in fact rather better, though not significantly better, than the heterosexual deviants. Contrary to expectation, however, the neurotic homosexual men had poorer relationships with their mothers than any of the other three groups. The author concluded that, among those homosexuals who are also manifestly disturbed neurotics, ambivalent or negative feelings to mother are more frequent than the usual stereotype of a close-binding-intimate relationship.

It may be objected that the typical voluntary patient, who is neurotically inclined, verbally expressive, and fairly well educated, gives a distorted picture of his upbringing because of a need to justify himself with a conventionally acceptable explanation of his condition. Miller (1958) found that homosexual prisoners, who are less educated, less fluent, and less likely to formulate psychological interpretations, nevertheless report similar parental influences. He studied fifty male homosexuals of effeminate type serving sentences in an American federal prison and found that a combination of overprotective mother and hostile or absent father was the commonest parental pattern.

The typically negative father and over-positive mother may work towards producing homosexuality by deterring sons from identification with things masculine and encouraging feminine identifications. Chang and Block (1960) compared a group of socially functioning male homosexuals with a control group using a psychological test which required the subjects to select adjectives descriptive of themselves and of each parent. By checking the same adjectives to describe both themselves and their mothers, and different adjectives to describe their fathers, the homosexuals revealed a stronger identification with mother, and a much stronger avoidance of paternal characteristics, than the male control group. If this is how parental influence works, one would expect male homosexuals with a strong feminine identification to have had a particularly unsatisfactory parental upbringing. Some confirmation of this comes from a survey by Nash and Hayes (1965) who found that passive, effeminate male homosexuals tended to have even worse relationships with their fathers than did active types of homosexual.

In most modern surveys, investigators have made a point of recruiting subjects through homophile organisations, or from other sources in the community, in order to produce samples of homosexuals who, not having felt the need for psychiatric treatment, may be presumed to be of homosexual orientation without being conspicuously neurotic. The results suggest that the disturbances in parental relationships observed in psychiatric samples also occur, though with less frequent incidence and in less extreme form, among homosexuals who have never been patients. This was the main finding of a research by Evans (1969), who gave 43 non-patient homosexual men, and a control group of heterosexuals, a questionnaire, adapted from Bieber's inquiry, and designed to explore the subjects' recollections of childhood interactions with their parents. The generally negative quality of the homosexuals' family relationships, and the typical combination of close, binding mother with detached, hostile father, emerged unmistakably in this survey, as in the previous studies of patient groups.

In a more recent investigation on similar lines, Thompson *et al.* (1973) studied parent-child relationships in a group of 127 white, educated male homosexual volunteers recruited through their friends, and compared them with 123 control subjects matched for age, sex and educational experience. Both groups came from the same geographical areas, mostly from Atlanta, Georgia. Questionnaires were given out and passed on to the subjects, completed privately, and returned anonymously. These included various masculinity-femininity tests, as well as a family background questionnaire containing 38 items concerned with parent-child interactions. The responses to the parental items were separately rated with reference to mother and father on scales designed to measure how closely relationships conformed to the classic stereotype described by Bieber. Although a wide variety of parent-son relations emerged, and some respondents reported ideal backgrounds, the male homosexuals as a group appeared very significantly more often mother-bound, and also more hostile to father, than the male heterosexual controls. Evelyn Hooker (1969), who studied non-patient samples of male homosexuals in California, reached similar conclusions. She found evidence for the anomalous parental constellations described by the psychoanalysts, but at the same time she felt this was only one of many influences at work in the development of homosexuals. A more recent study (Stephan, 1973), based upon a sample of 88 young male homosexuals who were active in the 'gay' movement, compared with a group of heterosexuals of matching age and occupation, produced essentially similar results. The homosexuals tended to have mothers who were more dominant and more affectionate than their fathers. As children they were often shy 'loners' who preferred the company of mothers, sisters or female friends to that of other boys. The survey of Saghir and Robins (1973) produced substantially similar results. Eighty-four per cent of the male homosexuals, but only 18 per cent of the controls, reported that their fathers were indifferent or uninvolved with them in childhood. In contrast, about two-thirds of the homosexual men, but only one-third of the controls identified primarily with their mothers. The homosexuals' mothers were frequently described as possessive, the dominant figure in the home, and the main disciplinarian. In later years, some of the homosexual sons began to resent the maternal tie. A number of them complained that their mothers had babied them and restricted them, forced them into feminine domestic activities, discouraged sports and boyish interests and hindered them in making dates with girls.

The American findings on non-patient samples are echoed in the results of an English survey by Westwood (1960), based on 127 homosexual volunteers from the community. He found that, in contrast with patient samples, a half of the men came from reasonably happy and complete parental homes. Even so, 38 per cent reported unsatisfactory relations with their father, and 44 per cent were of the opinion that their mother was possessive or over-protective in some way, and twice as many named mother as named father when asked which of the two was the more dominant parent. Eva Bene (1965b) compared 83 self-admitted English male homosexuals recruited from the community with the same number of married men of roughly equivalent age and social class. She gave to both groups a test consisting of a series of descriptive items of character or behaviour. The volunteers were asked to think back to their early years and to say which members of their family most closely fitted each description. Thirty-five per cent of the homosexuals, compared with only 13 per cent of the married men, thought that the item 'used to nag too much' fitted their mothers. A quarter of the homosexuals, but only 6 per cent of the married men, thought the description 'did not love me very much' fitted their fathers. Bene found a surprising ambivalence in the homosexuals' feelings towards their mothers, more of them than the married men endorsing negative evaluations such as 'used to be mean to me'. Apparently, the close-binding-intimate maternal relationship may come about at the cost of considerable resentment upon the part of the dependent youngster.

One pair of American psychologists (Apperson and McAdoo, 1968), who tried to elicit descriptions of parents by means of a questionnaire, obtained results slightly different from those reported by most investigators. Each subject, either a male homosexual recruited from the community, or one of a control group made up of soldiers and male hospital workers, had to select from a list of items of childhood behaviour which ones would have most 'bothered' his mother and which would have most bothered his father. The homosexuals reported, predictably, that asking questions about sex, or letting another child see them in the toilet, would have bothered their mothers. On the other hand they reported that certain items of unsocial behaviour (such as not returning a coin borrowed from a friend) did not bother their mothers. It seemed that homosexuals' mothers were not uniformly restrictive, they condemned sharply matters that offended puritanical sensibilities, but were over-indulgent and permissive about other areas of social training. The homosexuals' fathers, however, were just as expected from the descriptions of Bieber and others, being perceived by their sons as critical, impatient and rejecting.

In spite of all these congruent results, some doubts remain. A few investigators have obtained results that conflict with the accepted trend. Siegelman (1974a) compared 307 non-patient male homosexuals with 138 heterosexual male students, using a questionnaire on parent-child relations. As usual, the homosexuals reported more distant relationships with their fathers than the heterosexuals. Contrary to expectation, however, they also reported more rejecting or less loving mothers than the heterosexuals. When only those men who were free from neurotic tendency (indicated by low scores on the neuroticism scale of the California Psychological Inventory) were taken into account, no difference at all was found between the reported parental relationships of the homosexual and the heterosexual groups. Siegelman's results suggested that the disturbed parental relationships believed to be so prevalent among homosexuals may be a feature of neurotic homosexuals only.

A sceptical British psychiatrist, Dr. F.K. Taylor (1966) has pointed out that one cannot deduce with certainty that parental mismanagement causes homosexuality, since the recollections of adult homosexuals may be subject to bias. Zuger's observations of the parents of effeminate boys (cited on p. 53), made while the boys were still young, failed to reveal the expected shortcomings. Even if they really do behave as oddly as is alleged, the parents of a homosexual may merely be reacting to their child's innate peculiarities. A soft girlish boy might well arouse a mother's compassion and a father's contempt. The answer to these criticisms lies in long-term research, beginning with an objective assessment of parental behaviour from the moment a child is born and relating these data to sexual orientation in adult life. Something approaching this was done by McCord *et al.* (1962a). They had the good fortune to have access to a mass of psychological information on the upbringing and reactions of a large sample of Boston schoolboys who had been selected to participate in a delinquency prevention scheme known as the Cambridge Somerville Project. Observations began, not at birth, but around the age of eleven, when psychologists and social workers began to study the boys and take histories from their parents. Observation continued for at least five years, by which time sexual problems of adolescence had become evident.

Analysing the material sometime later, the McCords identified three kinds of sexually disturbed adolescent. The anxious, inhibited type feared any form of sex. The 'perverted' type indulged in a variety of disapproved activities (e.g. public masturbation, voyeurism, fetishism) in addition to ordinary heterosexual outlets. The 'feminine' attitude type were clearly unhappy in the male role, preferring girls' company and girls' pursuits, and being liable to overt homosexual activity. Compared with the sexually undisturbed youths of similar class and ethnic background, all three types of sexually maladjusted boys came from parental homes characterised by sexual anxiety and prudishness, maternal authoritarianism, quarrels between parents, and paternal punitiveness. The result fitted neatly the theory that a repressive, anxiety-ridden type of upbringing favours the development of sexual disorders of all kinds. The McCord study also brought out, yet again, the importance of the father (McCord *et al.* 1962b). The fathers of the 'feminine' type adolescents were especially unsatisfactory. Half of them were absent from home most of the time, and most of them neglected or openly despised their sons. With an absent father, or one whose rejecting or aggressive personality presented the child with an unattractive image of masculinity, a sexually repressive atmosphere in the home was particularly likely to generate homosexual or 'feminised' sons. The investigators commented that these boys had been exposed to a degree of parental mishandling perfectly obvious to outside observers at the time, which could not be explained away by bias in recall. In many cases the parental peculiarities probably preceded the birth of the son, and could not be merely an adverse reaction to the son's effeminacy.

Systematic observations by social psychologists (Hetherington, 1966) have shown that, even among quite healthy families, paternal absence, due to military service or similar circumstances, has a feminising effect upon small boys, who became noticeably less aggressive and more dependent than boys with fathers at hand. The presence in the home of a substitute father greatly reduces this tendency (Santrock, 1970). Such findings confirm the importance of paternal influence in protecting boys from feminising influences, and presumably also from homosexual development.

The results of modern investigations into the family backgrounds of male homosexuals confirm the importance of parental influence and vindicate the beliefs of previous generations of clinicians. They do not, however, take one much further than the psycho-social recipe for the development of homosexuality in boys suggested long ago by Terman and Miles (1936) 'Too demonstrative affection from an excessively emotional mother – a father who is unsympathetic, autocratic, brutal, much away from home, or deceased.' How this recipe works remains to be explained.

3. *Some psychoanalytic explanations*

Of all brands of psychological theorists psychoanalysts have had the most to say about the causes of homosexuality, but their views receive increasingly sceptical appraisal. The musings of neurotic patients in the intimacy of the analytic hour, their fears and fantasies, their dreams and free associations, and above all their recollections of the far-off emotional crises of early childhood, supply the raw data of psychoanalysis. This highly subjective material, interpreted in the light of analysts' personal experience and predilections, produce theories more imaginative than scientific. Even so, the method has proved a fruitful source of ideas about the origins of abnormal behaviour and has certainly enriched our understanding of human motives. Some psychoanalysts demand that one accept their theoretical system as a whole, as if the entire corpus of somewhat inconsistent speculations by Freud and his followers was made up of ideas of equal worth. This is not my approach. I prefer to select those notions which have some support from other lines of evidence, and those theories which have led to verifiable predictions.

Freudian theory asserts that individuals vary in attitude and behaviour because they discover, in the course of growing up, different personal solutions to universal human conflicts. The conflicts begin very early in life, as the infant's natural impulses collide with the necessary civilised restraints imposed by parents. Aggressive and sexual instincts cause the worst clashes, and sexual conflicts in particular have been held to blame for producing neurotic reactions. Analysts agree with poets and romantics that sexual love in the widest sense, which they call *libido*, provides the great driving force behind all human striving. It also provides a ready source of conflict. Analysts believe that libidinous impulses are as important in infancy as in adult life. The baby's need for mother, and the baby's joy in sensual cuddling and suckling, are the veritable precursors of adult thirst for love and adult urge for erotic contact. Even in childhood libidinal impulses pose a potential threat to family and social organisations. Inconvenient manifestations of sexuality on a child's part, and especially any signs of incestuous interest, provoke vigorous reactions. The control of forbidden sexuality appears so imperative that rational self-discipline will not suffice. The very existence of temptation has to be denied and banished from conscious awareness.

Psychoanalysis teaches that repression of socially undesirable impulses, which rids the individual of temptation to break the rules, takes place in infancy, and comprises one of the most important, and certainly the most indelible, forms of social learning. In some contexts it works most effectively. For example, the normal infantile fascination with excretion, and the impulse to smear and play with faeces, rapidly give way to an acquired conscious disgust. Usually an extreme modesty about bowel activities persists throughout life, but if madness or extreme senility supervenes the individual may revert to an infantile delight in playing with his own dirt. Repression takes a particularly large part in sexual training, but whereas people suffer no serious deprivation from the denial of pleasure in excrement, the denial of stronger libidinous impulses can produce complications. In their efforts to conquer completely all forbidden sexual desires some individuals repress too much, and so cannot enjoy uninhibited sexual relations with another person under any circumstances.

Too much repression is thought to be unhealthy and self-defeating. If instinctual needs are given too little outlet, they become like a grumbling volcano, quiescent but only partially subdued, liable to erupt any moment in disconcerting ways. When this happens, the incompletely repressed tendencies find expression in disguised form as neurotic symptoms, such as irrational states of anxiety without apparent cause. According to psychoanalysts, an examination of the situations that provoke such symptoms reveals that they tend to occur when circumstances of potential temptation stimulate the partially repressed impulses. For instance, one woman who suffered from travel phobia experienced no fear so long as her husband went with her. The psycho-analytic interpretation was that she had tried to repress her attraction to men other than her husband. Her neurotic symptoms came on when she was travelling on her own, because then she might meet other men, her true sexual inclinations might obtrude, and this would cause her panic.

Psychoanalysts look upon male homosexuals as persons who have over-learned childhood prohibitions against physical intimacy with girls and defended themselves against temptation by massive repression of all their heterosexual inclinations. If forced into close contact with women they become anxious and impotent. Their apparent revulsion is caused by panic at the threatened emergence of repressed desires. Their homosexual preference develops as a secondary consequence of their flight from women. Other men cause them less anxiety than women. It seems paradoxical that socially forbidden outlets should develop while socially permitted ones are repressed, but this state of affairs faithfully reproduces the childhood situation when sexual repressions were first instilled. At that age parents tend to place emphasis on the prohibition of physical intimacy with girls, leaving contacts with other boys relatively unrestricted.

It follows from this theory that psychosexual health depends upon discrimination in the process of repression. The preservation of an uninhibited sexual appetite for the legitimate marriage partner, while at the same time effectively repressing all socially disapproved tendencies, calls for a nice balance, which many neurotics fail to achieve. The most important factor in bringing about a successful adjustment is a favourable interaction between parents and child during the critical phases of development, which psychoanalysts believe take place during the first five years of life. A fearsomely repressive, puritanical upbringing risks producing a sexually inhibited adult liable to resort to all kinds of deviant substitutes for straightforward heterosexual intercourse. On the other hand, Freud believed civilised standards unattainable without some repression. In their natural, unrestrained state children appear to be totally undiscriminating – 'polymorphous perverse' – in their sexual inclinations. Without repression, we might all become anally and orally erotic, sadistic, incestuous and bisexual. According to Freud (1905a) 'Freedom to range equally over male and female objects – as it is found in childhood, in primitive states of society and early periods of history – is the original basis from which, as a result of restriction in one direction or another, both the normal and the inverted types develop.'

All children experience sexual prohibitions, but only a minority react adversely. Psychoanalysts find an explanation for this in the different ways of resolving the Oedipus Complex. Freud took the name from the legendary Greek foundling who, on returning as an adult to the land of his birth, killed a man who proved to be his father, and married a woman who turned out to be his mother. Overcome by guilt when he discovered what he had done, Oedipus gouged out his eyes as a self punishment. Freud saw in this legend a reflection of a universal tendency of boys to harbour 'incestuous' fantasies of ousting father and replacing him in their mother's affection. Such thoughts arouse intense guilt feelings and fears of punishment, especially punishment by mutilation and castration. Altogether the whole situation is so unpleasant and frightening that the thoughts are vigorously repressed, so much so that the crime of incest with mother becomes almost unimaginable to the civilised adult.

Put so baldly, and in adult language, the idea sounds implausible, but direct observations have confirmed that many children do indeed have such fantasies. In games like 'mothers and fathers', in scribbled drawings, in dreams, in fact in any situation which gives free play to the child's imagination, the theme of Oedipal rivalry, with fears of retributive disaster, find more or less open expression. The use of technical terms and adult vocabulary to describe such themes imposes a false impression of clarity upon chaotic infantile fantasies. Nevertheless, confirmation of their existence and their importance comes from other sources, from the folklore of primitive peoples, and from the ravings of psychotics, whose delusions break the bonds of repressions and display in brutal, undisguised form the self-same ideas. Of course incest guilt and castration fears are not clear-cut concepts attributable to explicit prohibitions, for parents rarely talk to children in such language. Modern parents do not try to control their child's sexual interests or masturbatory habits with crude threats to 'cut it off', but a sense of horrified disapproval communicates itself without words. The child has no need to understand the dictionary definition of incest in order to feel guilty about some of his secret sexual thoughts.

Freudian theory accounts for much sexual neurosis in terms of unresolved Oedipal conflict. Neurotics continue, unconsciously, to associate all their sex feelings with the incestuous desires they fought against in childhood, so they remain permanently guilt-ridden and inhibited. Boys who have had too intense and exclusive a relationship with mother in early life, exacerbated by an unsympathetic, condemnatory father, tend to develop particularly strong Oedipal fears. A common manifestation of this in adult males is the inability to perform sexually except with prostitutes. Nice women are too like mother, hence forbidden fruit, pure and untouchable. Homosexual males go one stage further and become cold towards all women, because any kind of heterosexual feeling arouses their incest guilt. For them, the female form inspires terror instead of pleasure. The absence of male sexual organs suggests castration. In his dreams the homosexual may visualise womens' genitals as a dangerous, biting instrument ready to trap and injure him (Fenichel, 1945).

Evidence for these interpretations comes from the rich harvest of fantasy produced by free association during analytic sessions, but even without this esoteric technique one can often discern the classic Freudian themes running through the life histories of male homosexuals. The special attachment to mother, and the fear or dislike of father, have been amply documented in the earlier part of this chapter. The spectacle of bachelor son and lively mother (or mother substitute) who gets taken about and fussed over like a girl friend, is only too well known. This de-sexualised ritual continues the mother-son symbiosis established in childhood, and represents a safe way of life that protects the son from having to come to terms with women of his own age.

The following case, seen as a hospital patient, illustrates more vividly than abstract discussion the kind of disturbance Freudian theory seeks to explain:

This man came under psychiatric scrutiny at the age of 30, after suffering for some eight years from unexplained muscular aches and pains, tired feelings, and recurrent moods of depression, when he would spend all his time moping indoors. He was haunted by thoughts of inferiority and fears that he would fail at anything he tried.

Because of his chronic lack of confidence, he would undertake only undemanding work far below his intellectual capacity. He drifted aimlessly from one boring job to another. He was single, living alone, with no close friends.

It soon emerged that his social invalidism stemmed from an extreme sense of guilt about sporadic homosexual experiences, coupled with an even deeper aversion to heterosexuality. He came from the typical homosexual's family background. He had been his mother's favourite. He used to stay in with her of an evening and feel no need for other company. When he was twenty, she died, and it was then, when he felt especially lonely, that he started visiting drinking bars on his own and his homosexual experiences first began.

At school, he had been unusually ignorant about sex, and was greatly troubled by other boys' obscene talk. In youth, he became very shy of girls, feeling clumsy and gauche in their company, and being dreadfully over-sensitive about the shape of his nose. He masturbated in solitude, thinking of girls, but could never be intimate with them, except in imagination, because of a phobia of making a girl pregnant. He thought that about the most terrible thing that could happen. He remembered vividly his mother, who had strict, old-fashioned ideas about sex, saying she would feel like killing a son who got a girl into trouble.

He also had the typical homosexual's unsatisfactory relationship with father. He complained that his father had never taken much interest in him, and never found time to attend school functions as other parents did. As a child he was nervous, afraid of the dark and a nail biter, but when he complained his father commented unsympathetically, 'You're weaker than I thought you were.' When his father re-married, following his mother's death, he disapproved strongly and left home.

Crippled with self-blame, he could obtain no joy from life. He held strong religious convictions, but kept away from his church because he felt it would be a mockery of religion for a homosexual to attend services. His homosexual relationships were circumscribed and largely anonymous. He never went with the same man more than once, he hated to be kissed or fondled, and he liked sex to take place in the dark as then he felt less ashamed. He had one friendship with a girl, but they never had intercourse. She would cuddle him in doorways, and he would become excited when he felt her body pressed against his, but then his pregnancy phobia would overcome him, and he would have to hurry away.

In this example, mother-fixation, excessive guilt, fear of heterosexual contact in spite of evident desire for it, and the sense of hopeless inferiority (castration complex) fit perfectly the Freudian explanation. In clinical experience one finds many cases running equally true to form. If the dynamic behind most, or even many, instances of male homosexuality consists of flight from mother-son incest, it should be possible to confirm the theory by showing, experimentally, that homosexual feelings are in fact stimulated by incest threat. Silverman *et al.* (1973) accomplished this feat by using a tachistoscope to present an appropriate stimulus subliminally. They flashed the words 'fuck mommy' before the subjects' eyes for a fraction of a second, brief enough to produce an effect, not long enough for the subjects to perceive consciously the content of the message. They also presented other kinds of stimuli to compare the effects. Before and after looking into the tachistoscope, the subjects looked through a series of pictures of ten males and ten females, each of which they had to rate for sexual attractiveness. The subjects who participated in the experiment were 36 male homosexuals recruited by advertisement in the *Village Voice* (a Greenwich Village tabloid) and 36 men of similar age range who considered themselves at least predominantly heterosexual. Following subliminal viewing of the incest stimulus the homosexual subjects, but not the heterosexuals, displayed a significantly increased tendency to select and rate as attractive the photographs of males. The 'threat' or 'shock' of the incest stimulus had apparently had the predicted effect of plunging them further into a defensive, homosexual stance.

Other attempts to investigate empirically psychoanalytic hypotheses concerning homosexuals have either failed to obtain confirmation, or have had only slight success (Kline, 1972). For example, De Luca (1967) used the Blacky Pictures with 20 male homosexuals and 40 male controls. This is a form of projection test utilising cartoons depicting a family of dogs in situations relevant to psychoanalytic theory. The subjects have to tell a story about each picture to illustrate what they think is going on and how each of the characters is feeling. The content of their stories, and the response they make to leading questions about the pictures, show which situations arouse anxiety. For example, persons with an unresolved Oedipus complex might be expected to respond peculiarly when confronted with the picture showing the dog Blacky watching his parents making love. Persons with marked castration anxiety might be more disturbed by the picture showing one of the dogs apparently about to have his tail cut off. Although psychoanalytic theory suggests that homosexuals should be peculiarly sensitive to such situations, De Luca found no significant differences between the responses of homosexuals and controls in this regard.

Lindner (1953) applied the Blacky Test to 67 prisoners guilty of sexual offences and to other prisoners matched for age, race, intelligence, marital status and length of sentence. The sex criminals gave more indication than the other prisoners of Oedipus complex, castration complex, and so forth, but no significant difference was obtained between the men guilty of homosexual offences and the men guilty of other sex crimes.

The failure of the Blacky Test to produce confirmatory evidence must not be taken as a firm refutation of Freudian theory. Projection tests of this kind are notoriously inefficient measures. Imprecision in interpreting and scoring the responses makes for a wide margin of error, so that many individuals must be tested before definite trends emerge. Both the surveys cited used rather small samples of homosexuals.

Although flight from incest is an easily recognised and extremely important theme among male homosexuals, it is not universal. For example, many homosexuals react to heterosexual situations with indifference (see page 25), or perhaps with mild interest, but certainly without the panic or revulsion expected from Freudian theory. Many are not in the least inhibited, as would be expected of individuals who have repressed too much, but seem to enjoy a variety of guilt-free sexual experience with a wide range of partners. Oedipal theory explains the power of the smothering mother, ogre father and puritanical home to excite archetypal fears and repress heterosexuality, but it fails to account for the numerous cases of male homosexuality developing without benefit of this particular parental constellation. Examples of men who lead active bisexual lives run counter to the notion that a taste for forbidden forms of sexual expression must always be a substitute for repressed heterosexual desire.

Psychoanalysts try to tinker with Freudian theory so as to stretch it to embrace all cases. They might, for instance, interpret the apparent absence of panic in a male homosexual when confronted by a woman as merely a successful defense against fears too awful to admit. Such 'heads I win, tails you lose' types of interpretation become less and less plausible as one moves away from the anxiety-ridden neurotic types and tries to explore the causes of homosexual orientation among less disturbed personalities.

Psychoanalysts continue to regard homosexuality as a second best substitute form of sexual expression, dictated by neurotic fears, but they have to admit that many people find it a workable substitute. Homosexuals have a better time than sufferers from impotence, or from sexual fixation upon small children, who can never attain full physical and emotional satisfaction. As Dr. K. Soddy (1954) once put it, homosexuals can achieve a stable and secure emotional adjustment which leaves other aspects of their character and intellect free to develop normally. Older psychoanalytic writings seemed to imply that insight into neurotic conflicts would produce the wish and the possibility to achieve a more 'mature' sexual adjustment. This overlooks the simple point that a minority life style that has been found viable and personally rewarding assumes a dynamic of its own. The conflicts that first drove the individual on to a particular path become less relevant as life proceeds. A contented heterosexual has no cause to fret about when or why he repressed his potential homosexuality; he has enough fulfilment, and enough problems, without the complications that might ensue from a reawakening of such inclinations. Some homosexuals feel the same about trying to recover a potential for heterosexuality. Insight into some of the repressions that may have determined their homosexual orientation no longer seems important to them.

4. *More psychodynamic theories*

Freud's early ideas about Oedipal conflict and incest fear as the basis for homosexuality were merely a prelude to the plethora of elaborations, modifications and alternatives that he and his later followers have since produced. Theories that possess the imprimatur of the orthodox psychoanalytic school have been reviewed by Weideman (1962) and Socarides (1968), while a slightly wider range of psychodynamic views on the topic has been helpfully summarised by Saul and Beck (1961). One point comes over forcibly from all these contributions; different theories are needed because the fantasies of homosexuals do not all run along the same lines. In some cases the classic theme of incest guilt predominates, in others a homosexual orientation appears to be associated with fears or conflicts of a different order.

Freud himself complicated the theoretical issues by postulating stages of sexual development through which all normal infants must pass, which he called the oral, anal and phallic phases. He believed that the first step in development, the oral phase, consists of a concentration of the initially diffuse bodily sexual feelings upon the mouth area, which becomes the first erotic zone. During this oral phase the infant derives his greatest satisfactions from sucking activities. Later, around the third year of life the anal zone gains temporary predominance, and during this phase the infant delights in bowel movements, spends an inordinate time on the chamber pot, and has to be persuaded to let go his stool (Freud, 1917). At about the age of four, the anal stage gives way to the phallic stage, and the penis or clitoris becomes the prime source of erotic pleasure.

Parental mishandling may, it is said, delay the infant's development from one phase to the next, or cause the transition to remain incomplete. Infants frustrated during their oral phase by rigid breast feeding time tables, or by abrupt weaning, may develop an 'oral fixation'. In adult life this fixation reveals itself in symbolic guise in character defects. For instance, 'oral' characters may allow themselves to be ruled by irrational mood swings, or they may crave succour, that is emotional or material support from others, instead of cultivating independence. Anal fixation, Freud (1908) suggested, might manifest in literal form as homoerotic anal sexuality, or might show up in obsessive orderliness, parsimony and obstinacy. He interpreted obstinacy and pleasure in hoarding as relics of the infantile delight in holding back faeces. The urge to tidy and clean up he saw as a reaction against temptation to do the opposite – to play with dirt.

This aspect of Freudian theory is more than usually speculative and controversial, and has been severely criticised, even by fellow analysts (Chodoff, 1966). Claims have been made that direct observation of small children bears out Freud's description of oral, anal and genital phases (Isaacs, 1933), but the more objective studies of this kind supply little confirmation (Murphy, 1957). It has been possible to show that children cut short in breast feeding during their first six months indulge in more than usual amounts of thumb sucking (Yarrow, 1954), but evidence that breast deprivation promotes thumb-sucking does nothing to confirm the erotic nature of the behaviour or its significance for later personality development. In Freud's conception, the influence of the first stages of infantile sexuality upon homosexual development works indirectly, by colouring the Oedipal conflicts, which assume importance during the genital phase, with oral and anal impulses left behind from earlier phases. Many psychoanalytic case reports on individual homosexual patients have sought to demonstrate the presence of character traits and attitudes derived from pre-genital fixations, but that such features are commoner in homosexual than in heterosexual neurotics is very much open to doubt.

Kline (1972), one of the few psychologists to test this aspect of Freudian theory empirically, constructed a personality questionnaire which successfully identified persons possessing a cluster of traits which analysts would call typically 'anal' characteristics. He applied the test to homosexual men under treatment at a clinic. Freudian theory predicts that practising homosexuals, because they express anal eroticism overtly, should have few of the anal personality traits which develop when anal erotic tendencies are repressed. Kline found that in fact, according to their response to his tests, the homosexuals were not significantly different from a control group of students.

Freudian theory seeks to explain personality problems seemingly unconnected with sex in terms of difficulties during infantile phases of sexual development. For instance, frustrations experienced during the latter part of the oral phase, when sucking gives way to biting, stimulate the infant to more and more biting activity. The full effect of this situation comes out in adult life in the form of a hostile, malicious, sarcastic, jealous personality. The child analyst Melanie Klein and her associates (1952) were particularly interested in the oral phase, and held that oral frustrations provoked the infant into cannibalistic fantasies of swallowing mother's breast, or even eating up mother whole, and were responsible for many personality and sexual problems, including homosexuality. The guilt feelings and dread of reprisal aroused by such fantasies were so fearsome as to turn boys away from women altogether. The homosexual relationships that ensued were, unhappily, still coloured by sadistic fantasies derived from oral frustration. These unpleasant tendencies showed up in the delight taken by homosexuals in causing their partners physical pain during sexual encounters, and also by the psychological satisfaction some homosexuals derived from humilitating their lovers by attitudes of contempt, derision or disgust. Saul and Beck (1961) quote one example of a male homosexual who had very little regard for his lovers, and had strong wishes to ridicule and degrade them. During sexual activity he had fantasies of urinating upon his partner or castrating him. His sexual life served the double purpose of satisfying erotic impulses and at the same time enabling him to discharge powerful destructive, hostile feelings.

Phenomena of this kind are, of course, all too familiar in the context of heterosexual relationships, but psychoanalysts believe that homosexuals, because their condition reflects disturbance in early development, are particularly prone to work out their aggressions or play out their infantile rituals upon their sexual partners. Instead of seeking another person to love and to share their life, they really want a puppet with which to act out their sick fantasy. Of course homosexuals dispute these interpretations, maintaining that neurotically distorted relationships are no more prevalent among homosexuals than among heterosexuals.

Psychoanalysis possesses a considerable repertoire of disgreeable labels, nearly all of them applied sooner or later to homosexuals. The label narcissistic, in Freudian theory, applies to persons whose sexual development has been arrested at the very early narcissistic stage, a time when erotic feelings are diffuse, not yet focused upon any particular erotic zone, and not associated with any person outside the infant himself. Narcissists love themselves, or any object that presents a flattering reflection of themselves, but seem incapable of loving other persons for their own sakes. The narcissistic person is a vain, self-glorifying individual who delights in admiration but gives little warmth in return. Ferenczi (1955), among others, laid great stress upon the narcissistic quality of homosexual love. The narcissistic type of homosexual might be expected to take great interest in his own appearance. If he has a feminine identification this may lead to the extravagant use of perfume or make-up, if he has a masculine ideal he will prefer the latest adolescent male fashion, particularly tight pants or other items which emphasise male physique. These exhibitionistic traits go along with a shallowness in personal relationships. Having captured the interest of a lover, the narcissist makes unrealistic demands upon the lover's exclusive attention, only to turn away as soon as some more promising admirer comes upon the scene. This fickleness stems from the impractical nature of the goal, which is to have a lover fit into the unreal mould of the narcissist's glorified self-image.

Psychoanalysts emphasise the complex interdependence of character patterns and sexual behaviour. The narcissistic homosexual, besides loving his own self-image, often has a close attachment to, if not a positive identification with, his mother. He wants to be as like his mother as possible. It helps him to do this if he chooses, as a love object, a boy like himself, whom he can love as his mother once loved (or should have loved) him. Narcissistic individuals with grandiose ambitions or a grandiose self-image may seek out as love objects persons who appear correspondingly grand. This may take a specifically sexual form, for instance, in the man who chooses lovers with a large penis or superlative physique. Saul and Beck cite the example of a narcissistic man who was particularly excited sexually by successful and socially prestigeful businessmen. 'When his unconscious wishes for adulation and omnipotence were uncovered, analysed, and worked through, the homosexual attraction became greatly attenuated.'

Freud (1905a) recognised that infantile sexuality might set the scene, but it could not complete the drama. Early experiences might create a predisposition towards homosexuality, but later events made their contribution to the ultimate outcome. He cited such factors as unhappy experiences of heterosexual intercourse, fear of venereal disease, and exclusive associations with the same sex at school or in the army, as significant influences. In his analysis of Leonardo da Vinci, Freud (1910) noted that female dominance in the home, by encouraging a feminine identification, increased the likelihood of a boy so predisposed taking the homosexual path.

Psychoanalysts today, as well as Freud himself in his later works, emphasise that a homosexual orientation represents a complex psycho-social adaptation, not just a straightforward expression of infantile erotic interests. Apart from the defensive function of forming a protective barrier against incest guilt and castration anxiety (Freud, 1919) a man's sexual orientation can serve other purposes, for instance, enabling him to resolve painful conflicts arising from sibling rivalry, maternal dominance or dislike of masculinity. By choosing a homosexual partner, a youth may withdraw from competition with more successful brothers, avoid arousing mother's jealous disapproval of young women, and opt out of the social responsibilities of a prospective husband and father. In short, homosexuality can be a means of expressing, in the sexual sphere, personality problems of a non-sexual kind. Clara Thompson (1947) thought that many cases of male homosexuality were the result of abnormal dependency needs. Karen Horney (1945) came to similar conclusions when she suggested that the struggle for ascendancy in sexual relations between men provided a means of acting out abnormal urges to subdue and conquer others, or alternatively to submit to and placate others. Ovesey (1969) identified a special category which he called the male pseudo-homosexual. These men resorted to deviant sex practices less from erotic need than from fear of self-assertion and from a compulsion to seek out situations of dependency.

Applied to actual cases, psychoanalytic interpretations appear more credible, and the multiple explanations for the same behaviour less confusing, than when stated as abstract verbal formulations. Socarides (1968) quotes at length one text-book illustration, the case of patient 'A', a young man who seems to have been a walking testimonial to psychoanalytic theories of homosexuality. An exclusive practising homosexual for some years, and a frequenter of public lavatories who had already had one police warning, 'A' came for treatment because he feared the ruin of his career unless he acquired some heterosexual competence.

'A's' whole life had been dominated by an aggressive, shrewish mother who controlled his every move, criticised his friends, especially girls, and abused him unmercifully and threatened to desert the home if he showed the slightest resistance to her wishes. His father, a passive, yielding man had long since given up all opposition to this domestic tyrant, so all family decisions were left to her. Psychoanalysts maintain that a defensive 'identification with the aggressor' is a common reaction in such situations, and 'A' did just that. He grew up very closely attached to his mother, in spite of her cruelties, and many of her attitudes he adopted as his own. He joined in with ridiculing his father, and he developed his mother's biting tongue, using it against those he felt inferior to him. In sexual matters his mother behaved provocatively towards him, parading about the house in states of undress, allowing him to sleep with her frequently until he was thirteen, and confiding to him that she hated sex with his father. During analysis, 'A' recalled vividly his guilty sexual interest in his mother and his childhood desire to fuse their bodies together as he lay with her. But the pleasure was tinged with fear of engulfment. 'She's gloating at me, she's enjoying it, too, and she has control and power over me.'

Socarides noticed that all 'A's' homosexual contacts were brief and casual, with no prolonged affection, and that they happened most often when he was feeling anxious about something. His sexual encounters had an aggressive quality, and at one point he described unmistakably sadistic fantasies towards his sexual partners. 'I want to jab harder into his rectum with all my might ... I'd like to punch and kick him at the same time ...' The sexual ritual was serving multiple functions one of which was the expression of rage against his parents. He was simultaneously revenging himself against a father who had failed to protect him and enjoying sexual release in spite of mother's interdictions. By choosing a submitting male, he avoided the threat of feminine domination and the guilt of symbolic incest. When he felt daunted by social difficulties, and thus reminded of his awful dependence upon mother, the sex gratification restored his confidence.

The analyst assumed the role of the good and effectual father, guided 'A' on the techniques of heterosexual intercourse, helped him to see his mother's ways as destructive and sick, encouraged him to take decisions on his own, and gave him insight into the sterile, unreciprocal quality of his homosexual encounters, 'with the other person merely a device for the enactment of a unilateral emotional conflict'. Heterosexual potency developed fairly soon, but it was a long time before 'A's' suspicions of women and fear of domination were quelled, and he frequently lapsed back into homosexual conduct when lonely and unsure of his ability to separate himself from his mother.

Socarides' patient was aggressive towards his sexual partners, but such is the fluidity of psychoanalytic theories that similar interpretations have been used to explain an opposite style of behaviour, the control of personal aggression by excessive submissiveness. Another analyst, J.H. Brown (1963), had earlier published the history of a particularly submissive minister of religion whose homosexual habits were attributed to this mechanism. In early life this man had had a close, dependent attachment to a mother who literally spoon-fed him up to the age of nine. He recalled a pronounced fear of his critical, punitive father, who liked to ridicule his puny build and sissy ways, but would do nothing to help or encourage him to learn masculine skills. His early sexual experience consisted of wrestling games with an older boy during which he was regularly over-powered and 'forced' to suck his friend's penis. He developed strong sexual fantasies in which he derived pleasure from being taken by force by stronger males. In his ordinary life he was a habitually mild, non-assertive character and doubtful about his competence to perform the male role in heterosexual courtship.

Brown interpreted this man's problem as a perpetuation of the childhood Oedipal situation. The combination of fierce father and seductive mother, by arousing incest guilt and castration anxiety, had frightened him off heterosexuality. His continued need to placate the father image was responsible for his neurotic compulsion to demonstrate his submissiveness towards more powerful men.

Some analysts consider a homosexual orientation akin to madness. As Joyce McDougall put it (1972): 'The erotic expression of the sexual deviant is an essential part of his psychic stability and much of his life revolves around it.' The kinky sex scene resembles a play with the essential clues missing. The fact that the true meaning escapes the deviant preserves him from unbearable anxiety. Too much delving into the unconscious symbolism of the sexual ritual can sometimes precipitate collapse into madness. McDougall envisages a chain of events roughly as follows. When it dawns upon the mother-bound boy that she actually belongs to father and not to him, he experiences a tremendous upsurge of hatred towards her. The possibility of retaliation from the all-powerful, engulfing mother causes him to seek protection by choosing to love a penis, symbolic of paternal power. This symbolism is not consciously understood by the patient, whose 'real father is invariably held to be valueless or regarded as absent'. McDougall cites the case of a man suffering from a compulsion to search each night for different partners for fellatio, in the (conscious) belief that one day he would find a person he really loved. In practice, he constrained his partners to fulfil a rigidly prescribed role in the sex scene, after which the relationship always came to an abrupt end. One night, however, he found himself more interested in the man than the penis. On that occasion the partner happened to be an older man. During analysis the patient realised, to his horror, that he had up till then carefully avoided becoming involved with his sex partners because he did not wish to recognise that the one penis he was searching to possess was his father's. This insight was too much for him. He immediately gave up homosexual adventures and began associating with a woman, but simultaneously developed delusions and hallucinations and was soon quite mad.

This brief glimpse of psychoanalytic thinking bears witness to the bewildering variety of interpretations advanced. This fact, coupled with the enormous volume of psychoanalytic writings, the esoteric language employed, and the absence of any verification for most of the assumptions involved, makes it extremely difficult for an outsider to appraise. Psychoanalysts must be given credit for calling attention to many interesting and curious features of homosexual behaviour, but some of their explanations seem unnecessarily complicated, and likely to apply only to a minority of peculiar and neurotic cases. Nevertheless, the intuitive insights which have come out of clinical case studies are valuable as a source of ideas and helpful as starting points for research of a more systematic and objective character.

5. *Position in the family as a factor in producing homosexuality*

The theory that over-intense mothering causes homosexuality in sons suggests that boys brought up as only children should have a high incidence of homosexuality. Lacking the companionship and alternative socialising influence of other children in the home, and exposed to the full force of undivided parental attention, the only child becomes highly parent-centred, and in consequence particularly vulnerable to deviant parental attitudes. Other positions in the family constellation have been said to carry a similar risk. The youngest of a large family, for instance, especially a boy born after a long interval to an ageing couple, may evoke particularly intense parental feeling. Also at risk are boys reared by solitary widows or deserted wives, with no adult male in the household to act as substitute father. Boys with many brothers, however, should have a low risk of homosexuality, since any unhealthy maternal influence must be diminished in intensity through being spread thinly.

Translated into testable observations, one could predict an association of male homosexuality with fatherless families, only children, elderly mothers, and a relative absence of brothers. Statistical inquiries have partially substantiated several of these predictions. Evidence for a raised incidence of homosexual tendencies among fatherless boys has already been cited and need not be repeated (see pp. 39, 87, 93). Evidence that male homosexuals tend to have elderly mothers has been put forward by Slater (1962) and by Abe and Moran (1969). These investigators made use of the files at the Maudsley Hospital, London, where they found 291 male cases with a diagnostic label 'homosexuality' in which both paternal and maternal ages at the time of the patient's birth were on record. Abe and Moran compared the distribution of these mothers' ages with corresponding national statistics, relating to births in the years under consideration, which were to be found in the Registrar General's reports. The mothers of male homosexual patients were on average more than two years older than mothers in the general population. Although the difference may not seem very great, the trend was consistent, and in statistical terms highly significant. The age of the fathers of homosexual patients were also examined and found to exceed the average from population statistics by over three years.

This result was unexpected, since according to theory mother's age matters more than father's age. Of course, given elderly mothers, one also expects to find elderly fathers as well, since women tend to marry men of corresponding age or a little older. The fathers of homosexual patients, however, were not only older than the population at large, but the gap between their average age and that of their wives was greater than usual. The high maternal age in this sample of homosexuals was apparently merely a secondary consequence of high paternal age. Mothers could still be held responsible, of course. It might be argued that the kind of woman likely to produce a homosexual son marries for reasons other than sex, and therefore tends to select an older man.

Saghir and Robins (1973) failed to discover any significant difference in maternal age at birth between heterosexual and homosexual samples, whether male or female. The supposed association between homosexuality and raised maternal age has been attributed by some authorities to biological rather than to psychodynamic factors. Certain medical conditions traceable to chromosome abnormality, notably mongolism (Down's Syndrome) as well as some forms of epilepsy and mental deficiency (possibly attributable to obstetric complications which increase with age), are all more prevalent among the children of elderly mothers. On the theory that homosexuality arises from some chromosomal or neurological deficit, an association with elderly mothers would not be unexpected. Abe and Moran argue that, since the raised maternal age in homosexual samples is secondary to raised paternal age, the biological explanation is unlikely. If the mother's physical condition were the decisive factor, father's age would be irrelevant, since older women with younger husbands would be equally at risk. As Moran (1972) points out, the influence of an elderly father could conceivably be genetic, supposing, for instance, that sperm from ageing testes carries damaging mutations. This is, however, most unlikely. In view of the relative infertility of male homosexuals, many of whom never marry, no known genetic mechanism appears capable of producing such a high incidence of affected individuals as actually occurs. If elderly fathers are important, it must be for some psychological reason, such as the inability of old men to inspire sons with an adequate image of masculinity.

The small statistical correlation between parental age and homosexuality in sons has an interest more academic than practical. In any event, homosexuality is probably only one of a range of psychological peculiarities that occur slightly more often among the sons of elderly parents. When Robertson (1972), also at the Maudsley Hospital, compared the ages of mothers of male homosexual patients and mothers of male neurotic heterosexual patients, both were rather high, but the difference between them was statistically insignificant.

In his study of the Maudsley sample, Slater (1962) examined the ages of the children in the families of male homosexuals. He found that the homosexual member tended to come late in order of birth. This could be regarded as another reason, in addition to maternal age, why homosexuals may stand a greater than average risk of biological anomalies. On the other hand, the finding could equally well be held to support the view that boys born late into a family, because they tend to receive more attention from the mother, stand a greater risk of becoming homosexuals. In any event, survey results do not always support the contention that position in the family has any significant association with homosexuality (Manosevitz, 1970). Siegelman (1973) compared 150 male homosexuals with 108 male heterosexuals, and 99 lesbians with 97 heterosexual women, but in neither case did any distinctive contrasts emerge, either in regard to birth order or family size. Similar negative results were reported by Saghir and Robins (1973).

Psychological theories suggest that the number of siblings born before or after him is less important than whether the boy occupies one or other of the two vulnerable positions of only son or youngest son. This contention was confirmed in the survey by Westwood (1960) who found that 80.0% of his sample of 127 male homosexuals had been reared as either only sons or youngest sons. Martensen-Larsen (1957) in an earlier survey had noted a similar phenomenon.

It has been held by some investigators that if a male homosexual has any siblings he is more likely to have brothers than sisters. The suggestion was first put forward by Lang (1940) on the basis of an investigation of the family composition of 1,517 male homosexuals whose names were on a German police register. Lang found that they had a total of 2,534 brothers, but only 2,034 sisters, a male-female ratio of 124 to 100. Lang believed that some of the apparent females in these families were chromosomal males who had undergone a complete physical sex reversal, due to some as yet unidentified biological defect. The psychological sex reversal was not always as complete as the physical reversal, hence the homosexual orientation. As will be realised from the previous discussion (see page 61), Lang's theory has been disproved by modern chromosome research showing that male homosexuals are in fact true genetic males. Nevertheless, the excess of brothers in samples of male homosexuals needs an explanation.

Some more recent investigations have yielded figures supporting the contention that male homosexuals have an excess of brothers over sisters (Nash and Hayes, 1965). No significance can be attributed to such findings, however, unless comparison has been made with an adequate control group. Spencer (1959), in an investigation of Oxford undergraduate males, discovered an excess of brothers over sisters in a ratio of 81 to 66, which agreed with what Lang had reported. Among Spencer's students, however, it was the control group rather than the homosexuals who had the most brothers. A similar observation was reported by Morrow *et al.* (1965), who discovered a brother to sister ratio of 125 to 100 for normal male students. They suggested that such figures could easily be accounted for if, in the normal population, there is a tendency for certain families to have children all or mostly of the same sex, in which case selecting male children for research would automatically produce a sample of male biassed families. Quite apart from this possibility, one can imagine that the process of educational selection might produce students from predominantly male families. These criticisms will not account for the findings of Saghir and Robins (1973, p.142) who discovered a significant deficit of sisters among the siblings of a sample of male homosexuals compared with a control sample of male heterosexuals of similar age and socio-economic status. The mean number of brothers the homosexuals and the heterosexuals had was similar, 1.0 and 0.9 respectively. The mean number of sisters was 0.80 and 1.43 respectively. A similar, though slightly less marked deficit of sisters was found in the siblings of lesbians compared with unmarried heterosexual women.

In the present state of knowledge, the relevance of sibling sex ratio remains doubtful. Most psychologists would have predicted an association between homosexuality and an excess of sisters, on the assumption that too much feminine influence interferes with the development of masculine identity. If the opposite proves to be the case, the explanation need not necessarily be biological. An all male family, like an all male boarding school, could be looked upon as a homosexual learning situation. However, until the facts become clearer, one need not be too concerned about possible implications.

6. *Learning theorists' explanations*

The motivational explanations developed by psychodynamic theorists, in which infantile fears and yearnings play so large a part, have to be inferred from the recollections and verbal reports of their clients. Many psychologists despair of ever being able to verify such subjective material, or of guarding themselves against imaginative fantasies, which can be as misleading as they are beguiling. Most academic psychologists prefer to work with simpler, behaviouristic concepts developed from direct observation and experiment. They like to use laboratory rats rather than human subjects. The behaviour of rats can be scrutinised and manipulated without ethical complications, and their responses can be interpreted without bothering about the animals' thoughts or motives. The simple principles of learning derived from this behaviouristic approach work well enough in laboratory situations. Learning theorists assume that socialisation processes in children, the learning of socially acceptable behaviour in real life, operates on similar principles.

A strictly behaviouristic psychologist conceives of all living organisms as machines that have built-in self regulating mechanisms to maintain or restore physical equilibrium in the face of environmental changes. Any disturbing influence from outside elicits a drive to action to restore the balance. In the face of a noxious or painful stimulus, the automatic reaction takes the form of an avoidance response calculated to restore the status quo. Disturbance can arise internally, for instance when a fall in blood sugar elicits the hunger drive and makes the animal responsive to the taste of food. In psychological terms, stimuli which lead to restoration of equilibrium are pleasurable or rewarding. It is a first principle of learning that animals tend to repeat actions which are rewarding and to cease behaviour which is not rewarding. The reinforcement of behaviour by reward (known as operant conditioning) and the extinction of behaviour that is unrewarded, or that leads to painful disturbance, are conceived of as automatic processes, a natural consequence of the way the nervous system is constructed. The fact that in human beings these processes are sometimes accompanied by mental states, such as recollections of past similar situations, or decisions to take a particular course of action, is irrelevant to the basic principle. The conditioning effects of reward and punishment are believed to take place inexorably, regardless of whether the individual is aware of it, or of what he thinks or feels about it.

Another form of learning is classical conditioning, so called because it was the first of the processes discovered by Pavlov, the great pioneer of learning theory. Some forms of behaviour, such as blinking the eyes when a puff of air reaches the face, are automatic reflexes. They do not need to be learned, they occur the first time the relevant stimulus appears. If, in the individual's experience, puffs of air tend to occur in conjunction with some other stimulus, then that also will in time produce automatic eye blinking. If a person is made to hear a buzzer each time he feels a puff of air on the face, then he will soon begin to blink to the sound of the buzzer even when no puff of air accompanies it. The reaction is quite involuntary, the subject cannot prevent himself blinking to the noise however ridiculous it seems. Psychologists believe that many of our emotional attitudes and anxieties are produced by such conditioning experiences. For example, a life-long aversion to particular foods may originate in long-forgotten battles with parents who forced their child to eat when he did not want to do so. According to some learning theorists, aversive conditioning, that is the linking of particular situations with painful experience, is one of the most powerful determinants of character. Avoidance, distaste, anxiety and panic are natural responses to painful stimuli. By means of punishments for rule breaking, parents condition children to produce these avoidance responses whenever disapproved behaviour is undertaken or contemplated. Social conscience in the adult is said to be the product of consistent aversive conditioning in childhood.

The basic processes of learning are most conveniently studied in the laboratory, where situations can be artificially simplified, the stimuli under investigation carefully controlled, and other factors eliminated. Countless experiments have been devoted to determining the optimum intensity and timing of stimuli, or to discovering the frequency and consistency of the rewards and punishments necessary to establish and maintain a conditioned response. It has been found, for example, that stimuli need not be particularly intense in order to be effective in conditioning, so long as they are consistent. In fact, too intense or too painful stimulation risks a breakdown of the learning process, resulting in paradoxical or chaotic behaviour. Consistency and timing are the most important factors.

The application of such principles to human learning, whether in the sexual field or elsewhere, requires an enormous conceptual jump and involves many unverifiable assumptions. The adult's sense of modesty, for instance, which requires the genitals to be adequately clothed, may be explained as a conditioned response to infantile experiences of punishment for indecent exposure. Direct verification of this is impossible, since the supposed conditioning experiences have not been observed and recorded. Moreover, the explanation seems over-simplified. It ignores the symbolic meaning of nudity, and it fails to account for the peculiar infrequency of breaches of this particular rule. Nevertheless, psychologists have gone a long way towards producing verifiable predictions about human behaviour based upon the principles of learning theory.

Although learning theorists and psychoanalysts start off with highly contrasting methods and philosophies, some of the practical implications of their theories turn out to be surprisingly similar. Both schools of thought recognise that some sexual responses are innate, unlearned mechanisms which, like the sucking of a hungry baby, can be evoked by internal states of disequilibrium. Thus, a paralysed man with a severed spinal cord, who has no sensation from or control over his genitals, may still have penile erections in response to local irritation, although he will not know about it unless he happens to be watching. Both schools also recognise that most sexual behaviour involves social interaction, and this is a learned activity determined, for better or worse, by life experience. Both schools agree on the importance of steady, consistent childhood training. Both schools point to the desirability of parents with a matter-of-fact attitude to sex training, capable of tolerating certain behaviour, while plainly disapproving others. They both agree that anxious parents, unable to talk about sex, who over-react when confronted with inconvenient manifestations of childhood sexuality, are apt to create the problems they most fear. Heterosexual curiosity curbed by reactions of disgust may be replaced by homosexual developments. The difference in the schools lies in their explanations. Psychoanalysts maintain that parents communicate their own sexual anxieties to their children. Learning theorists believe that the reasons for failure to acquire appropriate and stable patterns of sexual behaviour lies in faulty conditioning due to confused training.

In the present state of knowledge, learning theorists are not in a position to give precise accounts of human social learning. The conditioning of infants in the course of interaction with their parents does not lend itself to exact, systematic observation. Social psychologists tend to accept certain psychoanalytic notions, not for any great supporting evidence from behavioural studies, but because the views sound plausible and do not positively conflict with learning theory. Where the expectations of learning theory are more clear cut, they can be seen to differ in several important ways from accepted psychoanalytic doctrine (James, 1967). For example, learning theory points to the relative specificity of conditioning experiences. Faulty learning in one situation does not necessarily imply faulty learning in other situations, so the fact that sexual arousal has been conditioned to occur in response to socially inappropriate stimuli does not mean that other forms of behaviour will also be deviant. Unlike much psychoanalytic theorising, which tends to view homosexuality as an indication of serious emotional disturbance affecting the whole personality, learning theory envisages homosexual responses being acquired by individuals otherwise normal, conventional and socially competent.

Some deductions from learning theory are unverifiable, others conflict with factual observation. The belief (shared with the psychoanalysts) that human beings are potentially responsive to either sex, developing a preference for heterosexuality as a result of experience, could be verified by testing the responses of different age groups to homo- and hetero-erotic stimuli, but the social taboo against arousing the sexuality of children ensures that no such experiments will be done. Any behaviour that achieves sexual orgasm must presumably be powerfully reinforced by the pleasurable quality of that experience. From time to time case histories are published which support the idea that a powerful erotic stimulus, experienced at a critical stage of development, may condition a person's future sexual preferences for all time. The story of the shoe fetishist who was once tickled by the toe of his nursemaid's shoe is rooted in psychiatric folklore. Gebhard (1965) relates a similar case of a boy in the full flush of pubertal excitability who underwent a painful surgical manipulation while being caressed and comforted by a brunette nurse. He developed sado-masochistic interests and a particular attraction to brunettes with the same hair style as this nurse. A literal application of this conditioning principle would lead one to expect the activities that produce an individual's earliest orgasms to be self-perpetuating. The fact that most people become heterosexual is puzzling in view of the likelihood of the earliest orgasmic experiences being brought about by self-masturbation or by homosexual contact. If the first experiences of overt sexual relations with other persons take the form of seduction by someone of the same sex, this should condition the individual to a homosexual orientation. Such evidence as is available (see pages 16, 217), suggests the contrary, that homosexual seduction in childhood has little bearing on adult sexual orientation. On the other hand, some evidence exists to suggest that precocious sexual development, by causing a child to seek repeated sexual contact with peers of his own sex, may contribute to a permanent homosexual orientation (see pp. 19, 223-4).

Clearly, there must be more to the establishment of permanent sexual orientation than early physical contacts. In humans fantasy plays an important role. The thoughts which accompany orgasm may be more important than the mechanical technique of stimulation. Some psychologists (McGuire *et al.*, 1965) have suggested that masturbatory activity reinforces pre-existing homosexual interests, since the conjuring up of favourite sexual thoughts is an intrinsic part of the experience. Of course pre-existing heterosexual interests might be similarly reinforced. The important point is that in humans sexual fantasies may develop, and perhaps become fixed in masturbatory practices, before sexual contacts with other people commence. The sense of gender identity, which seems to be developed in infancy, probably predetermines the direction of the earliest sexual fantasies, so that later experiences of masturbation and sexual orgasm simply reinforce pre-existing inclinations.

If, as some theorists believe, learning experiences at adolescence or later continue to exert a considerable influence upon sexual preference, one might expect that any social circumstances which serve to hinder heterosexual contacts, while providing opportunities for homosexual contacts, would favour a high incidence of homosexuality. The sociologists Ashworth and Walker (1972) suggest that this expectation can be seen to be fulfilled in three well-known situations. Prisons and other one-sex institutions, which discourage or prevent heterosexual contacts, are known to favour the development of homosexuality. The male section of the theatrical profession is said to include a disproportionately large number of homosexuals, a feature usually attributed to the traditional tolerance of the theatrical community, which permits opportunities for homosexual behaviour not available elsewhere. In the opinion of Ashworth and Walker, this feature also reflects the handicaps experienced by male actors in the marriage market. Most of them are not held in much esteem socially, they receive irregular and low earnings, and their profession involves much travel and unsocial hours of work. Compared with men in more prestigious and stable employment, they have little to offer a woman. The authors find similar reasons for the high incidence of male homosexuality in traditional Moslem society. The stratified social system which puts a high price on brides, protects the virginity of the unmarried, and permits wealthy husbands to have several wives, inevitably leaves some men deprived of heterosexual contacts. The jocular attitude towards such matters in Moslem society permits men to develop homosexuality as a substitute form of sexual satisfaction. Aside from the problems of establishing the facts, and of ruling out alternative interpretations, these sociological theories tend to neglect the distinction between transient homosexual behaviour during a period of heterosexual deprivation, and the development of a true homosexual preference. Social pressures upon adults may be more effective in influencing current behaviour than in determining long-term sexual orientation. Learning theory differs most importantly from psychoanalytic teachings in the practical implications for treatment methods. If the conditioning effect of sexual practice determines sexual orientation, then a change in habits should produce a corresponding change of orientation.

Learning theory points to the possibility of deconditioning the homosexual response by abstinence, or by associating homoerotic reactions with punishing shocks. At the same time, positive conditioning of heterosexual responses might be brought about by exposure to heterosexually seductive experiences, or by training in masturbation while viewing pornographic materials designed to stimulate heterosexual fantasy. Psychoanalysts disapprove of this mechanical approach and do not believe in its effectiveness. They contend that the patient cannot benefit from exposure to heterosexual situations until the nature of his fears and his emotional resistance has been analysed, and the emotional blockage removed. The comparative results of behaviouristic conditioning techniques and psychoanalytic methods of treatment, and their bearing upon this theoretical controversy, are dealt with in Chapter Nine.

7. Hints from animal behaviour

Animal behaviour is relatively simple, and influences which affect it are not too difficult to identify. Ethological studies can provide valuable insights into the causes of individual variations in behaviour. Sometimes influences found to be important in animals are later discovered to play a part in human affairs. Of course outwardly similar behaviour can have different contexts, and analogies between animal and human situations have to be viewed critically. For example the fact that mice become aggressive when confined together in a restricted space suggests a possible cause for the association between human violence and over-crowded housing. The analogy does not take one very far, however, unless the nature of the stress in overcrowded animal communities, which might be anything from excessive competition for food to fear of body contact with other animals, prove to have something in common with the stresses which cause irritation among overcrowded humans.

Many species of mammals, including the primates, who are closest to man in evolution, have been observed in their natural state to behave in a seemingly homosexual fashion. From this it has been argued that homosexual responsiveness forms part of our evolutionary heritage and as such cannot be properly described as 'unnatural'. If men and women become exclusively heterosexual because social pressure constrains them to forego the bisexual habits of other mammals, then from a biological standpoint, exclusive heterosexuality merits the epithet 'unnatural' just as much as exclusive homosexuality.

This argument has been challenged on the grounds that the animal behaviour in question does not represent a true counterpart of human sexuality. In purely physical terms, however, no ambiguity exists. It seems that the more intelligent species, those that come closest to mankind in brain development, learning power and versatility, tend to display the greatest variety of sexual behaviour, including homoerotic and autoerotic stimulation. Male dolphins, for example, will attempt to masturbate against the flanks of smaller males in a manner similar to their behaviour during heterosexual arousal. A definite pairing of two male dolphins has been reported. The two kept together during the mating season and paid no attention to females (McBride and Hebb, 1948). Among primates, even when the situation permits access to the opposite sex, unmistakably sexual behaviour sometimes occurs between pairs of males. In the case of females, apparently homoerotic activity commonly takes the form of mutual grooming and licking of the genitalia. In males, pairing usually occurs between a mature dominant male and a juvenile. The dominant animal mounts his partner, clasping, thrusting with the pelvis, and sometimes apparently achieving penile penetration and ejaculation (Ford and Beach, 1952). These observations come as no surprise to the countryman, who knows that cows begin to mount each other when they are ripe for breeding, and that a young bull can be used as a 'teaser' to induce mounting and ejaculation when semen needs to be collected from a breeding bull for purposes of artificial insemination. Indeed, the sight of domestic dogs mounting each other and making copulatory movements is an all too familiar street spectacle.

Doubts about the significance of all this arise for several reasons. First, homosexual behaviour evidently takes place much more readily when animals are deprived of the opposite sex. Although, on occasion, they will deliberately choose one of their own sex, an exclusive homosexual preference, such as develops in humans, does not seem to occur among animals in the wild. A certain degree of ambisexuality comes naturally to them, but not an exclusive homosexual fixation.

A second and more fundamental reason for questioning the relevance of these ethological observations is that animals sometimes use sexual gestures for expressing social dominance or submission. In many species the threatening or aggressive behaviour which maintains safety, status and territory appears indistinguishable from the gestures, rituals and modes of attack employed by courting males (Tinbergen, 1964). Male animals of certain species, when losing a fight, often turn away and present their rears to the aggressor in the manner of a female ready for sex. The gesture produces an immediate pacifying effect. The active homosexual tendencies which some vigorous male animals seem to display may serve the purpose of asserting their superiority over smaller and younger males. This cannot be the whole story, however, since the homosexual behaviour of animals is not limited to occasions of conflict; on the contrary, it can lead to the establishment of alliances in which the stronger member of the pair protects the weaker (Denniston, 1965).

In some animals, mounting behaviour occurs as a natural response to sexual arousal. Rats that have failed to ejaculate with one female will jump on to any other rat, either male or female, in an attempt to reach a climax. In his eagerness, the mounting animal may simply fail to identify correctly his partner's sex. Disregard for the gender of the other animal might be no more than a sign of sexual excitement. When mounted by another animal, male rats almost invariably pull away and refuse to reciprocate. Exceptionally, some male rats react with a feminine stance to the approach of other males, but apparently more from excessive excitability than from homosexual drive. These same animals copulate vigorously when with a receptive female rat. Indiscriminate excitability will not, however, account for the behaviour of those monkeys who make a leisurely and preferential selection of another male, and it will not account for the behaviour of acquiescent monkeys, who adopt a collaborative posture and participate with the sexual aggressor in genital manipulations.

Ford and Beach (1952, p.140) suggest that primates and humans share a propensity for homosexual alliances because they both have a well-developed capacity for learning from their exploratory behaviour. 'As a consequence of prepubertal homosexual play the male can learn that sexual satisfaction is derivable from coitus with other males.' Powerful support for a learning theory of homosexuality comes from the observation that animals segregated among their own sex may gradually come to prefer their own sex even after heterosexual opportunities have been restored. Long ago Jenkins (1928) showed that prolonged segregation of male white rats induced homosexual behaviour which in some animals persisted indefinitely after the segregation ceased. Male rats given electric shocks whenever they copulate with females can be conditioned into becoming exclusively homosexual (Rasmussen, 1955).

A study of the ways in which animals learn their sexual habits might well teach us something about human sexual learning. Most lower animals respond to sexual stimulation more or less automatically without having to discover what to do or needing to imitate their elders. Higher animals, such as apes and chimpanzees, have to learn to copulate. Although patently excited by a receptive female the young primate's early attempts prove clumsily ineffectual. Given every opportunity for natural experience, some male apes need years of practice before they can copulate efficiently.

Not just the mechanical techniques of copulation but also the more complicated social behaviour necessary to secure a mate has to be learned. In an earlier chapter dealing with the learning of gender identity (see p. 44) researches were cited which demonstrated the importance to developing monkeys of the presence of others of their kind if they are to be able, when grown up, to behave in acceptable fashion and find a sexual partner. Mason *et al.* (1968), in a review of the social development of monkeys and chimpanzees who had been artificially isolated in early life, produced an alarming catalogue of maladaptive behaviour, sexual and otherwise. Monkeys reared in small, enclosed cages without contact with their mother or their siblings were utterly unfitted to cope with life subsequently. They spent their time in pointless rocking, clasping or sucking movements. In contact with other monkeys they became either terror-stricken or violent. Animals that had been exposed to less damaging degrees of deprivation interacted more with other animals, but with grossly inappropriate conduct. For example, some males became physically aroused in the presence of a female, but instead of proceeding to make further contact they began solitary and idiosyncratic masturbation. Deprived monkeys who make some attempt to copulate fail to take up a suitable position (Mason, 1968). Harlow and Harlow (1965), pioneers in the field of monkey deprivation research, give harrowing descriptions of the behaviour of socially deprived female monkeys who become pregnant. Lacking maternal skills normally learned by monkeys through contact with their mothers, these monstrous creations of science beat and trample their offspring, rub their faces in the floor, and would kill them off altogether if the experimenters were not at hand to rescue them.

These observations suggest that the sexuality of primates serves important social as well as reproductive functions. The ability to control aggression, to form bonds with other animals of the same species, and to pursue collaborative goals seems intimately bound up with the learning of sexual responses. The same may well be true of human relationships. Infant monkeys seem to need intimate body contact with other monkeys, and young monkeys to need the opportunity to rehearse sexual behaviour in play among their peers, in order to react appropriately when they become adults. Only recently has our society permitted anyone to ask the question whether children have similar needs.

CHAPTER SIX

Homosexual Living:
Past and Present

1. *Historical records*

Imagine trying to figure out how people actually behave sexually by studying marriage laws, religious writings, newspaper reports of scandals and the works of prurient novelists. Systematic social surveys being a recent innovation, the historian has only this kind of material to go upon. Knowledge of homosexual conduct in previous ages depends upon piecing together snippets of information from documentary evidence at once biassed and selective. Denigration of an enemy by means of accusations of homosexual depravity is an ancient sport. When just a few people could read or write, only the tiny literate minority set out their beliefs and attitudes, what the mass of the population felt about sexual matters remained unrecorded. The vastly different meanings attached to homosexual behaviour in different periods presents another difficulty. Contemporary arguments about personal freedom in the sexual sphere would have been unthinkable when homosexuality was inseparable from witchcraft and heresy. One may perhaps deduce something about the past by working back from our modern understanding of sexual behaviour, but historical interpretations are too uncertain to provide lessons for present day social policy, although some have tried to draw them. One can, however, assert with confidence that the prevalence of homosexuality today does not arise solely from recent changes. Whenever a society has left behind sufficiently detailed records, descriptions of homosexuality in one guise or another feature among them.

Many of the earliest references to homosexuality are found in religious writings. Those contained in the Bible have a special interest in the West because they document the origins of a Judeo-Christian tradition of antagonism towards any manifestation of sex outside purely procreative functions performed by married couples. While the New Testament gospels remain curiously reticent in giving specific directives on sexual conduct, the Old Testament reflects the values of an aspiring Jewish tribe living in an age when survival depended upon producing and preserving as many children as possible. Onan's wasting of sperm (through coitus interruptus), labelled a terrible sin, has been used as theological justification for the condemnation of masturbation, a point of view which, until relatively recently, received massive support from medical pundits who declared the habit unhealthy in the extreme and liable to cause sexual perversion, physical decrepitude and finally insanity.

The word sodomite, an abusive term for a male homosexual, originates from a story told in Genesis 29. A group of men from Sodom storm Lot's house demanding 'Where are the men who came to you tonight? Bring them to us, that we may know them.' (The Hebrew word translated as 'know' can mean 'to copulate'.) Lot proffers his own virgin daughters in the place of his guests, but the intruders will not accept. A similar story appears in Judges 19. A Levite and his concubine are staying as guests of an old man in Gibeah. Some local men, 'sons of Belial', storm the house and want the Levite. The host offers the concubine so that they will not rape his guest. In this version, the men accept the concubine and 'abuse her all night'. They let her go in the morning and she returns, only being now so contaminated she receives no gratitude for having saved her man, but is killed and her body dismembered into twelve pieces.

In Genesis, the story of Lot is followed by the grim statement that, as a punishment for the wickedness of its citizens, the Lord destroyed Sodom and all its inhabitants with a shower of brimstone and fire. Christians have always assumed, although the contrary has been argued (Bailey, 1955), that the sins in question were homosexual. Biblical references to 'sodomites', and their banishment by the kings of Israel (I Kings 15, 22), do not necessarily refer to uncomplicated homosexuality. The original Hebrew refers to 'kedeshim' which in the modern English version is translated as male cultic prostitute. These were probably priests of the ancient cults of the Great Mother, male eunuchs or transvestites, who offered their bodies in the temple as a form of religious sacrifice. Their homosexuality must have constituted a double abomination, for besides detracting from the goal of tribal proliferation, it was also associated with the ritual of an alien religion. On the other hand, some references in the Old Testament, notably Leviticus 20 – 'If a man lies with a man as with a woman, both of them have committed an abomination; they shall be put to death ...' – appear to condemn homosexual practices under all circumstances. A special horror of homosexual temptation between blood relations is exemplified in the story of the curse Ham brought upon himself through catching sight of his father lying naked in his tent (Genesis 9).

The sparse and obscure references to homosexuality scattered about the Old Testament were of course greatly amplified by later Christian authorities. St. Paul, well known for his sexually repressive doctrines, and for the saying 'better to marry than to burn', predictably condemned homosexuality in the strongest terms. In his Epistle to the Romans (I, 27) he referred to the punishments men may expect who 'leaving the natural use of the woman, burned in their lust one toward another ...' Centuries later, the same sentiments poured forth in the edicts of Justinian. In the year 538 (Novella 77) this Christian emperor declared: '... certain men, seized by diabolical incitement, practice among themselves the most disgraceful lusts, and act contrary to nature: we enjoin them to take to heart the fear of God and the judgment to come ... because of like impious conduct cities have indeed perished, together with the men in them.' This puts in a nutshell the essence of the traditional attitude to homosexuality, a tradition that has inspired the criminal laws defining homosexual acts as unnatural, or offensive to God, and prescribing the severest penalties (Brinton, 1959).

Jewish rabbinical law incorporates similar prohibitions. Marriage and procreation is a sacred duty, celibacy forbidden. Masquerading as a member of the opposite sex is specifically condemned. For acts of anal intercourse between males, whether committed for secular reasons or as part of a heathen religious rite, both participants merit death by stoning (Epstein, 1948, p.136). Whatever some persons may believe about the actual habits of some of its adherents, the Moslem religion also officially condemns homosexuality, although not in quite such violent terms as in the Judeo-Christian writings. The Koran (Khan, 1971) repeats in several places the biblical story of Sodom and the transgressions of the people of Lot. 'Lot, whom we sent, rebuked his people: Do you realise you practise an abomination of which no people in the world before you has been guilty? You approach men lustfully in place of women. You are people who exceed all bounds' (ch. 7, 81-3). Otherwise, the emphasis in the Koran is upon kindness, chastity, the wickedness of wife stealing, the avoidance of over-indulgence, rather than upon the particular sinfulness of what Christian dogma calls unnatural forms of sex. At one point (ch. 76, 19), an ambiguous phrase in the description of the pleasures of paradise promises, as a reward for the virtuous, that: 'They will be waited on by ageless youths, looking like scattered pearls.' This expression may not have the shockingly impious meaning attributed to it by the cynical, but it does suggest that an awareness of homoerotic beauty was not considered out of place even in the most serious and sacred of Moslem texts.

The secular Moslem literature of the Near East includes numerous and fantastic adventure tales, many with a strong erotic content, both heterosexual and homosexual. Jealous love affairs between males, and the shameless infatuations of older men of substance chasing after impish youths, are made to seem a commonplace part of life. Sir Richard Burton (1885), the renowned explorer, horrified English Victorian society when he produced an enormous ten volume translation of the tales of *A Thousand and One Nights*, together with a *Terminal Essay* in which he discussed at length the historical and contemporary sex life of the people he had studied in Africa, Asia and throughout the world.

Burton's rambling and speculative discourse, a strange mixture of travellers' tales and painstaking scholarship, covered a great range of homosexual topics, including romantic male loves in classical Greece, male brothels in Karachi, the debauches of the Caesars, lewd treatment of French prisoners by the Egyptians during the Napoleonic Wars, the kept boys of rich religious Moroccans, and the male temple prostitutes who in ancient times served in the name of the great sexual mother Goddess, variously known as Ishtar, Aphrodite, Venus, Mylitta etc. Burton believed in a 'Sotadic Zone' of homosexuality embracing Southern Europe, North Africa, Turkey, Iraq, Afghanistan, Kashmir, China, Indo-China and Japan. Within this vast area 'the Vice is popular and endemic, held at the worst to be a mere peccadillo'. In contrast, races elsewhere 'practise it only sporadically amid the opprobrium of their fellows, who ... look upon it with the liveliest disgust'. No one any longer believes in this division of the world into contrasting sexual compartments, but at least Burton deserves credit for calling attention to the many different times and places in which homosexuality, in one guise or another, has been observed and recorded. No society is ever likely to be able to ignore or eradicate this fundamental human tendency completely.

Burton included China in his 'Sotadic Zone', but opinions differ on the extent of homosexual practice in ancient times. Owing to the disapproval of later more puritanical and censorious periods, facts are hard to establish. Van Gulik (1961) points out that the ancient handbooks on sexual practice, being exclusively concerned with conjugal relations, ignore homosexuality, but that literary texts adopt a neutral attitude, so long as the relationship is not abused for profit or an individual's emotions exploited. In the first and second centuries B.C. several emperors were pronouncedly bisexual. Wu (140–187 B.C.) had several close homosexual favourites, one of whom was killed by another favourite for misbehaving with a woman of the harem. A later emperor, Ai-ti (6–1 B.C.) is said to have cut off his sleeve with his sword because he wanted to move without disturbing his favourite who was lying asleep on top of it, hence the origin of the term 'the cut sleeve' as a Chinese literary expression for male homosexuality. These scattered historical and literary references do not support the theory that homosexuality was more particularly widespread in ancient China than anywhere else. Van Gulik (1961, p.48) argues that impressions of nineteenth- and early twentieth-century observers that male homosexuality was rampant in China were mistaken, created perhaps by the social etiquette of the time, which was tolerant of homosexuality in theatrical performances, and of men holding hands in public, while confining heterosexual relationships strictly to private life. Other commentators have suggested different explanations. The dullness of Chinese womenfolk, due to their repressed, secluded lives, and the casual social attitude towards homosexuality, which some persons looked upon as a chic amusement, may have encouraged the use of male brothels, which undoubtedly flourished in large cities of Peking and Canton.

However far back one delves into historical records, there is no escaping homosexual themes. Overtones of romantic love between two men are to be found in one of the oldest poems in existence, the *Epic of Gilgamish*. Originating in 2,000 B.C. or earlier, and preserved in cuneiform script on Assyrian clay tablets, it has been rendered into English by R.C. Thompson (1928). Gilgamish, a great warrior leader, dreamed that a man still more powerful than himself fell upon his shoulders and could not be shaken off. His companions crowded round and kissed the stranger's feet while Gilgamish 'held him to his breast like a woman'. Soon after, Gilgamish actually meets such a person in the shape of Enkidu, and the two men fight over the sexual favours of a female courtesan. Gilgamish is subdued, 'his fury abated', 'his ardour quelled'. The woman was relinquished and the two heroes, becoming inseparable friends, set off on adventurous expeditions together. The Goddess Ishtar then falls in love with Gilgamish and wants him for her husband, but he spurns her. In a jealous frenzy she sends a bull to destroy them, but Enkidu kills the bull, and wrenching off the creature's penis flings it at her. For this upstart behaviour the Gods cause Enkidu to die, leaving Gilgamish to lament and mourn the remainder of his life. This epic story of male love inspiring warriors to almost supernatural heroism introduces a theme that recurs again and again in later ages. The legends of classical Greece are among the best known examples of this kind.

Unlike the Jews, and unlike most other civilised peoples we know about, classical Greece went through a period when love between men achieved a degree of official acceptance never seen since (Licht, 1926). In his *Symposium* Plato rehearses, with obvious relish, many moral and philosophical arguments for the superiority of male love to the ordinary love between men and women. The character Phaedrus puts the often quoted view that homosexual love inspires bravery and moral rectitude: 'And if there were only some way of contriving that a state or army should be made up of lovers and their loves, they would be the very best governors of their own city, abstaining from all dishonour, and emulating one another in honour, and when fighting at each other's side, although a mere handful, they would overcome the world.' The character Aristophanes argues for the existence of a special breed of specially valiant men who, as natural lovers of youth, have no interest in marrying women, except in obedience to the law. Throughout the *Symposium* the supposed virtues of homosexual attachments – loyalty, purity and so forth – are contrasted with the coarse lustfulness of heterosexual unions.

Classical Greece was uncomprisingly a man's world, and Plato's *Symposium*, like much of Greek literature and art, reflects an extreme undervaluation of women. Courage, nobility of mind and all the admired virtues are represented as essentially manly attributes. Women's place was in the home. Women were not expected to go out and about, or to take part in politics or intellectual discussion. For stimulating companionship men looked to each other, or sought the company of educated courtesans (*hetairai*). Some authorities have attributed Greek mens' partiality for homosexuality to their contemptuous attitudes to their women (Flacelière, 1962; Hunt, 1959), but this explanation fails to account for the fact that other societies have kept their women subservient without necessarily idealising male homosexuality.

Plato's *Symposium* undoubtedly reflects an important trend in Greek culture. Nude male forms, some very masculine, others with slender youthful figures resembling pubescent girls, dominate the art of the period. Greek pottery vases depicting overt sexual scenes frequently include men and boys making love to each other. Greek poetry includes innumerable love lyrics of an ambiguous or frankly homosexual character (Fitts, 1956). Greek mythology is replete with stories of the homosexual loves and jealousies of the Gods (Graves, 1955). One of the best known concerns the youth Ganymede, carried off by an infatuated Zeus to serve as his lover and to act as cup-bearer to the Olympian Gods. Male love was held to serve a useful purpose in society. As an inspiration to bravery in battle, homosexual ideals were put into practice in military organisation. The elite body of soldiers known as the sacred band of Thebes, for long believed invincible in battle, consisted of pairs of lovers fighting side by side. After their final defeat at the battle of Chaeronea, their conqueror, Philip of Macedon, is said to have wept at the sight of their dead bodies, whose wounds revealed that none had turned his back upon the enemy. In the Dorian states, a youth of good family was positively expected to form an attachment to an older man who would act as mentor, training him in the manly virtues, guiding him in the duties of a good citizen, and setting him an honourable example to follow. One apologist for Greek love (Eglinton, 1971) argues that even today a sexual relationship with a mature man brings out the best from a youth while helping to tide him over the difficult period of adolescence. So long as the older man remains primarily heterosexual, and does not become too possessive, the youngster's normal sexual development is encouraged rather than retarded.

In an important review of historical records of homosexual behaviour, Karlen (1971) points out that the homosexual phase in Greek culture emerged long after the Mycenaean period described in Homer. Unlike the later Greek writers, Homer did not credit the Gods with homosexual inclinations. For instance, Homer never suggested that Zeus was in love with Ganymede, merely that he chose the youth for his outstanding beauty. Even when the homosexual trends in Greek society were at their zenith, attitudes remained somewhat ambivalent. The educational argument for pederasty collapsed if the relationships fell short of the ideal, if old men lusted after boys promiscuously, or if fickle youths doled out their favours in return for benefits received, or if the mentors presented an example of effeminacy instead of manly valour. Such unedifying spectacles must have been well-known. They are vividly and sarcastically portrayed in the comedies of Aristophanes. Although romantic relationships between men and youths were tolerated, physical acts of sex were severely constrained, if not actually illegal. Solon's laws, dating from the sixth century BC, proposed a penalty of death for men who crept into the boys' gymnasium in Athens for immoral purposes, and a public whipping for any slave having relations with a free-born youth. Plutarch riled against the corrupting influence of homosexual tutors, and Socrates' partiality for youths may have led to his condemnation and death. Karlen argues that the literary apologists were quite likely unrepresentative, and that attitudes of mockery and disgust towards homosexuality were in fact widespread. Plato himself recanted in his later years and condemned homosexual relations as unnatural and degrading. The truth of the matter will never be fully known, but it is certainly more complicated than the customary representation of classical Greece as a unified pro-homosexual culture.

Sexual life in ancient Rome (Kiefer, 1951) was apparently less restrained than in classical Greece. The literature of the Roman Empire suggests much greater freedom for women, and the possibility of extra-marital adventures for both sexes. Four great works of the period, the *Satyricon* of Petronius, the *Satires* of Juvenal, the *Epigrams* of Martial and the *Lives of the Caesars* by Suetonius, combine to give an impression of a society in which every kind of perversion flourished unchecked. Doubtless they gave an exaggerated picture, concentrating upon the habits of the ruling class, who were the only people with much spare time for sexual dalliance. Juvenal, a poor and embittered man, sought to expose the moral and sexual licence that he felt threatened Rome. He hated the absurd posturings of effeminate males, the hypocrisy of husbands married only for appearances, who pay their wives to keep quiet about the men they take to bed with them, and the moral corruption of young men who pander equally to the sexual demands of master and mistress. The diatribes against young dandies using perfume, letting their hair grow long, or wearing scanty and revealing clothes, have a curiously modern flavour. So also have the descriptions of male homosexuals seeking pick-ups at the Roman baths (Highet, 1961). Petronius provides a cynical parody of the homosexual intrigues, quarrels and jealousies prevailing among the wealthy classes. In Karlen's view 'the hysteria and sentimentality of the affairs is instantly familiar to anyone today who has spent time in homosexual milieux'. Certainly Petronius' stories have a wickedly humorous twist. One tale recounts (§ 85-7) how Eumolpus, by declaring he would celebrate with a substantial gift if he succeeded in having sex without waking up his partner, succeeded in inducing a handsome boy to submit to his embraces while pretending to be asleep. Because he didn't receive the expected gift, the boy would not cooperate when Eumolpus tried again a few nights later. 'Just go to sleep or I'll tell father,' said the boy. Undeterred, Eumolpus seduced him forcibly, and so successfully that the boy kept wanting more throughout the night until, exhausted, Eumolpus himself flared up:

'Just go to sleep or I'll tell your father.' Suetonius gives factual details of the extraordinary debaucheries of the Roman emperors. Julius Caesar, described as 'every woman's man and every man's woman' used his gift for pleasing men sexually to further his political career. According to Suetonius Caesar's own soldiers ridiculed the conqueror of Gaul for allowing himself to be vanquished in bed by King Nicomedes of Bithynia (§ 49). Tiberius had a palace in Capri devoted to sexual orgies, where young men and girls were kept for group sex and small boys trained to suck his genitals. When two boys he fancied resisted his assaults he had their legs broken (§ 44). Nero was credited with incest with his mother. He also had his favourite boy Sporus castrated so as to make him more like a girl, after which he went through an elaborate marriage ceremony with Sporus as the bride. The twelve emperors were all sexually deviant to a greater or lesser extent. They were not so much homosexuals as completely abandoned, sadistic pansexuals, willing to try anything for kicks, with no regard for the suffering they might cause the unfortunate objects of their lust.

In the later days of the Roman Empire, the developing Christian sect had to compete against many other cults. Prominent among them were the worshippers of Cybele, whose adherents demonstrated their devotion to their Goddess in frenzied and bloody rituals, during which men slashed and castrated themselves (Frazer; 1951). The provocative processions of painted eunuch priests of this rival cult must have re-established in the minds of early Christians the ancient link between homosexuality and heresy. When, following the Emperor Constantine's conversion, Christianity became more or less the official religion, state laws against homosexual practices were gradually introduced, culminating in a penalty of death by burning at the stake. Before long, as Gibbon sagely commented, the ancient rulers found these new laws afforded a convenient method for disposing of political enemies. Those against whom no other crime could be imputed could be charged with pederasty, often on the slight and suspicious testimony of a child or servant.

A heavy load of responsibility for these developments rests with the early Christian fathers, whose doctrines equated sin with sex. St. Augustine regarded procreation as a regrettable necessity and thought celibacy the ultimate virtue. He condemned severely any form of sexual conduct with a pleasurable rather than a purely reproductive motive. When the Church became powerful, the way these doctrines were applied is revealed in the medieval penitentials (McNeill and Gamer, 1938). These were handbooks of guidance to confessors explaining the gravity of various sins and giving an appropriate scale of punishments. They were peculiarly comprehensive in regard to sexual misconduct. For example, they specified penalties for adopting anything other than the 'missionary' position during marital intercourse or for having sex during menstruation. Homosexual offences, especially anal intercourse, merited severe punishment. The

Columban Penitential, written about 600, imposed upon monks the same penance (ten years) for sodomy as for homicide. Lesser degrees of sexual contact attracted proportionately smaller penalties. The seventh-century *Cummean Penitential* distinguished between kissing between males, mutual masturbation, mouth genital contacts, insertion of the penis between the thighs and full anal intercourse. The use of an artificial phallus by nuns, homosexual incest between blood brothers, the abuse of boys by older men, the adoption of the passive role in sodomy, and the sin of habitual indulgence, were all singled out by one or more of the penitentials as particular offences, each requiring a specific punishment (Bailey, 1955).

The belief that homosexuality was a sign of heresy persisted throughout the middle ages and provided a religious justification for many gory persecutions. Westermarck (1939, p. 372) comments that throughout the Middle Ages and later, Christian legislators thought that nothing but a painful death could atone for these sinful acts, and in France offenders were actually burned for this crime as late as the second half of the eighteenth century. During the Middle Ages heretics were accused of sodomy almost as a matter of course. The French word *bougre*, from which comes the English term buggery, derives from the Latin Bulgarus, meaning Bulgarian, and was originally applied to a sect of heretics who came from that country in the eleventh century. An example of the linking of the two sins was the annihilation of the Knights Templars, which followed from confessions under torture by the Inquisition, and was accomplished by means of forced admissions to homosexual as well as heretical practices (Legman, 1966). In the witchcraft era women became the most frequent victims of accusations of heretical and magical rituals involving all manner of perverse sexual orgies (Summers, 1928). The readiness with which such accusations found acceptance reflected the prevailing religious attitude towards women, which emphasised Eve's role as temptress, and encouraged pious men to view the female as dangerous bewitching and sinfully sexual. According to Karlen (1971, p. 93), admiration for female virtue ran counter to traditional beliefs about the origins of sexual sin. For this reason, the medieval fashion of courtly wooing, when troubadours serenaded their chaste ladies, was at first strongly opposed by the Church of the day.

Denunciations by church authorities of the idea of sexual freedom, and particular condemnation of homosexual practices, have continued in Western culture into modern times. The Bishop of Rochester (1954) arguing against reform of the laws on homosexuality, wrote: 'Homosexual practice is always a grievous sin and perversion. Defective sexual intercourse between two persons of the same sex can only be gross indecency under the guise of expressing affection. Even if safeguards could eliminate the corruption of youth, and the practice could be confined to inverts of mature age, it would remain the perversion of a wholesome instinct to an unnatural and loathsome end.' At about the same time the then Archbishop of

Canterbury (1953) pronounced: 'Let it be understood that homosexual indulgence is a shameful vice and a grievous sin from which deliverance is to be sought by every means.'

In recent years the attitude of churchmen towards homosexual sins has noticeably softened, and individual clerics have made brave, if embarrassed attempts to evolve a more liberal theology, one that might permit the acceptance of homosexuals as members of a Christian community. Notwithstanding these developments, the historical force of orthodox Christian tradition seems fundamentally irreconcilable with sexual permissiveness. In spite of the humanitarian ideals of many religious people, the official Christian churches, including the Church of Rome, remain the most powerful pressure groups opposing birth control, abortion, divorce, pre-marital intercourse and homosexual freedom.

Accounts of homosexual behaviour in Europe during the last half-millennium are so numerous that only a professional historian with leisure to compile several fat volumes could do them justice. As the purpose of the present book is to review current knowledge the reader interested in pursuing these historical byways must look elsewhere. The writings of Karlen (1971), Taylor (1953, 1958, 1965) and Brinton (1959) will be found particularly helpful. Sources of information on homosexuality in the past include legal enactments, records of trials, parliamentary proceedings, biographies and fiction. In spite of the wealth of material, the place of homosexual behaviour in the life of the community in previous ages remains something of a mystery. The ecclesiastical burnings, and later the civil trials and occasional executions of prominent persons condemned for homosexuality, testify to the persistence of official abhorrence of sexual variants and to the equal persistence of compulsive defiance by individual homosexuals. Unfortunately these dramatic events reveal nothing of the extent of the gulf between official attitudes and the every-day conduct and opinions of the common man. Pornographic literature and scandal-mongering accounts of the behaviour of particular groups (notably foreigners, the nobility, priests and nuns) suggest that semi-covert flouting of the official rules was always fairly common, even when the penalties for exposure were extraordinarily severe. The facetious treatment of the topic in literature and the theatre suggests that pederasty, though officially a high crime, was always a commonplace vice and to ordinary people a subject of derision more than horror.

To support their argument that homosexuals are in no way inferior, homophile writers like to quote references to the irregular sexual habits of famous historical personages, especially those universally recognised as powerful or gifted individuals (Garde, 1964; Kayy, 1965; Graham, 1968). In many cases the attribution turns out to be no more than a suspicion based upon flimsy evidence. For example, Oscar Wilde, and many others after him, have credited William Shakespeare with bisexuality because of his love sonnets apparently written for a man with the initials W.H. The circumstances were too obscure to make any confident deduction, and in any case extravagant poetic language in the context of ordinary friendship was not so unusual in Shakespeare's day. Much better evidence exists for the homosexuality of Francis Bacon. The sex preferences of many artists, from Leonardo downwards, have been suspect, but owing to the secrecy which attaches to such matters, conclusive evidence rarely emerges. On the other hand even when facts indicative of an artist's homosexual interests have been well known to historians they have tended to refrain from comment. A case in point is Michaelangelo's fascination for male nudes, and his passionate attachment to the young aristocrat Andrea Quaratesi, the subject of the famous portrait drawing in the British Museum. Historic facts about intimate lives are most plentiful in regard to royal persons, since they were constantly exposed to contemporary public comment. The story of the infatuations of Edward II of England for Piers Gaveston and Hugh le Despenser, which led to his downfall and murder, formed the theme of one of Marlowe's plays. The method of killing, by the insertion of a red hot iron in the rectum, may have been inspired by his vengeful queen as a punishment for sodomy, but more likely it was chosen so that the king's body would not show obvious signs of external violence. The homosexual inclinations of at least two other English kings is beyond dispute. William Rufus behaved so scandalously that, after he was killed by an arrow while hunting, the church refused burial on consecrated ground. The tastes of James I of England gave rise to equal scandal, with his rapid transfer of affection from one favourite to another, and his jealous patronage of Somerset and later of Buckingham (Ashton, 1969). The habits of Henri III of France, son of the intimidating Catherine de Medici, his fondness for cross-dressing and the homosexual favourites he kept at his court, gave the protestant minority ample scope for scandalous lampooning, and subsequent generations every opportunity to read about his conduct.

At the beginning of the present century Kaiser Wilhelm II of Germany caused great embarrassment by choosing to surround himself with homosexual courtiers. By this time, however, the press had become powerful, and a publicity campaign against homosexuals in high places succeeded in bringing about convictions, or expulsions from office, of numbers of prominent men. Krupp, head of the famous armaments firm, accused in the newspapers of keeping a male harem, committed suicide. General Moltke was tried for homosexuality and dismissed from the army. An Aide-de-Camp to the Kaiser was imprisoned, while his brother, Count Friz Hohenau, was forced to resign from the diplomatic service after a newspaper had revealed him to be the victim in a homosexual blackmail case. Prince Eulenberg, another diplomat, and a personal friend of the Kaiser, was called as a witness at Moltke's trial. Having denied committing indecencies with the defendant, he was then prosecuted for perjury (Igra, 1945).

In England, every century has had its homosexual scandals, and many are recounted by Montgomery Hyde (1970). In 1541 the Rev. Nicholas Udall, then Headmaster of Eton, was imprisoned after confessing homosexual involvement with two Eton schoolboys. In 1631 the second Earl of Castlehaven was tried by the Lords for buggery, sentenced to hang, but subsequently beheaded after an appeal for mercy to Charles I. He was found guilty of committing buggery upon a manservant while the man was engaged in sexual intercourse with the Earl's wife. The servant was hanged, after protesting in vain that he had given evidence against the Earl on the understanding he would not himself be punished. In 1726 Mary Clap was sentenced to imprisonment and the pillory for keeping a disorderly house in Holborn where men gathered to dance together, put on a pretence of feminine ways, and then repair to more secluded rooms to make love. Such homosexual clubs, called 'mollies', were apparently quite well known at the time. One of the clients of Mary Clap's establishment, Will Griffin, was convicted of buggery and hanged at Tyburn, together with two others similarly charged. In 1739, the Warden of Wadham College, Oxford, was charged with attempted sodomy against a student, but succeeded in fleeing to France. The aura of 'fashionable vice' which, in spite of official condemnation, attached to homosexual affairs in this period is reflected in the novel *Roderick Random* by T. Smollett, first published in 1748.

The early nineteenth century saw the sensational exposure of another homosexual brothel at the White Swan in Vere Street, London (Holloway, 1813). Six men were sent to prison after being stood in the pillory in the Haymarket, where they sustained many injuries at the hands of an unusually brutal crowd. Their arrests followed the confession, just before he died, of a soldier called White who, like most convicted sodomists at the time, was publicly hanged for homosexual offences. White had apparently been particularly popular at the White Swan, where athletic young men taking passive sex roles were known by appropriate feminine nicknames.

During the greater part of the nineteenth century, minority sexual interests flourished more discreetly among the intelligensia, some of whom, like John Addington Symonds (1891) and Edward Carpenter (1908), went so far as to write books advocating tolerance for homosexuals. Apart from occasional hushed up affairs, such as the sudden resignation in 1859 of Dr. Vaughan, the respected head of Harrow School, the really great scandals came after the passing of the Criminal Law Amendment Act of 1885, which permitted the prosecution of homosexual acts other than buggery. In 1889 a furore arose following a police raid on a male brothel in Cleveland Street, London, close to what is now the post office tower. The proprietor had already fled, but two men, one a clergyman, were arrested and convicted of indecency. It appeared that gentry visiting the house enjoyed the rather poorly paid services of the local post office messenger boys. A newspaper campaign followed, accusing the authorities of suppressing evidence. Apparently the patrons of the establishment included some very noble persons, one of whom, Lord Somerset, was tipped off to leave the country just before the issue of a warrant for his arrest. He is said to have threatened to implicate Prince Edward Victor, late Duke of Clarence, the eldest son of the Prince of Wales, should the authorities persist with the case. From documents recently released by the Public Record Office it appears that the Prince of Wales and the Prime Minister, Lord Salisbury, took action to try to prevent more prosecutions. A number of the messenger boys were paid to take trips abroad to hinder investigations (*The Times*, March 11 1975).

Among scandals that were not hushed up was the case of the runaway Member of Parliament, de Cobain. He fled abroad in 1891 when he learned that his private life was under investigation and was subsequently dismissed for failing to obey the Speaker's summons to return. When he did unwisely return in 1893 he was convicted for acts of gross indecency committed three to five years previously and sent to prison.

The year 1895 saw the greatest scandal of all, the imprisonment of the dramatist Oscar Wilde after no less than three sensational jury trials, during which a parade of self-confessed male prostitutes and blackmailers gave evidence for the Crown and then went free. Wilde's ostentatiously high-camp taste and manners were quite renowned, but his downfall only came about, as so often happens in these affairs, when an accidental circumstance brought out publicly the details of his physical sex life. One of Wilde's homosexual friends, young Lord Alfred Douglas, happened to be on extremely bad terms with his father, the Marquess of Queensberry. With a vindictive determination to cause trouble, the Marquess left a card at Wilde's club alluding to his homosexuality. In response to this public provocation Wilde foolishly brought a libel action. Queensberry produced witnesses to Wilde's sexual affairs with young stable lads and the like, the case was lost, and Wilde himself was soon brought to trial (Hyde, 1948). The jury disagreed at first and he was made to stand trial again. Apparently the authorities dared not do other than prosecute to the utmost for fear of still more press criticism of protecting vice in high society. The press in fact almost unanimously hailed Wilde's imprisonment with sanctimonious expressions of justice well done. Only W.T. Stead in the *Review of Reviews* took a more moderate line, pointing out that those who 'corrupt girls' do more harm but arouse much less indignation. He also commented on the 'tacit acquiescence' in homosexuality at public schools where boys are allowed 'to indulge with impunity in practices which, when they leave school, would consign them to hard labour'.

The prevalence of homosexual and bisexual interests among famous people of the past can only be guessed at from occasional scandals and convoluted references by discreet biographers. Historians of the future will have the benefit of fuller and franker documentation as biographers become less and less squeamish about revealing personal details that would once have been thought too distasteful or too reprehensible to mention. Michael Holroyd (1971) shows no such squeamishness in describing the sexual proclivities of Lytton Strachey and his friend, the Cambridge economist John Maynard Keynes. Knightley and Simpson (1970) are equally frank about Lawrence of Arabia, as in Robin Maugham (1966) when discussing the sex life of his famous uncle Somerset. The homosexuality of E.M. Forster has become common knowledge with the publication after his death of his autobiographical novel *Maurice*. And so it goes. Nor do writers any longer need to wait for posthumous revelations. Autobiographical accounts describing romantic friendships as frankly as heterosexual affairs, as for instance in a recent work by the actor Emlyn Williams (1973), come as no great surprise and create no great stir. Even relatively unknown characters can obtain some attention by writing sexual autobiographies (Hutton, 1958, Ackerley, 1971). They need not limit themselves to writing. A semi-autobiographical British film, *A Bigger Splash*, depicting homosexual and heterosexual loves with equal frankness, was released in 1974. It was directed by Jack Hazan and played by the artist David Hockney, Peter Schlesinger and others, appearing as themselves.

Historians can make use of fictional accounts of the homosexual way of life in different periods, but never have these been available in such profusion as in the last few decades. Serious novelists have taken to exploring the theme in earnest, with results often more illuminating than the dry, questionnaire bound products of social science. Writers of distinction like Christopher Isherwood (1964), James Baldwin (1956), Jean Genet (1966), Compton MacKenzie (1956), Thomas Mann (1965), Angus Wilson (1952), Arthur Miller (1955), Simon Raven (1959), Roger Peyrefitte (1958) and Gore Vidal (1960) have all contributed their share. The *Play Index* for 1968 to 1972 (Fidell, 1973) lists 28 plays in English under the topic 'homosexuality' and another five under 'lesbianism'. Many such plays, such as *A Taste of Honey* (Shelagh Delaney, 1959), *Suddenly Last Summer* (Tennessee Williams, 1958) and *Staircase* (Dyer, 1966), have been made into highly successful films (Tyler, 1973).

2. *Anthropological evidence*

Cross-cultural comparisons of sexual attitudes and practices point to broadly similar conclusions as historical studies. They show that, in the sexual sphere, human societies in different parts of the world develop very different concepts of what is normal, tolerable or possible. Apart from the Kinsey studies in America, and a few more limited surveys in Europe, there have been hardly any scientific studies of the incidence and character of homosexuality in other parts of the civilised world. Judging from travellers' observations and historical writings (Mantegazza, 1932; Mathers, 1930; Lewinsohn,

1958; Edwardes and Masters, 1962) it appears that, at least until recently, that is before the world-wide proliferation of communist conformity and American official morality, in many parts of both the Near and Far East relatively little moral importance was attached to variations in sexual tastes and pleasures. More or less open manifestations of homosexuality, at any rate between men, evoked little concern and were extremely prevalent. Whether these impressions would stand up to systematic scientific inquiry is another matter. Melikan and Prothro (1954) tried, by means of a confidental questionnaire, to compare the sexual attitudes and practices of male Arab and American students at the American University of Beirut. Setting aside the obvious objection that these students might be untypical of Arab students elsewhere, the results did not support the simplistic notions that Arabs are 'more' homosexual. Higher proportions of Arab students were sexually experienced, both heterosexually and homosexually, but curiously the mean age for first homosexual intercourse was a year later among the Arab students, 13 rather than 12. A highly indirect method of judging the prevalence of homosexual behaviour was reported by Sechrist and Flores (1969). Inspection of the sexual graffiti on lavatory walls in the Philippines revealed that the proportion of homosexual themes was significantly less than in the United States.

Most crosscultural comparisons of homosexual behaviour have been carried out on primitive societies. Being small, cohesive groups, with well-defined regulations and relatively uniform patterns of social behaviour, they are easier to analyse and describe than vast, modern civilisations, such as that of the Americans or the Europeans, which are complex, pluralistic cultures where different standards coexist among different groups or classes within the same nation. Even in Eastern countries, which are often cited as examples of homosexual permissiveness, certain classes or religious sects adopt highly condemnatory attitudes. Carstairs (1956), a British psychiatrist who spent some time in India, has described the extreme disgust with which high caste Hindus of the North abhor homosexual practices, and the great contempt with which they regard the *hinjras*, transvestite males, who dance, beg and prostitute themselves to men. Although treated as the worst of outcastes, the prevalence of beggars of this type shows that homosexual activity must go on in a secret, guilt-ridden way in spite of puritanical denials.

The authoritative and much quoted review by Ford and Beach (1952) is still the most convenient source of information about homosexuality in primitive cultures. Making use of the Human Relations Area Files of the Yale Cross-Cultural Survey, they analysed observations from 200 primitive societies. Among the 76 societies about which relevant observations were on record, a majority of 49, that is 64 per cent, permitted some form of homosexual behaviour, not necessarily for everyone, but at least for some members of the community. The other societies discouraged homosexual conduct, sometimes with severe formal punishments, such as whipping of children and execution of adults, and sometimes by means of ridicule and contempt. In these more repressive societies adult homosexual behaviour was usually said to be very rare and secretive or not to occur at all, but it may have been more frequent than outside observers were allowed to know. For example, in his famous study of the Trobriand Islanders, Malinowski (1929) concluded that male homosexuality occurred only among the natives who were confined in white men's gaols or workers' barracks. In their home villages men discovered in such practices would feel so shamed and would be held in such contempt they would be likely to commit suicide. However, the fact that the Trobrianders' language included some common words and playful expressions descriptive of homosexual acts suggests that such behaviour may not have been so unthinkable as Malinowski's informants led him to believe.

In some of the societies surveyed by Ford and Beach a limited number of openly transvestite males, called *berdaches* (see p. 47), after going through the prescribed ceremonies, were accorded special status and permitted to take up a woman's role, sexually and otherwise. Men associating with these effeminate individuals, or actually taking one as a wife, were not considered abnormal, since the *berdache* was officially regarded as having become a woman. Whereas in some of the societies homosexuality was apparently limited to this small, institutionalised group of effeminates and their 'husbands', in other cultures it was permitted, sometimes even required, for all male members of the community at some stage of their lives. For example, among the Keraki of New Guinea and the Kiwai Papuans, young men submitted to anal intercourse as part of their initiation into manhood. The Kiwai maintained it made men strong (Landtman, 1927, p.237). Men of the Siwan tribe in North East Africa went still further, discussing their male and female love affairs with equal frankness and lending their sons to each other for anal intercourse. In most of the societies where male homosexuality was practised, it took the form of pseudo-copulatory activity rather than oral-genital contacts or mutual masturbation. Except for the few individuals permitted a sex role reversal in societies which had a *berdache* system, none of the primitive cultures in the survey, however tolerant they might be of homosexuality as an incidental form of sex expression, recognised a permanent, exclusive homosexual orientation as an approved or practicable life style or as an alternative to marriage. In some societies it was regarded as a form of behaviour appropriate only to the young.

Lesbian practices were much less often reported. Ford and Beach found some information about it in only 17 of the peoples surveyed, and in only a few cases was any evidence forthcoming as to the nature of the sex practices involved. The Australian Aranda women were said to indulge in masturbation of the clitoris and tribadism, the Chukchee of Siberia and the Mbundu and Nama of Africa were said to make use of an artificial phallus.

Money and Ehrhardt (1972) review the sexual habits of several contrasting primitive cultures. Among the Batak people of Sumatra, at the onset of puberty boys and girls leave the parental home to go to live in separate one-sexed communes of adolescents. In the boys' house the youth learns from others a little older than himself how to participate in homosexual partnerships. Marriage is obligatory, and at the appropriate age a young man leaves the bachelors' quarters to undertake the prescribed courtship and marriage rituals. He returns to tell the others of his accomplishments, thus communicating realistic expectations of heterosexuality to the inexperienced, segregated young men. In this culture there is no divorce; extramarital affairs are forbidden, and the tradition of homosexual segregation of the young ensures that for both sexes marriage is their first and only heterosexual relationship. The homosexual practices which are permitted between boys and young bachelors include mutual masturbation and anal intercourse, but not fellatio. In this the Batak people differ from the Kukukuku, of highland New Guinea, among whom oral homosexual relations are required for all youths and young men, because the swallowing of semen is believed necessary for strength and virility. In the case of cultures like that of the Batak, where a premarital homosexual phase is obligatory for all, the consequential postponement of first heterosexual contacts serves the interest of population control, which can be an important requirement for a people confined to a limited environment with scanty resources.

Among the Marind Anim of Southern New Guinea, a head-hunting tribe, a similar system of sex segregation at puberty was enforced. Boys spent their days in a house specially set aside for them returning at night to stay with a married couple, other than their parents, appointed as their mentors. It was customary for the male mentors to have a homosexual relationship with the boy in their care. Once married, however, the young man no longer had to obey his mentor. Unlike the Batak, the Anim permitted married men to have sexual relationships with other mens' wives, provided the affair was pre-arranged with consent, and provided it did not lead to the break-up of a marriage.

In the small Melanesian island community referred to by William Davenport (1965) as East Bay, youthful heterosexuality was discouraged but homosexuality widely tolerated. Nudity was the rule for both sexes up to puberty, and exploratory sex play by infants was allowed quite openly. After the age of five, however, boys and girls were strictly forbidden to touch each other, and girls were kept more and more at home and apart from boys. Boys continued rough-and-tumble sex play with each other beyond this age, grabbing and pinching at each others genitals, but they learned to avoid touching girls. In adolescence, heterosexual contacts were still forbidden, and even considered harmful, but masturbation was permitted and regarded as a normal, safe outlet in both sexes. Between young bachelors living in the mens' house homosexual partnerships involving mutual masturbation and anal intercourse were frequent and perfectly acceptable, as were homosexual relations between older married men and boys. Although anal intercourse was widely considered enjoyable no one in the tribe appeared to understand how mouth-genital contact could afford pleasure. Marriages were arranged by a kinship system, and married couples enjoyed intercourse frequently and uninhibitedly. In spite of the fact that married men often had extra-marital relations with boys, heterosexual intercourse was generally considered preferable, and exclusive, obligatory homosexuality was unknown.

As can be seen from these and other examples, heterosexual and homosexual permissiveness do not necessarily coincide. The Andamese, the Ute Indians of Colorado, and the Tahitians (Opler, 1965) all allowed heterosexual love affairs among the young and unmarried, while condemning homosexuality. In contrast, the Cubeo Indians (Goldman, 1963) condemned extra-martial heterosexuality but were indulgent towards homosexuality. In large parts of the Arab world heterosexual morality has been traditionally rigid, with women kept secluded, inaccessible and socially uneducated, so that men look for companionship among their own sex. Under these circumstances, as in ancient Greece, homosexuality flourishes, and comes to be regarded as a peccadillo rather than a serious transgression. Westermarck (1906), an anthropologist who lived in North Africa and observed these pressures in every day life, believed there was a direct connection between the repressive social regulation of heterosexual relationships and the prevalence of homosexuality.

All human societies have marital and family institutions, and these arrangements require some degree of regulation of sexual behaviour. Anthropological evidence shows that whereas incest taboos are almost universal, regulations concerning homosexual behaviour and extra-marital or pre-marital heterosexual behaviour vary enormously. The same culture can be permissive in one respect and strictly prohibitive in others. Some cultures have been open and permissive about homosexuality in all age groups, at least among males, others have sought to limit it to the young, others have allowed it only for a small group of individuals who have passed through a ceremony to change their sexual status, and others again have condemned homosexuality under all circumstances. While overt manifestations of homosexuality are obvious in permissive societies, no one knows how much secret homosexual behaviour occurs in societies which proclaim an official prohibition. In permissive cultures bisexual behaviour appears common, but permanent, obligatory exclusive homosexuality, which precludes normal marriage, is rarely reported.

3. *The 'gay scene' today*

Homosexual men have always enjoyed facilities for fraternising with others similarly inclined, but the long conspiracy of silence about sexual minorities helped to keep their meeting places discreetly away from public attention. Today, with all the descriptions and comment about the 'gay scene' in the media, and with sociologists writing books about it, few heterosexuals can remain ignorant of the existence and character of these resorts, even though they may have no inclination to explore them personally (Achilles, 1967; Fisher, 1972; Hooker, 1965a; Hoffman, 1968; Leznoff and Westley, 1956; Sonenschein, 1968; Weinberg and Williams, 1974; Yankowski and Wolff, 1965).

In the larger cities of America 'gay' life has become obtrusively public to an extent not yet attained in the United Kingdom. In New York, for instance, the currently permissive attitude towards the sale of explicitly sexual material, and to the showing of 'blue' films, reveals the substantial homosexual component in pornography. They must reflect a corresponding interest among a substantial minority of the public. A proportion of the cinemas dedicated to 'adult movies' (that is spectacles of sexual intercourse with a minimum of story-line to link them) offer homosexual films exclusively. Scenes of oral and anal sex between groups of males dominate their programmes. In the 'adult only' sections of pornographic book shops, stocked mostly with picture magazines of sexual activity, entire shelves are given over to homosexual themes. These same shops sell novels about homosexuals, psychological books with juicy case histories of deviant sex, a range of guides to the gay places to visit in America and Europe, and selections of pamphlets and newspapers issued by the homophile organisations.

The gay guides, and the advertisements in gay papers, leave the reader in no doubt where to go and what to expect. They reveal a vast trading enterprise ready to cater to homosexuals. Under the names of towns like New York and San Francisco so many bars are listed that they have to be grouped according to district. If the clientele of a bar has a particular character (such as 'rough trade', 'leather crowd', or 'drag queens') this is specified. The bars themselves vary in style, some being indistinguishable from any ordinary drinking place save that the seats in one corner are occupied almost entirely by men. Other bars are much more blatant. In some the customers all look like midnight cowboys, and the walls are strewn with pictures of male bodies and advertisements for drag shows and gay resorts. At one time certain of these bars possessed side rooms with very dim lights, where customers could retire for quiet orgies between drinks, but in the unceasing war between police and homosexuals this particular freedom was for the time being curtailed at least in New York, following a series of police raids in 1971 (Hunter, 1972). Many of these public bars are indifferent to whether males or females dance with their own or the opposite sex. Some establishments ape the hell's angels image, with clients dressed in leather and chains, and the walls decorated with whips and other sadistic emblems, in addition to the inevitable pictures of near-naked motor-cycle riders. Others specialise in female impersonators, and hold competitions among their customers for who can put on the best act.

Another type of commercial enterprise much advertised in the gay guides is the homosexual steam bath patronised by men looking for easy sex. In addition to their crowded steam rooms and darkened dormitories they have small private bedroom cubicles for hire which the occupant can make use of to entertain whoever takes his fancy. Notwithstanding official notices urging decorum and decency, unofficially every provision is made for promiscuous sexuality, including even a supply of lubricants in the vending machines purveying male cosmetics. One of the New York baths, the Continental, widely advertised and commented upon in the press, has become a real show place. The facilities include an expensive restaurant, a discotheque, and a Saturday night cabaret with leading artists. To all of these sections women are admitted. The male facilities include nude bathing (watched by the mixed cabaret audience) steam rooms, a dark room, and free blood tests in case someone has contracted VD. The owner is quoted as commenting: 'I've found all the authorities very realistic ... they know that homosexuality is here to stay ... The Baths does not moralise ... It does recognise Reality ... The Baths sells Sex' (Stone, 1973).

Specialised bars and baths by no means exhaust the facilities offered to the American homosexual. The names of eating places, swimming pools, cinemas, hotels, clubs, beaches and holiday resorts are all to be found in the guides. Some of these places, such as Fire Island (Goodman, 1966), have gained a world-wide reputation. In addition to the commercial establishments, the guides also advise on those free, but more dangerous, public places regularly 'cruised' by homosexual men on the look-out for pick-ups or prostitutes. When they become too notorious, so that the public complains, newspapers run exposure articles, and the police swoop down, the favourite locations are liable to abrupt changes. In spite of a waxing and waning of activity in response to police pressure, certain traditional areas, such as parts of Central Park, Forty Second Street, the public conveniences attached to bus and railway termini, or the off-street parking places where covered trucks accommodate nightly orgies, maintain their character over many years.

The comparatively blatant display of homosexuality in her cities contrasts ironically with America's repressive laws and hostile attitudes towards sex deviants. In England the scene is active in a more subdued style, but nevertheless the international gay guides, such as Spartacus (1976), find a great many places to list. Apart from the specialist clubs, many of the public bars and other places mentioned are not exclusively homosexual and their owners are not always pleased by the publicity. Information about such facilities is no longer restricted to a homosexual underworld. For instance, a number of them are described in *Alternative London*, a guide book of places of interest to young radicals (Saunders, 1974). The London University Students' Guide (1974) includes an article mentioning the 'Gay' societies available to students, listing the telephone numbers of homophile organisations, and urging the thousand or so gay students expected each year, as well as the 'many more who "swing both ways"' to 'cast out old prejudice and help your friends to be glad to be gay'.

Paradoxically, the new permissiveness, with its attendant publicity, has probably brought about, in real terms, a considerable clamping down on the more blatant manifestations of homosexuality in public places. Hyde (1970) quotes the reminiscences of older homosexuals who look back upon a time when they could visit certain cinemas, parks, boarding houses, Turkish baths or back street urinals, in the confident expectation of enjoying unhampered sexual exchanges. Today, with local authorities so much more alive to the problem, and policing stricter, English homosexuals have less opportunity for such activities. The old cinemas have either been knocked down or the purity lights turned up. The old urinals have been swept away to be replaced by modern edifices, fewer in number, but well-lit and often shut over night. Urban parks, once open, have been fenced so they can be gated at dusk. Any Turkish bath or sauna in England that got its name into a gay guide and allowed its customers to behave without restraint would risk swift closure. Furthermore, as the enormous gap in income and life style between the social classes in England has lessened, middle-class homosexuals no longer find it so easy to entice the young working-class male with a display of affluence and sophistication.

Even in England, some well-known cruising grounds still flourish. In the London area, part of the unfenced commons at Putney and Hampstead come alive on dark evenings with loitering figures, glowing cigarettes and rustling bushes. Although they are frequently used for group sex as well as for picking up, visitors to these places take considerable risks, since the locations are as familiar to potential robbers or to police as they are to homosexuals. *Gay News* (No.54, September 1974) warns readers: 'The police have also been active in London, and we're told that officers are taking the names of people on Clapham Common at night. Apparently they have been arriving in cars without lights and setting up traps in the bushes with car batteries and headlamps.

'Heavy patrolling has been taking place at the same time on the Putney towpath. Again, the police are using cars. Mind how you go ...'

Public bars and private drinking clubs supply the main facilities for socialising in England as they do in America, though with slight differences reflecting their English setting. As a rule only the clubs have an exclusively homosexual clientele, most of the public bars with a gay reputation have a greater or lesser admixture of straight patrons, and are therefore less blatantly gay than their American counterparts. According to Weinberg and Williams (1974, p.41) the reluctance of respectable Americans to have any dealings with known homosexuals means that many of the gay bars in New York City, especially the after-hours drinking places, are still controlled by organised crime and operated by underworld characters. This helps to infect the gay scene with other socially deviant phenomena, notably drug abuse and organised prostitution. Contrast this with the comments of the proprietor of the A and B (Arts and Battledress) Club in London, interviewed for a homophile magazine. 'I would say we had hardly, little if any interference [from the police], we've never excited their interest. We've always kept a pretty firm hand you know ... If this [club] was run by people who like brash, criminal, loud or over-effeminate types, then obviously we wouldn't get that respectable element. They would go elsewhere ... If we know that someone is a male prosser [prostitute] – it's out, out! ... We've never come across [protection rackets] thank God, because we've nothing to conceal ... [In America] the clubs pay the Mafia who pay the police ... We don't get this from one side or the other' (Davies, 1973). It would be nice to attribute the more orderly character and less extreme segregation of English bars to a greater community tolerance of the presence of deviants, but common sense suggests that it is more likely the result of better policing. British police are less constrained by civil liberty legislation, less often exposed to offers of substantial bribes, and less likely to encounter militant resistance.

In Britain the police, with the help of local licensing authorities, are still able to clamp down successfully upon any display of homosexual activity that becomes too blatant. In December 1974 the owners of one of London's oldest cinemas were refused a renewal of their licence by the local authority after police had given evidence of homosexual activity taking place in the auditorium. The cinema was allowed a six months' reprieve following an appeal and a change of management. The objections followed the publication in *Spartacus Gay Guide* of the comment: 'Action in the seats and in the toilets. Don't bother about what is on the screen.' The same month, following raids by plain-clothes policemen at a private sauna club for men in Kensington, some twenty men were arrested, twelve of whom were subsequently charged with offences of gross indecency, buggery, or keeping a disorderly house. Police officers, dressed in towels, had mingled with the clients, entered cubicles where indecencies were taking place, and secured arrests (*Gay News*, 65, February 1975). Also in the same month, a club in the Earls Court area of London, a well-known resort for young homosexuals, lost its licence, in spite of an appeal to the Department of the Environment. It was argued that the existence of the club, however well run in itself, aggravated the problems of street loitering and male prostitution in the neighbourhood (*Gay News*, 61, December 1974). While this was happening north of the Thames, the Father Red Cap, a well-known public house in South London, was closed following police summonses against the licensee and his manager for allowing a disorderly house. The place had been called the 'gayest pub in London' and witnesses alleged they had seen there couples of the same gender doing obscene things together. The new licensee, before re-opening, 'read out the riot act to the gay fraternity … He would not, he told them, let them use the club room and he would not be staging drag shows. At the informal opening of the pub his policy of non-encouragement of gay customers gained some weight with the presence of more than two handfuls of plain-clothes and uniform police …' (*South London Press*, 3 January 1975).

Most public houses in England are owned by a few large breweries, and they are not always particularly pleased to have one of their places singled out as a homosexual resort. Citation in a 'gay guide' can be the kiss of death for manager and patrons alike. Sometimes the compilers of the guides are over-enthusiastic. The inclusion, without justification, of well known places with a reputation at stake can cause a stir. The managing director of the Gloucester Hotel, Weymouth (once the summer palace of George III, and the place where British sovereignty over the American colonies was signed away) is reported to have said, in response to a recent unwanted citation: 'It's quite ridiculous and I'm glad to have the chance to say so. The last thing our cocktail bar is is a centre for homosexuals. It is a normal pleasant hotel bar and I've never heard of such a suggestion before' (*Gay News* 70, March 1975).

Although the homosexual's first contacts with others like himself have usually to take place in some public facility, once having taken that plunge, he can gain an entry to more private circles. Male homosexuals typically attach themselves to a loose network of acquaintances visiting each others homes for parties. On these occasions, when they can let their hair down in safe company, a great deal of camp sex talk and gossip goes on. Rather more often than would happen in heterosexual society, gay parties develop into snogging sessions if not outright orgies. A heterosexual couple meeting new friends and inviting them back for a drink would not ordinarily expect their guests to start disappearing into the bedroom, but in the homosexual world it would cause no surprise. This male emphasis on quick sexual contact with the minimum of preliminaries is aptly summed up by a remark in Crowley's play *Boys in the Band*, spoken by a visitor just arrived at a gay party: 'Who do I have to fuck to get a drink around here?' Although some of these gatherings are rather like after hours extensions of the gay bar scene, others, more private, and usually attended by persons who have been friends for a while, approximate to the picture of conventional entertaining in heterosexual society, with the emphasis on food and conversation rather than sex. Like everyone else, perhaps even more so because he lacks a wife and family, the homosexual needs companionship, and persons with whom he can talk over the ordinary problems of life without pretence. Homosexual cliques, though sometimes ridiculed for their clannishness, precious ways, snobbery and intolerance of straight society, do fulfil an important social function, and one that possibly becomes more important as the individual grows older.

Observers have commented on the high valuation of youthful good looks in male homosexual circles. A man of thirty already begins to feel at a disadvantage in the hunt for fresh conquests, and in the expectation of being propositioned by someone he would find attractive. In the gay bars, especially those that function more as sex markets than places for chatting with friends, no one takes much notice of a stranger unless he has a young and attractive appearance. Even very presentable young men hesitate to make a first approach, so there is usually a number of lonely, apparently aloof individuals, staring into space, waiting hopefully, not unlike the sad females lining the walls of dance halls. Men who continue to visit the bars in middle age strive to dress and look younger than their age, but unless they have money to throw around, or hospitality to offer, their efforts go unrewarded. Except for the bars where male prostitutes can be procured at a price by clients of any age, older men tend to drift away into private cliques made up of persons more their own generation.

In America and Western Europe homosexuals no longer depend entirely upon public resorts for gaining an entry into the gay world. Like other minority groups they now have their own organisations, and these provide many more facilities than the bars, namely clubs and meeting places that are more than just 'meat racks', lectures, discussion groups, legal and personal advisory services, and introductions to kindred spirits. In addition, these organisations act as education and propaganda centres, issuing pamphlets and news sheets combating official discrimination, and trying to improve the image of the homosexual in his own eyes as well as those of the public at large.

The semi-official recognition presently accorded homophile organisations in the United States and Europe came about quite suddenly. Despite years of dedicated struggle, the pioneers of homosexuals' rights in previous generations never lived to witness the hoped-for change. In Germany, Magnus Hirschfeld, a great pioneer of sexual research and sexual freedom, lived just long enough to see his work destroyed by the Nazis. In 1903, in collaboration with a pressure group called the Scientific Humanitarian Committee, Hirschfeld conducted a primitive but pioneering social survey to discover the incidence of homosexuality among male students and factory workers. When his research report was published, Hirschfeld was successfully prosecuted and fined for disseminating indecent writings. In 1919, profiting by a more liberal post-war atmosphere, he started the Institute of Sexual Science in Berlin, a library and research centre for studies of sexuality and its deviations. In 1933, at the instigation of the Nazi press, students raided the premises and carried off the collection of books and documents, all of which were publicly burned. The same year the newsletter of the Scientific and Humanitarian Committee appeared for the last time, the editor having been arrested and sent to a concentration camp.

Following the revolution of 1917, the Russian Bolsheviks legalised homosexuality as part of their official policy of sexual freedom, and in the years that followed official Bolshevik representatives attended meetings of the World League for Sexual Reform. An Institute of Sexual Hygiene, somewhat similar to the Berlin Institute of Sexual Science, was set up in Moscow. With the advent of Stalinism, however, there was a sudden about-turn. In 1934 anti-homosexual laws more stringent than ever were re-introduced, and mass arrests of actors and artists on grounds of homosexuality took place in Moscow and Leningrad. Since then, no more has been heard of homosexual liberation in the Soviet Union.

In England, Havelock Ellis and Edward Carpenter started, in 1914, the British Society for the Study of Sex Psychology, but as an institution it failed to outlast the initial enthusiasm of its founders. It was not until about twenty-five years ago that establishment circles in the English-speaking world began to break the long conspiracy of silence and for the first time to take serious notice of the existence of an important and sadly aggrieved homosexual minority. The rapid development of the present-day national homophile movements became possible after the last world war. Technical improvements in methods of reproducing and distributing propaganda literature helped, but more importantly an increasing permissiveness towards frank discussion of sex, and a questioning of traditional standards, produced a more receptive audience. The movements grew out of tiny, semi-clandestine groups, operating with secret subscription lists, and producing pamphlets for very private and very restricted circulation. The sudden expansion began first in the United States during the fifties (Sagarin, 1969, ch.4; Gunnison, 1969; Parker, 1972). At the time, public attention had been alerted by the two Kinsey reports, with their revelations as to the extent of sexual unorthodoxy in society, and their pleas for sexual tolerance. Also in the fifties, the witch hunts inspired by Senator McCarthy kept alive a continuous controversy on the place of homosexuals in American society. Certain politicians sought to gain advantage by accusing their opponents of un-American activities, namely radical affiliations or homosexual tendencies. Government agencies were blamed for employing dangerous perverts (United States, 1950) and the risks of allowing homosexuals vulnerable to blackmail to engage on defence work or to join the foreign service became a topic of much political and even psychiatric debate (*Psychiatry*, 1955). In the face of these patently exaggerated attacks upon a hapless minority, liberal voices began to rise in their defence, and people began to pay attention to views put forward by homosexuals themselves.

One of the first and still one of the most influential of the American homophile organisations, the Mattachine Society, took its name from a court jester who told the truth while hiding behind his mask. It was founded in 1950, and in 1954 it dropped the mask, obtained a corporation charter, and set up an official headquarters in San

Francisco. Today, the organisation is split up into independent chapters, one of the largest being the Mattachine Society of New York, which runs an office headquarters and a substantial library and information centre in the Greenwich Village area. Their telephone advisory service, manned by young volunteers, answers all kinds of queries from strangers, wanting to know anything from the address of the most active steambath, or the name of the most sympathetic clinic for VD treatment, to a request for an introduction to a homosexual with sadistic interests. (All three of these inquiries were overheard in the space of an hour while the author was consulting the Mattachine library).[1]

Apart from arranging a certain number of social activities, such as costume balls, beach parties and travel excursions for homosexuals, the main effort of the New York Mattachine Society goes into civil rights campaigns. They have been particularly active, for instance, in opposing the use of liquor licensing laws as excuses for police raids on gay bars. The Mattachine Society of San Francisco concentrates more upon its counselling and referral service for individuals in difficulties, maintaining for the purpose a network of personal contacts with sympathetic lawyers, psychiatrists and bail bondsmen. Civil rights activities and social functions are left to another San Francisco group, the Society for Individual Rights. One of the pressure group techniques used by this society is to invite the candidates in local elections to answer questions about their views on homosexual issues. The politicians' replies, or their refusals, then receive publicity, favourable or otherwise, in the organisation's monthly magazine *Vector*. In 1975, each of the candidates for the office of mayor was obliged to make a public declaration of his attitute towards civil rights for homosexuals.

Other pressure groups, such as the Mattachine Societies, believe in working with the system to try to change it. They make use of legal arguments, they exploit the rhetoric of liberal reformers and the idealism of social justice for all, they try to secure a legitimate hearing for their views through the media, and they project an image of sweet reasonableness patiently waiting for a bigoted society to see the light. They demand no more freedom for themselves than is already enjoyed by respectable, restrained, heterosexual citizens. More recently, however, the younger and more radically inclined elements have formed groups dedicated to militant confrontations with the establishment. The most active of these, the Gay Liberation Front, came into prominence in New York in 1969. That summer, the New York police raided the Stonewall tavern, a seedy homosexual bar in Greenwich Village, arrested the management for liquor licence violations, and turned the clients into the street. Instead of dispersing quietly, the homosexuals and their sympathisers attacked the police

1. The author would like to record his indebtedness to the officers of this society for their help in supplying many helpful references and much useful information.

and a full scale riot developed. The inevitable arrests and beatings which ensued furnished the new movement with the martyrs and the grievances they needed. The Stonewall incident, seized upon as a rallying point for protest marches and anniversary processions, quickly established itself as a key event in the folk history of gay liberation, in the minds of enthusiasts quite comparable to the Peterloo Massacre.

The Gay Liberationists, a collection of loosely affiliated activist groups dominated by young radicals, view the campaign for homosexual freedom as one part of the wider struggle of all oppressed individuals fighting against the coercive, authoritarian, capitalistic, jingoistic, racialist, sexist society (Altman, 1971; Humphreys, 1972; Teal, 1971; Tobin and Wicker, 1972). Many of them embrace a variety of causes – black power, decriminalisation of marijuana, worker's revolution, women's liberation – but not always to the gratification of the other social groups with whom they claim an identity of interest. Their tactics of confrontation and disruption horrify the older representatives of established homophile movements, who fear to 'rock the boat' or incite a 'puritan backlash'. Impatient of shamefaced anonymity, the Liberationists parade in public sporting labels like 'Gay is Good', chanting slogans such as 'Out of the Closets and into the Streets', and flaunting outrageous mixtures of male and female attire that defy the conventions of homosexual drag as much as they affront the standards of straight society. Scornful of the 'closet queens' who fear to admit their homosexuality openly, and intolerant of the rules of modesty prevailing in straight society, Liberationists love to make a show of embracing in public, dancing in the nude, and generally cocking a snook at conventional respectability. They see themselves as the protagonists of sexual liberation for all. Carl Wittman (1974) author of an influential manifesto on gay liberation argues: 'We know we are radical, that we are revolutionaries, since we know that the system we're under now is a direct source of oppression, and its not a question of getting our share of the pie. The pie is rotten.' He thinks it wrong for homosexuals to mimic the roles laid down by an oppressive straight society. He sees traditional marriage as 'a rotten oppressive institution', 'fraught with role playing', and believes that homosexuals who try to settle down with a steady mate in imitation of straight conventions do so because they hate their true selves and are trying to appear as much like heterosexuals as possible. He advocates instead freedom 'for people to live alone, live together for a while, live together for a long time, either as couples or in larger numbers; and the ability to flow easily from one of these states to another as our needs change.'

The homosexual activists' tactics, though usually stopping short of violence, employ a variety of harrassments, including sit-ins, picketing, invasion of meetings and noisy heckling. The invasion of heterosexual dances by militant homosexual couples seems to be a favourite sport. Luckless officials or election candidates, themselves the relatively helpless instruments of public opinion, are made to declare their attitudes to issues such as the employment of homosexual teachers. The San Francisco branch of Macy's, the well-known department store, was once picketed by militants protesting about the arrest of men using the store's lavatory for sexual purposes. One gay liberation activist boasted to the author that he had succeeded in forcing a particular church to admit self-declared homosexuals to its congregation by threatening to make public the names of those ministers who were known to the gay community to be homosexuals. He proposed to adopt the same tactics in relation to university teachers in order to persuade the university to give facilities to a student liberation group.

The advocates of gradual homosexual reform come under as vigorous an attack as the police and other authorities who administer anti-homosexual regulations. Laud Humphreys (1972) describes how a national conference of homophile organisations, called together in San Francisco in 1970, was brought to an end by invading gay revolutionaries. At a delegates' dinner, the dignified atmosphere was destroyed when two young men, protesters against the hypocrisy of both straights and gay reformers, stripped off and danced a nude can-can. Next day the revolutionaries forced their way into the meeting and started passing motions supporting the Black Panthers and calling for immediate withdrawal of American forces from Vietnam.

In England, the homophile movements, like the gay bars, reflect on a smaller scale the American scene. At the most establishment end of the spectrum, a small private charity, the Albany Trust (31, Clapham Rd., London SW9 0JD), with an impressive list of respectable supporters (most of them married and without suspicion of personal involvement in the gay life) struggles to provide an information and referral service, and to produce an occasional journal, *Man and Society*. The Trust aims to be broadly educational and to appeal to the liberal-minded in straight society. It has the support of various church groups, and its journal contains many articles concerning the ethics of homosexuality, as well as reviews and comments on the progress of counselling services and civil liberties for homosexuals.

This establishment image, with its medico-religious associations, contrasts with the Gay Liberation Front Manifesto (1971), which bears a clenched fist on the cover, talks about oppressed groups, and warns: 'We do not intend to ask for anything. We intend to stand firm and assert our basic rights.' The Manifesto attacks the family as an institution of sexual oppression: 'How many of us have been pressured into marriage, sent to psychiatrists, frightened into sexual inertia, ostracised, banned, emotionally destroyed — all by our parents?' It attacks the patriarchal sexist society, with its stereotyped roles of masculine dominance and feminine submission, that places women and gays in a position of permanent inferiority. It attacks the institution of compulsive monogamy, based on property ownership and emotional exclusiveness. It advocates a new, liberated life style, with gay communes and collectives acting as focal points for developing new levels of self-awareness and personal interaction.

The Campaign for Homosexual Equality (PO Box 427, 28 Kennedy Street, Manchester M60 2EL) is a less radical group, which concentrates on homosexual issues rather than trying to transform society. It was developed from the North Western Homosexual Law Reform Committee, started in 1964 by Alan Horsfall, a Labour Party councillor in Lancashire. It was not until 1970, when, under its new name, it launched an advertising campaign in the national press, that it began to expand into a national movement. At present (1975) it has a subscribing membership of some five thousand, a full-time paid secretary at head office, and more than a hundred local groups in different towns all over England. In spite of some widely publicised rebuffs from a few local authorities (in 1971 Burnley Council refused to allow CHE to open a club, and in 1972 Weymouth Council rejected its application to hold an annual conference in the town) the organisation is now well established. It has done a great deal to ensure that homosexual meetings and social occasions can now take place without subterfuge in respectable hired halls, including, for instance, the famous Brighton Pavilion.

More forthright and activist than the Albany Trust, but less politically revolutionary than Gay Liberation, CHE exists to press for equality for all, regardless of sexual orientation, within the existing legal and social system. It seeks to change the laws that control homosexuals differently from heterosexuals and to expose social discrimination and harrassment. It concerns itself with education on homosexual issues, in schools, in society at large, and within its own membership. It undertakes welfare functions, endeavouring to counter the problems of anxiety, guilt and isolation felt by many homosexuals. It cooperates with existing counselling services and promotes new ones specially for homosexuals. It organises social groups and meetings at which homosexual men and women can gather for social, educational and recreational purposes away from the predatory situation and ghetto atmosphere associated with commercial gay bars. It takes an interest in specialist issues, such as relations between homosexuals and the churches, the trade unions, the press, the youth services and the medical and social services.

CHE gatherings tend to be older, more earnest, more disciplined and more middle-class than the Gay Liberationist happenings, where discussions are noteworthy for confrontation rather than content. Some CHE members in London produced, until recently, when it folded up from shortage of funds, a lively and informative magazine *Lunch*. Among other things, the magazine featured some detailed, frank and factual accounts of the circumstances surrounding recent prosecutions of homosexuals. Such information would be difficult to obtain from any other published source.

The more radical homosexual press is calculated to shock the susceptibilities of the establishment. Though less way out than Gay

Liberation's *Come Together*, the main activist paper *Gay News* (1a, Normand Gdns, Greyhound Rd., London W14 9SB), with its boldly-worded advertisements for sex mates, has scant respect for the constraints observed by most English publications. Started in May 1972, it was the subject of a police prosecution for obscenity in April 1974. The magistrates dismissed the charges, but the organisation was made to pay most of the legal costs, amounting to nearly fifteen hundred pounds, and had to appeal to its readers for help.

The homosexual activists in England can be almost as militant as their American colleagues. For example, in September 1974, when the British Medical Association held a conference on psychosexual problems at the University of Bradford, without inviting representatives of homosexual organisations to attend, a large group of activists first picketed the conference room and then invaded the meetings, bringing the proceedings to a halt. The Chairman (a High Court judge) and one of the speakers felt obliged to leave. A young man in radical drag took over the microphone, and the intruders more or less dictated the terms on which the meeting could continue. One of the remaining speakers (the present writer) was permitted to talk for a few minutes on condition that a 'free for all' discussion followed. This was agreed, and after an hour or more of predictable exchanges of opinion the conference proper was allowed to resume.

Homophile organisations maintain that homosexual orientation presents no problem, except to the heterosexual bigot, but this does not prevent them from recognising that many homosexuals feel the need for help in coping with a hostile world, or from promoting counselling services to meet the demand. The Campaign for Homosexual Equality runs a befriending advisory service called Friend, with branches all over the country, which provides help for homosexual and bisexual men and women who are lonely, frightened or in some trouble. It is affiliated to the National Association for Mental Health and has the support of a body of well-equipped counsellors.

Icebreakers (BM/Gay Lib. London WC1 6XX), has a telephone service (01 274 9590), on the lines of the facility run by the Samaritans to help potential suicides, but staffed by homosexual volunteers. They began as an offshoot from a London Gay Liberation group who were dissatisfied with the quality of professional advice from psychiatrists and social workers. They believed that persons with direct experience of homosexuals' social problems were in a good position to help others similarly placed. In their first year of work they received over two thousand calls. They are a small group (22 men and women at the time of writing) claiming no special expertise, but offering time and a sympathetic ear for callers wanting to discuss personal problems. They let people know of gay meeting places and organisations, but do not act like a marriage bureau, though they hold occasional informal socials in private homes where lonely homosexuals can foregather. Many of the calls they receive come from married people. Others come from persons, especially women, living in small towns and rural areas and isolated from homosexual contacts. Lonely old people, whose sexuality is regarded as 'dirty', and lonely young people, whose sexuality is forbidden by law, likewise frequently call.

According to a Campaign for Homosexuality Equality pamphlet (CHE, 1975) young persons who realise that their sexual orientation is predominantly homosexual often feel left out and lonely, and compelled to hide their emotions from parents, teachers, and friends. Youth organisations and schools fight shy of the subject and try to deal with it by getting rid of staff or clients suspected of homosexuality. A unique organisation in England, Parents Enquiry (16 Honley Road, London SE6 2HZ) gives advice both to young people and to parents who have a homosexual son or daughter. Many parents, quite unprepared for the discovery that their offspring is homosexual, react with bewilderment, guilt, or rejection. Parents Enquiry helps parents to accept and be reunited with their homosexual son or daughter. The need is considerable. Over a recent twelve-month period, in London alone six thousand young people contacted the organisation.

Gay liberationists seek not only to combat the homophobic attitudes of society, but to try to free homosexuals from their own feelings of unworthiness. The need for this has been argued most forcibly by Hodges and Hutter (1974) in a recent liberation pamphlet. They point out that gay people, being reared as alien cuckoos in heterosexual nests, learn to loathe homosexuality before they discover that they are homosexuals themselves. Their ingrained sense of shame compels them to remain in hiding even when they have little to lose by coming out and openly joining liberation movements. Like genteel office workers, they reject the union in favour of the imaginary advantages of identifying with the management. They prefer such minor advantages as the continued pursuit of hobbies like Church or youth work, to honest disclosure. In truth they would rather be loved for what they are not than admit what they really are. Persons in positions of privilege and influence, like the late E.M. Forster, who had in his later years 'the undemanding security of a life fellowship at King's College', chose to maintain silence when an example of standing proud would have given comfort to many less fortunately placed homosexuals. Homophile writers themselves often fail to break out of the trap of self-denigration, especially when they try to make excuses for aspects of gay life which should be seen as positive assets. Easy access to sexual contacts by mutual agreement without the tiresome preliminaries of heterosexual courtship rituals, freedom from the constraints of child rearing, and the possibility of long-continued harmonious cohabitations unencumbered by the rigidly enforced sexual fidelity that makes for so much bitterness in traditional marriages, are all features that some heterosexuals might envy.

Well-meaning liberal ideas sometimes aggravate the situation. The notion that everyone is potentially bisexual contributes nothing towards a recognition of the differing needs of the average homosexual or heterosexual. The condemnation of gay clubs as ghetto situations carries the unwarranted assumption that ordinary clubs will allow gay people to seek each other out, to talk in endearments, to dance together and to kiss each other, as freely as heterosexuals can. The absence of crude legal discrimination is cold comfort to homosexuals who find themselves in an alien society where every institution, from housing estates to dance halls, caters only to the needs of heterosexuals. True homosexual equality means the homosexual millions making their presence felt, and this would mean a radical change in every walk of heterosexual life.

Despite their way-out image, their defiance of social coventions and assumptions, and the likelihood of their methods of agitation proving counter-productive, the Gay Liberationists have got on to one really crucial issue. They see the need for a genuine sexual revolution. The repressive outlook that has brought about so much unhappiness in the past may well have been a prime cause of compulsive homosexuality. As the psychoanalyst Robert Lindner (1956) points out, infantile responses to the onset of sexual sensations are heavily censored, shame and guilt are attached to erotic play in childhood, and when eventually, at a relatively late age, some use of the genital organs is permitted, highly restrictive conditions as to time, place, person, method and manners are laid down. Lindner views homosexuality as a form of rebellion against this tyranny, satisfying sometimes to the individual concerned, but hardly an ideal solution for mankind in general. He sees the growth of homophile agitation as a step in the right direction of greater freedom, but believes the movement doomed to failure in the face of traditional repression instilled from early childhood. The increase in tolerance that seems to have been achieved may be only apparent. Acceptance of homosexuals as a minority deserving more of sympathy and understanding than punishment diminishes the brutality but preserves the apartheid. In this way society avoids having to face a radical revision of attitudes towards child rearing, sex education, gender roles and marital fidelity, all of which are highly relevant to the problems of sexual minorities.

Lindner's scepticism about the true extent of the sexual revolution has been largely borne out by the experience of recent years. The influence of the sexual liberation movements upon, for instance, sex instruction in schools, or upon adolescents' knowledge of the techniques, difficulties and possible complications of sexual contacts, has so far proved less than might have been expected. Whether, in the long run, real sexual freedom from secrecy and guilt will emerge, and if it does what effect it will have upon the incidence of what is now called deviant behaviour, remains to be seen.

4. *The camp subculture*

The mannerisms, dress and language affected by male homosexuals when they get together in clubs or elsewhere provides a rich source of material for music hall acts and a constant affront to conventional ideals of masculine behaviour. In England, the humorous mannerisms adopted by some popular television comedians have given the watching millions a glimpse of the wrist-dropping, the flippant phrases, the sexual allusions, and the falsetto intonation that are important ingredients of 'camping it up'. The origin and purpose of such conduct has now become a topic for serious scrutiny by academic sociologists.

Camp clothes and camp manners have some obvious uses. The clothes are usually ahead of fashion, attention-seeking and meant to be sexy, all of which helps when out hunting for a partner. The manners and language serve as a membership badge advertising the wearer's right to acceptance by the gay group. Camp expressions can be used tentatively at first, then more floridly, as a means of establishing that a new acquaintance really does belong to the band and is a safe subject for sexual propositioning.

In homosexual circles the gestures, the styles of dress, the 'in phrases' and the slang vocabulary are constantly changing. They must change in order to keep ahead, to maintain the identity of the group, for straight society tends to pick up and often to take over what was once almost exclusively the prerogative of a sexual minority. For example, the tight pants and long hair, which became in the sixties the accepted standard for all young males, were once considered almost a homosexual uniform. The memory of that association was doubtless responsible for much of the virulence of parental disapproval when the fashion first began to spread. In America, the plain, short-haired image, once the hall mark of the respectable young, now that it has become unusual, risks being taken over again by homosexuals. Expressions like 'get you dear', at one time unheard of outside gay circles, are freely used by the heterosexual young.

The sociologist, Mary McIntosh (1973), in an insightful analysis of gay slang (*parlare*), points out some significant characteristics. Some of it consists of technical jargon for sexual activities – *trolling, cottaging, noshing, rimming* – but much more of it refers in ambivalently emotive terms to homosexual characters. 'The world is peopled with, on the one hand, *fags, queans, aunties* and *duchesses* and, on the other, *chickens, minnies, pretty faces* (some of whom may be trade), with a few *dykes* and *quean's dollies* or *fag hags* on the side-lines.' These terms are often used in a mocking, or frankly derogatory way. *Chicken* is not really an endearing term for an attractive youth so much as a label for a prospective sex object. 'That's a bitch' means he's feminine in bed, but the words have overtones of bitchiness. *Queen*, or *quean*, carries with it implications of effeminacy and when, as is usual, it occurs in phrases like 'silly old queen' or 'she's a screaming queen' the implications are unflattering. Camp language, used in this way, is a form of minstrellisation (as the sociologists say), male homosexuals playing up to the stereotype of the effete, effeminate, histrionic character society expects, like black persons playing up to the 'nigger minstrel' image of fun-loving, banjo-strumming, grown-up children. Homosexuals who deliberately display their campness in heterosexual company do so as a form of defence. By seeming to laugh at themselves they avoid being laughed at first. The preservation of camp conventions among themselves suggests that they have half-jokingly accepted the low valuation put upon their relationships by heterosexual society.

Bruce Rodgers (1972), in a comprehensive and scholarly analysis of American gay slang makes the same point. Much of the vocabulary 'is more vulgar, barbaric, cruel, racist and sexist than any speech you will ever encounter ...' People and events are spoken of cynically or disparagingly. For example, 'jungle meat' for a black man, 'chicken house' or 'pimple joint' for a place frequented by youngsters, 'meat market', 'fruit bin' and 'pansy palace' for a homosexual meeting place, 'chicken freak', 'youth worker' or 'bronco buster' for a man who likes youths, 'stuffed turkey' for a touch of middle-aged spread and 'pig pile' for group sex. The terms used in prison slang are especially cruel. The 'wolf-pack' hunts a 'first-cop' (sexually inexperienced newcomer) to have a 'gang-splash' (group anal rape) the first, second and third rapists being 'welcome wagon, sloppy seconds and bloody thirds'. The raped man becomes a 'punk' or 'prison pussy'. As Rodgers points out, 'Slang flourishes in the ghetto. Those who struggle to leave the ghetto shake off the language first and then decry its message.' Many gay militants abhor the contrived lingo of the ghetto faggot because it puts the gay world in such an unfavourable light. 'They consider the jargon yet another link in the chain which holds the homosexual enslaved.'

The camp subculture may strike the outsider as uncomfortably self-mocking, but to some of its more dedicated adherents it represents a safe and satisfying haven, a kind of protective mutual admiration society. Like other unpopular minority groups, homosexuals over-compensate by putting on superior airs. As Ruitenbeek (1963) puts it, this type of homosexual 'cultivates a snobbery of his own, a "wit", an interest – often superficial – in the arts. He lives fast and moves often; today he is in New York, tomorrow in California ... Settling down is abhorrent, the non-homosexual world unbearably dull.' Having no family ties, male homosexuals can indulge in elegant clothes, extravagant interior decor, frequent theatre-going and adventurous travel. So long as he preserves the manners and appearance acceptable in gay circles, wherever he goes he has easy access to congenial company, no lack of invitations, and can enjoy the feeling of belonging to an elite that rises above the petty limitations of the straight world.

The hedonistic outlook of the camp subculture, and its preoccupation with the delights of sex, are well illustrated by 'Arcangelo' (1971) in what must surely be one of the most humourous, scandalous yet strangely insightful accounts of the gay life ever written. It takes the form of a satirical and highly explicit sex guide, supposedly addressed primarily to young men wondering how to be happy though gay, but also 'designed to amuse, enlighten and instruct all manner of readers'. The author adopts the ethic of a Tennessee Williams character who believes the world is divided between happy people who know the pleasures of sexual love, and miserable, maladjusted wretches who watch with sick envy. His opening chapter on prostitution refers to 'disposable people', men whose chief qualification is to become instantly aroused at the jingle of money. He advises the neophyte to patronise sexually frustrated college men in preference to the professional hustler, who is apt to belong to the 'We fuck but we don't kiss' brand of homoeroticism. For those contemplating taking up the trade themselves, he warns against the low pay, about what a slum female could expect, the long hours of waiting, and the need to give the customer whatever he pays for, even if that happens to mean submitting while 'gagged in a bathful of old whisk brooms'.

Advice, equally sage and cynical, is given the young man on choice of clothes. He should not advertise sexual wants too blatantly, since that only makes for unnecessary martyrdom when it comes to getting a job or trying to enter a college, where some minor official may have the power to block entry. 'Simplify your clothing. It's how you look without it that's most important.' The chapters on techniques of sexual intercourse, heterosexual and homosexual, are considerably franker and more practical than most marriage manuals. The author explains that the strong sphincter muscle around the anus can be adapted to a milking, massaging movement that no vagina can match. He suggests practice with an artificial phallus, to avoid a painful first experience and to get the knack of flexing the sphincter muscles so that the lover has greater satisfaction. The comments on homosexual marriage are enough to warn off many candidates. Relations that start off on a 'high voltage sexual basis' can never be maintained at that level for long. If the sex act is the only thing two people enjoy doing together they will soon find each other's company boring. If one holds the lease on the apartment the other is like an Arab wife disposed of with the formula 'I divorce thee' repeated thrice. What happens when the needs of two male careers conflict? If the couple have invested together in real estate, in imitation of heterosexual unions, they can't solve the problem by sawing the sofa in two.

The advice on how to stage a homely orgy is less intimidating. Drop hints in advance to persons who might be interested, they need not be persons one would mix with on other social occasions. Empty the room of hard obstacles, scatter low cushions, organise a supply of liquor (but not too much) and have available erotic pictures and some ready-prepared pot for those who feel more voluptuous when they smoke. Guests are expected to have whom they please and leave when they please and not to be disappointed if their fellow revellers are not all works of beauty. 'One doesn't go to orgies for aesthetics.' As the author says 'If a good gang-shag has any advantage over any other sort of sexual performance, it seems to me to be its indifference to and rather neutralising effect upon emotional love.'

One noteworthy feature of the homosexual subculture is the ostentatious display of artistic taste. As with clothes and social manners, the trend is sometimes taken deliberately to humorous extremes, as when a huge crystal chandelier appears in a tiny bed-sitter, or a very ordinary bedroom houses a four-poster crowned with carved eagles. The artistic pretensions of the homosexual subculture probably stem in part from a craving for attention and status, and in part from the traditional toleration of homosexuals in the art world, which encourages homosexuals to seek work in these fields as designers, dealers, or theatre employees. The supposed concentration of male homosexuals in some of these occupations naturally arouses unfavourable comment. For example, the sometimes grotesque and inconvenient features of feminine high-fashion have been attributed to the malignant influence of male homosexual designers. Against this, the homophile propagandists contrive to suggest that a homosexual temperament endows a man with special artistic sensitivity, if not with actual creative talent (Ruitenbeek, 1967). Well-known writers who have been homosexuals, such as Gide, Proust, Maugham, J.A. Symonds and Wilde, are constantly cited in this connection (Reade, 1970), but who is to know whether they would not have been equally creative had their sexual orientation been different? The illuminating portrayals of homosexual situations by gifted writers like Christopher Isherwood, Angus Wilson or Colette depend upon oustanding perceptivity and talent for expression and cannot be a mere by-product of an author's own erotic development. However, given the necessary talent, the homosexual's situation of an outsider looking in on the doings of mainstream society can be turned to advantage. An important factor in creative art is the presentation of everyday images in new, questioning and challenging forms, and outsiders, social misfits, and ambisexuals are in a position to view life from unusual and often revealing angles.

Membership of the homosexual subculture, unlike membership of, for example, the black minority, need not be a full-time occupation. Many men prefer to change their image with the day of the week, one day passing for straight among mates from work or neighbourhood friends, the next day, at a conveniently safe distance, camping it up in gay company. The extent to which a homosexual mixes freely in gay society depends upon other factors besides personal inclination. Leznoff and Westley (1956), who surveyed a Canadian community of male homosexuals, divided their sample into the overt, or fully committed members, and the secret types who visited occasionally but tried to avoid a too frequent or too public connection with the gay scene. They found that the overt types mostly occupied low-status jobs, loss of which would not matter, or else worked in some form of personal service, such as hairdresser or interior decorator, where their position would not be affected if their homosexuality became known.

The covert types more often occupied professional or managerial positions. Many of them admitted that they felt forced to preserve secrecy. One man, recently promoted, described his attitude to the homosexual group as follows: 'For the first time in my life I have a job I would really like to keep and where I can have a pretty secure future. I realise that if word were to get around that I was gay I would probably lose my job ... I don't mind seeing them once in a while at somebody's house, but I won't be seen with them on the street any more.'

Enthusiastic youngsters sometimes fail to appreciate that homosexuals in responsible jobs must 'pass for straight' most of the time in order to be allowed to continue to function. The author knows of one student who always wore a Gay Liberation badge and railed against closet queens, but the moment he started work he threw away the badge and became fearful that his new colleagues suspected him.

The all-too-visible gay bar scene, upon which public impressions and sociological analyses of the homosexual subculture have been largely based, cannot be taken as typical of the everyday life-style of most homosexuals. Even for many of the regular patrons, gay-bar socialising represents no more than a weekly Saturday night escape from an otherwise conventional and possible lonely existence. Carol Warren (1974), a Los Angeles sociologist, tried to delve deeper than most of her colleagues had done into the less public aspects of homosexual social life. She made friends with a circle of gay men, attended their parties, got herself asked out on dinner dates, and made good use of conversational opportunities to probe attitudes, observe manners and listen to accounts of homosexual living.

Notwithstanding some irritating excursions into professional theorising of doubtful explanatory value, Warren's book contains some shrewd observations that might have been hard to come by through conventional interview techniques and sampling methods. The predominantly middle-class homosexuals she met pursued their work and their careers like other middle-class Americans, limiting their unconventionality to leisure hours, when they were free to exchange visits with friends of their own choosing with whom they felt safe to relax and play camp. She noted that whenever these men had to pass from gay to straight company they automatically changed their manner in many subtle ways, substituting a conventionally masculine tone and stance for the gestures and expressions natural to homosexual circles. Most of her informants appeared to reject as low class 'trash' what she called the 'career homosexual', the individual, usually of lower education, unstable work record and no particular stake in the straight, respectable community, who spends his full time in unconcealed homosexual philandering. Such persons have no need for periodic constraints upon their dress or manners, and no hesitation in advertising their commitment to gay protest movements. For the most part, the older and more middle-class homosexuals preserved fairly successfully a double persona, one for relatives and

business, one for gay company. She met only one individual who had
experienced public exposure. He had been divorced by his wife when
she discovered him in a sex act with the man next door. Warren
noticed, however, that homosexual men with little recent experience
of socialising with women sometimes gave themselves away in normal
company by their excessive politeness and outmoded manners. Most
of the older men lived in well-cared-for, elegantly ordered homesteads.
If they did not actually belong to a wealthy income bracket, they
managed to put up a show of elitist tastes and manners, in order to
keep up with the expectations of the group. Most of the older men
shared their establishments with another man of similar age, taste,
and education in what amounted to an unofficial marital set-up. They
did more of their socialising in each other's homes than in gay bars, a
habit which the younger homosexuals attributed to the older men's
lack of success in outside competition for sexual contacts. Some
marital partners strove to remain sexually faithful, but commonly
there was an understanding that each partner could have occasional
one-night stands with outsiders, or alternatively both partners
together shared sexual contacts with some visiting third party. Unlike
their pseudo-marital arrangements, which followed the style of
heterosexual marriages in being largely confined to partners of similar
background, these occasional outside sexual contacts were often with
men of a younger generation, lower class and different ethnic group
with whom they shared no interest save sexual activity. Their more
permanent companions were generally persons who would not by
their manners or their appearance spoil a respectable front. For the
same reasons these men neither mixed with nor approved of persons
indulging in public transvestitism or in chasing small boys. Their
attitude was not quite 'Thank God I'm normal', but 'Thank God I'm
a normal queer'

Warren's picture of a cosy, self-contained, insular society, enjoying
the morale-boosting effect of a shared secret life, and viewing the dull,
straight world outside with a tinge of contempt, reflects the particular
segment of male homosexual society in California into which she
managed to gain an entry. The men described by Warren had the
intelligence, the money and the social opportunity to construct a
shield behind which they could enjoy a partially liberated homosexual
life without losing the contacts with conventional society, or the social
habits of their class, upon which their status and incomes depended.
These discreet libertines may be no more typical of homosexuals at
large than the more blatant characters whose lives revolve around the
gay-bar scene. The difficulty with all such research is the impossibility
of obtaining a truly representative sample. In one sense, of course,
there can be no such thing, since homosexual lives run to patterns as
diverse and individualistic as heterosexual lives. The forms of
adjustment open to a homosexual depend very much upon his
particular position within the complicated and stratified, as well as
pluralistic and changing, culture of the present age.

5. *Behind the gay scene*

Homosexual life as seen by the public is just the tip of a very large iceberg. Its contours give no indication of the shapes below the surface. According to the most reliable surveys, at least 5 per cent of the population, men and women included, are seriously involved in homosexuality for a signicant part, if not for the whole, of their lives. Only a tiny fraction of the totality of homosexuals in the community are accounted for by the membership of homophile groups or the regular patrons of the big-city gay bars. Most studies of homosexual life histories have been based upon samples taken either from a medical clientele or from members of homophile groups and their friends. How the great silent majority organise their lives remains unclear. From what little is known it seems plain that homosexual life-styles vary as much as heterosexual life-styles, and that often they are unobtrusive and undramatic. From an individual's sexual orientation one cannot predict what his personality will be like, what beliefs, social attitudes or moral ideas he will hold, what intelligence he will have, or what sort of career he will pursue. One cannot know how he will handle the challenges of school and work and perhaps military service, or how he will react to the crises of love, separations, sickness, and ageing which everyone must face. Some homosexuals conform to, or even try to emulate, the expected stereotypes, but most real-life histories are more notable for their individuality than for their patterning. The following examples illustrate the remarkable contrasts in attitude and circumstances between homosexuals who have accepted their orientation as a matter of course, carrying on with their lives without worry and fuss, and those who have felt it a crippling handicap and allowed it to blight their whole existence.

The case histories of self-torturing neurotics so often quoted in psychological texts, and the troubles of homosexual living revealed by sociological surveys, highlight some very real problems, but give an exaggerated impression of unrelieved gloom. This needs counter-balancing with examples, no less important for being undramatic, of individuals who have come to terms with a homosexual orientation and found it no obstacle to contentment and fulfilment. The autobiographical notes which follow were written by one such person, a well-respected professional man in his sixties, who happens to be known to the author. Admittedly, his social and educational advantages gave him unusual freedom to choose his own way of life, but the outcome was attributable more to stable temperament than social circumstances:

I was born in a country district. Father, an army officer, was away from home most of the time until I was six. Mother was a woman of superior education, capable, with considerable organising powers and intellectual interests. She was, to an extent somewhat ahead of her time, a strong believer that women should be individuals first, and wives and mothers second. My brother and I were brought up in an atmosphere of love and affection, coupled with firm influences towards duty and loyalty. As small children we spent our daily routine in the charge of a nursery maid, a young local woman of warm character, to whom I became very attached. At the age of ten I went to boarding school, following my brother who preceded me by a couple of years.

I admired Father but, looking back, would guess he was shy towards young people and did not know how to express his affections. Spontaneous, spur-of-the moment behaviour was something I never achieved with him. Mother was affectionate, and up to the time she was killed in an accident, just before I left school, I was very much attached to her by deep ties. Within a year of her death Father re-married. Instead of establishing a better communication, now I was old enough to be company for him, the circumstances of his re-marriage put a sullen distance between us.

It must have been before I was 6, I can remember having dreams about rescuing some handsome boy from danger and feeling warmly attracted to him. Once, when I was about 8, I vividly remember stumbling accidentally upon Mother while she was standing naked in her dressing room. I was horrified, deeply repelled at the sight of her body, which unexpectedly bore some ugly scars from an old accident, and I ran away without speaking. Nor did Mother ever say a word about it.

At the age of 12 or so, I made particular friends with a fellow boarder at school, and much enjoyed a holiday spent at his home. I had no special skill and little confidence at games, but when I was with this particular friend I felt some confidence for the first time, and there was quite an element of showing off together during dancing lessons in the gymnasium. A few years later, at public school, a friend got me to join a group of boys who introduced me to masturbation and ejaculation. I soon found I was popular with other boys as a sex partner and, equally, very soon found that sex with boys was a wonderful experience. At first it was the sex act not the person that mattered, but in a term or two I had begun a lasting affair with a handsome boy called Tony, slightly older than myself. This lasted for the whole of my remaining time at school. I am surprised now at the risks I took to visit his dormitory, night after night, but we were never caught. I also had sex with several other boys whom I liked, but that did not seem to matter to Tony, since we knew the two of us liked one another best. In my last days at school, a housemaster got to know about our activities and there was an inquest and a lot of spreading questions and interviews. I was lucky in having chosen as friends boys who turned out to be discreet and not to panic when questioned. Tony turned up later at the same university as myself, but the short interval had made a change, his school days were over and it was obvious to me he had started a new phase. He got engaged that same year, married soon after finishing university, and I hardly saw him again.

During holidays at home I accepted that sex and family life did not mix. We had the usual parties with girls present, but I had grown awkward about dancing with girls. I cannot remember ever having been curious about girls at this time, and certainly never had any sex play with them.

I worked steadily at university and did not have much sex life, but I did get to know a teacher who had around him a circle of homosexual undergraduates, and this was a very pleasant and formative circle of friends. For about five years after graduating, I worked in London, shared flats with homosexual friends, and had a fair amount of casual sex, though this was not what I was really looking for. Then came the war and five years as an officer in the army, where I led a very celibate life. After demobilisation I returned to life in London, locating various prewar contacts, some of whom have proved life-long and valued friends. After one somewhat frustrating love affair with a young man who did not find me physically exciting, I met John. He was ten years younger than me, but I came to find him more and more attractive and sympathetic and we began an affair. I was able to provide a home for the two of us and we have lived together ever since. I have had nearly thirty years of lasting affection and shared life with John, and count myself lucky to have done so.

Living together has not presented us with social problems. John's parents accepted me freely and generously, and I became fond of his parents, particularly his father. My nearest relatives were my brother and his wife. I have always assumed my brother is aware of my homosexual relationship, and his wife let it be known, by various allusions, that she understands, but the situation has never been discussed explicitly, and they have never treated John as one of the family in the way his folks treated me. I know John resents the one-sided situation that exists.

I would say I am more independent than John is. He worries more about what people think of him. Certainly I have never thought of my homosexuality being a specially important or even a specially interesting part of my character, no more so, that is to say, than heterosexuality is to people who are heterosexual. I believe that most people, when not adopting 'public' attitudes which they believe are expected of them, do not find the subject specially important or interesting.

I can recall only two occasions when I have been embarrassed by unwanted sexual approaches from women. Otherwise my being homosexual has not landed me in any awkward situations and I am content to be as I am. I often feel an attraction to a woman or girl seen casually in the street, and I remember once feeling strongly attracted to a girl I saw in a Lesbian club. My immediate reaction was 'If only you had been a boy'. I feel it impossible to disentangle whether this was a self-deceiving rationalisation or an indication that heterosexual feelings are not as deeply submerged as they seem. I know that homosexuality is said to result from a blockage of ordinary leanings to the opposite sex, but for myself I have never seen much point in trying to seek out its origins. What is certain is that at the level of conscious life I am happy to be as I am and have no wish to be changed.

This example contains most of the common elements of a male homosexual history. The description of the parents reads like a slightly attenuated version of the classic dominant mother plus (psychologically) absent father. The recollection of shock at mother's nudity might be thought to echo the Freudian theory of incest guilt. The reference to awkwardness and dislike of sports suggests boredom with certain conventionally masculine pursuits. The boarding school experiences may have encouraged a homosexual orientation, although Tony, the main sex-partner at that stage, who was presumably not so predisposed, apparently became satisfactorily heterosexual soon after leaving school. The reason for quoting the case is to show how, given particular circumstances and temperament, pressures towards homosexuality can sometimes produce their effect apparently without worry or conflict, and can result in a way of life that, to the individual concerned, seems perfectly natural, acceptable and ·unproblematic. This man himself commented that, owing to our educational habits, boys' pubertal years come in the middle of a quite long period of sex-segregated life. 'Given this situation, I guess that I settled into a homosexual way of life with less worry than if my early influences had orientated me towards a heterosexual life, which as things were would have had less opportunity to develop itself.'

Here is another example, also known to the author, of a longstanding homosexual marriage:

Apart from the vaguest of memories of some erotic play with a girl when he was a young child, Peter said he had always been interested exclusively in his own sex. He participated in the sex games and mutual masturbation that took place between boys at school, but not until late adolescence, when his friends talked a lot about girls while he remained uninterested, did he realise he was different and begin to read about homosexuality. He passed through a period of celibacy, followed by a phase of sporadic furtive contacts in 'cottages', not from choice or shame, but simply because he did not know about the availability of gay society, which in those days was much less publicised. He was well into his twenties when he met a more sophisticated homosexual, who introduced him to bars and parties. He quickly acquired a taste for the 'gay' life, becoming exceedingly promiscuous, as well as enjoying a number of short-lived passionate love affairs. After a few years of this, he fell in love with a slightly younger man: They set up an apartment and are still living together nearly a quarter of a century later.

Peter was a successful scientist. He was an easygoing personality who got on smoothly with his colleagues, but he avoided intimate friendship, and kept his private life carefully apart from his professional associations. There was nothing about his unremarkably masculine physique and manner to arouse suspicion. He particularly avoided involvements with women, laughingly remarking that his only woman friend was his mother. Like so many male homosexuals, he regarded his mother as the important parent, and spoke of his father in disparaging terms.

Like any ordinary newly married man, Peter gave up his promiscuous roamings when he found a partner to live with him. He started to take an interest in shared domestic comforts and in plans for achieving a secure and substantial home, which would have a separate apartment for his parents on their retirement. This all worked out quite well, and Peter's partner changed his surname so that he could pass as Peter's brother as far as neighbours were concerned. Marital relationships, however, soon became, on heterosexual standards, somewhat unorthodox. Peter resumed his promiscuous interests, and even went so far as to import into the household a succession of brief 'affairs'. The partner tolerated rather than approved these developments, but as Peter always considered him first in all important practical matters, he came to terms with the situation. Eventually, one of Peter's importations stayed so long that it was evident the establishment had become a *ménage à trois*. All three spent holidays together, and all three enjoyed sexual contacts with outsiders from time to time.

In middle age, a neurological complaint that had threatened Peter since youth finally worsened and he became intermittently paralysed and was compelled to give up scientific work. This challenge, that might have proved disastrous to many a heterosexual partnership, was successfully met by the other two members of the triad also giving up their jobs, and all three clubbing together to open a small business. The venture proved a practical success and a happy solution to a difficult situation. The locality was noted for a high incidence of gay residents, and all three were soon making new acquaintances in the gay community.

Like many homosexuals, Peter and his friends displayed ingenuity and adaptability in avoiding damaging confrontations with straight society, while arranging their lives to suit their sexual proclivities. By any ordinary standards for measuring social adjustment – freedom from neurotic breakdowns, regular earning-capacity, preservation of lasting and cooperative relationships – Peter would be assessed as normal. The proportion of reasonably adjusted and happy homosexuals in the community is probably greatly underestimated, because the discontented, exhibitionistic or neurotic are always more likely to come to notice in social surveys and clinical work. Reports of things going well don't make interesting news.

The next example illustrates the situation of a man unable to reconcile himself to being a homosexual:

Edward came from a Roman Catholic family of middle-class education and social background. At a relatively early age he obtained a responsible post in a public organisation which brought him into friendly contact with most of the leading citizens in his community. To all outward appearances· Edward seemed a conventional pillar of the establishment. He attended all the right functions, often accompanied by the young lady to whom he had been unofficially engaged for some time. However, ever since adolescence he had been having numerous clandestine homosexual experiences, mostly with casual pick-ups. He had also had one lasting attachment, of an essentially platonic quality, to an older homosexual who died prematurely of cancer. His sexual responses to women were feeble in comparison with his passionate reactions to young men, but sufficient to let him pass for normal. He intended one day to settle down to a socially successful marriage, but was in no hurry to name the day.

Edward knew all about the gay scene from his older friend, but he avoided participation in it, and did not classify himself as 'one of them'. He preferred to spend his time in 'normal' bars, drinking freely, and chatting to all and sundry. His sexual activities most often took place after closing time with whatever male drinking companion he had acquired in the course of the evening. One night he left a bar in company with a young soldier, which was not unusual. The pair went behind a hedge, obstensibly to urinate, but soon started mutual masturbation. At this point two policemen who had watched them disappear together sprang out from the other side of the hedge and arrested them in the act. Edward was sentenced to a mere conditional discharge, but his real punishment came when he found himself cold-shouldered in the social circles that had previously been so welcoming, ordered to resign from his post, and encouraged by his relatives to move out of the district. He developed a bitter grievance about his spoiled career and social prospects and an irrational grudge against the police for bringing what he considered an unnecessary charge against him. He still refused to see his behaviour as anything more than a drunken indiscretion.

For the next twenty years, Edward went on bemoaning his fate. Although he managed to obtain some interesting jobs, involving a lot of travelling, he always regretted the more prestigious position he might have held but for his criminal conviction. He continued with his casual sexual adventures, frequently choosing coloured men or aggressively working-class types, whom he affected to find uninteresting and revolting once he had been to bed with them. He felt disgusted with himself afterwards. In spite of his own behaviour, he liked to moralise about the promiscuous habits of homosexuals. As he grew older he chose sex partners much younger than himself. He said he was looking for a soul mate, and that physical sex didn't matter. He had a short, intense affair with an unstable homosexual youth who had been in a mental hospital with a diagnosis of 'psychopathy'. They lived together for a time, but quarrelled and sulked incessantly, until finally the youth absconded with a homosexual policeman. Later on, he formed an attachment to an aggressively heterosexual Indian teenager, and although they spent a large part of their spare time together no overt sexual contact took place.

Edward reached middle age lonely yet promiscuous, one moment gloating over some new sexual adventure and the next disgusted with himself, fearful of growing old, and still talking – but only talking – of the women he had known in the past and might have married. Unable to face up to the demands of heterosexual life, and equally unable to accept a continuing sexual relationship with another man without upsurges of shame, Edward at 50 remained as confused about his needs and goals as he had been in youth.

6. *Fulfilment and disillusionment*

Individual case histories chart the different courses a homosexual career may take. Some bear witness to the possibility of great satisfaction and fulfilment, others to the likelihood, in the long run, of sad disillusionment. As to which represents the more probable course experts differ. Everything depends upon how the research worker selects his sample. Whatever the ultimate prognosis, however, most observers find that the stage of first 'coming out' as a self-admitted homosexual represents a turning point in life which individuals experience with relief and a sense of fulfilment. Barry Dank (1971) studied the coming out process in a sample of male homosexuals contacted through a homophile organisation in a large American city. The term 'coming out' can mean several things, admitting to oneself that one is a homosexual, making a semi-public admission of the fact by appearing in gay bars, or declaring oneself to the public at large, for instance by wearing a gay liberation badge. Some people call any homosexual who has not passed through all three stages a 'closet queen', others limit the expression to those who decline to mix in gay circles, or to those who refuse to think of themselves as homosexuals.

Dank found that, even in a contemporary American city noted for liberated ideas, considerable time elapses between a male's first experience of an erotic preference for his own sex (modal age range 10-14) and his recognition of himself as a homosexual (modal age range 15-19). A lapse of five years was usual, and in a fifth of cases the interval exceeded ten years. Even extensive involvement in homosexual activity does not necessarily cause a man to classify himself as homosexual, especially if he has no contact with gay circles and believes true homosexuals to be effete creatures with whom he has nothing in common. Dank quotes one man's reaction to his first introduction to a gay bar as a sudden realisation that not all gay people are dirty old men or idiots or silly queens. 'I saw gay society and I said "Wow, I'm home".'

Dank found that the social experiences leading to coming out were not necessarily associated with gay bars, but were liable to occur wherever males were segregated together, in institutions, in the military, in college dormitories or in YMCA hostels. Men could experience strong homosexual feelings and have numerous furtive sexual contacts, but until coming into contact with some social situation, such as naval service, that opened their eyes to the true sexual orientation of many apparently normal men, they would never think to identify themselves as 'queer'. It takes some practical experience of homosexual reality to counteract the unfavourable public image. Once having identified as 'one of them' men strive to maintain self respect by convincing themselves that 'gay is good' and queers are nothing like so bad as they are painted.

Acceptance of a homosexual identity, even though it may come very late in the day, brings relief to many conflict-ridden sufferers. Dank quotes one case of a man of 65 who, following an introduction to a religious organisation for homosexuals, suddenly discovered himself at home with and able to talk freely to gay people. Up till then he had been miserable, socially isolated and fearful of any contact with known homosexuals. 'It's a tremendous emotional break-through. I feel comfortable and relieved of tensions and self consciousness. My effectiveness in other fields has been enhanced 100 per cent ... I'm alive at 65.'

As Dank himself noted, following the coming out experience, men who had previously maintained a certain amount of sexual activity with women tended to abandon this in favour of exclusive homosexuality. They may have merely been giving expression to a previously inhibited preference, but some sociologists (McIntosh, 1968) have argued that an identification with gay society involves pressures to conform to a homosexual sterotype, just as identification with straight society involves pressures to conform to the heterosexual stereotype. The dominant belief among gay circles is that a homosexual orientation is the natural endowment of a privileged minority, and any effort to change it, or to revert to heterosexuality, is unethical and dangerous. Apart from the influence of such opinions, the process of immersion in gay social life inevitably causes some lessening of normal social contacts. The conscious adoption of a gay label may therefore help to exaggerate or to perpetuate a homosexual trend. If society were more tolerant of varieties of sexual preference, people might feel less pressured to choose between 'gay' or 'straight' communities, and bisexual life-styles might become more prevalent.

The stereotype of the gay person as a happy social rebel, one who has overcome outmoded moral limitations, and discovered a new, satisfyingly independent life style, has great appeal to some young people. Adolescents in conflict with parental ideas and standards are apt to fasten upon subcultural groups, such as prohibited drug users, political or religious extremists, or sexual minorities, because these groups provide an oppositional ideology, and a sense of identity and importance, which can be exploited to good effect in confrontations with parental authority. In this way some youngsters may come to adopt totalistic ideologies, for example in allegiance to exclusive homosexuality and a rejection of all ordinary social life and standards, for the negative reason that they deride conventional beliefs rather than for the positive reason that they suit the individual's particular needs (Gonen, 1971). The same point was made by Horowitz (1964) who conducted a survey into the self-concepts of male and female homosexuals on behalf of the lesbian organisation the Daughters of Bilitis. It was noted that some individuals used homosexuality as an instrument of revolt against social and parental restrictions, as a means of gaining a sense of identity and significance.

The joys of coming out are sometimes short-lived. Dispassionate observers find the gay scene anything but enticing. As Karlen (1971, p256) comments, homosexuals themselves have to admit some truth in the play *The Boys in the Band*, which depicts gay life as 'replete with jealousy, competitiveness, insecurity, malice, tantrums and hysterical mood shifts'. The obsessive preoccupation with sexual topics wherever gay circles foregather gives the impression 'that homosexuals are devoted to full-time sexual musical chairs'. The romantic newcomer searching for a permanent love-match is in for a disappointment. Few love affairs between males are lasting. All too often they degenerate into boredom or jealous quarrels, leaving one or both parties sadly disillusioned.

Homophile enthusiasts may challenge the accuracy of these observations, based as they are upon a noticeable but not necessarily typical segment of the gay community. However, the fact that many male homosexuals find it difficult to stay together in pairs for long has been substantiated by numerous surveys (Saghir and Robins, 1973) including those conducted by the most sympathetic of inquirers (Liddicoat, 1961). Many homosexuals restrict their sex life to casual acquaintances, avoiding sexual involvement with their closest and most enduring friends because the possessiveness and jealousy which sex arouses destroys amicable relationships (Sonenschein, 1968). In his English survey, Westwood (1960) reported that 47 of the 127 men in his sample said they would not wish to have an affair. One man, fed up with jealous arguments said: 'I don't want any more emotion with my sex. I suppose you could call me disillusioned.' Others felt that a pseudo-marital situation held no attraction. One commented: 'I can't abide the idea of someone stopping at home wearing an apron – an apology for married life.' Others felt it not worth the social difficulties that might arise. One man put this attitude in a nutshell: 'It's impossible for me to have an affair in my position ...'

Nevertheless, affairs do occur and sometimes last, as in two of the examples quoted earlier in this chapter. A quarter of Westwood's sample were presently living, or had lived together in homosexual couples for five years or more. Some of these relationships, combining companionship, sexual fulfilment and shared activities, resembled ideal heterosexual marriages. One man described his affair as 'a good deal happier than any of the marriages my two sisters and two brothers have made'.

Homophile writers who admit the unsatisfactoriness and impermanence of male affairs usually attribute the fact to the malevolent attitude of straight society. In large cities single people living somewhat anonymously can nowadays share apartments without provoking comment, but in most places landlords, employers, neighbours, social services and interfering relatives all frown upon households not composed of conventional family units. These social difficulties do not really explain the frequent break-up of male affairs from internal dissension rather than outside pressure, or the observation that affairs between female homosexuals often last longer. Social disapproval may account for some men feeling reluctant to set up a homosexual ménage in the first place, but they often have other reasons for their reluctance, notably a preference for a variety of sexual partners and a dislike of being tied down, either socially or sexually, by a permanent lover.

The contrast between the minority of idyllic partnerships and the majority of conflictual ones suggests a difference in temperament and needs between different categories of male homosexual. Psychoanalytic writers have eagerly seized upon the relative rarity of lasting relationships as evidence of the defective character development of homosexuals. For example, Greenspan (1971) argues – on what grounds he fails to make clear – that male homosexuals are rebels without courage, frightened to show their true selves even to their sex partners. By trying to act a role to please the other person, they soon run into boredom and frustration. On the other hand, as homophile writers unceasingly point out, homosexual unions experience less coercion from outside to maintain their status quo. Many heterosexual marriages might break up from boredom or sexual jealousy were it not for the pressure of parental responsibilities, economic constraints and social tradition. The more liberated among homosexual propagandists see no reason to value permanency or exclusiveness in homosexual relationships because that pattern happens to suit heterosexual families. As with so many topics, the information presently available is insufficiently comprehensive or reliable to allow one to dogmatise about a young homosexual's prospects of finding contentment either in a lasting union or in some other mode of living.

One argument against a too-ready acceptance of a gay identity, at least for those who feel they have some choice in the matter, rests upon the belief, shared by many sympathisers with gay liberation, that a homosexual orientation often leads to loneliness and disillusionment in later life (Allen, 1961). Laud Humphreys (1972) remarks upon the discomfiture experienced by older members of the homophile movements when they find themselves ousted by the younger generation and no longer wanted, either sexually or socially. When male homosexual affairs based upon ephemeral sexual attraction reach breaking point, the older partner finds himself on the shelf, still yearning for the solace of sexual companionship, preferably with a younger person, but unable to obtain it. The comforting belief that older people cease to want physical sex expression has been shown to be false. Pfeiffer *et al.* in a follow-up study in America (Palmore, 1970) found that 50 per cent of normal men continued heterosexually active at 72 to 77, and 20 per cent continued so into the 80s and 90s.

In 1973 an English organisation, Age Concern, which campaigns on behalf of old people, brought out a pamphlet about the emotional needs of the retired and elderly. It is a well-documented fact that many old persons retain a desire and a capacity for sexual activity (Felstein, 1973), but the pamphlet mentioned sexual needs only cursorily and made no reference whatever to homosexuality. Struck by this omission, a branch of the Campaign for Homosexual Equality brought out its own Pamphlet (reviewed in *The Times*, 22 March 1974) appealing for some attention to be paid by research workers and social agencies to the needs of ageing homosexuals, especially of the elderly homosexual living alone. Widows and widowers may have their children and other relatives to turn to, but single persons living alone, and especially the many single men with a homosexual orientation, seem particularly vulnerable to loneliness and loss of contact with others of their kind. The compilers of the report had not conducted a systematic survey to substantiate this plausible contention, but they reproduced a number of sad testimonials from elderly men describing their experience. One man wrote: 'As one gets older the sexual drive often diminishes and with it the energy and enthusiasm to continue the hunt. It is so much easier to sit and mope ... Sexual satisfaction through "cottaging" or furtive meetings like ships that pass in the night on public benches or in parks or commons become increasingly hazardous and frustrating as one gets older, not the least because one comes to feel like one of the "dirty old men" of popular mythology ...' Another man, aged 67, wrote: 'It seems to me that there is a generation gap and that older men still appear as the legendary "dirty old man" in view of the young – respect for grey hairs, but not someone to go to bed with. For my part I feel exactly the same as I ever did, but without quite as much of the desperate urgency, and a greater need for companionship, because so many of my former friends have all either died or moved away.'

As further illustration of the frustration of the elderly male homosexual, the CHE report quotes a number of personal advertisements from the newspaper *Gay News*. A typical one read 'Bachelor, 53, tired of wandering and loneliness, 45 miles north of London, longs for permanent loyal friendship with one slightly younger, kind, fond of home, sincere, and intelligent.' This man (like many others who give similar ages in their appeals) has, as the CHE authors rightly comment 'nearly twenty more years left of his "three score years and ten" life span.' An awesome prospect!

But need it always be such doom and gloom? No law prevents old people of either sex sharing accommodation if they can find someone to do so. As one man quoted in the CHE report remarked, homosexuals used to managing independently are perhaps 'better suited to live alone, however desperately lonely it may be, than married persons who on the death of a partner are sometimes overwhelmed'.

Two New York researchers (Francher and Henkin, 1973), who collected life stories from members of the local gay community, made the same point in a different way. They noted that often the homosexual faces and overcomes his worst crisis early in life when his orientation alienates him from the parental home and loses him the support he could otherwise have from relatives. This leads to a building up of independent interests and concerns, free of the usual commitments to heterosexual and family roles, together with stronger links with like-minded peers. Homosexuals may not have families but they often have friends who help them at times of illness or social need. Having never had to adjust to family life, they do not face the difficult readjustments heterosexual men have to make if the role of family man comes to an end in old age.

The previously cited survey by Weinberg and Williams (1974) produced evidence that, in the United States especially (but to a lesser extent in Holland and Denmark), male homosexuals do become isolated with age. Compared with younger homosexuals, those past 45 visit gay bars and clubs less often, have sex less frequently and more often reside alone. On the other hand, they found that older homosexuals worry less about the possibility of exposure of their orientation, less often think of themselves as looking or behaving effeminately, have more settled opinions about themselves, and are less likely to want psychiatric help. This apparent contentment among older homosexuals, in spite of their more restricted sexual life, may reflect a lowering of aspirations, and a willingness to come to terms with the inevitable. Older people make a better adaptation to their situation than young people believe possible. Finally, as the surveys mentioned in Chapter Two go to show (Calleja, 1967; Hader, 1966) age does not deter everyone. Notwithstanding all the supposed obstacles, some men manage in their old age either to revert to homosexual practices or to take them up as a new means of satisfaction.

The inconclusiveness of these reflections brings out the strange ignorance and uncertainty which still surrounds human sexuality and makes generalisation difficult. Most of the important questions remain unanswerable. Is it correct that, on average, male homosexual couples become sexually bored with each other quicker than heterosexual pairs? Is it true that middle aged heterosexual males find pleasure with partners of similar age more readily than do homosexuals? Is it true that homosexuals are more easily 'turned off' by the sight of an ageing body? If these generalisations hold true for male homosexuals, do they also apply to lesbians? Even more fundamental, what governs the association between youth and sexual attractiveness, age and sexual repulsion? How is it that some races, such as the Japanese, enjoy a reputation for finding ageing persons sexually interesting, whereas in England and America such a taste would rank as a perversion and be labelled gerontophilia? None of these questions has been properly researched, though all of them have more importance for human welfare than most of the topics of psychological research encouraged by government patronage and university tradition.

CHAPTER SEVEN

Female Homosexuality

1. The incidence and quality of lesbian sexuality

The male dominated literature on homosexuality has, until recently paid scant attention to lesbianism. Comparatively few surveys have included women subjects, and opinions about the incidence of female homosexuality, its causes, and its effects upon life style and personality, have remained speculative and unreliable. The small amount of scholarly or scientific information available is excellently reviewed by Kenyon (1970; 1974) and some other recent studies have been summarised by Rosen (1974). Inquiries into lesbianism cover much the same topics as those dealing with male homosexuality. The incidence of lesbian orientation, the way it first manifests and subsequently develops, the possibility of hereditary or glandular causes, the influence of parental upbringing, the relationship to masculinity-femininity identifications, the association with personal conflicts and neurotic tendencies, and the manner in which different social systems accommodate lesbians in the community have all been described, discussed and argued, but on the whole with even less conclusiveness than in the case of male homosexuality. Most survey workers have found lesbians less willing and less frank informants than male homosexuals (Saghir and Robins, 1973; Thompson *et al.*, 1973).

Kinsey's figures for the incidence of female homosexuality have been briefly cited already (see p. 12). He found that, by the age of 45, some 13 per cent of women had experienced homosexual contact to the point of orgasm, but this may have been an overestimate, for his sample included an excess of single women. Homosexual activity among Kinsey's female sample was largely confined to the single female and to a lesser extent to those who become widowed or separated. By the age of 40, 24 per cent of the females who had never married had experienced homosexual contacts, compared with only 3 per cent of the married women. Only about a half to two-thirds of the women who had had homosexual contacts had ever reached orgasm by that means. Only 4 per cent of the total sample had had continued involvement in homosexual contacts over more than three years. Even among single women aged 30 or over, although about 18 per cent were to some extent actively homosexual, only about 5 per cent were more or less exclusively lesbian in their habits (Kinsey rating 5 or 6). A permanent and exclusive homosexual orientation appears to be less common among women who identify themselves as lesbians than among men who identify as homosexuals.

Kinsey's approach, which concentrates upon the purely physical aspects of behaviour, has definite limitations, particularly when applied to the study of female sexuality. Women can participate in sexual intercourse while remaining relatively passive and unaroused. Because of the pressure to hold on to husbands for financial support and social status, the heterosexual behaviour of some women may not necessarily correspond to their actual psychological preference. Furthermore, women appear to have a greater propensity than men for forming close, passionate attachments to persons of the same sex without necessarily having physical contact and orgasm, and without categorising the relationship as homosexual. Katharine Davis (1929), who conducted a questionnaire survey of 2,200 women, found that more than a sixth of them had had overt homosexual experiences, but that as many again reported intense emotional relationships falling short of physical contact. Her incidence figures were probably exaggerated by her dependence upon subjects (mostly college graduates) prepared to fill up questionnaires, but there is no reason to doubt her discovery of the importance of emotional relationships. In another American survey by Landis *et al.* (1940), female psychiatric patients were compared with 153 normal females belonging to women's organisations. Among the normal group the incidence of overt homosexuality was 4 per cent and 2 per cent in single and married women respectively, but the incidence of intense emotional attachments was as much as 17 per cent and 30 per cent respectively.

The course of homosexual development runs differently in men and women. In the female, homoerotic fantasies with intense emotional feelings usually precede overt physical contact by a period of years. In a sample of confirmed lesbians in Philadelphia (Hedblom, 1973), 70 per cent reported having been aware of homosexual fantasies before the age of 15, but only 34 per cent had had actual physical experience by that age. As with males, the first contacts usually occur by mutual consent with no clear distinction between seducer and seduced. Again, as with males, the process of 'coming out' into a circle of homosexual friends usually occurs some years after the first overt sexual experiences. In the case of women, however, the coming out process consists of introductions to a circle of special friends rather than, as in the male, entry into gay bars or pick-up places. Hedblom's study confirmed the belief that lesbians have more contact with the heterosexual world than male homosexuals; 90 per cent had 'dated' men during their homosexual careers, and over 50 per cent had had sexual contact with a male. Even so, nearly half of them were living in a stable relationship with another woman at the time. In contrast to male homosexuals, many of whom like 'to play the field', nearly all the lesbians said they preferred a lasting, faithful relationship. The patterns reported by Hedblom reproduce in almost identical form those found in other surveys of lesbians. For example, Saghir and

Robins (1973) noted that 80 per cent of their sample experienced intense emotional attachments, often with an erotic component, before they were 14 years old, although only 24 per cent engaged in overt sexual practices, such as 'necking' or genital manipulation, before they were 15. The translation of a vague awareness of 'being different' into a full realisation of being homosexual tended to occur later in women than in men. The 'coming out' process, when the lesbian discovers the gay network and begins to patronise specialised clubs, or participate in homophile organisations, was often delayed to the mid-20s or later. Many lesbians never took the plunge at all, but stayed on 'within the framework of very few relationships and of very restrained sexual activity' (p. 232).

In the Saghir and Robins survey only about a quarter of the women, compared with almost all of the men, reported having had seven or more 'casual-transient contacts', and most of these had lasted several months, whereas male 'transient' relationships were mostly one-night stands (p. 223). These did occur among the lesbians but were 'the exception rather than the rule' (p. 313). Nearly all of the lesbians had had relationships with another woman involving strong emotional and sexual attachment lasting more than a year, whereas a substantial proportion of male homosexuals (39 per cent) had never had an affair lasting so long. 'During young adulthood (age 20-29), 82 per cent of the females but only 41 per cent of the males were involved in a homosexual relationship lasting more than one year' (p. 225). Once established, however, a stable affair was as likely to last a long time, four years or more, among male homosexuals as among lesbians. Female homosexuals were much more likely than male homosexuals to remain sexually faithful to each other for the duration of the affair, but ultimately the majority of pairs broke up, usually in less than three years. Among the older females, loss of romantic feeling, or the intrusion of a heterosexual interest (a relatively rare event in male homosexual affairs), were the usual reasons given for the break-up of an affair. Among the younger females, however, family pressures and family moves were the commonest reasons for parting.

The relative stability of lesbian relationships was brought out particularly strongly by a survey conducted by the Daughters of Bilitis (1959) using a mailed questionnaire. Failure to reply may have caused some bias, but of the 157 who responded 72 per cent said they were at present living in a stable relationship with another woman. Their relationships lasted on average four to five years. Clearly, the casual, roaming sex adventurer, so common among male homosexuals, is a relative rarity among lesbians, at least among the kind of women who belong to organisations and answer questionnaires.

Saghir and Robins also confirmed the lesbian propensity for heterosexual involvements. Four-fifths of the lesbian group reported having had sexual intercourse with a man. This was more than in the control group of unmarried heterosexual women, only three-fifths of whom had experienced intercourse. Most of the lesbians who had had intercourse with a man had never attained orgasm by that means. This result paralleled the findings of another American survey (Gundlach, 1967), in which three-quarters of the lesbians who were questioned had had intercourse but only a third had attained orgasm. Simple curiosity, or a need to confirm their true sexual preference, impelled many of the lesbians to heterosexual experimentation, but most of them found the experience unrewarding, both emotionally and sexually. Had it turned out differently, of course, they would not have remained lesbians and become members of the survey sample. Even so, 44 per cent of the lesbians had maintained some heterosexual relationship for a year or more. More frequently than homosexual men, lesbians embarked upon marriage, but most became divorced or separated after a year or two. They were also more often prepared to contemplate a marriage of convenience to a homosexual spouse, and more likely to form close friendships with heterosexual persons.

In males, the comparative arousal value of heterosexual and homosexual stimuli is readily assessed by measures of physiological response, notably volume changes in the penis. Various methods of investigating sexual preferences in females by means of physiological measurements have been proposed (Zuckerman, 1971). A device for registering volume changes in the clitoris has been designed by C.T. Tart. Another of the accompaniments of female sexual arousal, swelling and colour changes of the vaginal walls and labia, due to increase in the genital blood flow, can be registered indirectly from increases in the local temperature. Changes in skin temperature in other parts of the body accompany the sex flush that occurs in the majority of women during states of arousal. Alterations in the acidity of vaginal secretions provides yet another possibility for measuring sexual response. So far, these techniques have not been exploited in the interests of research into homosexuality. In addition to the reluctance of lesbian women to participate in physiological investigations, another barrier to this line of inquiry is the relative insensitivity of many women to the pictorial stimuli that commonly evoke a swift response in men. Sooner or later, however, some enterprising investigators will overcome the technical difficulties, and we shall have physical data on the arousability and preferences of homosexual females comparable to those steadily accumulating about males.

Of course simple physiological arousal is only a part of the story in the complex business of human relationships. Sexual fidelity, for example, a quality said to be more characteristic of lesbians than male homosexuals, is less quickly measured.

The importance of the emotional factor 'in female homosexuality has been emphasised by every observer. It came out unusually clearly in a study of American women prisoners by Ward and Kassebaum (1965). Homosexual affairs were much more obvious in women's than in men's prisons, and estimates of the proportion of inmates involved varied from a half to three quarters. Most of these were 'jailhouse turnouts', women who had not been homosexual outside of the prison. The obvious explanation – sex starvation – did not really fit. Incidents of sexual coercion and group assaults, common to male prison homosexuality, were not in evidence. When asked to mark on a list of items which aspect of imprisonment they found hardest to bear very few women (only 5 out of 293 questioned) chose 'lack of sexual contact with men'. The item 'absence of home and family', chosen by 43 per cent, four times as many as chose any other item, was clearly a much more important deprivation. Missing the warmth and support of husbands, lovers and relatives, and lacking the tradition of social rebellion and inmate solidarity which sustains men in prison, these lonely women readily succumbed to sexual proposals from anyone prepared to show an affectionate interest. At least initially, emotional much more than erotic needs governed their reactions.

Opinions and survey findings vary somewhat in regard to the possible influence of early sexual experience. Most investigators seem agreed that the first physical seduction usually occurs in a context of pre-existing emotional or erotic attachment, and cannot be the original cause of a lesbian orientation. Some evidence has been found for the view that unpleasant first experiences with men influence some girls away from heterosexual development. Rosen (1974) considered that the quality of a first sexual experience, whether positive and pleasurable with a woman, or, as in many cases, discomforting and negative with a man, to be an important factor in the confirmation of a lesbian orientation. Kenyon (1968b) found that 41 per cent of lesbians compared with only 25 per cent of heterosexuals said they had, as small girls, been disgusted or frightened by the sexual behaviour of a man.

Although Kenyon's study was carried out in England, the findings resembled those of most American surveys. A total of 123 English, non-patient lesbians, obtained through a homophile organisation, completed an anonymous questionnaire. Only 37 per cent of the lesbians were exclusively homosexual, 58 per cent had had experience of heterosexual intercourse, and 19 per cent had been pregnant. However, a third of the lesbians with experience of heterosexual intercourse reported obtaining no pleasure from it or even postiively disliking it. Only 1.6 per cent of the control group of married women made a similar comment. A half of the currently married lesbians, compared with only 5.7 per cent of the heterosexuals, reported poor sexual adjustment to their husbands. It would seem from this that a number of lesbians participate in heterosexual intercourse for reasons other than strong erotic motivation.

Kenyon also confirmed the relatively late development of homosexuality in the female. In his sample the mean age for first awareness of homosexuality was 16.11 years, 60 per cent of cases being fifteen years or over before experiencing homoerotic feelings. The first physical experience came on average five years later, 40 per cent being aged 20 or more at the time, with a mean age of 21.45

years. In contrast, only 5 per cent of the married women admitted to having been aware of homoerotic feelings at any stage.

As mentioned previously (see p. 23), Kinsey found lesbians' especially in the early stages of their sexual careers, less venturesome in their lovemaking techniques than male homosexuals. Nevertheless, compared with heterosexuals, both lesbians and male homosexuals, perhaps because of their experience with a number of different partners, and the anatomical barrier to conventional intercourse, tend to acquire some sophistication in the use of different methods of stimulation. This could perhaps account for the greater sexual responsiveness of lesbians in comparison with heterosexual women. Charlotte Wolff (1971, p. 55), on the basis of a survey of English lesbians, concluded: 'I have no doubt that lesbianism makes a woman more virile and open to any sexual stimulation, and that more often than not she is a more adequate and lively partner in bed than a "normal" woman.' In his more matter of fact way Kinsey had made the same point when he observed that the proportion of females who reported experiencing satisfactory orgasms was higher among lesbians than among married women.

The relative ease with which lesbians achieve orgasm could be connected with the habit of masturbation. Kenyon (1968b) noted that a much higher proportion (80.5 per cent) of lesbians than of married women (41.5 per cent) admitted they had sometimes indulged in masturbation. Saghir and Robins (1973, p. 216) found that a higher proportion of lesbians (79 per cent) than of single heterosexual women (44 per cent) admitted to masturbation, and on average the onset of the habit was at an earlier age among the lesbians. Some women find manual manipulation more effective in promoting climax than stimulation from the penis. Kinsey noted that among women in general, of those who admitted having masturbated themselves very few, only about 5 per cent, had failed to reach a climax by this means. In contrast, as many as 17 per cent of women who had been married for five years reported that they had never succeeded in achieving orgasm during intercourse with their husbands.

Practice in self stimulation probably facilitates the attainment of orgasm during sexual contacts with other persons, but traditionally the habit has been disapproved of on medical as well as moral grounds. The commonest method of masturbation consists of rhythmic stimulation of the clitoris, and psychoanalytic theorists have long held that this produces a less satisfactory or less 'mature' form of orgasm than vaginal penetration. Freud believed that some women have a physical constitution which predisposes them towards lesbianism. Women endowed particularly strongly with clitoral sensitivity will have a correspondingly reduced interest in being penetrated vaginally and will prefer a more active, masculine method of sexual arousal. Recent evidence, in particular the physiological research of Masters and Johnson (1966), gives no support to these notions. Even among the most heterosexually satisfied women, stimulation of the clitoris plays a crucial part in the neurological reflexes leading to orgasm. Physiologically, female orgasm is a uniform phenomenon which does not vary whether the stimulus that sets if off is directed to clitoris or vagina. The clitoris has a richer supply of sensitive nerve endings than the vagina, and the effectiveness of vaginal intercouse in arousing women depends to a large extent upon the indirect stimulation to the clitoris which occurs during male thrust movements. Seymour Fisher (1973), who investigated the subjective experiences of orgasm in normal married women by means of elaborate interviews and questionnaires, found that his subjects could readily distinguish the quality of the sensations produced by clitoral and vaginal stimulation respectively. The former was more often described as a sharp or exotic sensation, the latter as soothing or comfortable stimulation. The women differed considerably in their preference for one or the other sensation, and this appeared to influence the stimulatory techniques whereby they attained orgasm during marital intercourse. Manual stimulation of the clitoris by the husband before penetration, and again after his ejaculation, was required by many of the women in order to reach a climax. Four-fifths of the women said they sometimes needed a final push from manual stimulation to reach orgasm, and 35 per cent said they needed this more often than not. Among these normal women, no connection was found between a preference for either vaginal or clitoral stimulation and sexual responsiveness, frequency of orgasms, marital harmony or personality factors. In view of these findings one can perhaps forget the theory that a predilection for clitoral stimulation denotes emotional immaturity, sexual maladjustment or lesbian tendency.

In all probability the sexual happiness achieved by some female couples has more to do with psychological than physical attributes. They appreciate each other's emotional needs more directly and intuitively than they can hope to know those of a person of the other sex. Contrary to popular belief, many lesbians show surprising readiness to switch roles in love making, sometimes being the passive 'feminine' recipient and sometimes the active 'masculine' stimulator. This easygoing reciprocity may well contribute to sexual harmony. In her sample, Wolff found that in their dreams and sexual fantasies, as well as in their actual sex exchanges, lesbians enjoyed both male and female roles. She concluded that lesbians differed from heterosexual women in their ease in changing from sexual aggressiveness to feminine surrender and also in the relative rarity of sexual frigidity.

As with male homosexuals, lesbian manners, attitudes and dress styles vary enormously. The majority do not fall easily into either the 'butch' or 'femme' categories. The small minority of swaggering 'dykes', wearing cropped hair and men's fly-buttons and talking in gruff expletives, parody male manners as crudely as mincing fairies parody normal women. These grotesques stand out in the public mind, but in reality modern lesbians are mostly inconspicuous. Indeed, as Charlotte Wolff emphasises, many take special pains to appear feminine to avoid suspicion. In the days when only men's opinions counted, female reformers, political activists and rebels of all kinds, including lesbians, wore severe costumes, felt hats and flat heels as a uniform that had a social rather than a sexual symbolism. A few prominent female couples affecting outstandingly mannish attire – such as the nineteenth-century 'Ladies of Llangollen' (Mavor, 1971), or the lesbian novelist Radclyffe Hall and her friend Una, Lady Troubridge (1963) – may have helped to establish an exaggerated public stereotype. Of course, even today, many lesbians, like many male homosexuals, choose to wear on occasions trendy clothes, faintly suggestive of unconventionality, which are calculated to attract the interest of persons of similar inclinations. In Kenyon's sample, 42.3 per cent of lesbians, compared with only 2.4 per cent of married women, answered 'yes' to the question 'Do you like to dress in male type clothing?' This does not necessarily imply any deep sense of masculine identification. Asked about the qualities they looked for in an ideal sex partner, 28.3 per cent mentioned feminine attributes, 20.2 per cent mentioned masculine attributes.

Saghir and Robins (1973) found that a smaller minority of lesbians than of male homosexuals adopted a consistently masculine or feminine position during love-making. Except among some older women, who tended to become habitually 'male' in their approach, versatility in this respect was the general rule. Some connection was apparent between strong preference for a male position in love-making and a feeling of being unfeminine in personality and attitude, but no significant connection between the common experience of being a tomboy as a child and subsequent sexual practice emerged from this study. On the other hand they did find that lesbians, more often than male homosexuals, thought of themselves as being untypical of their sex in such matters as aggressiveness, choice of clothes, gestures, occupational preferences and social attitudes and interests. Less than half believed themselves 'appropriately feminine', although the vast majority appeared so to outside observers. Over half the lesbians, compared with less than a fifth of heterosexual women, said they had been tomboys as children, avoiding girl playmates, dolls and feminine domestic activities and preferring sports and boys' pursuits. Unlike sissy boys, who constitute a smaller and more socially disapproved minority, these women did not suffer on account of their peculiarity. Moreover, little connection was found between the lesbians' self-assessments of their masculinity or femininity as adults, and their childhood histories of tomboyishness. Only a small minority of the lesbian sample displayed consistently masculine characteristics in their adult social relationships in the heterosexual world, or in their dealings with their sexual partners.

As with so many issues concerning homosexuality, an investigator's views about masculinity – femininity among lesbians seem to depend upon the nature of the sample he has been able to study. Charlotte Wolff, like most investigators who have taken their opinions from present day, middle-class volunteers, plays down the butch-femme dichotomy, but others who have carried out surveys in different social settings sometimes report quite contrary findings. Rita Bass-Hass (1968), who studied a sample of overt lesbians in the community, described a definite division between stud (butch) and fish (femme) types, the former tending to be more importunate in sexual relations, to take the lead socially, and to enjoy some kind of privileged status in the gay pecking order. The 'fish' were judged by themselves and their stud mates to be much like women in a male-dominated heterosexual culture. The ideal 'fish' was young, pretty, successful at securing dates, yet demure and sexually faithful. A 'fish' who slept around too often was soon relegated to the unwanted class of 'sluts', but the studs, who were in a prestigious minority, enjoyed much greater liberty to switch partners at will. The studs tended to be deeply committed to lesbianism, whereas the 'fish' had affairs with men and were apt to be lured away from the gay life. Bass-Hass noted that, as in the case of homosexual men, older lesbians, finding themselves less sought after, tended to retreat into small groups of established couples, and at the same time to abandon the extremes of stud and femme role-playing that had been expected of them as members of the gay scene.

Out of the 195 lesbians in the Bass-Hass survey, 120 were white Americans and 75 non-whites. The contrasts between these two groups provided another instance of external social pressures determining lesbian patterns. Most of the white lesbians came from over-protective, sexually restrictive homes. They had never tried, or been encouraged, to form liaisons with men. Their earliest sexual relationships, usually beginning between the ages of 17 and 22, were with women. The non-whites came from sexually permissive homes, often with an absent father and a mother openly involved with a series of men. They tended to have considerable heterosexual experience in their 'teens, but to turn away from men in their early twenties. By this time they had come to view the males in their black community, possibly realistically, as harsh, exploitative, unfaithful and economically undependable. They turned to lesbianism in their late twenties in the hope of finding relationships more companionable and secure than those they had experienced in the heterosexual world.

Ethel Sawyer (1965, quoted in Karlen, 1971) also studied black lesbians. Her subjects came from a very overt, gay-bar setting in St. Louis. It was a world of 'pugnacious studs and flirtatious fish', with a great deal of enraged jealousy manifest in fights, stabbings and suicides. Really long-lasting affairs, of five years or more, were exceptional. 'Friends were often only waiting for the right time to pounce on each other's lovers.' When Sawyer concluded her investigation, only one of the subjects had kept to the same partner throughout the duration of the inquiry.

Sawyer's sample came from an extremely deviant setting, but observers of more conventional lesbian affairs have commented on the stormy, hot-house atmosphere that so often prevails. Charlotte Wolff commented forcibly on the extreme jealousy of many lesbian couples. 'They guarded each other like prison warders' (p. 151). This often led to aggression, which 'is more extensive and more intense in lesbians than in heterosexual women'. Wolff described the scenes of alcoholic violence she had witnessed, involving interventions by doctors or police. She concluded that aggressiveness, both constructive and destructive, is an important characteristic of the lesbian personality. It manifests constructively in intellectual freedom, social independence, concern for women's rights, and rejection of exploitation as a sex object, but also destructively in jealous rages and possessiveness. The stressfulness of lesbian relationships arises from the strength of the emotional tie, from the absence of the wider responsibilities and commitments present in a heterosexual marriage, and, of course, from the self-questioning and defensiveness of persons who have to conceal their true selves from a disapproving society.

2. *Lesbianism ancient and modern*

Observations of primitive communities and of animals tend to support the belief that overt homosexuality occurs less often in the female than in the male. In their survey of sexual behaviour in primitive communities, Ford and Beach (1952) found far less evidence of lesbianism than of male homosexual practices. The apparent difference might be attributed to the unobtrusiveness of female sexual habits, especially when the investigators happen to be Western males, but this explanation would not account for the scarcity in society of institutionalised methods for coping with lesbians analogous to those used for male homosexuals. In the history of Western civilisation, the laws against homosexuality have almost always been directed at males. In primitive communities with institutionalised systems for the ceremonial changing of an individual's sex role, it seems to be much more often men who assume women's clothes and functions rather than the other way around. The Mohave Indians studied by Devereux (1937) were exceptional in permitting public sex reversals for both men and women and in openly sanctioning female homosexuality. In animal studies, as was mentioned earlier (see p. 116) sexual pairing of females is relatively uncommon among primates, and when it occurs it does not usually lead to orgasm (Kinsey, 1953, p. 449), although recent observation of stumptail monkeys shows that it certainly can do so (Chevalier-Skolnikoff, 1974).

Historical records contain many fewer references to lesbianism than to male homosexuality. Although both receive mention in classical literature, the attention paid to male sexuality is much greater, but of course masculine affairs generally were regarded as more worthy of notice. In male-dominated societies, as in Greece (Licht, 1926), lesbian activities in the women's quarters seem to have been treated with an amused tolerance, so long as they did not interfere with masculine satisfactions. This could reflect a masculine undervaluation of female sexuality, but it might also stem from the prurient interest taken by males in lesbian behaviour. To this day, pornographic materials intended for heterosexual males commonly depict scenes of group sex in which the women, but not the men, are involved with each other as well as with the opposite sex.

Literary and historic references to lesbianism are frequently cited by writers wanting to show the importance of the homosexual minority in both sexes. Damon and Stuart (1967) compiled an extensive bibliography on the lesbian in literature. A scholarly and historic review of the subject has been produced by Jeanette Foster (1958), sometime librarian to the Institute of Sex Research at Indiana University. Unfortunately a great many literary works, fictional and otherwise, are most untrustworthy as sources of impartial information. Many of the books about lesbians have been written by men to satisfy the prurience of male readers, or to propagate the moral dogma that lesbians are miserable, depraved creatures (Wysor, 1974).

Surviving fragments of Sappho's poetry are the earliest literary records of lesbian love. Born about 612 B.C. to a distinguished family, she lived at Mitylene on the island of Lesbos. She ran an establishment that was in effect a finishing school where she taught young ladies of quality the arts of music, verse and dance. Her poems of romantic passion, addressed to young ladies, avoid describing specific sexual acts, but the lesbian feelings come through explicitly enough (Sappho, 1965). She was probably not an exclusive lesbian, since she married and had a daughter, Kleis, to whom she was devoted. Some authorities have tried to picture her sentiments as purely romantic, without lewd connotations, but the burning of her works by the early Christian authorities suggests that her reputation as the prophetess of female homosexuality is not without foundation (Foster, 1958; Weigall, 1933).

Literary commentaries on lesbianism have been, from earliest times, more critical than complimentary. In Juvenal's sixth *Satire* lesbian practices are associated with courtesans, prostitutes and general debauchery. He depicts women of the highest rank competing with prostitutes in tests of erotic skill and endurance during sexual acts with each other. In the romantic literature of the middle ages, the occasional lesbian theme appears in the guise of a woman masquerading as a man and thus arousing forbidden passion. In the Italian story *Orlando Furioso* by Ariosto (1907), first published in 1531, Bradamante, a young female Amazon type, puts on armour and rivals the male knights in deeds of bravery. A young princess falls for her, thinking her to be a man, and continues to pine for her even after her true sex is revealed. The situation is saved by a double masquerade. Bradamante's twin brother, impersonating Bradamante, visits the princess, who welcomes him to her bed, where she discovers the convenient sex change, which the brother explains away as a piece of magic. Sir Philip Sidney (1912) published a similar story in English in about 1590. The hero dresses up as an Amazon to gain access to a beautiful princess. She conceives a passion for him, but believing him to be a woman, is tormented by the seemingly unnatural direction of her feelings.

In the seventeenth and eighteenth centuries, references to lesbianism became more realistic and also more scandalous, especially in continental writings. In 1665 Brantôme (1933) published a colourful portrayal of the goings on at the French court where sexual morals were apparently extremely free, lesbian attachments very much taken for granted, and bisexual philandering commonplace. Works purporting to reveal the sexual irregularities of officially celibate nuns are well exemplified by the novel *La Religieuse*, by Diderot (1938), first released in 1796, but actually written some years before the revolution of 1789. The story, in autobiographical style, describes the struggles of an illegitimate girl, forced into a convent by her family, to withstand the onslaughts of a lesbian Mother Superior.

From the nineteenth century onwards, realism becomes more fashionable in literature, and authors strive to depict homosexuality as it appears in everyday life and as it is experienced by ordinary people. Some of the best-known writers, especially in France, have made the attempt, but, as Jeannette Foster (1958, p. 549) aptly put it: 'Even the best authors are scarcely able to free their work of all controversial overtones ... Negative writing ... manipulates circumstances to the end that variant experience shall always prove disastrous.' Moreover, the defenders of homosexuality do little better. 'Fearing public opinion too much to betray unqualified sympathy, they, too, strain circumstance to prevent their appealing characters from enjoying happiness.' One of the most famous novels of Emil Zola, *Nana*, portrays a heterosexual heroine gradually drawn into an underworld of interlinked prostitution and lesbianism, and finally engaging in an active lesbian love affair which ends with the premature death of one of the participants. Balzac, in the story of *The Girl with the Golden Eyes*, tells of a mysterious and sequestered beauty who displays so much voluptuous sophistication that her lover puzzles over the fact that he found her a virgin. Her sexual experience actually derives from an affair with a wealthy and jealous lesbian who has kept her shut away. This woman, discovering the girl's infidelity, kills her in a jealous rage. As an added twist to the tragedy, the rival lover and the lesbian prove to be half-brother and sister.

In a more modern setting, Sinclair Lewis (1933), in the novel *Ann Vickers*, describes an equally morbid situation. A smart woman executive pursues and seduces a character called Eleanor, who has been through an exhausting series of casual affairs. Once having secured Eleanor, the woman loses interest and turns her attentions to other females. The situation drives Eleanor into a neurotic decline and eventually to suicide.

For a more understanding and less tortured account of lesbian affairs one has to turn, perhaps not unnaturally, to women authors, and most notably to the *Claudine* novels of Colette. At school, the young Claudine falls for a pretty young woman teacher, but the lesbian headmistress has her eye on the same one, so Claudine finds herself abandoned. Later, Claudine marries a man considerably older than herself. When she develops a passion for another married woman, her husband is so compliant as to provide the two of them with a secret love nest. Claudine then discovers her husband making use of the nest and of her woman friend for himself. After a stormy interlude, their marriage settles down to a happier if more conventional mould, untroubled by further sexual indiscretions.

Contemporary biographers, novelists, playwrights and film makers have become at least as frank in their treatment of lesbianism as in the presentation of male homosexuality. Nigel Nicolson (1973), for example, used his late mother's diary to enliven his biography of his famous parents, Vita Sackville-West and Harold Nicolson, with accounts of her tempestuous lesbian love affairs. Some of the modern dramas on the topic, such as *The Killing of Sister George* (Marcus, 1965) have consisted of somewhat stereotyped and unsympathetic presentations of butch and femme characters, but others, such as the recent French film *Emmanuelle*, depict lesbianism much more as the modern liberation movements might wish, namely as an enjoyable and legitimate alternative form of erotic fulfilment.

3. *Personality problems and parental background*

Most writers who base their views upon clinical experience with patients or offenders conclude that lesbians are generally unstable and neurotic (Bergler, 1951; Bacon, 1956; Caprio, 1954; Kirkham, 1966; McDougall, 1970; Romm, 1965; Wilbur, 1965). For the most part such views have been based upon individual case reports, or have reflected the general impressions gained by therapists in their dealings with lesbian patients. Swanson *et al.* (1972) tried to be more systematic. They compared 40 women seeking psychiatric treatment who admitted to lesbian interests and experiences with 40 female heterosexual patients of similar age attending the same clinic for working women, with the same psychiatric diagnoses – mostly anxiety, depression or personality disorder. The lesbian patients differed from the heterosexual patients in having a higher incidence of drug or alcohol abuse and attempted suicide. They frequently reported disorganisation and conflict in their parental homes. Very few described their parents in favourable terms, and 75 per cent felt their parents had rejected them. They were, however, no worse in this respect than the heterosexual patients. Conflict with parents loomed large in the histories of all categories of patient, and was not a distinguishing feature of the lesbian group.

Studies based upon patient groups have great difficulty in distinguishing between characteristics arising from a neurotic disposition and characteristics intrinsic to lesbianism itself. To avoid this problem investigators in recent years have carried out surveys of non-patient lesbians recruited from the community, usually with the aid of homophile organisations. The result of some of the reports that have appeared in Anglo-American periodicals are summarised in the following table:

Some Published Surveys of Lesbians
(Based upon women who were not psychiatric patients)

INVESTIGATOR	SAMPLE	METHOD	FINDINGS
Liddicoat, 1961	50 non-patient lesbians from the community (in S. Africa) compared with 50 women from a research institute	Interviews	Lesbians more often came from disruptive or unhappy parental homes. Lesbians as a group not more neurotic, or socially unreliable, but more prone to anxiety
Armon, 1960	30 non-patient lesbians and a matched group of mothers whose children were participating in an educational research project	Personality testing (Rorschach and figure drawing)	Few clear-cut differences in personality traits in the lesbians as a whole, but a significant tendency to aggressive attitudes and unfavourable evaluation of the female role. Projective tests of little use in identifying individuals of lesbian orientation
Bene, 1965a	37 lesbians from a homophile organisation, 80 married women from a market research organisation	Family Relations Test, interviews	Lesbians more often hostile towards and afraid of their fathers or describe him as weak and incompetent. Parents more often said to have wished for a son
Kenyon, 1968a, 1968b	123 lesbians from a homophile organisation, 123 married members of women's organisation	Personality testing (Maudsley Inventory, Cornell Medical Index)	Lesbians rather higher on neuroticism, but nowhere approaching the level of neurotic patient groups. Lesbians had poorer work records, more frequently reported poor relationships with father or mother and discord in parental home;

INVESTIGATOR	SAMPLE	METHOD	FINDINGS
Kenyon, 1968a, 1968b (cont.)			lesbians more often suffered from depression and reported frightening sex experiences with a male in early life
Freedman, 1968	62 lesbians from the Daughters of Bilitis group and 67 women from a volunteer national service organisation	Personality tests (Personal Orientation Inventory, Eysenck Personality Inventory)	Lesbians not more neurotic or less socially adjusted, but more independent, inner-directed and less rigid than heterosexuals
Gundlach and Riess, 1968	202 middle-class lesbians from a homophile organisation, 206 heterosexual women of similar educational level	Questionnaire	Lesbians less neurotic and better socialised, more often only children
Kremer and Rifkin, 1969	25 adolescent girls suspected of lesbianism by teachers	Interview	Fathers hostile, detached, exploitative. Mothers overburdened, ineffectual
Saghir and Robins, 1969, 1971, 1973	57 lesbian members of a homophile organisation, 43 single heterosexual women	Interview	Greater prevalence of alcoholism and attempted suicide among lesbians, but no significant difference in the prevalence of neurotic disorders
Hopkins, 1969	24 lesbians from a homophile organisation, 24 heterosexual women	Interviews, personality testing (Cattell 16PF)	Lesbians more independent, resilient, self-sufficient; not necessarily more neurotic
Wolff, 1971	108 lesbians, mostly middle-class, obtained through homophile groups and 123 women of similar social class from public organisations	Interviews, biographies, questionnaire	Lesbians more aggressive, tense, less socially adaptable, more erotic, more often from parental homes with unloving father, indifferent mother, more often only or elder child, more often say parents would have preferred a son

INVESTIGATOR	SAMPLE	METHOD	FINDINGS
Thompson *et al.* 1971, 1973	84 non-patient lesbians and a group of 94 presumptively heterosexual women volunteers matched for age and education	Personality and attitude tests (Adjective Check List, Semantic Differential)	No important differences in personal adjustment or self evaluation. Lesbians more self confident than heterosexuals, more often report unsatisfactory relationship with father, more often distant from both parents
Wilson and Green, 1971	100 lesbian volunteers and 100 matched heterosexual women	Eysenck Neuroticism Scale, California Personality Inventory	Lesbians lower on neuroticism, higher on dominance, endurance and intellectual efficiency
Loney, 1972, 1973	11 non-patient lesbian friends of a student, 12 heterosexual women friends	Elias Family Adjustment Test	Lesbians mostly living in homosexual marriages, 36% had sought treatment for homosexuality. Unfavourable comments about parents, particularly fathers, frequent
Siegelman, 1972b	84 non-patient lesbians from homophile groups and 84 female students who identified themselves as heterosexual	Personality testing (Schier and Cattell Neuroticism Scales, Crowne and Marlow Social Desirability Scale)	Lesbians in some respects better adjusted, lower on depression, higher on self-acceptance, not more neurotic
Rosen, 1974	26 lesbians from the Daughters of Bilitis	Questionnaire and Adjective Check List	Lesbians within the range of normality for personal adjustment and selfesteem, but some tendency to be unduly anxious and not to enjoy life to the fullest extent. Most felt closer to their mother than their father, but critical descriptions of both parents were quite frequent

The results of these surveys might have been expected to provide an immediate answer to the question whether lesbianism is a personality disturbance or a healthy alternative to heterosexual living. In point of fact, the results appear at first sight so much at variance with each other as to cast doubt upon the reliability of psycho-social research methods. Some of the findings suggest that lesbians fall comfortably within the normal range as regards personal adjustment, and may even be on average slightly superior to heterosexuals in such qualities as self-reliance and independence. Other findings suggest that lesbians are often unhappy and neurotic individuals driven into sexual non-conformity by their own personality problems.

The difficulties in the way of obtaining a representative sample account for some of the differences in results. Older studies which used as subjects prisoners, prostitutes and mental patients biassed their results in the direction of a high incidence of character abnormality and social maladjustment. Modern studies based on student volunteers or members of homophile organisations introduce a different bias, this time towards the more vocal, better-educated and socially assertive types. As Loney (1972) points out, the policy of eliminating all subjects who have had contact with treatment agencies may produce a sample of untypically healthy (or perhaps defensive) individuals. Samples easily recruited from visible and cooperative sources, such as gay student groups, will inevitably under-represent socially isolated individuals who might feel too frightened or ashamed to volunteer as subjects for research.

Apart from variations produced by sampling difficulties, the use of personality tests creates additional problems. Tests provide some protection against the inevitable personal bias introduced when interviewers record their own subjective judgments about clients, but they have their disadvantages. Responses are apt to be affected by the subjects' intelligence, educational background, understanding of the matters the tests seek to probe, relationship to the investigator and attitude towards the supposed purpose of the inquiry. To match lesbian subjects and heterosexual control subjects in all these respects is virtually impossible.

Test scores deviant from the average for heterosexuals do not always imply abnormality or inferiority. Hopkins (1969), who used Cattell's 16 Personality Factor Test with 24 lesbians, found significant personality differences, but not necessarily to the discredit of the lesbian sample. All but one of her subjects came from an English lesbians' organisation (The Minorities Research Group), and each was paired with a heterosexual woman of similar age, occupational group and intelligence rating. The lesbians produced scores indicating that, as a group, they were significantly more independent, resilient, reserved, dominant, bohemian, self-sufficient, and composed than the heterosexual women. Apart from the quality of reserve (derived from Factor A, indicative of a detached, critical, cool, 'schizothymic' tendency) most of these items would count as deviations in the direction of superiority rather than inferiority – unless of course one prefers women to be subdued, conformist and dependent. Hopkins carefully refrained from speculating as to the cause of the differences.

Freedman (1968) found lesbians more candid in their responses than heterosexuals, as indicated by lower scores on Eysenck's lie scale, and also more self-accepting and aggressive. Wilson and Green (1971) found lesbians actually less 'neurotic' on the Eysenck scale than the heterosexual controls and also more competent and dominant. Siegelman (1972b) also found lesbians less 'neurotic', less 'depressive', more goal-directed and more self-accepting than heterosexual women. Giannell (1966), who interviewed and tested a sample of lesbians contacted in homosexual bars in Toledo, Ohio, commented upon their poor sense of reality, which enabled them to behave as if social conventions did not exist, their lack of inhibition, which enabled them to pursue a homosexual life-style without moral qualms, and their frustrating life histories, which impelled them to seek outlets for aggression, independence and non-conformity. Compared with a group of college girls of similar age on their responses to the Edwards Personal Preference Schedule, the lesbians appeared to have a high need for nurturance, autonomy and aggression and a low need for deference. Whether these characteristics reflect maladjustment, as Giannell obviously thought, or valuable qualities of social assertiveness, as gay liberationists might claim, is a matter of taste. As Riess *et al.* (1974) point out in a recent review, studies using personality questionnaires for the most part reveal lesbians as certainly not neurotic and on the whole more dominant, autonomous and self-assertive than heterosexual women, in fact more like the ideal male. Unfortunately, such results cannot tell us whether the quality of social unorthodoxy typifies lesbians in general or merely those who join a homophile organisation, or whether the quality of independence is part of the lesbian's underlying character, or a result of experience in managing her affairs without a male partner.

Perhaps the most important conclusion from the application of personality tests is the absence of any clear evidence for a generalised neurotic disturbance among lesbians. Even where studies have found some degree of neurotic tendency among non-patient lesbians (Kenyon, 1968a, 1968b) the scores have been less anomalous than those typically produced by neurotic patients.

The insensitivity of standardised personality tests, or their inapplicability to the relevant areas of disturbance, might account for their failure to detect the personality defects supposedly associated with a lesbian orientation. Scepticism concerning the mental health of the lesbian population has been expressed by investigators who have concerned themselves with factual information about lesbian attitudes and way of life as revealed in extensive interviews or questionnaires. Virtually every investigator has reported that lesbians, more often than heterosexuals, tend to describe disruptive or unhappy parental homes and conflict-ridden childhood relationships with their parents. This feature holds true not only for patient groups, but also for lesbians who are living normally in the community and showing no overt disturbance (Bene, 1965a; Kenyon, 1968b; Thompson *et al.*, 1973; Loney, 1973; Wolff, 1971; Siegelman, 1974b: Rosen, 1974).

In Siegelman's survey, 63 non-patient lesbians were compared with 68 heterosexual women, using the Parent-Child Relations Questionnaire (Short Form 2). In comparison with heterosexuals, lesbians described a greater degree of psychological distance from both father and mother, less family security and more friction between parents. The more distant relationships reported by lesbians could not be explained as a consequence of neurotic tendency. The difference still held true even after all but the more stable women (identified by low scores on neuroticism test) were eliminated from the analysis.

In the survey of Saghir and Robins (1973) 44 per cent of the lesbians (compared with only 17 per cent of the heterosexual women) described their parents as always quarrelling or drinking heavily. Very significantly more of the lesbians than of the heterosexual women had lost a parent by divorce before reaching the age of 10. Most of the lesbians had poor relationships with their mothers and tended to identify with their fathers, the reverse of the trend reported by heterosexual women. The authors (p. 302) see this evidence as for an association between homosexuality and difficult childhood relationships with parents, but they point out that the parents may not be solely responsible. The temperamental peculiarities of the pre-homosexual child, the tomboyish girl for example, may exacerbate the strains within the family, inviting parental rejection, which in turn has an unfavourable effect upon the child's personality development.

In Kenyon's survey the great majority of married women (83.7 per cent) but only a minority of lesbians (46.3 per cent), answered 'yes' when asked if their parents were happily married. Very few married women (0.8 per cent), but a substantial proportion of lesbians (21.1 per cent) said they got on poorly with their mothers. A much higher proportion of lesbians than of married women reported poor relations with father (30 per cent compared with 8 per cent). Charlotte Wolff (1971) obtained similar results. As many as 37.0 per cent of lesbians in her survey, compared with only 9.8 per cent of heterosexual women, described their mothers in terms suggestive of indifference or outright negligence. Thirteen per cent of lesbians had neglectful fathers compared with only 2.4 per cent of heterosexual women. Eva Bene (1965a) found that, to a very significant extent, lesbians were more often hostile towards and afraid of their fathers, and also less affectionate towards their mothers than heterosexual women. In a more recent survey by Poole (1972) in which a questionnaire was administered to 50 heterosexual women and 50 self-admitted lesbians, 44 per cent of the lesbians, compared with only 10 per cent of the controls, recalled their mothers as having been lacking in affection and understanding. Only 4 per cent of heterosexuals compared with 36 per cent of lesbians thought their mothers had been unhappy in their marital or maternal roles. Whereas a majority, 68 per cent, of the lesbians, recalled their mothers as disapproving of sex, only 28 per cent of the heterosexual women did so. While confirming the presence of parental disturbance of one kind or another, these empirical surveys do not, on the whole, bear out the psychoanalytic theory that poor relationships with father are more characteristic of lesbians than poor relationships with mother.

Kenyon reported that 28 per cent of lesbians, compared with only 10 per cent of controls, thought that their parents would have preferred a boy. Bene (1965a) and Gundlach and Riess (1967) also found parental wish for a son a significant distinguishing feature of their lesbian samples. Charlotte Wolff (1971, p. 119) noted that the mothers of lesbians, more often than the mothers in her control group, showed undue preference for their sons. Wolff commented that a girl's realisation that her mother would have preferred her to be a male may have a particularly injurious effect. She concluded: 'These maternal attitudes strike at the very root of a daughter's being, and are an essential cause of the development of lesbianism.'

Parental regret at having produced a girl rather than a boy does not mean that they would necessarily wish the girl to act like a boy, although that might be how the child interprets the situation. In Kenyon's survey all the married women and the majority of the lesbians (81 per cent) thought they had been brought up and treated by their parents as a girl. Even so, that left a significant minority of lesbians who thought otherwise.

Psychiatrists believe that unhappy home life as a child, and poor parental relationships, are the cause of much unhappiness, character defect, and even mental breakdowns in later life. In view of the evidence that many lesbians have been exposed to this misfortune, it would be surprising if the experience left no scars. In point of fact, there are indications in some of the surveys that lesbians do tend to suffer more than heterosexual women from psychiatric complaints, particularly depression. In Kenyon's questionnaire study, 19.5 per cent of the lesbians, compared with only 5.7 per cent of the controls, reported having had a 'nervous breakdown' in the past. Nearly 5 per cent of the lesbians, but only 0.8 per cent of the controls had required in-patient treatment for their illness. 'Depression' was much the most common form of breakdown. Charlotte Wolff found that her lesbians differed very significantly from heterosexual women in their greater liability to react badly to stress, by losing their composure and emotional equilibrium. Of course none of this proves that lesbians have a particularly morbid susceptibility to neurosis. Heterosexuals might have just as many breakdowns if they were exposed to the difficulties that lesbians have to contend with in society. Kenyon recorded that similar proportions of lesbians and heterosexuals (26.9

per cent and 27.7 per cent) reported having had one or more neurotic traits, such as nightmares and phobias, during childhood. This could be interpreted as evidence that, before the malevolent effects of social rejection take their toll, lesbians are no more neurotic than heterosexuals.

Saghir and Robins (1973, p. 270) found practically no difference between lesbians and heterosexual women on various indicators of personality make-up. For instance the proportions of women whose answers implied inability to express anger, poor self-confidence, inner tensions, low self-esteem, avoidance of competitive situations, or feelings easily hurt, were similar in both groups. Although they had excluded from the sample anyone with a history of hospitalisation for psychiatric disorder, 37 per cent of the lesbians had had psychotherapy at some stage, compared with 26 per cent of the heterosexual controls. More strikingly, they found that 35 per cent of the lesbians, compared with only 5 per cent of the heterosexuals, were or had been excessive drinkers or definite alcoholics. Otherwise, psychiatric symptoms, such as anxiety states, depressive reactions and pre-menstrual depression, were no commoner in lesbians than among heterosexuals. They did have, however, a slightly greater incidence of attempted suicide, 12 per cent as opposed to 5 per cent, usually during a depressive episode following the break up of a romantic relationship.

Whatever one's views of the strengths and weaknesses of the lesbian character in general, there is little doubt that for some young girls homosexual behaviour represents a blind groping in any direction that promises some assurance of love in a predominantly hostile world. Criminologists have shown that rootless adolescent boys from broken, disordered or rejecting homes, who lack firm goals or sense of identity, often seek a solution in the world of delinquency, dedicating themselves to beating the system by thieving and skiving. Girls from similar backgrounds often take to unconventional sex lives, dedicating themselves to promiscuity, prostitution and lesbianism (Cowie *et al.*, 1968). In a survey of clients of a day centre for homeless girls, Timms (1968, p. 34) reported that, out of a group of 38 girls, aged 16 to 21, as many as 23 volunteered the information that they believed themselves to be lesbian, 8 had illegitimate pregnancies or were pregnant, and all save one admitted to illicit drug-taking. The chaotic sexuality which characterised these rootless adolescents was illustrated in a number of case histories quoted in the pamphlet. One of these described Eileen, a girl of 21, the child of quarrelsome and long-separated parents. Although mannish in appearance and attire, experienced in numerous lesbian affairs, and never at a loss for money from her female admirers to meet her immediate needs, she still dreamed of being a mother. She became pregnant, as a result, she said, of intercourse with a stranger while she was drunk. She had ideas of keeping the child with the help of her latest lesbian partner. In view of her impulsiveness, lack of means and the instability of her relationships the prospect seemed highly unrealistic. The eventual outcome of the situation was never fully revealed, because she suddenly made off, and the social workers never heard from her again.

The 25 lesbian schoolgirls, aged 12 to 17, studied by Kremer and Rifkin (1969) presented a similar picture of chaotic social and sexual life. Most of them belonged to a 'bathroom gang' who aggressively molested other girls in the toilets at their school. They came from broken-down homes in a poor neighbourhood of New York. Unlike middle-class lesbians who complain of over-intense parental relationships, 18 of the girls had fathers who were dead, separated or unknown, and most of their mothers were overburdened, inadequate and rejecting. Two had experienced incest with a father or step father, and most of them had good reason for regarding their substitute fathers with fear or hostility. Their lesbian proclivities comprised only one aspect of all-embracing disturbance, manifest in unruly, aggressive behaviour and serious personality problems.

4. *Theories of causation*

Biological causes for lesbianism cannot be dismissed, but from the few investigations that have taken physical factors into account little positive evidence has emerged. The old surveys of body build by Henry (1941) and his collaborator Galbraith, from which he concluded that lesbians tend to have broad shoulders and narrow hips, indicative of an immature form of skeletal development, have never been confirmed. Kenyon (1970) who depended upon measurement made by the subjects themselves found no consistent difference between lesbians and controls except for shorter average height in the former. Endocrinological influences have been discussed earlier (see p. 63). The weight of present evidence favours the view that increased androgenic hormones may heighten female sexual responsiveness, and possibly induce active, tomboyish behaviour in girls, but does not cause lesbian orientation. The literature on homosexuality in female twins is very scanty (Pardes *et al.* 1967), but the existence of recorded cases of identical twin pairs, one lesbian and the other not (Koch, 1965; Parker, 1964) shows that environmental influences can override an hereditary predispostion.

Debate about the causes of lesbianism mostly centres upon psychological factors and environmental influences. As in the case of male homosexuality, psychoanalytic theorists have advanced a large number of imaginative and complicated hypotheses which are exceedingly difficult either to verify or to disprove. Freud's main contributions to the subject appear in his case reports of homosexuality in women (1905b; 1920), and in his later discussions of female sexuality (1925, 1931). According to psychoanalytic theory, all children have their first experience of a love relationship with their mothers. In boys, this situation persists throughout the Oedipal phase of childhood, during which father becomes a hated rival and mother the object of libidinal desires. Incest taboo, and the fear of punishment by castration, serve to prise the boy away from his mother so he can fall in love with other women. In contrast, girls start life in an inverted Oedipal situation, clinging to the parent of the same sex, and viewing father as a rival. Freud had some trouble in explaining how the girl transfers her feelings from mother to father and ultimately to other men. He believed that the distress girls suffer when they discover that they lack a penis, their anger, resentment and sense of inferiority, cause them to blame mother for the situation. They may believe that she has castrated them as a punishment for masturbation. They therefore turn to father for consolation.

According to Freudian theory, continuing penis envy is responsible for many of the peculiarities of feminine psychology, from resentment of supposed masculine superiority, to the desire to engulf, incorporate and thus to possess the penis. As one possible consequence of penis envy, a girl may identify so closely with her father as to become effectively a phallic male figure herself, pursuing other women in imitation of him. On the other hand, if she feels rejected or abused by her father during the Oedipal phase, a girl may regress back to the earlier and comparatively blissful union with her mother. This paves the way for a permanent rejection of men because she can never trust them to provide the depth of love and security available from a mother or mother substitute. Anthony Storr (1964) believes this yearning for a substitute mother, upon whom they can lean with child-like dependence, impels some lesbians to form partnerships that are doomed to failure because they are based upon unrealistic and unattainable demands and expectations.

Numerous elaborations of these themes advanced by different psychoanalysts have been summarised by such writers as Khan (1964) and Socarides (1968), but they are too complicated and confusing to attempt to review them systematically here. If either a boy or girl develops a too intense Oedipal attachment to the parent of the opposite sex, guilt and fear associated with the incest taboo may cause a revulsion against all heterosexual situations. In girls, the difficulties may begin even earlier. Because they must first renounce their primary source of love and nurture in order to transfer libidinal yearnings to the father, girls tend to enter the Oedipal phase later than boys. The prolonged period of exclusive and dependent attachment to mother colours to a considerable extent subsequent sexual attitudes. If the experience with mother has been frustrating, so that resentful and ambivalent feelings carry over into the Oedipal phase, this makes for a sensitive and turbulent paternal relationship, and consequent risk of regression to maternal and feminine attachments.

It would seem that intense, ambivalent maternal relationships feature prominently in the development of homosexuality in both sexes. Lesbians are not usually so dramatically father-bound as male homosexuals are so often mother-bound. Apparent hostility to father is very common. Helena Deutsch (1944) suggested that a brutal and sadistic father may induce a revulsion against all men and a search for relationships analogous to the original mother-child situation when father was excluded. On the other hand, superficial antagonism may conceal deep attachment. Catherine Bacon (1956) believed that some women seek refuge in lesbianism because they fear to arouse father's anger by showing preference for another man. Regression to an infantile maternal fixation often involves a reawakening of extremely hostile feelings derived from periods of helpless dependency and murderous aggression towards the mother, who can be powerfully threatening and punishing as well as a source of all-embracing love. The explosively aggressive quality of lesbian loves has been held to reflect the aggressive elements in the original mother-daughter relationship. Socarides (1968, p. 70) states unequivocally: 'In all homosexual women there is an intense unconscious aggressive murderous hatred against the mother and reproachful feelings towards the father.' In their lesbian affairs, women re-enact the mother-child situation, some taking the part of the active, caring mother managing her child, others adopting the role of passive yet selfishly demanding and chronically unsatisfied child. These are just two possible patterns among a total of nine 'clinical types' of lesbian described by Socarides. In a previous generation, Ernest Jones (1927) had listed three. First, the women who crave acceptance as a man among men, who often complain bitterly of the injustice of male dominated society. Secondly, those who enjoy femininity vicariously through other women, though they cannot accept to be feminine themselves. Thirdly, those who cannot tolerate penetration by a man's penis, though they seek analogous forms of stimulation by another woman. Jones explains all three attitudes as alternative forms of denial of femininity, arising from a too-close identification with father.

Among the welter of psychoanalytic ideas and interpretations the importance of early upbringing stands out clearly, but no single pattern of family disturbance emerges as the main cause of lesbianism. In reviewing the psychodynamic theories Cornelia Wilbur (1965) cites no less than 16 different factors, among them father fixation or mother fixation, childhood seduction (real or imagined), penis envy, paternal seductiveness, paternal rejection, maternal absence, witnessing parents in sexual intercourse, sibling rivalry, a continuation of childhood bisexuality, tomboy interests, disillusionment with father (because he is weak or domineering), inability to identify with mother (because she is hostile or competitive), fear of the consequences of heterosexual intercourse (such as unwanted pregnancy, injury from vaginal penetration, venereal disease), fixation on the clitoris due to masturbation, and finally social segregation of the sexes and social taboos about mixing with males resulting in the first sex contacts being homosexual.

Until much more painstaking research has been done one explanation seems about as good as another. No doubt innumerable pressures impinge upon the development of sexual orientation, and no one factor is likely to provide a sole and sufficient cause. The outcome in any particular individual, which must depend upon a balance of interacting influences, is not necessarily a simple black-or-white distinction. More often than male homosexuals, many lesbians are neither totally exclusive nor permanently fixed in their sexual preference. The effect of counterbalancing influences later in life, and the prospects of change for those who wish it, are topics rarely included in discussions of causation, but they are of great practical importance and will be considered in a later chapter.

5. *The lesbian life*

Until recently women's organisations, comparable with those that promote the interests of male homosexuals, hardly existed at all. Little could be discovered about lesbians' life styles because they kept quietly and unobtrusively to themselves. That state of affairs changed abruptly with the upsurge of Women's Liberation and Gay Liberation. Now, both in Europe and America, active organisations have grown up which publish magazines for lesbians, and provide social and counselling services similar to those available to men. At the same time, some of the male homophile organisations have opened their doors to lesbians, although, as might have been predicted, they do not always get along together or agree on social policy.

In England the chief lesbian organisation is Kenric, which produces a monthly newsletter. In addition a monthly magazine *Sappho* (BCM/Petrel, WC1), and another called *Arena Three*, begun by the Minority Research Group, are also available. The Albany Trust concerns itself with the sexual troubles of both men and women. At one time the Trust employed a female caseworker with a special interest in women's difficulties, and the Trust's publication, *Man and Society*, has carried articles by and about lesbians. Women also belong to and participate in the discussion groups, protest marches and other activities of the Campaign for Homosexual Equality.

A major contribution to the public image of the lesbian movement has been made by self-declared homosexual women writing books about their personal lives and their struggles for social acceptance (Aldrich, 1955). Two women, Del Martin and Phyllis Lyon (1972), both among the founders of the Daughters of Bilitis, after having 'lived together as lovers for nineteen years' put out a book dedicated to all the 'daughters throughout the world who are struggling with their identity as Lesbian/Woman'. Jill Johnston (1973), another American lesbian activist, published her own account of her public debut as 'a political and social lesbian'. Sidney Abbott and Barbara Love (1972), drawing upon 'their own experiences and those of other lesbians' combined to present to the world 'a liberated view'.

In common with the accounts produced by male homosexuals, lesbian writings reveal a tension between the desire to put the homosexual life-style in a good light, to support a 'gay is good' philosophy, and the desire to point out the miseries caused by the hostility of straight society and the inflexible opposition of its official institutions. These authors make it crystal clear that lesbians labour under a double grievance. Already treated as inferior in status to men because of their sex, they suffer additional denigration on account of their sexual orientation. They resent the way their perceptions of injustice are written off as 'masculine protest' or 'penis envy'. They are angered by the misleading myths that circulate concerning lesbians, some of them obviously originating in the blinkered masculine approach of medical authorities. Not so long ago proper ladies had to stay still in bed so as not to shame their husbands with an uncouth display of passion. This denial of a woman's sexual needs lasted a long time, and still affects the double standard applied to such matters as the sexual fidelity of men and women. Lesbians have particular reason to object to the questionable theory of the superiority of vaginal over clitoral orgasm, which implies scepticism that women can satisfy each other fully without the help of man. Masculine conceit, and the reluctance of male researchers to put their assumptions to the test, must be partly responsible for the conventional wisdom that asserts that love between women is always neurotic, immature, unsatisfying, impermanent or destructively possessive. Martin and Lyon blame the pattern established by male-dominated heterosexual unions for the phenomenon of 'butch' – 'femme' role playing. They believe that lesbians get caught up in a tradition that does not really suit them. Most lesbians need another woman like themselves to share life on an equal footing. They have no need to caricature the conventional division of functions between a man and wife with young children to look after. After some time together, many lesbian couples find that they can easily abandon the butch-femme roles that they once thought sustained their relationship. Jill Johnston (1973, p. 176) makes the same point. 'The butch or diesel dyke is fast disappearing.' The butch role is just a stylistic imitation of the heterosexual male's superiority games. 'The woman in relation to herself is not a butch or a femme but a woman. She is not naturally a role playing animal.'

Even the bold women who have publicly cast off the shackles of conventional morality without disaster admit that the great majority of their fellow lesbians still prefer to lead a secret, double life. The pressures compelling this deceit, and the sad consequences which it sometimes entails, are much the same for lesbians as for male homosexuals. Martin and Lyon, for example, describe the discomfiture they experienced in the early days of their association, before their respective families had been told of the nature of their relationship. Each one had to go away separately on visits to fulfil family obligations and to participate in events from which the other was necessarily excluded. At times of crisis, the insecurity of an unrecognised 'marriage' becomes especially acute. For example, one has heard of a possessive next-of-kin separating a dying woman from her partner and proceeding to sell their joint possessions. The sheer mechanics of living as a married pair in a shared home presents difficulties. The official guardians of such services as joint banking accounts, home loans and credit financing expect to deal with heterosexual married couples, and treat other forms of partnership with deadly suspicion.

Lesbians who do not expect to marry must support themselves to survive, so a career, or at least a decent job, is particularly important to them. Fear of exposure to employers or colleagues at work worries lesbians. Many gain their livelihood as teachers, social workers, probation officers, police women, doctors or in government offices. Until recently, known homosexuals were never recruited for any of these types of employment, and lesbians have every reason to fear that a revelation of their true sexual orientation would seriously damage their career prospects, even if it did not result in outright dismissal. Abbott and Love (1972, ch.1.) describe what they call the 'debt paying' type of lesbian who, in return for apparent social acceptance, leads a stultifying existence pleasing the boss, becoming indispensable, and creating an impression of unassailable respectability. They quote examples of women of this type who have been sadly disillusioned when, some malicious person having informed upon them, they find themselves suddenly without job and their years of dedicated work wasted. Martin and Lyon (1972, p. 195) observe that some lesbians, especially those who have fought their way to a management position despite discrimination against women, feel extremely threatened by the presence of other homosexuals in the same firm. As a cover, 'she may even go to the extreme of spreading rumours about another employee in order to direct attention away from herself'. The perils of exposure begin early. The same authors quote (p. 170) the example of a 16-year-old pupil at a Californian Catholic school caught kissing another girl. The teachers held a tape recorded trial, attended by the parents and student council representatives, and expelled both girls, at the same time warning them that should they apply for admission to another school the tape would be sent on with their scholastic records. When the girls did in fact try to enroll in another school, the registrar, duly forewarned, told them primly, 'We can't have anyone like you in this school.' Thus, by being made an involuntary drop-out from the educational system, a career can be blighted before it starts. These girls belonged to devout religious families, which presents yet another hazard. To the orthodox Christian, lesbian activities are wicked and unforgivable. Any woman who takes her religion seriously must either deceive the priest and the other church members, and bear a load of guilt, or else confess and find herself socially, if not theologically, beyond redemption.

The necessity for constant vigilance in keeping up a facade of heterosexuality produces in some lesbians a feeling of almost unbearable strain. Some situations are particularly aggravating –

office parties, for instance, when women are expected to produce a husband or boy friend, or vacation periods, when everyone chats about their holiday plans, and the lesbian feels impelled to invent a cover story to conceal the fact that she intends to visit a gay resort with her female lover. Interference from well-meaning relatives, who want to introduce her to prospective boy friends, and importunate males, who must be allowed some encouragement, if not some actual sexual gratification, in order to preserve her heterosexual reputation, add to the difficulties of the lesbian in hiding. The daily task of systematic deception and frank lies, the necessity to spend most of her time in the company of straight acquaintances with whom she must be eternally on her guard, can become in time a wearing, demanding process, leading to depression and psychosomatic ailments. Those too afraid, or too isolated, to discover and visit gay meeting places, or to join lesbian organisations, risk becoming suddenly indiscreet when their habitual restraints are worn away by great loneliness. A minority of lesbians escape from the situation by abandoning all attempt at respectability, and joining up with other rejects of society in the subculture of drop-outs, drug abusers, prostitutes, delinquents and self-advertising homosexuals who frequent the seedier night spots of the big cities. Others conceive of death as the only solution. As Abbott and Love say, 'every lesbian knows of women who have taken this final route out beyond their peripheral and despised position in society into nothingness'.

Saghir and Robins (1973) point out several respects in which lesbians seem better off in society than male homosexuals. Growing old, for instance, causes them less apprehension, more of them believing, perhaps unrealistically, that they will grow old in a stable lesbian relationship. Many expect to compensate for old-age loneliness with involvement in non-sexual activities. Unlike male homosexuals, none of the lesbians thought they would ever resort in later life to paying money for sexual relationships (p. 312). Since few lesbians go in for 'cruising' in search of casual sex, they are not subject to the same risks of assault, robbery, intimidation or arrest. Most lesbians felt their sexual orientation had not impaired their social life and work careers, possibly because, as women, they came under less suspicion of homosexuality than their male counterparts. Over half of the lesbian women thought that their parents definitely did not know of their homosexuality, although they may possibly have suspected it. However, of the four lesbian women in the sample who had joined the American military, two were discharged when rumours about their sexual orientation began to circulate, although no complaint of actual offenses was made against them. The one deprivation felt more often and more acutely by lesbians than by male homosexuals was the absence of a family home with children.

Whether by tradition or by natural inclination, women seem less inclined than men to rebel against the conventional rules of law and morality. In striving to retain some remnant of religious faith, in struggling to build a home and maintain a permanent one to one love relationship based upon more than passing sexual fancy, the lesbian sets herself standards and undertakes responsibilities which many male homosexuals would consider unrealistic or unnecessary. Whereas a few male homosexuals concern themselves with children, lesbians quite commonly have a feminine interest in babies, actively desire parenthood, and if they become mothers strive to do their duty by their offspring as well as any heterosexual woman.

There is a relatively high proportion of latecomers to homosexuality among females. Many of them are women in retreat from unsuccessful marriages and unhappy relationships with men, and of course some of these women already have children. Sometimes the situation arises, as in the case of Jill Johnston (1973, p. 70), because a woman who knows her own lesbian inclinations nevertheless feels 'driven into the desperate expedient of marriage as the illusory solution to a problem ...' In other cases the woman only realises the nature of her problem after years of marriage. When a marriage breaks up due to a wife's attachment to another man she does not necessarily lose the custody of her children, but if she leaves the marital home to set up with another woman her fitness to keep her children may be vigorously contested. Martin and Lyon (1972, p. 133) state: 'We know of only one case where custody of children was awarded to a declared lesbian mother.' Fear of loss of their children holds some married lesbians captive, others manage to secure divorces with pretexts that conceal the true reason, but thereafter live under the threat of discovery. Martin and Lyon cite one case of a mother of three children whose divorced husband was a gambler and a drunkard. After four years of sharing life with a lesbian partner, a childless married relative of the husband turns up and threatens to expose her as an unfit mother and apply for custody of the children. They could offer the unfortunate mother no comfort for 'there is no known case where a judge, given the choice between a homosexual and a heterosexual household in which to place the care of children, ever ruled in favor of the homosexual one'.

A development which may indirectly bring some relief to lesbians who feel socially oppressed is the adoption of their cause as a proper concern of the Women's Liberation movement. Many thoughtful commentators, notably Simone de Beauvoir (1963), Kate Millett (1970), J. Stearn (1965) and D.W. Cory (1964), believe that some women become lesbians out of revulsion against male domination. That being so, it is hardly surprising that lesbians should have taken a leading part in feminist movements. They are, after all, risking nothing that much matters to them by incurring the displeasure of men. The more radical among Women's Liberation theorists openly identify with the ideal of total freedom for women, including freedom to practice lesbian sex (Firestone, 1970). In radical circles the term political lesbian has sprung up to describe women who deliberately seek out lesbian experiences so as to be able to proclaim independence of men even in the matter of sexual pleasure. As Abbott and Love (1972) point out, such women receive something less than a unanimous welcome from those with a life-long commitment to exclusive lesbianism.

The women's movements in America for a long time stood officially aloof, concentrating upon civil rights issues, and avoiding confrontation with the issue of lesbian liberation. Privately, however, women's liberation leaders felt angered and threatened by the 'lavender menace' which might tarnish their image and detract from their effectiveness in the eyes of the establishment they wanted to influence, which was of course predominantly heterosexual and predominantly male. One of the most prominent leaders of the feminist cause, Kate Millett, repeatedly challenged at meetings by gay activists, finally admitted on a public platform her own bisexuality. Her admission was published, with highly uncomplimentary comments, in *Time Magazine* (8 December 1970). This event helped bring matters to a head. After a period of turmoil, during which lesbians tried to pack committees and storm meetings, and some were ignobly expelled, the National Organisation for Women finally decided, in the words of Abbott and Love, not to let the lesbian issue split the organisation down the middle. They passed a resolution acknowledging 'the oppression of lesbians as a legitimate concern of feminism' and additionally resolved that 'a woman's right to her own person includes the right to define and express her own sexuality and to choose her own life-style'.

CHAPTER EIGHT

Social Problems

1. *Homosexuality and mental illness*

Psychological tests applied to ordinary homosexuals in the community do not reveal any strikingly large incidence of individuals of manifest neurotic disposition (see pp. 31-4, 185). Nevertheless, psychiatric clinics and counselling services have to deal with many homosexuals, some of whom experience acute mental breakdowns, some of whom are chronically tense, unhappy, neurotic characters incapable of relaxing and enjoying normal human contacts. The presence of this troubled minority, which seems disproportionately larger among homosexuals than among heterosexuals, convinces many clinicians that, in some cases at least, a causal link exists between homosexuality and mental instability. Whether the mental instability predisposes towards the development of a homosexual orientation, or whether it arises later in response to the social difficulties imposed by a disapproving heterosexual society is a secondary issue, and one much more difficult to clarify.

Relatively high incidences of completed or contemplated suicide among homosexuals have been noted by several authorities (Van Schumann, 1965). In some cases threat of legal exposure and social disgrace is the immediate cause. In the days when police drives against homosexuals were more prevalent, newspapers occasionally reported such cases. For instance, when eleven males were brought before Evesham Magistrates' Court in April 1956 on charges of homosexual indecency, a defending solicitor remarked that three others who might have been with them were facing a higher tribunal (*Evesham Standard*, 13 April 1956). Following police questioning, one man had gassed himself, one thrown himself under a railway train, and a third, an old man of 81, had died of cerebral haemorrhage after receipt of the police summons. A growing fear that being homosexual means being trapped in a life-long situation of misery and frustration may also lead to suicide (Weisman, 1967). The strain of keeping up a conventional front while pursuing a secret sexual life sometimes becomes unbearable. Evelyn Hooker (1961) in a biographical study of one such case, described how the man concerned became increasingly alcoholic and attempted suicide six times over a period of five years. Swartzburg *et al.* (1972) report an interesting example of an attempted dual suicide by two male students. Both were homosexuals, and known to each other, but they were not emotionally involved together. Each one, for his own independent reasons, was feeling depressed on account of unwanted homosexual inclinations and problems in personal relationships. They decided upon a cooperative suicidal bid, collecting a hoard of sedative pills, and retiring together to an unused building, where they washed down the pills with whisky. As the first student began to lose consciousness, the second lost his nerve, made himself vomit, and called the police.

Among double suicides generally, homosexuals do not figure very largely, according to the few surveys that have been published. Out of 58 incidents of suicide pacts investigated by John Cohen (1961) only one was a male homosexual pair. The majority were ageing married heterosexual couples in failing health or otherwise difficult circumstances, who had decided they had no worthwhile future and wanted to die simultaneously. In a Japanese survey, Ohara (1963) found that 4 per cent of double suicides were homosexual pairs, more often lesbians than male homosexuals.

Clearer evidence is available for an over-representation of homosexual individuals among solitary suicides. An American medical authority on forensic matters (Rupp, 1970, comments that: 'Almost weekly we see in the newspaper an account of a serviceman who commits suicide while on leave or while AWOL. A careful background check in such cases usually reveals evidence of homosexual connections.' He goes on to quote one homosexual serviceman's suicide note addressed to his parents pleading: 'Please do not mourn for me for I was sick and this is my way out of a sick life'. Self-disgust and repudiation of an unacceptable destiny provide motives for homosexual suicide just as powerful and as frequent as external social crises, such as blackmail or threatened dismissal from work. The association of suicide with homosexual problems among young soldiers was established more systematically in a British survey by Karl Lambert (1954) who studied two hundred sufferers from neurotic conditions and found a history of attempted suicide or severe depression to occur much more often among those with homosexual tendencies. In an earlier study, O'Connor (1948) reporting on a small series of suicides and attempted suicides, found a homosexual problem underlying some 50 per cent of cases. Some particularly rich descriptive material on homosexual suicide has been published by Hendin (1969) in a study of suicide in the black ghetto of Harlem in New York. Four out of the 12 case histories of male suicide quoted by Hendin were homosexuals. A reaction of rage and frustration, turned inwards against themselves, characterised Hendin's suicidal cases. Suffering the double stigma of a racial and sexual minority, contact with white men as sexual partners afforded a temporary but ultimately unsatisfactory form of escape from feelings of personal inferiority and rejection.

In the Saghir and Robins (1973) survey, in which white American volunteer homosexuals, mostly single, were compared with unmarried heterosexuals, 7 per cent of the homosexual men, but none of the male heterosexuals, were found to have made a serious suicidal attempt at some time in their lives. Owing to the small size of the sample, this difference, though distinctly suggestive, was not statistically significant. The investigators explored other indices of mental instability. A history of excessive drinking, frequent changes of job, dropping out of college before graduation, depression for which the sufferer sought medical help, and reports of psychiatric illness or alcohol problems in parents or siblings, were all more frequent among the homosexuals than among the controls.

Unmarried persons, homosexual or otherwise, are known to have a greater incidence of psychiatric morbidity than married persons. The Saghir and Robins findings suggest that homosexual single men are slightly worse off in this respect than heterosexual single men, but the differences they noted were relatively slight. The great majority of both homosexuals and controls were working regularly and productively, disabling psychiatric symptoms were reported only rarely, and not significantly more often by the homosexuals than by the heterosexuals. A systematic comparison in regard to history of specific psychiatric disorders, such as morbid anxiety, depressive episodes, and psychosomatic symptoms, yielded no appreciable difference between the homosexuals and the control group. In short, this careful scrutiny of a sample of homosexual males drawn from the community, as opposed to one drawn from clinics or penal establishments, produced no evidence of extensive psychiatric morbidity, but some evidence of a marginally raised incidence of social maladjustment in comparison with unmarried heterosexuals. These conclusions are entirely in keeping with the relative normality of the psychological test responses obtained from groups of volunteer homosexuals (as in Hooker, 1957, 1958; Manosevitz, 1971). Notwithstanding these results, the size of the maladjusted minority of homosexuals remains open to some dispute. If the more seriously disturbed are less likely to volunteer for research, they must necessarily be under-represented in the published surveys.

Drinking to excess, causing health problems or difficulties at work, was one of the features Saghir and Robins found more frequently among male homosexuals than among their control group. Psychiatrists have long recognised that seeking refuge in the bottle, or in drug abuse, is one way in which maladjusted and conflict-ridden individuals try to obtain relief from their unhappiness. When senses are dulled, self-criticism stilled, and a pleasant euphoria supervenes, anxiety and inhibitions dissolve away. Homosexual males have been credited with a particular predeliction for this form of escape. Bychowski (1956), for instance, argues that the weak personality structure which underlies the development of a homosexual orientation makes homosexuals susceptible not only to psychotic breakdowns (which will be considered later, see p. 207) but also to drug addiction and alcoholism. Others have suggested that homosexual problems, both overt and repressed, are detectable in a high proportion of the male alcoholic population. The claim seems never to have been properly substantiated. Botwinick and Machover (1951) once applied some masculininity-femininity questionnaires to a series of alcoholics in a Brooklyn hospital without finding any significant variation from the responses expected of a normal male population. On the other hand, Jacob Levine (1955) who studied records of psychotherapeutic interviews with 63 male alcoholics, found evidence of overt homosexuality in two cases and relative indifference to heterosexual intercourse in the majority. The patients' histories revealed, in many instances, that they had grown up without benefit of any satisfactory male figure with whom to identify, and had become unduly dependent upon their mothers. Even if one accepts these findings at their face value, they refer in the main to a connection between alcoholism and sexual inhibition in male patients, rather than between alcoholism and overt homosexual orientation in non-neurotic individuals.

Two further points about male alcoholics have been held to favour a homosexual basis for their problem. The wives of alcoholic husbands are often described as dominating women who obtain covert satisfaction from their husbands' weaknesses. The husbands, on the other hand, in spite of their frequent sexual incompetence, are often extremely jealous and suspicious of their wives' sexual infidelity. It is argued that a dominating wife is the type likely to be chosen by a mother-dominated, repressed homosexual, and that sexual jealousy may be a projection of the husband's own repressed desire to be unfaithful with men. While such recondite interpretations may be justified in some cases, simpler explanations are more convincing. A heavy alcoholic intake, by decreasing sexual potency, could give rise to jealous fears quite apart from any homosexual problem.

The psychoanalyst Karl Abraham (1927) long ago pointed out that, for the secret or partially repressed type of homosexual, bouts of heavy drinking, being regarded as a manly vice, could be used to obtain occasional homosexual contacts during states of intoxication, without destroying the masculine image. When sober, the sexual indiscretions can be conveniently disowned or 'forgotten'. The story of an apparently 'straight' man, who periodically disappeared on wild binges, during which his homosexual inclinations found some release, forms the theme of the American novel *The Lost Weekend* by Charles Jackson. This pattern of behaviour is probably less common today, now that everyone is so much more alive to the possibility of a homosexual explanation for otherwise mysterious conduct.

One prosaic reason for the development of heavy drinking habits by some male homosexuals is that so much of their socialising takes place in bars. Even outside of the specialised gay bars, one of the easiest approaches in seeking a sexual acquaintance is to offer the man a drink. In this way it may be that some homosexuals acquire drinking patterns they might not otherwise have chosen. Being usually unmarried and without dependents, the free-roaming homosexual male has an unusual amount of leisure and financial opportunity to spend freely on drink. However, notwithstanding all these influences, the fact remains that the great majority of male homosexuals have stable and moderate drinking patterns which cause them no problems.

Evidence against any close relationship between alcoholism and homosexual tendency in males emerged from an American follow-up study of a large sample of men whose behaviour and family backgrounds had been studied when they were schoolboys (a part of a delinquency prevention scheme known as the Cambridge Somerville Youth Project). Of 24 boys thought to have feminine tendencies only one became alcoholic as an adult, compared with 16 per cent of the normally masculine boys. However, 2 out of 6 boys noted for troublesome homosexual behaviour in childhood became alcoholics as adults, but these numbers were, of course, much too small to form the basis of any conclusion (McCord and McCord, 1960).

Serious mental disturbance seems to occur more often in individuals who feel guilty about their erotic interests, and struggle to deny and repress homosexual impulses, than in persons with a more accepting, matter-of-fact attitude. Psychoanalysts use the concept of repressed or latent homosexuality to explain the emotional malaise and irrational attitudes displayed by some neurotic patients. Although rather obviously unhappy and insecure in their heterosexual relationships, such patients firmly deny to themselves and others the idea that they might have inclinations towards their own sex. Some of them have a morbid fascination for the topic of homosexuality, and readily attribute homosexual motives to others. Placed in a situation that threatens to excite their own unwanted homosexual thoughts, they over-react with panic or anger. Repressed homosexuality may sometimes be the explanation why men of intelligence and judgment, who would never express themselves so crudely on other topics, indulge in wildly inaccurate and absurdly emotional pronouncements about homosexuality. In advocating castration or the gas chamber for sexual corruption of youths, they betray a need to compensate for their own inner guilt by vigorous denunciation of sin in others.

Over-sensitivity to the possibility of being or becoming a homosexual manifests in a variety of ways. Students' counsellors sometimes have to deal with young men suffering from an intense, obsessive preoccupation with fear of homosexuality. Unlike those who actually participate in sex with other males, most of these panic-ridden young men do not in fact become homosexuals. Their anxieties arise from confusion and inhibition in personal relationships not necessarily connected with sexual orientation (Hart, 1958). American psychiatric textbooks describe a more acute mental disturbance called Kempf's Disease, after the man who first attributed it to homosexuality (Kempf, 1920). It consists of a state of sudden feverish panic or agitated furore, amounting sometimes to temporary manic insanity, which breaks out when a repressed homosexual finds himself in a situation in which he can no longer pretend to be unaware of the threat of homosexual temptations (Glick, 1959; James, 1947). Situations of enforced intimacy between men, in ships, military camps or penal institutions, are liable to provoke these wild reactions from susceptible individuals. The unfortunate person who has, perhaps unwittingly, aroused the unwanted sexual feelings is likely to receive the brunt of the outburst.

Homosexual panic, or something near to it, probably accounts for some curious crimes of violence in which a powerful young man, after allowing himself to be solicited or perhaps seduced by an older male, suddenly turns upon the homosexual in a blind rage and batters him to death. The unnecessary fury of these attacks, the absence of material gain, and the reckless disregard of consequences, reflect the assailants' disturbed state of mind at the time, which cannot reasonably be put down to ordinary feelings of disgust, but which could be a reaction to the intolerable pain caused by the threatened collapse of a heterosexual self-image. Motives of robbery scarcely account for the many tragic cases known to the police in which the putrefying, naked body of an ageing homosexual is discovered, lying alone, stabbed or bludgeoned to death by the young man he had invited home. With youngsters poised on a knife edge between greed and temptation on the one hand, and shame and guilt on the other, the slightest wrong move may instantly transform an apparently willing sexual partner into a raging inferno of animosity (Kiel, 1965). From time to time the police become concerned about minor epidemics of this kind of crime. According to a report in *The Times*, 15 July 1975, Scotland Yard had assigned twenty detectives to loiter around certain public lavatories in London where a murderer was believed to make contact with homosexual victims. Two homosexuals, one an accountant and the other a solicitor, had recently been battered to death and robbed and others attacked and left severely injured.

The mental processes involved in these violent incidents are complicated by the close association in some men's minds between homosexual indulgence and loss of status and self-esteem. To them, homosexuality symbolises submission, defeat and degradation in place of masculine dominance. One psychoanalyst in particular (Ovesey, 1969) has argued that conflicts about the wish for social dominance, fear of slipping down in the pecking order, and consequent anxiety about relationships with other competitive men, is the main cause of many cases of male homosexuality. The man with a sense of inferiority has a pressing need to reassure himself of his ability to hold his own with men. In Ovesey's view, the unconscious power struggle, and the delight in dominating and manipulating the partner, sometimes transcends the sexual motive in homosexual relations. In such cases, Ovesey prefers the term pseudo-homosexuality, since conflict over sexual orientation is not the primary problem.

Be this as it may, there is no doubt that aggressive and homosexual fantasies form dangerous combinations. Woods (1972), in a discussion of the psychopathology of violent men, quotes the case of a fundamentally heterosexual man, unfairly defeated in business, who threatened to batter and cripple his rival. In a dream, the man found himself confronted by a cripple of tremendous strength, who stripped and raped him in front of deriding spectators. This mental link between social and homosexual insult no doubt contributed to the man's unnecessarily violent reactions. Even more dangerous examples of homicidal reactions to real or imagined homosexual threat are well known to the forensic psychiatrists who have charge of criminal mental patients, especially the so-called aggressive psychopaths, whose over-sensitivity to the slightest challenge to their hyper-masculine image is often connected with actual or imagined homosexual provocation. Murders of women prostitutes, such as the famous 'Jack the Ripper' sequence of stabbings and mutilations in the East End of London in the nineteenth century, are sometimes motivated by the urge to be rid of sexual evil in the self by destroying the supposed representatives of evil in society. Murders of homosexuals are often committed for similar twisted motives by aggressive psychopaths who cannot tolerate the presence of homosexual impulses in themselves or in others.

One such case occurred some years ago in England. After arrest and questioning a young man admitted committing three homicides. The first of his known victims was a homosexual he met late one night. They went together to a park. After having anal intercourse, he started to batter the homosexual, breaking his jaw and leaving him lying unconscious. A week later he met another homosexual, a man of sixty, whose body was subsequently found in a quiet lane with a fractured skull. A few months later another homosexual, aged forty-eight, was found lying dead at the same spot, with skull broken and brain lacerated. He eventually admitted battering this man to death. In between these two incidents he had killed a youth of fifteen during a country walk in what was described as a 'frenzied stabbing'. The killer was quite coherent and displayed no delusions or other signs of madness, but he declined to discuss his motives. He was well-known as a violent character, he had a criminal record, and he had attempted suicide several times following quarrels with a girl friend. A plea of diminished responsibility having been rejected, he was convicted of murder.

Of course, homosexuals who put themselves in compromising positions are in danger of attack, not only from individuals with pathological obsessions with sexual non-conformity, but from ordinary young delinquents whose exuberant aggression finds an outlet in the sport of 'queer bashing'. Some years ago a part of Wimbledon common became particularly well known as an after-dark meeting place for homosexuals. Youths would lie in wait for them and the London police received many anonymous telephone complaints from assault victims. This particular epidemic ended in the death of one man and the conviction of four youths for murder. The victim was found on the edge of the heath having been battered about the head with sticks by a group of twelve boys, who were later surprised and regretful to learn that he had died from extensive brain damage. One of the assailants explained at the trial how he had kicked the victim in the face a few times because the other boys were all looking at him and waiting to see what contribution he would make. Interviewed by a journalist subsequently (Gillman, 1971) the mother of one of the convicted boys, who was aged 15, reflected that her son was branded a murderer on account of 'Little bits of men. In this filthy hole.' A local youth commented: 'When you're hitting a queer you don't think you're doing wrong ... there's nothing to be scared of from the law because you know they won't go to the law.' A second youth commented: 'Once you've beaten one up you get confident and you're not so scared any more ... It's just someone you can beat up and get away with ...' Criminologists interested in the role of the victim in provoking crimes have become increasingly aware of the importance of homosexual behaviour as an instigator of crime (Sagarin and MacNamara, 1973).

Homophobia, exaggerated and irrational over-reaction against homosexuality, is not limited to those who have tried to repress their inclinations. Many individuals recognise only too clearly that they are homosexuals, but do so with a deep sense of shame. Infected with the traditional view that they are dirty perverts, unfit to assume responsibilities or to have any place in respectable society, they suffer a perpetual sense of inferiority. Hating themselves for being what they are, their sex contacts are kept secret and compartmentalised, virtually disowned by their more respectable selves. Like old-fashioned negro servants who shared their white employers' contempt for 'black trash', these miserable homosexuals, far from sympathising with others of their kind, have a sincere disdain for 'gay' society and all it stands for, a genuine suspicion of all overt homosexuals, and a pronounced tendency to join in the queer-baiting chorus. Like thieves or embezzlers, who recognise but do not like to think about their dishonourable status, they have no particular respect or liking for others similarly placed. Inevitably they project their negative feelings about homosexuals on to their sexual partners, so that satisfying love-relationships become impossible. Their chronic guilt and fear of exposure makes them oversensitive to social slurs, anxious about their positions at work, and unwilling to take on jobs that might interfere with their imagined need for extreme privacy. These self-punishing over-compensations for inner guilt are often interpreted by psychoanalysts as 'moral masochism' or 'paranoid tendencies', when in fact they are, at least in part, reflections of the homophobic attitudes prevailing in society at large.

Homosexuals have been accused of undue touchiness, a tendency to perceive disapproval even before it has been expressed, a paranoid suspiciousness of anyone who appears friendly, and a readiness to 'collect' grievances in order to prove how badly everyone treats them. That homosexuals do indeed sometimes exaggerate their social difficulties was suggested by some sociological research by Kitsuse (1962). He was interested to discover what caused American undergraduates to suspect some of their acquaintances of homosexuality, and to label them 'queer', and what were the consequences of such a diagnosis. He found that the belief in another person's homosexuality often began with the observation of some minor foible or unexpected attitude thought to be untypical of 'straight' hetrosexuals, and then built up into a stronger suspicion as the observer gradually recalled more and more details about the other person which fitted his idea of what a homosexual is like. To this extent the findings seemed to provide ample justification for wariness by homosexuals in their dealings with heterosexual colleagues, but the consequence of being suspected were often nothing like so dire as homosexuals feared. Sometimes it meant ostracism, but frequently it made no difference to ordinary social relations. No instances of physical violence or denunciations to the police were reported. Of course the subjects of the investigation were largely young middle-class intellectuals, a group which might well be more tolerant than the average American.

Evidence that homosexual males tend to hold themselves and their society in low esteem was collected by Kendrick and Clarke (1966), who applied an attitude measure to a group of homosexual men referred to a psychiatric hospital and a control group of ostensibly heterosexual volunteers. Given a series of topics to evaluate, by selecting from a series of descriptive adjectives supplied by the investigators the one they thought most closely corresponded to their own feelings, the homosexuals made more derogatory choices then the heterosexuals in relation to various aspects of social and family life. Such concepts as 'British justice', 'Sex', 'Punishment' and 'Myself as I am' evoked particularly unfavourable responses, but although the homosexuals' attitudes were distinctive they were not pathologically extreme.

Kendrick and Clarke's investigation might be faulted for using patients as subjects who, almost by definition, might be expected to feel dissatisfaction with themselves and their environment. Dickey (1961) carried out a rather similar survey of American homosexuals located through the Mattachine Society. Feelings of personal inadequacy were evaluated by noting discrepancy between ideal self-concepts and actual self-concepts on a personality questionnaire. It was found that men most committed to the homosexual role felt the least adequate, whereas those who identified with conventional masculine norms, sharing the interests of the average heterosexual male, tended to feel much more satisfied with themselves. The result echoes the findings of Siegelman quoted earlier (see p. 34) according to which, among male homosexuals, only those with a feminine identification manifest significant neurotic tendencies on personality tests.

Many psychiatrists still believe in a link between madness and homosexuality. Sigmund Freud originated the idea that paranoid schizophrenia (sometimes aptly called persecution mania) is associated with, if not actually caused by, homosexual conflicts. Typically, the deluded sufferer imagines himself the victim of wicked plots and scheming enemies. He may 'hear' voices, or 'feel' strange effects, which he attributes to malevolent influences, such as 'ray machines' or 'telepathic forces' manipulated by his enemies. Often he complains of disgusting thoughts or sexual sensations inflicted upon him from a distance. Freud suggested that such delusions have a thinly disguised homosexual flavour. The imagined persecutor represents, in reality, a person to whom the patient feels homosexually attracted. Panic at this unseemly truth produces a psychotic reaction. The resulting delusions take the form of over-compensatory denial: 'I don't love him, I hate him, he persecutes me.' Freud worked out this theory in detail in his analysis of the case of Dr. Schreber (Freud, 1911). This deluded Dresden judge had published an autobiographical account of his hallucinatory experiences, which included a belief that he was being emasculated, for purposes of sexual abuse, by his physician and imagined tormentor, Professor Fleisig (Schreber, 1903).

No psychiatrist would deny that homosexual preoccupations feature prominently in some schizophrenic delusions, but so do chaotic sexual ideas of all sorts, including incest, change of sex, sadistic mutilation and heterosexual activity. Efforts to collect statistical data about schizophrenic patients have yielded conflicting results. Planansky and Johnston (1962) reviewed 150 male psychotic patients in a veterans' hospital. They found a high incidence of sexual problems in the psychotic group, and although reports of overt homosexual behaviour appeared infrequently in the men's clinical or service records, over a half of the patients expressed some concern over homosexuality. Many of them heard hallucinatory voices accusing them of being queer, or had delusions that other men were trying to tempt or to coerce them into homosexual acts. However, heterosexual concerns were even more frequent than homosexual preoccupations, and chaotic ideas about sex, including imagined changes of identity or genital status, were more characteristic of these patients than specifically homosexual problems.

In another investigation using a psychological projection test, Grauer (1954) failed to confirm earlier claims that responses to the Rorschach ink-blot test reveal a higher incidence of homosexual fantasy in paranoid schizophrenics as compared with other types of psychotic patients. In an investigation of 75 female paranoid schizophrenic patients Klaf (1961) found that 43 had delusions of a sexual nature, but that 83.7 per cent of the sexually deluded women were preoccupied with heterosexual ideas. Furthermore, a majority of the schizophrenic women (61.3%) had male persecutors, contrary to the expectations of the homosexual theory.

On the other hand, some clinical evidence for a link between paranoid schizophrenia in men and homosexual conflict has been reported. Klaf and Davis (1960), in an investigation of hospital records of 150 male paranoid schizophrenics found evidence of preoccupation with homosexual thoughts in 23 cases. They also noted that in the great majority of cases (84.7%) the imagined persecutor was a man. In another survey (Moore and Selzer 1963), 128 male paranoid schizophrenics were contrasted with 77 male schizophrenics considered to be non-paranoid. Among the paranoid cases overt homosexual behaviour, or homosexual preoccupations emerging in the course of psychotherapy, occurred in 78 per cent compared with only 47 per cent of the non-paranoids. Silvano Arieti (1967), a leading exponent of American psychiatric opinion, has argued that homosexuality can precipitate a schizophrenic illness through the anxiety and conflict associated with unacceptable impulses. It would seem to follow that if a patient begins to accept his sexual impulses without panic, the risk of psychosis should lessen. One American psychotherapist (Brody, 1963) has published an example of a schizophrenic male patient who recovered from his psychosis when he found a means of escape from his family entanglements by becoming an overt homosexual.

Psychological conflict may contribute to the development of a schizophrenic breakdown in vulnerable individuals, but the conflict need not be about homosexuality. The delirium of madness, like the nightmares of the sane, are filled with fear, aggression and sexuality because these are common human preoccupations. The reasons why a minority lapse into madness must lie in some more particular causes, most probably in some as yet unidentified neuro-physiological dysfunction. The presence of homosexual impulses, whether overt or repressed, is too commonplace a circumstance to provide any real answer to this baffling medical enigma.

2. *Child molestation and other sexually deviant behaviour*

When arranging bookshelves intended to interest male homosexuals, purveyors of pornography often set aside special sections devoted to sadistic scenes (men being overpowered, tied up, whipped and subjected to all kinds of painful manipulations) or to paedophiliac interests (pictures of young boys, not yet past the earliest stages of puberty, shown in naked poses or engaged in frankly sexual games). The fact that pornography merchants find this worthwhile suggests that sado-masochistic and paedophiliac preoccupations are fairly common among male homosexuals.

The comparative prevalence of deviant sex interests among homosexuals and heterosexuals has never been scientifically established, but many psychoanalysts have convinced themselves that all kinds of sexual deviations tend to occur in conjunction with homosexuality. They regard homosexuality as only one among a range of possible substitutes for, or perversions of, normal intercourse, all of them dictated by fears of intimate contact with members of the opposite sex. Similar pressures and anxieties cause different individuals to develop different perversions. For example, the compulsive male exhibitionist, who tries to shock women by displaying his penis to them from a safe distance, but cannot tolerate a closer relationship, often has the same parental background and the same ambivalent anxious feelings about female sexuality as have many homosexuals. A resentful submission to maternal domination, an excessively prudish home atmosphere, and a passive, ineffectual father, are frequently described by both exhibitionists and homosexuals (Rooth, 1971).

In the perversion known as fetishism, a man's erotic interests are directed towards some inanimate object symbolic of the female, usually an article of feminine attire, from which he obtains sexual satisfaction without the need for contact with a real woman. In Freud's view, the essential psychopathology of this peculiarity derives from an intense infantile fear of castration, which makes it impossible for the man to accept the reality of the female genitals. The absent phallus constitutes too threatening a reminder of the vulnerability of his own genitals (Gillespie, 1964). Unlike the homosexual, who looks for another human being with a penis, the fetishist looks for an object that symbolises a female penis. The connection, in psychoanalytic theory, between the causes of male homosexuality and the causes of fetishism and other deviations are further emphasised by the contention that, in all these conditions the man has a tendency to identify himself with the female. Gillespie refers to cases in which 'the fetishistic act represented a passive, feminine masochistic identification with the suffering mother, and the fetish was her 'phallus'. He goes on to cite one of his own patients who had as a fetish mackintoshes and uniforms, which he gazed at when they were being worn by actual women, or put on himself. His fantasy consisted of women being tied up and forced to wear these clothes as a punishment. He frequently tied himself up in similar clothes when masturbating.

Sado-masochistic deviation, that is the need to administer or to submit to painful or humiliating rituals in order to attain orgasm, is regarded by some psychoanalysts as particularly close to homosexuality. Socarides (1968, p. 95) states: 'In sexual (erotogenic) masochists ... one finds a strong feminine identification may exist without homosexual object choice.' He cites Freud's famous 'wolf man' case as an example of a masochistic heterosexual approach being selected in preference to becoming a homosexual when normal sexual outlets have been blocked by neurotic fears (Freud, 1918). In another famous case of a beaten child, Freud (1919) thought that the beating fantasy had its origin in the boy's incestuous attachment to his father. By a slight modification into a fantasy of being beaten by a powerful man-like woman, such patients, at the cost of admitting a mild kinkiness, succeed in repressing their less acceptable homosexual urges. Socarides (p. 97) asserts quite confidently: 'In masochists strong homosexual tendencies are readily observed. All homosexuals suffer from a degree of psychic masochism.'

Such assertions are almost impossible to confirm or to refute because of the difficulty of translating vague labels such as 'psychic masochism' into the precise, practical terms needed for objective, statistical comparisons. In clinical experience overt, practising male homosexual patients rarely describe either fetishistic or exhibitionistic urges. They sometimes admit to a particular fascination for large genitals and bulging trousers but that hardly differs from the heterosexual male's fascination for big breasts and tight sweaters. They rarely confess to hoarding male clothing, or using male underwear as a masturbation object, in the way heterosexual fetishists use female articles. Except for the purpose of making contact in lavatories, homosexual men are not given to exposing their genitals from a distance in the manner of heterosexual exhibitionists. In any event such behaviour would have little meaning, for another man, being both familiar with and indifferent to the spectacle exhibited, would be hardly likely to gratify the exposer with the emotional response some women might display.

Sado-masochistic rituals seem to be the only overtly deviant routines shared by large numbers of heterosexuals and homosexuals alike. In the male homosexual context sadism is associated with wearing studded leather, chain decorations and other symbols intended to denote aggressive masculinity. Sadism is a sufficiently common interest to feature prominently in sex adverts, prostitution practice, and pornography, both heterosexual and homosexual. Contrary to what we might expect from psychoanalytic theory, sadistic rituals are usually additional to, rather than a substitute for, genital contacts. Although accidents can happen, and participants can get carried away and cause unintended injuries during a high pitch of sexual excitement, the vast majority of these encounters take the form of a relatively harmless playful situation, entered into voluntarily and repeatedly for the sake of the erotic pleasure derived. The painful, unhygienic and imprudent practice of fist fucking (insertion of hand and forearm into the rectum) has become prevalent in America. It is a popular subject for pornographic films, in which the passive party is often shown tied up and unable to resist the procedure. Rather more dangerous, from the point of view of fatal accidents, are solitary masturbatory rituals in which men tie themselves up into positions from which they may find more difficulty in extricating themselves than they anticipated (Resnik, 1972). How often sado-masochistic practices represent a late-acquired sexual taste, learned through contact with others of similar interests, or how far they reflect early-acquired predispositions of an unhappy, neurotic kind, as described by the psychoanalysts, is far from clear.

In rare cases, sadistic men lose all restraint, and will plan and perpetuate the most ruthless tortures, mutilations and murders in pursuit of their own sexual pleasures. Some of these individuals seem to be unfeeling psychopaths, who show little regard for other people in anything they do, but some become ruthless only when their lust is aroused. Lust murderers usually choose women victims, but some, like the mass murderer Ian Brady (Sparrow, 1966), who buried his victims in remote graves on the Yorkshire moors, attacked juveniles of both sexes. Occasionally, sadistic murderers have committed exclusively homosexual crimes. One particularly dreadful example was the American killer Dean Allen Corll of Houston, Texas, himself murdered at the age of thirty-three by one of his potential victims during a glue-sniffing party. After his death more than a score of bodies were unearthed, most of them buried in a boat-shed he had rented. He employed two teenage youths, who were subsequently charged with murder, to procure adolescent boys for sexual purposes. The victims were tied to a board, sexually abused and tortured, and then disposed of by shooting or strangling. Such cases are so excessively rare and puzzling that no generalisations about their psychology can be made with any safety. Notwithstanding some contrary opinions (Brittain, 1970; River, 1958), there is no firm evidence to suggest that a homosexual orientation has any connection with homicidal sadism.

More than any of the other conditions with which homosexuality may sometimes be associated, paedophilia, sexual interest in children, has attracted the attention of research workers and medico-legal experts. Their concern reflects the social furore which the detection of sexual offences involving children invariably creates. Admissions by prisoners, patients and volunteer subjects in sex surveys suggest that adult males, both homosexuals and heterosexuals, fall into three more or less distinct categories as regards the age range of the persons to whom they feel sexually attracted. The great majority prefer physically mature adults, a minority of ephebophiles prefer post-pubertal adolescents aged about twelve to sixteen, while a still smaller minority of paedophiles prefer sexually immature children under the age of eleven. Whereas ephebophiles are sometimes rather fluid in their responses, and capable of developing some interest in adults, paedophiles tend to be more fixed in their attachment to children, and readily put off by the appearance of adult sexual characteristics (Gigeroff et al., 1969). The work of the Czech psychiatrist Freund (1965a; 1967), who, as we have noted, pioneered the measurement of the changes in the volume of the penis as a more effective method of testing male erotic responses than asking questions, confirms these impressions. Most males, especially paedophiles, have a consistent preference for a given age range. They also have, within each age group, a consistent preference for either a male or a female as a sex partner. For most men the sex of the partner matters even more than the age (Freund, Serber et al., 1974).

Investigators have often noted (Westwood, 1960) the sentiments of incomprehension expressed by members of these various sexual groups for the interests and behaviour of other groups. One man, charged with offences with young boys (and at the time of writing serving a substantial prison sentence) told the writer he felt just as much revulsion at the idea of sex with grown-up hairy men as he knew ordinary homosexuals must feel at his activities with small boys. He regretted that he had not stayed permanently in India where, whatever the official attitude, in practice he had found that people are not much concerned to protect boys from homosexual experiences, and he had been able to pursue his interests without police interference.

Heterosexual ephebophilia in men meets with amused deprecation rather than horrified condemnation. Masculine interest in adolescent girls is catered for rather openly in pornography, and marriage to girls of fourteen or less is still a respectable practice in some parts of the world. A brothel trade in pubescent girls flourished in Victorian England, until the newspaper campaigns by the editor W.T. Stead roused the public conscience and led to a raising of the 'age of consent' to sixteen by the Criminal Law Amendment Act of 1885. This law may have modified the trade in child prostitutes, but it has certainly not suppressed the attraction many men feel towards pubescent girls. Females under the official 'age of consent', many of them involved with men much older than themselves, make an appreciable contribution to the official statistics of illegitimate births and legal abortions, but only exceptionally do these incidents lead to the identification and conviction of the offending heterosexual male.

Homosexual ephebophiles evoke much stronger condemnation. Incidents involving adolescent youths and older men are more likely to lead to conviction and imprisonment when they come to the notice of outraged parents or observant police. The resulting over-representation of homosexual as opposed to heterosexual ephebophiles among the clientele of the criminal courts gives an exaggerated impression of the prevalence of this sexual preference among the generality of homosexuals.

Paedophilia, in the strict sense of a positive preference for, or an exclusive interest in, sexually immature children is a relatively unusual deviation in either heterosexuals or homosexuals, and one that apparently occurs almost exclusively among males. Women hardly ever admit to a sexual interest in children, and are almost never prosecuted for indecent acts with children, except occasionally as accomplices to a deviant male. Even so, playful sexual fondling of small boys by nursemaids, child minders or older sisters is not unknown in the intimate confessions of male patients to their psychiatrists. Cultural acceptance of intimate contacts between women and children for the necessary purposes of maternal care and personal hygiene help to conceal any sexual motives that might be present. Nevertheless, very overt sexual acts with children, such as mutual masturbation, are usually committed by males.

Homosexual paedophilia and ephebophilia have probably always been commoner than most people realise, as the writings of nineteenth-century sexologists show (Tarnowsky, 1967). The salacious recollections of self-confessed paedophiles who have travelled widely (Davidson, 1971) bear witness to the extraordinary readiness of boys in more permissive lands to cater to the sexual desires of any older male willing to take an interest in them. Even in England, inquiries following the arrest of a staff member at a boys' boarding school or a youth hostel often reveal that whole classes have long been aware of their teacher's peculiarity, and that a large proportion of the boys have allowed sex play to take place. In one instance known to the author, the situation came to light when a teacher wanted to punish a boy for arriving late. The boy explained that he had expected a lift in the headmaster's car, but had been made to walk because he repulsed a sexual advance. In another case, the exposure came about when the headmaster refused to discipline two very badly behaved boys. He could not do so because they were blackmailing him with a threat to reveal his sexual habits. In both instances a considerable number of boys had been involved over a long period, a situation that might have continued indefinitely but for the unexpected event which led to inquiries being made.

Even quite young boys may actively encourage older men in sexual play. In the autobiographical account recorded by Tony Parker (1969, p. 61) the prisoner 'Wilfred Johnson', convicted of offences against boys aged eight to twelve, recalled his notorious reputation among the local kids. 'They talked about it among themselves I suppose, they knew where they could go and get a sixpence any time if they wanted one.' 'They'd be pushing notes under the door, they would, if I was out.' On one occasion when he was brought to court the police themselves mentioned that the boys had been pestering him. He lived alone with an ailing mother. After she died he took to drink, becoming ever more reckless in his conduct until one day the police walked into the room where he was sitting drunk, with boys larking around him half dressed. On that occasion he was sentenced to eight years preventive detention. His total of prison sentences amounted to over seventeen years. Imprisonment in such cases can mean a worse fate than usual. As Wilfred explained, all the time inside child molesters are scared to death that other prisoners will discover the nature of their crime. Everyone in prison holds offenders of this sort in contempt. He knew of instances of men being set upon while the prison officers just walked away. He dared not talk to people, or try to explain how it really was. If anyone seemed to be on the point of asking him about himself he would break into a cold sweat.

The frequency with which teachers and youth workers are discovered to have sexual contacts with boys in their charge (Plaut, 1960; Banis, 1966), in comparison with the relatively small numbers convicted for interfering with girls, has helped to reinforce the belief that persons of homosexual orientation are particularly liable to molest children. The difference could arise in part from the factor of opportunity. Conventional social habits of sexual segregation enforce the separation of girls from male teachers during washing, changing, sports activities and dormitory hours, but permit closer contact between men and boys.

The results of numerous surveys of detected paedophiles reveal substantial agreement about the usual characteristics of these offenders and about the nature and circumstances of their offences (Apfelberg et'al., 1944; Fitch, 1962; McCaghy, 1967; McGeorge, 1964; Mohr et al., 1964; Mulcock, 1954; Shoor et al., 1966; Swanson, 1968; Toobert et al., 1959; Wyss, 1967). Whether they choose male or female children, these offenders tend to be lonely, socially isolated and sexually inhibited individuals. Like other kinds of sexual deviant, they frequently come from parental homes in which sex was a taboo subject and sexual instruction completely lacking. Far from being arrogant individualists who deliberately flout conventions, they are generally timorous, shy characters whose relationships with other adults, even on a non-sexual level, tend to be distant and unsatisfying. Far from being unrestrained sex maniacs, their approaches to children are almost always affectionate and gentle, and the sex acts which occur, mostly mutual display and fondling, resemble the sexual behaviour that goes on between children. The use of presents and favours as inducements is much commoner than threats or force. Unwilling or unresponsive children are not pursued. The offenders are usually persons known to the child, such as relatives, lodgers, neighbours, or youth workers who have become friends, so that the sexual incidents arise in a context of easy familiarity. This is especially true of girls, perhaps because they are more protected than boys, and less likely to go unaccompanied to cinemas, parks, childrens' exhibitions, and the sort of places where encounters with adult strangers with paedophilic interests sometimes occur. Contrary to what might be expected, mens' public lavatories do not appear to be favourite resorts of the average homosexual paedophile, probably because the presence of other adults is inhibiting and not many young boys loiter around adult lavatories for sexual purposes.

It has been argued that sexual relationships between boys and older men are usually harmless (Ullerstam, 1966), or even positively educational and beneficial (Eglinton, 1971). In spite of the existence of a small paedophile liberation organisation in England, called PAL, there is no substantial support, even among the more radical gay liberationists, for acceptance of paedophilia as a legitimate life style. Paedophiles often convince themselves they do no wrong. Their sincere fondness for the objects of their sexual desire sometimes leads them into quite striking acts of charity in efforts to further the child's happiness or future prospects. Since they know they cannot expect other adults to understand or sympathise, they adopt a habitually defensive attitude, frequently denying a detected offence, or denying any continued interest in children, in spite of all the evidence to the contrary. A common plea of the detected offender is that he had been drinking at the time, and would never have touched a child in his sober state (McCaghy, 1968).

Various sub-groups of child molesters have been described. Some are lonely, elderly men who regress to primitive forms of expression as their sexual potency and ability to strike up relationships with other adults diminishes. I recall seeing one lonely widower who had been happily married for many years and manifested no previous homosexual interests. He was working as a caretaker on a building site. Young boys used to talk to him and accept cups of tea in his hut. One of them became particularly friendly, and some sex play took place. This boy invited others similarly inclined, until soon the old man acquired a sinister reputation and police came to question him. Smitten with guilt, he confessed immediately.

At the opposite extreme, and devastating for the public image that the more respectable homophile campaigners try to maintain, are the minority of unscrupulous and predatory homosexual paedophiles who put pressure upon and exploit young boys in ways no one could excuse. Some of these men are clearly criminally inclined in other ways besides their illicit sexual habits. *The Times* of 30 July 1975 reported the case of a man with a pre-existing criminal record for buggery and indecent assault who, by passing dud cheques, obtained some £3,000 worth of goods, in the shape of Meccano railway sets and other toys, which he used to attract and bribe the boys he wanted. One boy of eleven, whom he encountered in an amusement arcade, was said to have taken to male prostitution subsequently.

An even worse example was widely publicised in a television programme entitled 'Johnny come home', broadcast on 22 July 1975. This concerned a man with a criminal record, claiming to be a priest of a minority religious group, who ran hostels for homeless men and boys on an ostensibly charitable basis. He would pick up destitute youngsters arriving from the provinces at London railway stations, and offer them a place at a hostel, where they soon found that sexual services were expected in return. This man was also criminal in other ways, making substantial profits by charging different charities for the same boys. It seems that he was far from conscientious in seeing to the needs of his charges, and he had a number of homosexual associates to whom he could pass on boys who no longer took his fancy. The television interviewers filmed him in religious garb, recruiting clients, and describing his charitable activities in suitably sanctimonious terms. Before the film could be shown, as an example of good works, a murder had taken place at one of his hostels, resulting police inquiries had exposed the sex scandal and the frauds, the bogus priest was in prison, and several of his associates were charged with homosexual offences. The film was shown, instead, as an example of the dangers of being taken in by a respectable facade.

　　Adolescent offenders differ from older paedophiles in that their conduct often reflects a retardation in social and sexual development that may be expected to rectify itself given time. Some of them are distinctly below average in intelligence, and on a mental level close to that of the children with whom they misbehave. Usually they are isolated, passive personalities who find it hard to compete with socially more robust age mates (Shoor *et al.*, 1966). Those whose attachment to children persists into later life become the typical, fixated, exclusive paedophiles, who are liable to repeated convictions for indecent acts with children, and whose prospects of change are rather poor. The statistics show that the great majority of first offenders in cases of child molestation are never reconvicted. Many prosecutions, especially of youthful or senescent offenders, arise out of incidental circumstances unlikely to be repeated, or out of the frustration of young people who have not yet acquired acceptable techniques for forming relationships with persons of their own age. For the minority who appear before the courts a second time on a similar charge the likelihood of continued reconvictions increases dramatically, especially so in the case of homosexual offenders (Radzinowicz, 1957).

　　Aggressive sexual overtures, and a willingness to approach children of either sex, are unusual for child molesters. These features do appear with some frequency, however, among the minority of paedophiles who have criminal or antisocial tendencies in other respects besides their sexual habits. In a survey of men imprisoned for homosexual offences, forty per cent of whom had a previous conviction for a non-sexual crime, Schofield (1965a) found that a quarter of those sentenced for offences with young boys had also committed offences with young girls, and less than a quarter of them were exclusively attracted to boys. In contrast, in his earlier survey of homosexuals in the community (Westwood, 1960), the only three paedophiles he discovered all conformed to the usual pattern of more or less exclusive attachment to immature boys. He did, however, locate two men who admitted occasional casual experiences with boys under 13, although they normally preferred other adult males. These two were noteworthy for their complete disregard for the possible consequences of their behaviour. One of them said he just played around with a boy of 8 to see if he could get an erection.

　　Indiscriminate sexual behaviour of a casual, opportunistic kind, with adults or children of either sex, is characteristic of selfish, impulsive, aggressive, socially unrestrained individuals, the sort of people who are more concerned with immediate gratification than the personal qualities of the sex partner or the prospects of a stable love relationship. These individuals (often called psychopaths when their antisocial traits become extreme) usually commit non-sexual crimes as well, have frequent confrontations with police and other authorities, and consequently tend to turn up in prison samples more readily than the timid, outwardly respectable paedophile who is likely to be placed on probation or dispatched to a psychiatric hospital.

A massive study of thousands of convicted sex offenders conducted by the Indiana University Institute for Sex Research (Gebhard *et al.*, 1965, p. 205) confirmed the general belief that paedophiles form a group distinct from the ordinary homosexual population. Only 9 per cent of men convicted for homosexual offences with adults had ever had contact with children and only one per cent admitted a preference for children, although as many as a third had admitted some contact with sexually mature youths under the age of 16. At the same time the investigators identified an aggressive, predatory group 'succinctly described as criminally inclined men, who take what they want, whether money, material or women ... their sex offences are by-products of their general criminality.' These aggressive types were responsible for most of the violent assaults upon women, and occasionally for quite brutal attacks upon female children. Physical violence, though not unknown, was less common in cases of sexual interference with young boys. This could be taken to indicate that violent tendencies are less prevalent among homosexuals. Outside prisons and other closed male institutions, violent sexual assaults upon adult males, with or without forced anal intercourse, appear to be rare, but then one has to keep in mind that the potential victims, being of equal strength to the assailants, cannot be so easily subdued without the use of accomplices.

Apart from deliberate aggression, a panic reaction by a timid offender, desperately trying to silence a child who takes fright and threatens to call for help or otherwise betray him, occasionally results in tragic injury.

Parents worry themselves unnecessarily about the likely consequences of homosexual contacts between boys and older men. Evidence cited elsewhere in this book (see pp. 16, 223-4) suggests that sex play between youths, or between a youth and an adult male in the context of prostitution, do not produce a permanent homosexual orientation unless the individual already has a strong inclination in that direction. When samples of normal young men are questioned about their past experiences, a substantial proportion recall some sexual approach by an older male when they were children. Among the English youths studied by Schofield (1965b), 35 per cent described at least one such experience. Landis (1956), who investigated 1800 students of both sexes by means of a questionnaire, found that a quarter of the men recalled homosexual advances by older males when they were young, many of them describing several such incidents. Hardly any of them thought they had been deleteriously affected by the experience. Gibbens (1957) questioned 100 youths of 16 to 21 undergoing borstal training, asking if any adult male had ever tried to make a pass at them or interfere with them. The sample was divided into those with known homosexual tendencies and the remainder. The proportion who replied affirmatively, almost a third, was the same in both groups. Doshay (1943) studied 108 boy sex offenders aged 7 to 16. None had been convicted for other kinds of crime, but over a half hạd been involved in homosexual offences, either with older males or with other boys. Followed up in adult life, there was not a single instance of any further sex violation in their official records. Individual case studies revealed no sign of continued homosexual interests. He concluded that when a boy is brought before a court on account of homosexual behaviour this does not indicate any great likelihood that he will become a homosexual adult. In a follow-up study in Holland, Tolsma (1957) traced 133 men who had had homosexual contacts with adults when they were children. All but 8 were married and had not continued homosexual practices. A long-term and detailed follow-up by Bender and Grugett (1952) of a small group of child victims of molestation also led to the conclusion that the experience did not usually affect adult sexual adjustment adversely, provided the child was not in some way disturbed to begin with. As Bender, Burton and others point out children starved of affection or attention from their parents are peculiarly vulnerable. In addition to a liability to develop disorders of character and conduct, they try to solicit attention from other adults, and this lays them open to premature sexual experiences. Failure to take fully into account these antecedent peculiarities has led some psychoanalytic writers (Halleck, 1965) to attribute to sexual seduction disturbances which, in all probability, were the causes rather than the effects of their experiences.

Lindy Burton (1968), after reviewing many previous surveys of children involved in sexual incidents with adults, and describing a survey of her own, concludes that the experience 'does not have particularly detrimental affects on the child's subsequent personality development'. Gibbens and Prince (1963) who studied a random sample of children, contacted by Committees for the Moral Welfare of Children, noted that 85 per cent of the girls and 71 per cent of the boys knew and could identify the offender. Two thirds of the children had participated in indecencies on more than one occasion or with more than one adult. In some cases the incidents had been repeated many times and over a long period. This highlights the point, obvious from other studies (Rasmussen, 1943; Bender and Blau, 1937) that many of the children involved, even if they do not actively solicit sexual contact, are easily lured by small bribes or by reassurance from a trusted adult, and often become quite eager participants once contact is made. Subsequent distress, when it occurs, arises from the shock of discovery by others, and the ensuing police inquiries, family recriminations and court appearances. The prosecution of the offender, especially in a contested case, in which the child must give evidence that sends a former friend or relative to prison, can be particularly stressful. Gibbens and Prince noted that children from problem families were particularly likely to become sexually involved with household members, sometimes their own fathers. Other family members might then exploit the situation out of malice, or to obtain better accommodation from housing authorities. Such emotionally fraught situations are particularly stressful to the child. Homosexual molestation of a son by his father is, of course, much less common than incest with a daughter, but some cases have been reported in medical literature (Langsley *et al.*, 1968; Raybin, 1969). Usually they occur in a context of severely disordered family relationships, so that the possible effects of the sexual incidents cannot be separated from those due to other unfavourable influences in the boy's situation. The externally imposed stresses resulting from police inquiries and cross-examination of children by defending lawyers in the courts ought to be at all costs avoided. For instance, the police could employ an independent and experienced child psychologist to elicit from the child victim in private all the information required for the case. Some such scheme already operates in Israel (Reifen, 1972).

Sometimes spontaneously, but much more commonly as a result of detection and prosecution, paedophiles come to psychiatrists appealing for help to change their sexual habits. The possible methods of treatment for homosexuals, and the likelihood of change, form the topics of the next chapter. The considerations involved are much the same for paedophiles as for homosexuals in general, except that external pressures in the shape of social condemnation, or threatened imprisonment, are much stronger. The prospects of diverting the paedophile's interest from younger boys to older males are better than the prospects of conversion to heterosexuality, a point which needs taking into account when deciding the goals and strategies of treatment (Davison and Wilson, 1974). Unlike the ordinary homosexual, many homosexual paedophiles are conspicuously anxious, confused personalities who would find difficulties in social adjustment whatever their sexual orientation (Bell and Hall, 1971).

Claims have been made for the successful treatment of paedophiles by group discussion and individual psychotherapy (Resnik and Wolfgang, 1972), by conditioning methods (Barlow *et al.*, 1969; Kohlenberg, 1974) and even by training in masculine-decisiveness. In one case report (Edwards, 1972), a man who was in serious difficulties from compulsive homosexual paedophilia of ten years' duration became satisfactorily heterosexual after instruction in techniques of self-assertion. This unusually favourable outcome was doubtless made possible by the circumstance that the man had some heterosexual experience and was married. Previously a resentfully submissive husband, he derived much gratification from practising his newly learned dominating ways upon his wife.

In the case of some highly compulsive offenders, who risk repeated prison sentences of increasing severity if they do not curb their habit, purely suppressant techniques, using hormones as a form of chemical castration, seem to many medical men fully justified. On the other hand, as has been repeatedly demonstrated, a substantial proportion of paedophiles are relatively harmless individuals whose behaviour can be brought sufficiently under control by out-patient treatment (Resnik and Peters, 1967) or by the supervision of a probation officer (Gigeroff *et al.*, 1969). Even though their sexual inclinations may undergo no fundamental change, the development of new social and occupational interests often serves to decrease the compulsion to spend time chasing after children. An encouraging development in the penological field has been reported from Atascadero State Hospital, California, which contains a population of approaching two hundred paedophiles (Serber and Keith, 1974). In spite of aversive methods to produce conversion to asexuality or heterosexuality, many of the patients are found 'unamenable' to treatment and committed to prison via the courts. Into this traditionally punitive setting a retraining programme for paedophiles was introduced, based upon acceptance of a homosexual orientation and encouragement of participation in the homosexual community. Many of the paedophiles had limited their friendships to juveniles partly because they lacked the social skills needed to establish contact with adult homosexuals. Homosexual student volunteers were called in to act as models and instructors in an assertive training programme that included role playing and behaviour rehearsal in mock gay-bar settings and other situations calling for an appropriate social response. Swift improvement occurred in the patients' self-confidence, and in their willingness to discuss their problems frankly and to form self-help groups, as well as a lowering of tension and reduction in the hospital staff's overtly sceptical and disapproving attitude towards this class of patient. It remains to be seen whether the results will carry over after release, and serve to help these men to avoid further arrests for molesting young boys. The pros and cons of the available treatment methods are discussed further in the next chapter.

3. *Prostitution*

Information about the techniques of present-day homosexual prostitution, the life style and backgrounds of its practitioners, and the nature of its clients, can be gleaned from fictional accounts as well as from sociological inquiries. The former are often more graphic and convincing than the scientific studies, which are generally based upon small and selected samples of hustlers interviewed in dubious circumstances. The fictional works of John Rechy (1963, 1967, 1969) give a particularly vivid insight into the range of experiences encountered by the young American hustler. Richard Green (1972), describing similar experiences in a London setting, gives such explicit details of the prostitute's work that the book became the subject of an unsuccessful prosecution for obscenity, but the story lacks the psychological depth of Rechy's writing. The purportedly true confessions of some former male prostitutes (Marlowe, 1964; O'Day, 1964) are usually more dramatically salacious than informative. An exception is the short, insightful account by a student who became a temporary prostitute in London's Piccadilly (Lambton, 1973). An earlier and equally good account of male prostitution in London was published in a literary magazine by the novelist Simon Raven (1960), but the author gave no indication how he derived his facts. A longer and more modern account of the Piccadilly scene has been produced by Mervyn Harris (1973) who 'hung around' the area, got to know some of the youths trading there, and recorded their accounts of what went on. A similar investigation in America was reported by a young sociologist (Ginsburg, 1967) who wandered about the tenderloin district of San Francisco dressed like a prostitute, pretending to be on the game, and fraternising with the local hustlers who for a time took him to be one of themselves. A description of male hustling in Chicago was compiled by Ross (1959) on the basis of conversations with seven prostitutes and one 'well-educated' client. One of the most perceptive accounts of American male prostitution is included in a book by Cory and LeRoy (1963) which gives an insider's view of the gay life at that period. Most workers, however, have been content to conduct their interviews under professionally safer circumstances, that is after the prostitutes have been apprehended by the police or come to the attention of psychiatrists (Butts, 1947; Deisher *et al.*, 1969; Jersild, 1956; MacNamara, 1965; Reiss, 1961; Russell, 1971). The account which follows draws upon all these sources to construct a general picture of male prostitution, and the social problems to which it may give rise.

Whether from cultural restraints, or from difference in the quality of their sexual needs, women are conspicuously less inclined than men to pay for the pleasure of short term sexual encounters with strangers. Prostitution is essentially an enterprise catering to male customers. Brothels for women patrons, or freelance male prostitutes offering themselves to women, are relatively uncommon. In homosexual prostitution the same holds true, male 'punters' buy the services of male 'hustlers', but women selling themselves to lesbians, or brothels with a lesbian clientele, are rarities.

In present-day Western society homosexual brothels of any kind have been largely eliminated (Pittman, 1971). Benjamin and Masters (1964) were able to describe a visit to one male homosexual brothel in New York, located on Third Avenue somewhere around 50th Street, where no women were present, the 'madam' was himself an obvious homosexual, the boys mostly dressed up in military uniforms, and 'the atmosphere was businesslike, with no drinking, music or dancing'. Even these enterprising authors, however, had to admit that lesbian brothels and lesbian sexual exhibitions are rare 'curiosa', although descriptions of them have been published by some modern writers (Caprio, 1954).

Male hustling differs in important respects from ordinary prostitution, both because the traders are men and also because the relationships are homosexual. Most hustlers work individually on a free-lance basis. They organise their own activity, negotiate directly with their clients, and have no use for pimps or intermediaries of any kind. Unless they limit their sexual repertoire to passive roles without orgasm, their masculine physiology lacks the capacity to satisfy a series of customers in quick succession after the manner of women of the brothel. Many ply their trade part-time, and when not actually 'on the game', occupy themselves with other work, either legitimate or criminal. If they do have a full-time commitment to prostitution, they tend to enter into relatively long-term arrangements with clients, accepting overnight accommodation, or invitations to week-end sex parties, which provide them with more material benefits than a straight fee for a short time. Heterosexual clients, who are often married men, have less opportunity and possibly less inclination to invite women prostitutes into their homes. Moreover, the women being more organised and professional, the transaction has more chance to remain on an impersonal and commercial level. In a heterosexual context, material patronage extending beyond an immediate fee merges by imperceptible degrees into a culturally acceptable economic relationship between lover and mistress.

Benjamin and Masters (1964), quoting the evidence of Harold Call, president of the local Mattachine Society, describe organised 'call boy' rings operating in California to provide well-off male homosexuals, at a price, with rendez-vous, in suitably plush surroundings, with the youth of their choice, selected from photographs leaving nothing to the imagination. They also describe the well-groomed young men dressed in the height of fashion, operating quietly and skilfully in such places as the sky-top lounges of the smartest American hotels, ready to zoom in with appropriate casualness and aplomb once they detect the right look of interest on the countenance of some unaccompanied gentleman guest. At the pinnacle of their profession, these young men hope for something better than a one-night stand. They will stay with a customer indefinitely as a paid guest, enjoying affluent living conditions and extravagant holiday excursions, preferably with a pseudo-legitimate label, such as chauffeur, gardener or personal secretary, to camouflage the true nature of the services they render.

This degree of systematic application to the job is untypical. Most full-time hustlers are youths or young men in the age range 16 to 25, drop-outs from respectable society, disorganised in their habits, conspicuously work shy, living from hand to mouth. They gravitate to the groups of alienated young rebels, drug abusers and delinquents, living on their wits, who are to be found in the so-called vice spots of every big city. Many have drifted away or run away from unsympathetic, neglectful or conflict-ridden parental homes. Bored by the unrewarding drudgery of dead-end jobs and a drab, restricting family atmosphere, they are attracted by the prospect of a new and exciting life of pleasure, by the escape from set hours of work, and by the exercise of personal freedom unhampered by the carping criticisms of conventionally minded relatives.

Given this attitude and background, the close association between male prostitution and crime seems hardly surprising. Disinclined or incapable of organising themselves in the businesslike manner of the call girl with her own apartment, these youths resort to soliciting in the well-known streets ('meat racks'), public lavatories, or rough bars where homosexuals go to look for pick-ups. Soliciting is perhaps too strong a word for the exchange of meaningful glances, the slow idling past to see if the 'punter' will follow, or the casual remark that starts off a conversation. In England, at any rate, young hustlers are only rarely arrested for the offence of 'importuning', but their relative immunity owes more to police policy than to the success of their inconspicuous techniques of making contact. If anyone is to be prosecuted it is more likely to be the older man rather than the youth.

Youths trading in this way are typically improvident. Deisher *et al.* (1969) found that the majority of the hustlers they saw claimed to make at least a hundred dollars a week, but in spite of this most of them had no savings and less than one dollar in their pockets. Not infrequently, their entire worldly goods are stowed in a left-luggage office, and unless they make contact with a sufficiently affluent or hospitable punter they lack a bed for the night.

Under these circumstances, con tricks and petty thefts are inevitable. Robbery from customers (known as 'rolling'), with or without violence, is less common than might be supposed, but the frequency is difficult to discover since the victims are usually reluctant to compromise their reputations or risk prosecution for indecency with a youth under 21, by reporting the incident to the police. Some hustlers, referred to as 'rough trade', make a speciality of bullying and robbing clients. Some clients, judging by their repeated victimisation, and the characters they choose to invite home, must obtain a masochistic satisfaction from these incidents. Generally, however, the rough types tend to lose trade as the loose fraternity of hustlers and their regular clients get to know of their habits.

Contradictory opinions have been put forward as to the proportion of male prostitutes who are homosexual, or who become so as a result of experience. In his sample of 300 male prostitutes known to the Danish police, Jersild (1956) found that a third of them were under 18 and about four-fifths under 21 when they began work as 'rent boys'. The great majority were initially heterosexual and remained so even after years of experience in prostitution. Only about 15 per cent were true homosexuals or bisexuals. Few of these youths established any lasting relationships with the homosexuals they met, and the great majority drifted away from the homosexual milieu as they grew older. In contrast, Lambton (1973) writes of the 'Dilly Boys': 'There were all kinds of people, but the one unifying fact was that all of them were gay.' This statement accords with the often quoted homosexual quip: 'Today's (rent) trade is tomorrow's competition.'

Such contradictory views point to the variety of reasons that induce young men to become prostitutes. A youth with a positive aversion to bodily contact with males could never practice as a hustler. At best he might operate that not uncommon con trick which consists of enticing homosexuals into compromising situations in which money can be extorted or stolen before any sexual transaction takes place. The legitimate prostitute must be at least sufficiently bisexual to manifest some degree of sexual arousal when stimulated by a client. At the same time he may be predominantly heterosexual and find much greater erotic enjoyment with women than with homosexual clients. Although many full time male prostitutes are true homosexuals, many others find their work no hindrance to a robust heterosexual libido. The most convincing evidence on the point comes from Freund (1974, p. 30), who applied direct measures of penile reactions to erotic stimuli. The results of the physiological tests confirmed his impressions from interviews with male prostitutes that a considerable number were thoroughly heterosexual.

Some prostitutes consciously struggle to avoid the risk of becoming contaminated by their clients' sexual preferences. This is perhaps especially true in the case of young delinquents who look upon prostitution as just one among many available techniques of illegitimate gain. Reiss (1961), who studied young men in a penal institution, found that many had been involved in sporadic prostitution, but without defining themselves as real hustlers, and certainly without thinking of themselves as queers. Their peer culture permitted boys to go with queers without losing status, provided the motive was purely mercenary, limited to letting the queer perform fellatio upon them, and provided the process was carried out in a sufficiently impersonal manner. A queer client who broke the rules by using a term of endearment as if to a girl, by showing undue familiarity outside of the customary meeting places for trade, or by trying to prevail upon the boy to reciprocate the sexual routine, risked being beaten up on the spot, or as soon as assistance was at hand.

Less extreme forms of masculine defensiveness are apparent among the many male prostitutes who are prepared, given sufficient payment, to go along with any sexual routine, including submission to anal intercourse, provided the client promises never to tell what has happened. Harris (1973 p 72), maintains that 'scoring' (that is making a fee) without having had to do anything much sexually appears to be the main criterion of success when 'Dilly boys' gossip among themselves about their trade. Some of the boys are so anxious to preserve an image of detachment that they lie limp and seemingly in a day dream, leaving the client to fellate an apparent corpse.

The myth that youths are seduced into prostitution by the importunate advances of older men receives no confirmation from any observer. Nearly always, boys come to the game ready-primed by their more sophisticated peers with information about where to go and what to do. As Lambton (1973) put it: 'The punters were rarely attractive. But they were usually gentle, it was not a question of pawing and grabbing.' Most male prostitutes in Western society are fully mature young men, who know what they are doing, even though they may be well below the legal age of consent. Younger boys, aged 13 to 15, sometimes drift on to the scene. In March 1972, five men were sentenced at the Old Bailey to sentences of imprisonment ranging from one to six years for soliciting young boys in an amusement arcade near Piccadilly Circus. It was made clear that the boys involved were 'willing to enrich themselves by indecencies', but the judge, Sir Carl Aarvold, emphasised that even debauched youth is entitled to protection from further debauchery (Harris, 1973 p. 64). In his study of boy prostitutes below the age of 16, seen in the course of psychiatric practice with offenders, Craft (1966) mentions local epidemics of masturbatory activities in cinemas, through which boys discover a ready means of obtaining cash by prostituting themselves to older males.

Even when prostitution begins at an early age, a homosexual outcome is by no means inevitable. Owing to the small numbers involved, and the fact that the boys were subnormal or psychiatrically disturbed and from appalling home backgrounds, no generalisations can be made from Craft's study. Nevertheless, when followed up after five years, most of the young men who were outside institutions and working in the community were leading active heterosexual lives. The studies by Doshay (1943) and Tolsma (1957) referred to earlier (see p. 218) also showed that boys who had sexual contacts with older men did not become homosexual adults. These studies did not distinguish habitual prostitution from occasional seduction without money changing hands. It may be supposed that long-continued practice in homosexual activity, during years of prostitution, would lead eventually to an acquired preference for this form of sexual gratification. Many individual cases might be quoted in support of this view, but the commoner trend appears to be a reversion to heterosexual habits with increasing age. It is difficult to distinguish those who appear to become exclusive homosexuals during a career of prostitution from those who merely give up the struggle to deny the homosexual inclinations they have been aware of all the time.

In one sociological survey (Coombs, 1974) personal histories were obtained by informal interviews with 41 male homosexual prostitutes who agreed to meet and talk with the investigator at a coffee house and a bar patronised by hustlers, clients and their friends. Compared with a group of youths of similar age (average $19\frac{1}{2}$ years) and socio-economic status, a much larger proportion of the prostitutes, 64 per cent as opposed to only 15 per cent, said they had participated in homosexual activity at an early age. The average age for these first encounters was 9.6 years for the prostitutes, 9.2 years for the control group. In both groups, early encounters were nearly all associated with some kind of reward other than any sexual pleasure that might be derived. One youth recalled having been 'sold' by his alcoholic father when he was 10 to an old homosexual who gave him clothes and presents. Another recalled receiving bicycle rides when he was 12 in return for masturbation with an older adolescent. Later, when a prisoner in the Marine Corps brig, he was forced into repeated anal intercourse, then bribed to keep silent. He said he got used to it, decided to 'relax and enjoy it', and discovered he could make it pay well. Coombs concluded that a significant factor in the genesis of male prostitution is boyhood homosexual experience which teaches him to use sex to manipulate others and obtain reward. This type of learning does not necessarily change sexual orientation. Some youths with both early seduction histories and extensive commercial sex contacts with men claimed to be distinctly heterosexual in erotic preference. They felt prostituion was a relatively easy way of life. Most of them lacked stable homes and vocational skills, and had little motivation to compete for more legitimate work. As MacNamara (1965) had put it in an earlier study, immature and irresponsible youths drift into prostitution as a temporary method of survival 'not as self-destructive as suicide, narcotics addiction or alcoholism, nor as anti-social as an overtly criminal career'. An early acquired sophistication in manipulative sex may well influence which of these paths the socially vulnerable youth decides to take.

The career of the male prostitute does not last so long as that of a woman prostitute. As the bloom of youth recedes, the young man becomes rapidly less attractive to the average punter. The only exception to this would seem to be Japan where, according to Benjamin and Masters (1964), the fascination of age is such that younger clients will sometimes pay for older prostitutes. In Western countries, most rent boys have more or less retired by the age of 25. Those who acquire regular patrons, and those who find 'sugar daddies', may continue longer in the trade. For most of the hustlers, however, the possibility of becoming a 'kept boy', even if it arises, does not attract them for long. They are too wilful, too freedom-loving, too irresponsible and untamed, to allow themselves to be moulded into the patterns desired by older, possessive middle-class patrons.

There is no doubt that life on the game can be for some a slippery road to disaster. Jersild found that many of his youths had been erratically behaved or delinquent long before they took to prostitution, but many became considerably more delinquent subsequently. The joys of a parasitic life, the brief experiences of sudden splendour while being entertained by a wealthy homosexual, can be unsettling. For a youth who has lost the habit of regular employment, and lost the time he should have spent training for a trade, a resumption of routine existence is difficult and frustrating, especially when he has had a glimpse of living standards quite unattainable to him by legitimate means. Disillusioned by the real hardships of deviant living, many do in fact reconcile themselves to returning to the kind of life they wanted to escape, but others, seizing upon what seems a viable alternative solution, turn to crime. And of course the most readily available victims are their former patrons, whose habits and addresses they already know.

By all accounts the rent boys' clients have much in common with the clients of female prostitutes (Gibbens and Silberman, 1960). Many are physically unattractive, ageing individuals with little chance of winning a sex partner by their own unaided charms. Others are married men, or men too guilty or ashamed of their sexual needs to want anything more than swift, anonymous release with a stranger to whom they have no emotional commitment and no embarrassing social obligation. Others again are men with unusual sexual tastes, who may enjoy having themselves or their partners adorned with leather and chains or dressed in girls' underwear, or who may take pleasure in being whipped, or in urination rituals, or in acting out elaborate fantasies of the master-slave variety. Such specialised requirements stand more chance of being met by a partner paid to collaborate. As Harris (1973) points out, rent boys acquire a cynical and amused tolerance of even the most bizarre fantasies, and quickly learn how to play along and earn their clients' gratitude. At the other extreme are those clients for whom the physical act of love-making takes second place to a brief illusion of uncritical affection, or the opportunity to talk about their intimate troubles in a way they could not bring themselves to do in any other setting.

The peculiar difficulties of male homosexual living ensure that prostitution will continue to flourish. The persisting attitudes of fear and shame which militate against open and stable homosexual relationships, the prevalence of 'kinky' tastes, the high valuation placed upon the sexual conquest of good-looking, youthful partners, and the unenviable position of married men who cannot suppress and dare not confess their homosexual inclinations, are all circumstances which encourage a resort to commercial sex. On the other side of the fence, economic pressures, and the presence of groups of youths alienated from the conventional standards of society, ensure a continued supply of sex for payment. Over time, the balance of supply and demand may change. In England, for example, the numbers of ordinary young working men anxious to supplement their wages by occasionally sleeping with a punter have probably decreased. Simon Raven (1960) described public houses in London which were well-known as places patronised by soldiers and sailors only too ready to go to bed with anyone in return for a supply of drink and pocket money. Now that servicemen earn a great deal more than the pittance they used to receive, the economic need for them to hustle has decreased, and fewer appear interested in doing so.

Prostitution has always provided easy material for moralising; yet the trade does fulfil some very real human needs, and ought not to be condemned out of hand. The corrupting influence upon the young hustler of an undisciplined life of tax avoidance and quick gains, inevitably based to some extent upon pretence, has to be set against the fact that a certain proportion of these unsettled adolescents do eventually manage to find their feet, some of them indeed with the help and advice of the older men to whom they sold their sexual services (Harris, 1973). It used to be argued that heterosexual prostitution preserves respectable women from unwanted molestation. It could be argued equally well that the existence of professional hustlers prevents lonely and sex-starved men from trying to bribe or coerce younger and more innocent boys into homosexual practices. For all its dangers and problems, homosexual prostitution, like any other institutionalised human relationship, is neither wholly white nor jet black, but a varying shade of grey, according to the circumstances and characteristics of the individual participants.

4. *Venereal disease*

One unforeseen consequence of increasing frankness about homosexuality has been a proliferation of articles in medical journals on the transmission of venereal disease through homosexual contacts. Far from being relatively immune from venereal infection, as many used to like to believe (Schofield, 1964), male homosexuals run a particularly high risk of acquiring sexually transmitted diseases. All recent surveys agree that a disproportionate number of men attending VD clinics have contracted their condition through homosexual contacts. A research conducted for the Medical Society for the Study of Venereal Diseases (Willcox, 1973), drawing upon information from 176 British VD clinics, established that, in the year 1971, out of a total sample of 830 cases of recent syphilis in men investigated at English clinics, some 46 per cent were homosexually acquired. Previous researches at various London clinics had yielded even higher proportions of recent syphilis attributable to homosexuality, variously stated as 83.3 per cent (Waugh, 1972), 73.2 per cent (Fluker, 1966), 72.0 per cent (Jefferiss, 1966) and 68.5 per cent (Woodcock, 1971).

Syphilis, a potentially disabling and sometimes lethal disease, has been a relatively small-scale problem in Great Britian in recent years, and might have virtually disappeared, instead of having a troublesome resurgence, had it not been for the activities of male homosexuals (King, 1974). The high proportions of homosexually contracted syphilitic infections quoted from health service facilities are probably underestimates. Some homosexual patients will still pretend, if they can, that their condition was acquired heterosexually, while others, driven by shame, will pay for treatment privately in order to avoid exposing their circumstances at a public clinic. The particularly high proportions reported by London clinics, in comparison with a national figure of 46 per cent, and still lower figures of 9.5 per cent and 13.5 per cent for Wales and Scotland respectively, are partly accounted for by the tendency of homosexuals to gravitate to the metropolis, and partly by the sympathetic, non-condemnatory approach followed by venereologists at the London teaching hospitals. This has the effect both of persuading clients to tell the truth, and also of encouraging homosexuals to travel some distance to attend the clinics that have a reputation, through the grapevine, of being kindly disposed.

The spirochaete *trepanoma pallidum*, the germ which appears in huge concentrations in syphilitic sores, and which is carried throughout the blood and body fluids of acutely infected individuals, passes from one person to another by skin contact. It cannot gain entry through ordinary, unbroken skin, but it can get into cuts and abrasions, and it can penetrate the mucous linings of vagina, mouth and anal canal, and the delicate covering of the head of the penis, especially if vigorous sexual activity has produced tiny scrapes or tears. The germ needs moisture to survive long enough to penetrate. It is susceptible to antiseptics, so simple hygienic precautions such as swift and thorough soapy washing, or the application of a bacteriocidal ointment, are not entirely useless in lessening the risk of infection.

When the germ penetrates, a hard painless sore or chancre forms at the point of entry. This takes anything from a week to three months to develop, but most often appears after about three weeks. In a woman, the chancre often forms high up in the vagina where she may not be aware of it. In males, it usually forms on the penis, occasionally on the lips, sites which cannot be overlooked. Among those homosexuals who like to have a man insert his penis into their anus, a chancre may develop in or around the orifice, or deep inside the rectum. The sore may be invisible and painless, or alternatively may be mistaken for a haemorrhoid or for one of the benign skin conditions that affect the anal area. In either event, it will quite likely receive no treatment and will remain highly infectious. A promiscuous homosexual with such a reservoir of infection can transmit the disease in all innocence to a whole sequence of victims before the carrier is discovered. The diagnosis at this stage is not always obvious, even when suspected, since blood tests for this infection do not usually become positive until some weeks after the primary chancre has appeared.

Primary chancres are usually accompanied by swollen lymph glands producing lumps in the groins. Left untreated both sore and lumps disappear, but unfortunately this does not mean the disease is cured. The germs proliferate in the blood stream, and after a period of two to three months the secondary stage of the illness begins, characterised by vague malaise, slight fever, swollen glands, a variety of skin rashes, and sometimes painless ulcers in the mouth, throat or ano-genital region. During all this period of incubation, and during the secondary phase, the patient remains infectious, and the skin eruptions in particular are highly infectious.

Even now, if the patient is too frightened to go to a doctor, or if, as sometimes happens, the symptoms are quite mild and shrugged off as unimportant, the condition may remain untreated. In that event, the rashes and other disturbances once again subside, although they may recur with varying degrees of intensity in the years to follow. Once again the patient may believe himself cured, but reservoirs of infection are apt to persist in almost any part of the body, and to flare up at any time in unexpected ways, sometimes after an interval of many years, causing heart disease, spinal paralysis, softening of the brain or any number of other dire consequences.

With modern antibiotics, syphilis is an eminently treatable disease, and can usually be completely eradicated, leaving the patient free to pursue his sex life as before. Blood tests will detect the condition even during the latent or symptomless phases, and at any stage appropriate treatment can usually forestall or arrest the further progress of the disease. In view of the special risks of concealed syphilitic infection among persons of unconventional sexual habits, homophile organisations advise their members to have blood tests at least twice a year (Albany Trust, 1966).

The one sure method of prevention, sexual continence, holds little appeal, least of all to the promiscuous male homosexual. Simple hygiene and germicidal ointments may lessen risk, but are not very effective. Prophylactic doses of antibiotics are unwise, and indeed impractical if exposure to the risk of syphilitic infection occurs constantly. Moreover, some doctors believe that the indiscriminate use of antibiotics risks masking the symptoms of a syphilitic infection without completely eradicating it, thus introducing a condition even more dangerous and ultimately all the more difficult to treat.

Gonorrhoea, the commonest of the venereal diseases, manifests in males by an irritation or burning sensation during urination, followed by a yellowish purulent discharge from the penis. The germ passes from the genitals of one person to another during intercourse. The incubation period before symptoms develop is usually relatively short, two to five days. In the male, the inflammation is usually obvious and painful, treatment is sought promptly, and antibiotics are quickly effective. A woman with a gonorrhoeal infection deep in the vagina, or a man similarly infected in the rectum, may themselves experience no symptoms, but continue to act as carriers of the disease until such times as the repeated complaints of their sexual partners draws attention to the state of affairs. Rectal gonorrhoea may produce oozing and irritation round the anus, but this is easily overlooked. Only occasionally does it provoke more acute disturbance, such as burning pain, or blood and mucus in the stools. Warts appearing around the anus, due to secondary infection, also give grounds for suspicion, although they are not necessarily indicative of the presence of gonorrhoea.

Since Fiumara, Wise and Many (1967) cited some instances of gonorrhoeal throat infection in homosexuals, presumably contracted by fellating an infected male, similar observations have been reported by a number of others (Owen and Hill, 1972; Ratnatunga, 1972). In a Danish survey of 1,152 patients infected with gonorrhoea (Bro-Jørgensen and Jensen, 1973), bacteriological examination revealed the presence of gonorrhoeal infection in the throats of 10 per cent of female patients, 7 per cent of male heterosexual patients and 25 per cent of male homosexual patients. Most of the patients found to be so infected admitted mouth-genital sexual contact. The risk of acquiring a throat infection was greater from fellatio than from cunnilingus. A few of the infected patients had fever and inflamed tonsils, but most suffered no symptoms, although presumably they could infect others. These throat infections proved persistent and much more difficult to eradicate with antibiotics than gonorrhoea of the genitals. To sum up the position, gonorrhoea of the throat is yet another venereal complaint, relatively common, often symptomless, yet a potential source of serious complications, which is particularly prevalent among male homosexuals, due to their widespread use of mouth-genital contacts.

Among men with gonorrhoea seen at London clinics the proportion reported to have been infected by homosexual contacts, although quite high (about a fifth), is less than the proportion of syphilitic infections so acquired (King, 1974). The reason for this is unclear. Being a less serious illness, doctors may not feel the need to probe into its origin as carefully, or patients to confess so frankly, as in the case of syphilis, so the contribution of homosexual contacts might be underestimated. On the other hand, there are a great many more women carriers of gonorrhoea than women carriers of syphilis, so gonorrhoea rather than syphilis is the more usual complaint of male heterosexuals.

Infections of the urinary passage by germs other than the gonococcus, so-called non-specific urethritis, can occur in both heterosexual and homosexual men, but are thought to be particularly prevalent among those who habitually expose their penis to the wide variety of germs that inhabit the rectum. The causative organisms cannot always be identified, and sometimes the inflammation and discharge persists or recurs from time to time in spite of vigorous treatment with antibiotics.

Syphilis and gonorrhoea are not the only sexually transmitted diseases. A rare, but extremely serious and intractable condition, lymphogranuloma venereum, occurs most commonly in tropical and sub-tropical countries, but a few cases are turning up in Europe and America, possible due to the increasing habit of world travel. The disease produces cancerous swellings and abscesses which eat away the vagina and rectum, leading to severe ulcerative colitis and rectal obstruction. When this disease occurs in the rectum in males it is believed to be the result of infection during homosexual activity (Greaves, 1963). Unfortunately the condition responds poorly to antibiotics, and often leads to permanent painful disability.

Another rare ulcerative condition, lymphogranuloma inguinalae, is now known to be an infection caused by the organism *Donovania*, which thrives in faeces and lives inside the intestines. Venereologists believe that a likely method of contracting this disease is by homosexual practice, since ulceration surrounding the anus occurs only among those who are passive partners in anal intercourse (Goldberg, 1964).

Two common parasitic itching skin complaints, crab lice in the pubic hair and scabies of the genitals, are usually contracted by sexual intimacies with an infected person. Fortunately they are relatively innocuous and easily eradicated. The frequency with which the homosexual clients of VD clinics complain of repeated attacks of these infestations, as well as previous attacks of gonorrhoea, provides ample confirmation, if any were needed, of their promiscuous habits.

Finally, a possible association between liability to liver disease and homosexual habits deserves mention. Jeffries *et al.* (1973) found a significantly raised incidence of Australia (hepatitis-associated) antigen in the blood of venereal clinic patients, particularly so among male homosexual patients. The finding has been confirmed by other venereologists.

Nothing much seems to have been written about venereal disease among lesbians. It is assumed to be rare, but unless an infected woman chooses to report that her partner was a female, the doctor would have no cause to suspect the fact. However, since lesbians tend to avoid promiscuity, and to make love by embracing and manual manipulation, which do not easily transmit venereal infection, their way of life involves little risk of infection. But there are exceptions. A small minority of lesbians are highly promiscuous with both men and women. The prevalence of such conduct among young girl delinquents has already been noted (see p. 188). These girls also have a high incidence of venereal infection.

Medical warnings have failed to abolish cigarette smoking and are unlikely to have much effect upon social habits in the sexual field. The practice of anal intercourse, and the enjoyment of a variety of sexual relationships with different partners, seems an inescapable part of the male homosexual condition. The habit of holidaying in exotic places renowned for easy sex, but equally renowned for infectious diseases, adds a further quota of risk. The importance of public education in this matter, so that homosexuals become aware of the risks, cannot be over-emphasised. Some homosexuals have discovered that they can secure periodic blood tests without the embarrassment of visits to a VD clinic by volunteering as blood donors.

VD clinics could do more to lessen embarrassment. A recent *Which?* guide (1974), one of a series published by the Consumers' Association, criticises the lack of understanding of their clients' sensitivities displayed by the staff at some clinics, which has the effect of discouraging patients from returning for periodic checks. Braff (1962) pointed out that detailed inquisition into sex positions during love-making, to which homosexuals are sometimes subjected, is often unnecessary. The absolute anonymity of medical records and of statistical returns to government agencies needs to be repeatedly emphasised. Homosexual behaviour among the young is still a criminal offence in England, so young persons and their contacts have reason to be wary. Schofield (1964) quoted advice published some years ago by an American homophile organisation to the effect that homosexuals should keep away from public VD clinics because of lack of assurance that information given there 'is not also available to the public, the police and the courts ...'. English people probably have more confidence in the medical profession, but even so the construction of many VD clinics does not inspire confidence. Often clients have to enter hospitals by a special entrance, separate from all other out-patient facilities. In a small town, patients dislike visiting such places, because people who know them may see them going in and realise immediately that they are VD clients. Unfortunately, the organisation of VD services, and the attitudes of VD workers and fellow VD patients, cannot be altogether immune from prevailing community attitudes to sexual irregularities. The very existence of these separate hospital facilities underlines the fact that neither patients nor doctors fully accept that sexually transmitted diseases should be treated on exactly the same footing as any other illness.

5. *Homosexuality in prisons*

In comparison with the United States, very little has been published in England concerning sex in prisons. Official reticence in the face of an embarrassing topic, and the influence of the Official Secrets Acts, may be in part responsible, but, on the other hand, different social circumstances might account for prison homosexuality manifesting more dramatically and more violently in America. The United States has more men in prison per head of population, her institutions are larger and more overcrowded, her judiciary passes considerably longer sentences, and key posts in her prison services have been affected by political patronage.

One of the earliest and frankest accounts of sexual happenings in men's prisons in America was written by J.F. Fishman (1934), a one-time Inspector of Prisons. Among the factors contributing to homosexual behaviour he cited the absence of women, the close proximity of other men, the enforced idleness, the perpetual salacious talk, the breakdown of normal self-respect and social standards, and the presence among the prisoners of known prostitutes only too ready to proffer themselves shamelessly to all and sundry. He noted how the active homosexual or 'wolf' courts any newcomer who takes his fancy, pursuing his object with the pertinacity of one who has nothing else to occupy him. Some good-looking young prisoners take advantage of the situation to get as much as possible in return for their sexual favours. Others, more scrupulous or more sensitive, submit unwillingly, terrified of the consequences of refusal, and not daring to complain to the authorities for fear of reprisals from other prisoners. Fishman mentions numerous allegations that prison guards not only turn a blind eye to sexual abuses, but take advantage of their position in order to oblige inmates to gratify their own sexual demands.

Recent accounts of prison life suggest that little has changed over the years (Vedder and King, 1967; Sykes, 1958; Williams and Fish, 1974). Most prisoners come from the underprivileged segments of American society where masculine self-respect, denied the rewards of education and prestigious employment, depends upon physical dominance and assertive sexual conquest. Such men regard a resort to solitary masturbation as a confession of shameful weakness and personal failure. Having led aggressively predatory heterosexual lives outside, they transfer their outlook to the prison setting, preying upon weaker inmates for the dual purpose of maintaining their machismo image and at the same time achieving release of sexual tension (Buffum, 1972). The high proportion of black inmates in most American prisons contributes to the likelihood of homosexual conduct, since they have less inhibitions than whites and accept with little compunction any fellator or prostitute willing to provide them with an easy sexual orgasm (Huffman, 1960).

Sexual exchanges in male prisons lack the reciprocity of homosexual relationships in the free community. Men adhere to active and passive roles in a crude caricature of heterosexuality, the active partners boasting their masculine prowess, the passive partners being treated like girls and losing face accordingly. Sociologists have been struck both by the high incidence of prison homosexuality and by the way the prison subculture exploits homosexuality as a means of placing individuals within the inmate caste system. Clemmer (1958) estimated that some 40 per cent of male inmates participated in prison sex, although only 10 per cent were homosexually inclined under normal circumstances. Prison slang defines sexual habits and inmate status simultaneously. Lowest of all in the pecking order come the 'girls' or 'fagots', natural homosexuals who offer themselves spontaneously as passive partners. The 'punks' a stage higher up, have put up an initial resistance to sexual molestation, but have finally given way to force, threats or ingratiation from stronger or more experienced prison 'wolves'. Once he has yielded and been type-cast a 'punk', a prisoner can never regain the top status of 'jocker' or 'wolf'.

While some prison wolves are casual and promiscuous in their sexual conquests, others become 'daddies', courting, befriending and patronising one particular 'kid', who becomes their sexual slave. By dint of an appropriate show of dominance and possessiveness towards the punk who has become a substitute wife, the wolf manages to retain his masculine image and status. Any suspicion of 'flip-flopping', that is occasional reversal of sexual positions, allowing the wife to get on top sometimes, causes the wolf to lose status.

Horrifying stories of desperate fights for sexual supremacy have been reported by American prisoners. In a chapter entitled 'Sexual Perversion in the Prison' L.D. Johnson (1970), an ex-convict from Kansas, describes the furious jealousies, leading sometimes to murder, which can build up when a prison wolf discovers that the punk he believes he possesses completely is flirting with another prisoner. As Johnson sagely remarks, outside prison jealous lovers can get away from the scene and forget it, but inside prison the only escape from humiliation and frustration lies in acts of violence.

Johnson agrees with the sociologists Gagnon and Simon (1968) that the inmate who falls into the passive punk role usually does so because he feels the need for protection and sees the advantage of a close relationship with a powerful, high-status prisoner. A lonely, frightened young newcomer has to be unusually courageous and resolute to resist the insistent pressure from an experienced convict, especially if he accepts favours which automatically place him under an obligation. Sexual submission at knife point, or as a result of outright force, is the exception rather than the rule, although such occurrences are by no means uncommon, especially in institutions for young offenders, where discipline is lax (Ward, 1958; Huffman, 1961).

The outcome of various judicial inquiries into prison rapes leaves. little room for complacency. An especially revealing inquiry was conducted by Allan Davis (1970), a District Attorney in Philadelphia, following the complaint of a 19-year-old youth that he had been repeatedly raped by a gang of criminals while being transported in a sheriff's van after his arrest. The investigators interviewed over 3,000 prisoners and 500 staff. They found that virtually every slightly built young man was sexually approached within a few days of his first entry into the Philadelphia prisons, and that many of them were raped repeatedly by gangs of inmates. Others yielded to the domination of an individual tormentor in order to gain protection from indiscriminate assaults. The report quotes numerous eye-witness accounts of kids forcibly held down, screaming in agony and bleeding from the rectum, while one prisoner after another commits anal rape. Victims were too terrified of retaliation from other prisoners, or too ashamed of the consequences of a public revelation of their humiliation, to report incidents to the guards. Those who did so were often discouraged from making an official complaint. If they persisted they were put into virtual solitary confinement for their own protection, with nothing to look forward to but revenge attacks from the aggressors and their friends whenever they returned to the prison community.

The investigators estimated that nearly a thousand assaults took place each year, only a tiny fraction of which, perhaps 3 per cent, were reported. In addition, much of the supposedly consensual homosexual behaviour in the prisons was only made possible by the fear-charged atmosphere and the ever-present threat of rape. Obviously effeminate homosexuals and known prostitutes were supposed to be segregated, but guards cynically left their cells unprotected so that favoured prisoners could enjoy sexual relations. The existence within the prison system of a research project, for which volunteers lucky enough to be selected got paid for acting as guinea pigs, aggravated the situation by creating financial inequalities between inmates and thus enabling bribery and prostitution to flourish.

Comparisons between the victims and aggressors in sexual assaults showed that the latter were more likely to be older and stronger and negro, and more likely to be serious criminals with a history of violent crimes such as rape, aggravated robbery and assaults with intent to kill. Expressions commonly used by aggressors, such as 'Fight or fuck', or 'You'll have to give up some face', revealed a need to degrade and conquer as well as to obtain sexual pleasure. Such expressions of anger and frustration, prompted by inability to achieve masculine pride other than by sexual and physical subjugation, suggests that the motives for aggressive sexual assaults in prison have much in common with the motives which impel the same individuals to commit other kinds of violent crime when they are outside.

From time to time the explosive sexual tensions in prison reach the ears of the courts. In 1971, the Supreme Court of Missouri (State v. Green, 470 S W 2d 565) was called upon to decide whether to uphold a court decision refusing an escaped prisoner permission to run a defence that he had acted under compulsion in running away from prison to escape homosexual rape. The decision was upheld, but with a powerful dissenting opinion from Judge Seiler. The defendant in question, aged 19, alleged he had been homosexually ravaged at knife point by two inmates who picked the lock of his cell during the night. Two weeks later three inmates invaded his cell, knocked him unconscious as he tried to flee, and raped him. Twice the defendant had complained to a prison official but been told to defend himself, submit, or 'go over the fence'. Warned one day by four or five inmates that they were going to visit him that night to force him to submit again, he decided to escape. The dissenting judge took the view that the prisoner had been confronted with a horrifying dilemma not of his making, that he had acted under coercion, and that he should have been allowed to put that defence to the jury (Kadish and Paulsen, 1972, p. 129). More recently (March 1975), a prisoner who fled from a Californian jail rather than submit to rape fared better. Justice Robert Gardner of the Court of Appeal, fourth district, Southern California, ruled that conditions can get so bad that the prisoner has a human right to leave. He must, however, have done everything possible to defend himself against sexual attack before taking it upon himself to escape, and once outside he must give himself up to the police promptly.

The public is beginning to realise that for young men who are not tough, hardened criminals, and not sophisticated in the power games of closed institutions, being sent to prison may mean the additional shame and discomfort of sexual humiliation. The play *Fortune and Men's Eyes* (Herbert, 1967), converted later into a dramatic film, was supposedly based upon true experience in Canadian prisons. Depicting one man's struggle against the pressure of homosexual seduction, and another's pathetic and repeated capitulation to the wolves, it is well calculated to arouse attention and sympathy for individuals caught up in these prison conflicts.

Men's prisons in England are certainly not immune from the homosexual conflicts that beset closed, single-sex institutions all over the world, but by all accounts they experience the phenomena in relatively subdued, non-violent forms. A good deal of gossip, occasional passing of propositioning notes, and surreptitious meetings in wash rooms, would seem to be the norm, but discipline and close surveillance prevent more florid manifestations. Self-declared homosexuals with outrageous mannerisms, delighting in the girls' nicknames by which they are universally known within the prison, create a certain amount of uneasiness among prisoners anxious to avoid sexual temptation or involvement while inside (Morris and Morris, 1963, p. 187). These well-known 'bitches' are tolerated, perhaps jokingly flirted with, but are not really liked by the majority. Since they give the appearance of substitutes for women, more masculine prisoners can make use of them without loss of face or risk of being type-cast as 'queers'. One educated ex-prisoner, Heckstall-Smith (1954, ch.11) has written a lengthy and apparently realistic account of his experiences of homosexuality in English prisons. He blames the influence of ex-borstal boys and inmates of residential schools for delinquents, who have been used to nightly sex orgies in the dormitories, for spreading among prisoners a sordidly uninhibited attitude to homosexual indulgence. He thinks youths passing through such institutions become sophisticated in homosexual prostitution. In the adult prison, sex gossip, jealous intrigues and homosexual liaisons are going on all the time, and many married men, who would never have looked at a 'queer' outside, become involved. Some inmates, Heckstall-Smith believes, having begun homosexual affairs for the first time in prison intend to continue after release.

Most authorities assume that, as with sexually segregated male rats who have acquired homosexual habits, swift reversion to heterosexuality will take place once access to the opposite sex is regained. MacDonald (1961) points out that this may not necessarily follow in the case of human prisoners. Welfare workers are aware that men separated from their wives for long periods sometimes find difficulty in resuming their previous sexual performances. Although most men who have had homosexual experiences in civilian or prisoner-of-war camps like to forget all about it later, there are exceptions. Westwood (1952) describes one such case. A young RAF officer, captured in wartime when he was aged 21, who had no previous homosexual feelings, formed a deep attachment to another inmate of the prison camp, and went to live with him after their release. Two ex-prisoners, Davis and Telega, writing in a prison reform magazine (*Fortune News*, New York, April 1974) describe as a 'terrifying experience' the feeling of attraction for a person of their own sex that develops in prison in men who have never had that orientation or desire before. Telega, who was 19 on release after a three-year stint, commented: 'I acted towards girls the way I had three years earlier. They had grown but I hadn't. It took me a long time to catch up.' Davis remarked: 'After relating to men over a long period of time, what do you say to a woman? ... My adjustment was very difficult.'

Like so many matters concerned with human sexuality, observations on prison behaviour raise important questions as yet unanswered by any research. The proportion of men who develop homosexual interests when forcibly segregated from women has never been satisfactorily established. Just as they tend to lose interest in alcohol when it becomes unobtainable, many prisoners, instead of experiencing an upsurge of homosexuality report a deadening of all sexual feeling once their customary outlets are cut off. Younger prisoners more than older ones, on account of their strong physiological impulses and as yet unsettled behaviour patterns, may be particularly liable to fluctuations of sexual interest as a result of imprisonment. Rationally, one might expect lasting shifts of sexual orientation to be most likely to occur among those forced to pass through adolescence in closed institutions where they are denied normal socio-sexual learning experiences at a critical phase of development. The incidence and nature of problems of sexual orientation developing apparently as a result of imprisonment deserve close study. The investigations needed to explore these questions would be embarrassing, but well worthwhile. Although it creates problems, both personal and administrative, the system of conjugal visits, whereby rooms are set aside for male prisoners to receive their wives in private, has been found to have the effect of reducing the incidence of overt homosexual conduct within prisons (Nice, 1966).

Penologists have often pointed out that sexual tension is even more evident in women's prisons than in male institutions (Ford, 1929), and especially so in reformatories for juvenile girls (Halleck and Hersko, 1962; Taylor, 1965). Prison lesbianism, however, does not encompass forcible subjugation, and is usually more loving and less impersonal and less overtly exploitative than homosexuality in male institutions. This difference has been cited already as an example of the predominance of the emotional over the erotic in female sexuality (see p. 171). Rose Giallombardo (1966), who made a detailed study of a Federal Reformatory for women in West Virginia, was struck by the development of an inmate system of 'families' in which married couples were represented by homosexual alliances. The system enabled inmates to obtain emotional support from a small intimate group, and to continue some of the family roles (such as 'granny' and 'elder sister') so dear to women in the community outside. Prisoners assumed 'male' or 'female' characters, the former, within the limits of prison regulations, dressing in a symbolical masculine fashion, with short hair, no make-up, and stiffly starched and folded blouse collars. In their pseudo-marital alliances the women adopted roles appropriate to 'husband' or 'wife'. The male stud role, being perhaps more difficult to maintain, was less frequent, and carried a certain prestige. The stud was expected to protect the wife from criticism, to show her consideration and politeness, and to share with her any material possessions. The wife in her turn supplied 'services', sexual and otherwise, which might include doing the stud's cleaning and tidying chores as well as her own. Alliances were formed on a romantic basis, studs pursuing femmes with flowery notes ('kites'), and urging upon them the advantages of becoming a pair. Stable couples were recognised as such and admired by other inmates. A certain amount of philandering, especially by studs, exposed to the seductive charms of the many unpaired femmes, was tolerated, but not when it led to the break-up of a 'family'. This system of 'family' relationships gave the prisoners a focus of interest while they served their sentences and enabled many of the women to continue the social roles to which they were accustomed in working-class society at the time.

The 'play families' which exist in female institutions, and include mother-daughter relationships, as well as 'honey' or husband-wife roles, were first described by Selling (1931) and have been discussed again in some detail in a study of the Women's Reformatory at Occoquan in Virginia by Esther Heffernan (1972). She estimated that up to half of the inmates involved themselves in pseudo-families, in spite of disapproval by the prison staff, but the borderline between companionable and conjugal relationships was hard to define. In particular, she observed that overt physical sex contacts won less widespread approval among inmates than emotionally tinged role-playing. One prisoner was quoted as believing that most of the studs were 'just putting on an act', that if they were really sexually abnormal they would take pains to hide it. Certainly real physical intimacies had to take place very discreetly, owing to the strong disapproval of the staff and the firm disciplinary action taken against couples caught in the act. Actually, due to the connivance of other inmates, who did their best to shield their friends during occasions of intimacy, detected incidents were rare, but suspected liaisons were frequently broken up by administrative transfers.

Some New York psychiatrists (Bluestone *et al.*, 1966) have commented that homosexuality appears so prevalent in women's prisons that it would be useless to try to separate off the known homosexuals from the rest of the inmates, as is done in male prisons. Since women receive sentences of imprisonment much less frequently than men, the women in prison represent a highly selected and socially deviant group. According to Bluestone *et al.* the majority of female inmates of New York prisons have experience of overt homosexuality before entering prison. They mostly come from disorderly homes with sexually promiscuous parents. Many have been prostitutes, and mixed in circles where drug abuse and sexual irregularities are rife. Their prison sex behaviour is an extension and an exaggeration of their conduct outside. Being ineffectual, dependent personalities, prison homosexual relationships provide them with a form of emotional security they cannot achieve in the more demanding atmosphere of the heterosexual world outside. However that may be, lesbianism is common place in women's prisons, and Miller and Hannum (1963), who applied a battery of tests, including the MMPI, to women prisoners at another institution, discovered no significant difference between those who were known participants in prison lesbianism and those who were not.

Clearly, the character and prevalence of homosexuality in women's prisons must reflect the kinds of women sent to prison, the disciplinary regime within the institution, and whether homosexual liaisons become so much a part of the inmate subculture that those who do not participate find themselves ostracised. The situation in English women's prisons has never been investigated and reported by sociologists, so one can only speculate as to how far the American observations apply. Now and then some scandal reaches the newspapers, indicating that official silence does not mean absence of homosexual phenomena. In 1974, for example, a female prison officer was sentenced to six years imprisonment for conspiring to help the escape of a notorious woman prisoner serving a life sentence for her part in the moors murder incidents (see p. 211). Another inmate had warned the authorities that the two women were having a love affair, but she was not at first believed, and was disciplined for making a false accusation (*The Times* 2-3 April 1974).

CHAPTER NINE

Change: Spontaneous and Assisted

1. *Treatment attempts: the ethical issue*

The prospect of changing an adult's sexual orientation stirs deep feelings pro and con. Some authorities assert dogmatically that it cannot be done. The traditional medical view of homosexual orientation as an undesirable, restrictive and unhealthy condition, to be rooted out by any means available, moves the younger generation of radical homosexuals to righteous indignation. They consider it misguided and immoral to try to inculcate an alien sexual pattern for the sake of conformity to convention. The long-unquestioned medical assumption that homosexuality is necessarily bad, and associated with all kinds of abnormalities, strikes modern critics as suspiciously reminiscent of the similar ideas formerly promulgated by doctors to discourage masturbation (Hare, 1962). Homophile propagandists invariably express scepticism about the likelihood of achieving a successful conversion to heterosexuality. They see nothing incongruous in simultaneously claiming that many married people discover, relatively late in life, a homosexual preference, since they attribute such apparent conversions to a mere belated acknowledgment of the truth by persons who have had social reasons for hiding their real sexual orientation.

In response to frequent complaints that psychiatrists use their prestige to support the establishment in denigrating homosexuals and coercing them into conformity, the Trustees of the American Psychiatric Association, on 15 December 1973, adopted a resolution that: 'Whereas homosexuality per se implies no impairment in judgment, stability, reliability, or general social or vocational capabilities, therefore, be it resolved that the American Psychiatric Association deplores all public and private discrimination against homosexuals in such areas as employment, housing, public accommodation and licensing and declares that no burden of proof of such judgment, capacity, or reliability shall be placed upon homosexuals greater than that imposed on any other persons. Further, the American Psychiatric Association supports and urges the enactment of civil rights legislation at the local, state, and federal level that would offer homosexual citizens the same protections now guaranteed to others on the basis of race, creed, color, etc. Further, the American Psychiatric Association supports and urges the repeal of all discriminatory legislation singling out homosexual acts by consenting adults in private.' At the same time the organisation modified its official nomenclature, deleting homosexuality from the list of mental disorders (where it had previously appeared in company with such sexual deviations as paedophilia and voyeurism) and replacing it with a new category of 'sexual orientation disturbance', described as follows: 'This category is for individuals whose sexual interests are directed primarily toward people of the same sex and who are either disturbed by, in conflict with, or wish to change their sexual orientation. This diagnostic category is distinguished from homosexuality, which by itself does not necessarily constitute a psychiatric disorder. Homosexuality per se is one form of sexual behavior and, like other forms of sexual behavior which are not by themselves psychiatric disorders, is not listed in this nomenclature of mental disorders.'

This decision means that, according to their official spokesmen, American psychiatrists no longer consider homosexual orientation a matter for interference or treatment, so long as the affected individual remains undisturbed by his condition and does not want to change. Many prominent psychiatrists profoundly disagree with this new liberal attitude, and continue to regard homosexuality as a highly undesirable deviation, at least as serious as fetishism and exhibitionism, which still count as mental disorders. The new official line emerged following a symposium on the subject, led by Stoller and others (1973), which was held during the annual meeting of the Association and published subsequently in the American Journal of Psychiatry. Highly divergent views, passionately expressed, marked the occasion. Judd Marmor argued that there is incontrovertible evidence that some homosexuals are happy with their lives and have made a realistic adaptation to being members of a minority group. Ronald Gold, a representative of the Gay Liberation movement, argued that psychiatric interference makes homosexuals ill who would otherwise be healthy and happy. Socarides argued that the homosexual's inability to penetrate a woman's vagina and fertilise her is an obvious biological defect, and the opinions of contemporary social or political movements cannot change this fact. This continuing controversy reflects an unresolved confusion in psychiatric literature about the concepts of normality, sickness and deviance, especially as they apply to homosexuality (Pattison, 1974).

The older generation of psychiatrists seems to have been particularly firmly wedded to belief in the pathological nature of a homosexual orientation. Edmund Bergler (1951), who wrote a well-known book describing homosexual love as Neurotic Counterfeit-Sex, has always insisted that homosexuals are very sick people who would lead miserable lives whatever society's attitude towards them. Another American psychiatrist, Hervey Cleckley (1957), devotes the whole of a substantial book, entitled *The Caricature of Love*, to challenging the fashionable acceptance of homosexuality as not particularly pathological or regrettable. Cleckley blames the preoccupation of certain writers with homosexuality for fostering a false picture of life. Oscar Wilde's famous aphorism 'each man kills the thing he loves ...' reflects the disillusionment of a man committed to homosexual relationships. In Cleckley's opinion, Proust's admission that the invert seeks out the love of a man who loves women reveals an important feature of male homosexuals. Because they seek the unattainable, namely a heterosexual partner, they can never satisfy each other for long, and their attempts to form romantic unions inevitably fail. He quotes literary descriptions of unhappy homosexual lives, such as. Truman Capote's *Other Voices, Other Rooms* (1948) to show that a 'perverse' sex drive does not lend itself to genuine love. Descriptions of the life in gay bars shows how homosexual relationships are soured by peevish demands and characterised by outlandish promiscuity. The attraction of older men for toughs and hustlers reflects the element of disgust that enters into their desires. Cleckley thinks that homosexuals believe in the goodness of gay life because they know no better, being unable to appreciate at first hand what the mating of a man and woman really means.

More recent books take an essentially similar line, modified only slightly by the greatly increased dissemination of writings by homosexuals describing the realities of the gay world. For instance, in *Growing Up Straight*, a popular book explaining 'what every thoughtful parent should know about homosexuality', Peter and Barbara Wyden (1968) maintain that the attempts by homosexual organisations to achieve the ennobling status of an unfairly persecuted minority rests upon the propagation of misleading information about homosexual affliction. 'Most heterosexuals would probably be surprised to know just how harsh, cold and downright treacherous the homosexual life often is.' Apart from the everlasting fear of discovery under circumstances leading to loss of livelihood, homosexuals face risks of blackmail, venereal disease and 'especially the risk of having to lead a permanently driven, disorganised, unhappy and often lonely life'. It is a world 'where the accent on youth is so obsessive that men of 35 or over often cannot "make out" unless they pay for partners'. The authors regret the visible infiltration of well-off gay couples into certain notorious sections of American cities (sometimes known as 'The Swish Alps'), they deplore the availability of flourishing gay resorts ready to welcome any young newcomer wavering on the brink of a homosexual decision, and they object to the flaunting by gay communities of the institutional trappings of a respectable way of life.

The Wydens believe that homosexuals resist change, not because gay life seems rewarding, but because homosexuals are ruled by the fears that produced their condition in the first place. They challenge the pessimism of many psychiatrists about the feasibility and desirability of conversion to heterosexuality. They think too great

prominence has been given to the outmoded opinions of Sigmund
Freud (1935) who once wrote, in reply to a mother's request for advice
about a cure for her homosexual son: 'In a certain number of cases we
succeed in developing the blighted germs of heterosexual tendencies
which are present in every homosexual; in the majority it is no more
possible ... What analysis can do for your son runs on a different line.
If he is unhappy, neurotic, torn by conflicts, inhibited in his social life,
analysis may bring him harmony, peace of mind, full efficiency ...' In
practice, given a suitably sympathetic and confident psychotherapist,
the Wydens believe that many one time homosexuals abandon their
orientation with relief and come to function happily as heterosexuals.
They illustrate their point with some telling examples.

Dr. George Weinberg (1972), one of an increasing number of
psychotherapists to take an opposite standpoint, devotes a passionate
chapter of his book *Society and the Healthy Homosexual* to 'the case
against trying to convert'. He finds some of the treatment methods
employed, especially the aversive techniques, gruesome and
ineffectual. Therapists concentrate on putting an end to disapproved
behaviour, but give little thought to whether the patient will find
romantic fulfilment with the opposite sex or prove a satisfactory
marriage partner. A total disappearance of homosexual inclinations
rarely occurs, and Weinberg cites instances, counted as successes by
therapists, in which marriages have been marred by intermittent
lapses into homosexual behaviour. Therapists often underestimate the
richness of the love feelings they seek to eradicate, failing to appreciate
how ordinary human experiences, shared between lovers, create
bonds not easily broken. Moreover, a patient's sense of purpose and
identity may depend upon his homosexuality. Weinberg cites the
example of a successful creative writer who completely lost his ability
to work because an unwise therapist had provoked a deep shame for
the concealed love fantasies that had been his inner inspiration.

Green (1972) a psychiatrist with a long career as an investigator of
cases of gender confusion and hermaphroditism, and a man whom no
one could accuse of neglecting possible biological and hormonal
determinants of sexual orientation, after a lengthy review of the
evidence for the presence of physical and psychological peculiarities
among homosexuals, reached the conclusion that no convincing data
existed to prove that heterosexual orgasms and heterosexual loves
were necessarily superior to homosexual ones. He noted that the value
system by which heterosexuality was judged superior, and
homosexuality thought a suitable condition for treatment, was based
upon the now questionable social benefits of producing children and
contracting a permanent monogamous marriage. As to the latter, man
had, 'by fiat', 'joined company with geese and the painted shrimp,
who by instinct effect lifelong matings'.

Martin Hoffman (1968), another American psychotherapist who
disagrees with the disease concept of homosexuality, sees no call to
apply treatment indiscriminately. He quotes the psychoanalyst Van

den Haag (1963) who, in reply to a colleague's remark that 'all my homosexual patients are quite sick' retorted 'so are all my heterosexual patients'. Although not uncritical of some aspects of male gay life, notably the prevalence of 'one-night stands', the fragmentation of sex life from ordinary contacts, and the fetishistic concentration on youthful appearance, Hoffman remains convinced that many of the participants achieve a reasonable poise and suffer no undue anxiety. Society may label homosexuality a disease, as a matter of definition, but the assertion that all homosexuals are unhappy or neurotic is open to contradiction from factual observation.

Views similar to those of Weinberg and Hoffman find favour among sophisticated members of the intellectual establishment, especially in the United States. For example, a study guide on homosexuality issued by SIECUS (1973), the Sex Information and Education Council of the US, refers to an increasing respect for the diversity of human sexual behaviour and states that 'homosexuality is more and more coming to be viewed as a legitimate, not uncommon, and frequently rewarding form of sexual expression'. They point out that findings based upon carefully controlled samples suggest that homosexuals fall within the normal range of variation and are not consistently different from heterosexuals in their psychological functioning. They note that most homosexuals apparently overcome social discrimination, may win acceptance by their families and enjoy a wide circle of friends, and few are ever arrested or blackmailed. They remark that 'sensitive, intelligent parents do not insist that children become carbon copies of themselves', and they advise that 'the demand that a child conform to a sexual pattern which the parent happens to find personally rewarding, should be replaced by an interest in promoting a sexual way of life that is entirely congruent with the young person's deepest needs and interests'.

Controversy about the ethics of treatment for homosexuals hinges upon an evaluation of the advantages and disadvantages of homosexual life-styles, and an estimation of the prospects of achieving conversion to a secure and satisfying heterosexual orientation. Since the experts flatly contradict each other on these points, the reader may like to know this author's present views. Of course, any opinion must have an element of personal bias, and may perhaps be influenced by the individual's own sexual history. But bias can work in different ways. At a meeting of a Gay Liberation group at the London School of Economics a member of the audience objected to the speaker's rather clinical approach because he thought it derived from the prejudices of a 'straight' psychiatrist who could not appreciate the homosexual psyche. Another commentator expressed the less flattering conviction that the speaker's views represented the hypocritical protestations of a 'closet queen'. Either way, such comments distract people from the real issues. They reflect the fact that self-styled gay people have committed themselves to a particular view of their situation and will adopt any stratagem to refute the suggestion that the homosexual condition is less than an ideal state, or that young homosexuals might do well to consider the possibilities of change.

Whatever may be the situation in future, a homosexual orientation is still a considerable social handicap, and those wishing to lead an overtly homosexual style of life encounter many obstacles. Some gay people successfully surmount these problems, and lead contented, useful lives, but others feel chronically under stress. Even if love relationships between members of the same sex become fully acceptable, complete fulfilment would probably elude certain homosexuals. Sexual non-conformity can reflect an individual's difficulty in relating to others or in integrating love and sex, and these problems cannot be blamed entirely upon the attitude of straight society. For these reasons I do not agree with an attitude of complete neutrality towards the development of sexual orientation. On the whole, being heterosexual enhances a person's prospects of personal happiness and social integration. Therefore, when young people seek advice on the matter, it seems right to put this viewpoint to them.

The likelihood of success in changing sexual orientation, and the relative effectiveness of the various techniques used to stimulate heterosexual interests, are matters for research rather than ethical argument. Since these methods exist, persons who make a rational and informed decision that they want to try them should be allowed to do so, but any form of undue pressure or coercion to induce reluctant individuals to undergo such treatment is entirely out of place. In this, as in other contexts, the medical man has a duty to explain fully, to the best of his knowledge and judgment, what the treatments involve, how they work, and what outcomes may be expected. The desirable is not always attainable, an incomplete result may be worse than total failure, and the psychological costs of forsaking a settled style of life can be heavy. Some homosexuals yearn so desperately for 'normality' that they will undergo any procedure, however unpleasant, that offers some prospect of change. As was mentioned earlier (see p. 205) many homosexuals, affected by the homophobic attitudes prevalent in their environment, come to loathe and condemn themselves. They would do anything, and accept any suggestion, however flimsily based, that promised an escape from their guilt-ridden sexuality. The therapist should not accept a vehemently expressed desire for change as invariably indicative of good prospects for change. Some prospective candidates stand in greater need of a cure for their homophobia than of a conversion to heterosexuality. The experienced therapist avoids excessive enthusiasm, recognising that some individuals lack the flexibility to start a new way of life, and that others are too long fixed in their habits or too deeply wedded to an unconventional existence to justify attempts to alter their adjustment.

With these emotive issues relegated temporarily to the background, the remainder of this chapter seeks to elicit some basic information about the techniques of conversion treatment and their results.

2. *Expectancy, reassurance, encouragement, opportunity*

A policy of masterly inactivity sometimes works wonders. As was pointed out earlier (see p. 21) Kinsey's survey of males indicated a substantial shift towards heterosexual behaviour with increasing age. At age 20, only 81 per cent of males were predominantly heterosexual in their current behaviour (rating one or two on the Kinsey scale), but by the age of 45 this figure had risen to 93 per cent. Kinsey warned that the magnitude of this drift might have been exaggerated by the reluctance of older men to admit continued homosexual behaviour, but clearly a substantial number of men who are actively and exclusively homosexual in behaviour in their late teens or early twenties become heterosexual later in life.

The homosexual behaviour of some youths reflects nothing more significant than a relative lack of access to girls and a pressing need for an immediate sexual outlet. Most of these youngsters know very well that their basic interests are heterosexual, and have no cause to worry about their masculinity. On the other hand, some naïve young people, especially if they have not yet achieved their desired goal of heterosexual coitus, become anxious following involvement in homosexual incidents, because they fear the experience may have permanently unfitted them for a conventional sex life. Reassurance is all they need (Woodward, 1958).

The basic sexual orientation of the majority of persons becomes clear even before they reach puberty. By late adolescence or early adult life, the time when those troubled by sex problems tend to consult doctors, the typical homosexual knows full well, whether he likes it or not, that the strength of his erotic fascination for his own sex greatly exceeds any interest he has in the opposite sex. In such cases the advice 'Forget it, you'll soon grow out of it' is not merely inappropriate, but positively insulting. All the same, instances of young people genuinely unsure of their sexual orientation, and genuinely bisexual in their inclinations, do occur. These youngsters give the impression of being still very open to a push or pull in one direction or the other.

On occasions, even a well-established sexual orientation proves less fixed than at first appears. Although some militant homosexuals find such claims improbable and unpalatable, authenticated accounts have been published of apparently exclusive and long-standing homosexuals unexpectedly changing their orientation. One man, known to the present writer, was fully and actively homosexual in his younger days but later married, lost interest in gay life, produced a family and became exclusively heterosexual in both desire and practice. Some twenty years later his wife developed an incurable illness, his marriage broke up, and he reverted to exclusive homosexuality. Like a male version of a 'merry widow', he started dressing young, attending gay parties, and having love affairs with young men.

Liss and Welner (1973) report a particularly striking case of a man who had been an actively practising exclusive homosexual for eight years before spontaneously changing to heterosexual interests. The authors discounted the effect of the slight contact he had had with a psychotherapist as being in any way adequate to account for the change. In another case (Wellman, 1956), a young man undergoing psychotherapy experienced a sudden release from homosexual inclinations, not apparently as a result of treatment, but following a significant event in his life, namely a change in attitude towards him on the part of his mother, who had till then behaved in an over-possessive, over-controlling manner.

Another example of complete reversal of sexual orientation is described in an autobiography by Aaron (1972). The writer was a clumsy boy who hated games and had no mechanical aptitudes. He felt a 'sissy', clung to his mother's apron strings, and avoided contact with his supposedly unsympathetic father. He grew up an exclusive homosexual, and spent twenty years hunting promiscuous sex on the international gay scene. He was not entirely contented, having certain religious scruples, and feeling he was missing out on the satisfactions of family life. Eventually he confided in a woman who undertook to provide practical training in sex. After being taught female anatomy, and how to arouse a woman manually, he became excited himself and achieved penetration. At first he used homosexual fantasies to increase his potency, but after a time the need for this ceased. He married, and in time came to look upon having a wife and home and children as the natural order of things. Gay life, which was once all he knew, faded into history and became meaningless to him.

The fact that spontaneous reversals of sexual orientation can occur at all, even though rarely, points to the need for caution before dismissing the possibility of change in an apparently permanent homosexual. Until a person has been encouraged to try, one cannot declare with any confidence that he will not, given favourable circumstances and opportunity, discover a taste for heterosexuality.

The earliest medical approach to patients wanting to change from homosexual to heterosexual habits consisted of instruction, encouragement and the provision of easy opportunity, a combination that remains an essential accompaniment of sophisticated modern techniques. On the theory that the patient's difficulty lies in a failure to learn how to behave in heterosexual situations, success in practice attempts with the opposite sex should bring their own reward, and should result in the patient acquiring a taste for the delights of conventional sex. The Baron Albert von Schrenck-Notzing (1895), a German physician, was one of the first to claim success for the method of persuasion and exhortation. He employed authoritative suggestion to convince his male patients of their ability to perform sexually with women. He advised them, at times of sexual arousal, deliberately to substitute the image of a woman sexual partner for that of a man. He used hypnosis when suggestion in the waking state proved insufficient. He wrote: 'But even in deep hypnosis it is not always easy to implant sexual feeling ... I have always succeeded, however, with the exception of one case ... in inducing patients to attempt coitus. When heterosexual intercourse has been successful, as has been said, it may be regarded as the turning point for improvement, in spite of the initial disgust during and after coitus.' The use of prostitutes, paid to stimulate the client as long as need be to enable him to complete the act, provided the means for repeated practice regardless of initial failures and despite initial distaste.

In the days when all respectable brides were supposed to be sexually ignorant and upper-class bridegrooms were supposed to have had some practice in the arts of manhood with the help of female servants or prostitutes, it must have seemed quite natural to enlist professional prostitutes to help male patients over their sexual difficulties. In these more egalitarian and squeamish times, the idea has less appeal, but the use of dedicated female helpers or 'surrogates' amounts to the same thing (Masters and Johnson, 1970). They should not be too difficult to find. Following an earlier edition of this book the author had a visit from a young lady who had, by means of a tactfully light-hearted, playful approach, successfully seduced her inhibited and supposedly homosexual boyfriend. He promptly went off to practice his newly acquired talents with other girls. She was keen to have introduction to other homosexuals for whom she might perform a similar helping service.

Actual practice in heterosexual intercourse is still insisted upon, even by psychoanalysts, as an essential part of 'treatment'. Hatterer (1970, p. 91) insists that every attempt the male patient makes to engage in heterosexual activity should be encouraged and applauded as steps in the direction of heterosexual adjustment. Attempts at intercourse with prostitutes 'should not be passed over lightly. They represent a valuable attempt at some kind of hetero-erotic activity ...'

Schrenck-Notzing claimed success in 11 out of 27 males treated by directive methods. The results, like those of behaviour therapists today, were regarded with scepticism by many authorities, notably Magnus Hirschfeld (1920), who believed in the inborn and unalterable quality of homosexual 'inversion'. Such theorists preferred to believe either that the changes would prove no more than temporary, or that the patients were not 'true' homosexuals in the first place.

Success, in the eyes of Schrenck-Notzing and his contemporaries, meant the establishment of a capacity for heterosexual intercourse. But as Kurt Freund (1974) has so forcibly pointed out, a certain capacity for sexual arousal with women falls far short of a positive and stable heterosexual preference. In his experience of supposedly 'cured' homosexuals followed up over a period of years, he finds many instances of a reversion to former habits and inclinations or of an unhappy struggle to keep up appearances in heterosexual marriages which have become emotionally sterile and sexually frustrating. Over-persuaded by therapists, or driven by their own aspirations to social propriety, homosexuals force themselves to mix with the opposite sex and to have intercourse if they can manage to do so. Mistaking minimal sexual arousal for genuine heterosexual inclination they rush into marriage to try to consolidate their gains, but live to regret the step. The double disillusionment, when a shocked wife discovers how she has been deceived, and an unhappy husband finds his homosexual urges stronger than loyalty to wife and children, is a situation to be avoided. The likely consequences of this kind of debacle are illustrated by the sad biography of one man who went through the experience, ultimately paying for his secret visits to public lavatories with social disgrace, imprisonment and complete rejection by wife and children (Drakeford, 1971). The consequences to the wife can be equally disastrous. Henry (1955, pp. 16-25) describes the case of 'Ralph' who was pressured into marriage by a girl who did not know of his obsessive passion for boys. Years later, disillusioned by her husband's chronic lack of ardour, and realising that he was a homosexual, and in a frenzy of anxiety that their two small children might become similarly affected, she strangled them both and attempted to kill herself.

In such marriages the victimised wife often seems to have partly contrived her own downfall. Myra Hatterer (1974), who studied a group of 17 women married to men undergoing therapy for homosexuality, found that all of them had had psychosexual problems before marriage. They were excessively inhibited sexually, feared being inadequate in heterosexual relations, and had doubts about their attractiveness. They all had a history of conflictual relationships with their fathers, and some had competed unsuccessfully with their brothers for parental attention. Because of their insecurity, most of them, before finally marrying, had singled out one homosexual male after another in their search for an undemanding sexual relationship with a partner they could dominate psychologically. After marriage, hostility would erupt, with mutual recriminations about sexual inadequacy, but neither could break away because both felt trapped by their own fear of being unable to cope with a fully heterosexual partner. The birth of a child encouraged these dissatisfied wives to take refuge in maternal preoccupations, leading to a further worsening of the marital relationship.

Based on an admittedly very small and highly selected survey carried out in Belgium, Ross (1971) reported on the situation of married couples with one partner homosexual. Usually, the marriages had been entered into because of the initial failure of one or both parties to recognise and fully admit the homosexual condition. Sometimes marriage was undertaken as a refuge from homosexual temptation, or for the sake of establishing a home. Most of the marriages proved unhappy, because of conflict over the homosexual partner's declining interest in marital sex and increasing commitment to outside relationships. Occasionally, a workable adjustment was reached if both parties understood and accepted the need for extra-marital affairs. In one unusual example the wife agreed to and enjoyed group sex with her husband and other men, both obtaining satisfaction from the arrangement.

The Saghir and Robins (1973, p. 104) survey of non-patient volunteers from the gay community provides one of the few sources of systematic information about the marriages of men who continue a homosexual involvement. Sixteen out of the 89 questioned had married, but only 2 were still married at the time of the investigation. Most had got married rather reluctantly, under pressure from relatives or in an effort to reassure themselves and solve their homosexual problem. Most such men marry 'women who are strong-willed, demanding and pushy'. With the partners having such different expectations a break-up occurs almost inevitably, usually within three years. In spite of good intentions initially, the husband finds continued abstinence from homosexuality impossible, but the wife remains ignorant of the fact. 'Her demands on him socially and sexually help to accentuate the split.' The only two who managed to preserve their marriages did so because they fully enjoyed both heterosexual and homosexual contacts, and succeeded in concealing their homosexual activities from their wives. However, both these men suggested that if the present marriage terminated they would not seek another but would probably turn to men exclusively.

Faced with a troubled homosexual who wants to try to make some sexual contact with the opposite sex, but is held back by anxiety, social shyness and fear of failure, it seems reasonable to encourage the attempt and to provide simple practical advice. For those who have previously avoided mixing socially, learning to dance, accepting invitations to parties and making 'dates', are helpful preliminaries to feeling at ease with members of the opposite sex. Most males need to gain confidence and experience gradually, so first attempts at love-making are best limited to kissing and petting. Alcohol and relaxing situations help. Nowadays, some male homosexuals find an easy route into heterosexual activity through participation in group sex, where the presence of other males excites and encourages them, and where the success of the event does not all depend upon their own faltering performance. In the past, doctors condemned masturbation and pornography, but both have their uses as a preparation for heterosexual intercourse. Pornography gives the inexperienced individual explicit information about sexual positions and the sheer mechanics of intercourse. At the same time pornography stimulates sexual imagination and fantasy and provides potentially stimulating heterosexual images. If the homosexual finds such images powerful enough to excite him, or to provide a pleasurable fantasy during masturbation, he knows that he should not have much difficulty becoming similarly aroused in heterosexual situations in real life.

Helping a man who already wants to do so to experiment heterosexually is a far cry from the authoritarian exhortations and moral pressures which doctors once felt justified in bringing to bear upon their reluctant patients. Some authorities today would question the desirability of proffering any positive advice to a patient who has not been able to achieve heterosexual intercourse on his own initiative. Psychoanalysts believe that the problem goes much deeper than just lack of facility in heterosexual love-making. Consciously or unconsciously male homosexuals have an enormous resistance to intimacy with women. Their fears, suspicions and hostilities will not necessarily disappear when they gain some skill in the mechanics of heterosexual coitus. The danger is that they may, for reasons of prestige or material security or to avoid social disapproval, use their new found coital skills to form heterosexual relationships or marriages for which they are psychologically unsuited. Hatterer (1970), a therapist with no inhibitions whatever about encouraging homosexual patients to practice coitus, nevertheless warns of the likelihood of a reversion to former habits when, as so often happens, personalities clash and all the old hostilities re-awaken. He cites (p. 228) the example of a man with a doting but possessive mother who used him as companion and confessor in return for giving him money or anything else he demanded. When he started to go with the other women he expected them to treat him the same way. He felt angry and rejected when, instead of giving in to him in everything, they expected him to do things for them. On the other hand, if a girl pandered to him like his mother, that would not work either, for he would then begin to suspect her of wanting to possess and crush his freedom and individuality in the way his old mother tried to do. So long as a man carries with him fears and suspicions based upon infantile misconceptions of the opposite sex, heterosexual relationships are doomed to failure.

In spite of the acknowledged dangers of forcing change upon unwilling homosexuals, some therapists still feel justified in using highly directive hypnotic suggestions to inspire homosexual men with an aversion for contact with the male body, and to relieve their fear or disgust at the thought of intimate contact with women (Miller, 1963). Positive suggestions about the attractiveness of the opposite sex, and negative instructions about the nastiness of homosexuality, can be combined with optimistic psychological interpretations implying that the patients' difficulties in achieving a heterosexual adjustment can be overcome. Roper (1967), who applied this method to 15 homosexuals, found that those who became deeply hypnotised had a greater chance of changing their sexual interests. Most modern hypno-therapists avoid such crudely directive approaches, and employ suggestion to encourage the patient to ventilate his feelings and to bring his sexual fears into the open, rather than tell him what to do. Used in this way hypnosis, like conventional psychotherapy, aids self-analysis, but does not attempt to force the patient to make decisions before he feels ready to do so (Schneck, 1950).

3. *Physical methods of treatment*

Suppression of sexual feelings by means of drugs or surgery scarcely merits the term treatment, but such action is justifiable in exceptional cases, when a patient prefers sexlessness to an unwanted or dangerous sexuality. A male teacher, with desires exclusively towards small boys, unable to obtain sexual release in any way acceptable to himself or to society, who feels distracted and fearful at the continual risk of disgracing himself with his own pupils, may well find himself happier, less anxious, and an altogether more effective person, after taking medication to suppress his sexual feelings. Dangerous offenders, whether heterosexual or homosexual, with urges towards violent sexual assault, perhaps against child victims, occasionally plead for a state of sexlessness in preference to an intolerable burden of guilt and the near-certainty of spending the best years of life in prison. Some people, whose problems look to the outsider not so serious, can become quite overwhelmed by what seem to them to be totally unacceptable impulses. For example, the man who has become a slave to the dangerous habit of touring public lavatories every night desperately needs a period of sexual tranquillity during which, perhaps with the aid of psychotherapy, he can reorganise his life on a more sensible footing.

The oldest of all sex-suppressing procedures, castration, has been used in modern times in a number of countries, including Germany, Denmark, Finland and Holland. It has been made legally available under various circumstances, as a penal sanction imposed by the courts upon convicted sex offenders, as an alternative to imprisonment or long-continued penal detention, as a compulsory procedure applied to sexually troublesome mental patients in institutions, and as a treatment undertaken voluntarily on medical advice. German law, for example, introduced penal castration for sexual criminals officially evaluated as dangerous. The statute was passed on 24 November 1933, during the Nazi regime. Denmark, where the castration of sexual criminals became an acceptable preliminary to release from detention, operated a law, instituted on 1 June 1929, permitting castration provided the offender himself petitioned to have it done. Although doubtfully legal under the United States constitution, Slovenko (1965), writing in relatively recent times, noted that judges in isolated areas of America sometimes granted a sex offender probation or a suspended sentence on condition he agreed to surgical castration.

Surgical castration involves removal of the testes, leaving the penis anatomically intact, but cutting off the body's main source of androgenic hormone, thus bringing about a diminution in the urgency of sexual drive. The effects of the operation have been studied in a number of extensive follow-up enquiries. Bremer (1959) reported on the outcome of legal castrations carried out on 216 men in Norway during the years 1935 to 1949. Most of them were subnormal or psychotic patients under psychiatric care, but some were sex offenders not categorised as mentally ill and dealt with by the penal authorities. Sturup (1968, 1972), drawing upon his own long experience of practice in Denmark, and quoting results from Germany, Holland, Sweden and Switzerland, as well as Norway, found that of 3,120 male sex offenders so treated only 2.2 per cent were detected in any further sex crime. Considering that many of these men had committed serious sex offences on a number of different occasions before being castrated, the results were from a penological standpoint highly satisfactory, providing good evidence that castration reduces the propensity to sexual offences. It does not, however, prevent repetition of other kinds of crime.

Following castration it takes several months, sometimes years, for sexual interests to dwindle and impotence to develop. Some men never lose their virility completely, presumably because other glands than the testes produce sufficient androgens to maintain sexuality. This is one reason why the operation fails to provide an absolute guarantee against further sexual misconduct. Another reason is that diminution of sexual interest may not abolish temptation completely. Moreover, relative impotence does not necessarily prevent an attempted sexual attack or the manual molestation of a small child. Bremer cites the case of one assaultative offender who developed into a passive homosexual seducer following castration.

Castration sometimes causes troublesome side-effects, notably the formation of feminine contours of fat, loss of beard and body hair, the development of a smooth, puffy facial complexion, and during the early stages flushes and sweats similar to the symptoms experienced by women during the menopause. Genital deformity, which would otherwise occur from the collapse of an empty scrotal sac, is easily prevented by inserting plastic substitutes when the testes are removed. According to Sturup, physical disadvantages are less serious than popularly supposed, and most sex offenders who have had the operation have no regrets about their decision and are happy to be released from pressures they could not cope with. The temptation to combat physical changes, and to regain some sexual libido, by taking testosterone to replace the lost testicular androgen, has to be resisted. Some of the very few men who repeated a sex crime after castration had been taking androgens. C.T. Duffy (1965, Chapter 17) one time warden of San Quentin prison, shared Sturup's favourable opinion of the benefits of castration for sex offenders. In his view, most of the Californian convicts who submitted to the operation improved dramatically, became more cooperative, happier, better able to face the future, and were generally successes when paroled.

An even more radical form of surgery for reducing sex drive attempts to apply to humans neurophysiological information derived from animal experiments. It has been shown that, in the rat, the ventromedial nucleus of the hypothalamic region of the brain plays a part in the regulation of sex-hormone secretion. The German neurosurgeon Roeder and his collaborators (1966, 1971), using a stereotactic technique to insert the electrodes into very precise points within the brain, have tried the effect of destroying the ventromedial nucleus by electrical burning. They claim to have succeeded by this means in abolishing or reducing aberrant sexual drive in a number of homosexual paedophiles. Until the neurological processes involved are better understood, and possible side-effects investigated, any judgment about this form of treatment would be premature.

The effects of surgery being relatively drastic and irreversible, control of male sexual desire is in most cases better achieved with the use of suppressant drugs, the dose of which can be adjusted to suit individual needs. According to an old soldier's tale, tea given to them at the front was dosed with bromides to quell inconvenient sex urges, but more effective and less dangerous substances are available for the purpose. For many years, female sex-hormones, oestrogens, were frequently prescribed for male sex-deviants (Scott, 1964; Whitaker, 1959). Tablets had to be taken regularly every day, and the results were not immediate and not very reliable. Some men became impotent without losing their unwanted sexual urges. Distressing side-effects were common, in particular feelings of nausea and painful swelling of the breasts, which was not only embarrassing but carried some risks of producing cancer (Symmers, 1968). Heavy and prolonged doses effectively destroyed the active cells of the testes, producing effects similar to castration. Since candidates for this treatment were usually somewhat reluctant sex-offenders, a method had to be found that did not depend upon unsupervised daily doses. Field and Williams (1970, 1971), working at Wormwood Scrubs Prison in London, used an oestrogen preparation implanted under the skin to achieve a slow release of hormone over a period of time. A series of men given repeated implants, sufficient apparently to reduce their sexual drive, were found to re-offend after release significantly less often than imprisoned sex criminals dealt with in other ways. The use of an instrument to detect changes in heart or respiratory rate, skin moisture and increases in penile volume, during exposure to erotic material, helped to monitor the effectiveness of the hormonal suppressant, and also to assess the likelihood of further offences after release.

More recently, other sex-suppressant drugs that do not have the disadvantageous side effects of oestrogens have appeared on the market. One of these, benperidol, was tried out with promising preliminary results by Field (1973). However, a more systematic comparison, in double blind trials at Broadmoor Hospital by Tennent *et al.* (1974), indicated that benperidol was no more effective than a standard tranquilliser chlorpromazine, or an inactive placebo, in reducing physiological responses to erotic stimuli. It did, however, appear to reduce the incidence of sexual ruminations; but on the other hand it caused drowsiness, and sometimes stiffness and tremor, due to a side action on the extra-pyramidal nerve centres. Some psychiatrists find that tranquillising drugs used in the treatment of psychotic patients, some of which can be given in single slow-release doses effective over a period of weeks, are quite useful for decreasing libido in persons with sexual problems (Bartholomew, 1968). The most promising development, however, has been the introduction of cyproterone acetate (marketed by Schering Chemicals under the trade name of Androcur), a substance which acts by blocking the action of normal body androgen. Dosage has to continue for weeks or months before the full effect develops. Patients often experience drowsiness and fatigue, especially in the first few weeks, but more serious side-effects are rare. Trials by Davies (1970) on mentally subnormal patients who had committed sexual assaults or habitually masturbated in public indicated that the drug was surprisingly effective in reducing disapproved sexual activity. Cooper *et al.* (1972) used the drug with three men, a sexually assaultative married 'psychopath', who had committed incest and indecent exposure as well as homosexual activity and compulsive masturbation, a homosexual priest who had previously had tranquillisers and electrical aversion-treatment without benefit, and an elderly man agitated by unwanted erections and nocturnal emissions. All three patients experienced a beneficial reduction of sexual drive as well as a generally tranquillising effect. The first patient, who was investigated in hospital, showed a marked fall in plasma testosterone level in only a few days, and after a week could no longer produce a full erection even with prolonged masturbation. Bancroft *et al.* (1974), comparing the effect of oestrogen and cyproterone acetate on the sexual responses of patients in Broadmoor Hospital, found the two substances equally effective in reducing sexual fantasy and masturbation (judged from patients' reports), but only the cyproterone acetate significantly reduced erectile responses to erotic material. The authors concluded that, in view of the absence of serious side-effects, cyproterone acetate was the best of the presently available suppressant drugs.

Apart from libido-suppressing procedures, various bizarre methods of physical treatment have been applied to homosexuals from time to time. The use of electroplexy, that is the artificial induction of an epileptic discharge in the brain, ordinarily used only in the treatment of severe depression resistant to drugs, has been reported by several workers, generally without satisfactory result (Liebman, 1944; Thompson, 1949; Glueck, 1956). The neurological operation of lobotomy, now out of fashion, but once used fairly extensively in an effort to control agitated or aggressive mental patients, was found to increase rather than to decrease sexual activity, including homosexual behaviour (Zlotlow and Paganini, 1959). Some time ago, Silverman and Rosanoff (1945) published the results of an encephalographic survey of 53 homosexual prisoners. They reported a high incidence of abnormal brain rhythms of a kind found among psychopathic, psychotic or brain-damaged patients rather than among normal persons. As so often in such investigations, they failed to allow for the obvious possibility that the abnormalities in question had more to do with their subjects being unsocialised, aggressive prisoners than with the fact that they also happened to be homosexuals. A more recent survey, based upon a less abnormal group, namely prospective candidates for aversion therapy, yielded no evidence of the kind of clear-cut abnormalities reported earlier, but did find a raised incidence of persisting slow waves following a test period of deliberate, forced heavy-breathing. This sign, commonplace in children, when it occurs in adults is said to indicate cerebral immaturity, and to be sometimes associated with personality disorder. The investigators concluded that they had probably discovered a significant feature of homosexuality, a degree of cerebral immaturity related to 'retardation or failure of psychosexual development with increased susceptibility to sexual trauma or seduction' (Papatheophilou *et al.*, 1975). They did not, of course, discuss the likelier explanation that being a psychiatric patient, rather than being a homosexual, was the reason for the 'immaturity'. In any event, the peculiarity was not such as to suggest any particular form of treatment. Recently, neurologists have become interested in a specific malfunction of the temporal lobe of the brain as a possible cause of certain cases of aberrant sexual behaviour (Kolarsky *et al.* 1967). It has been suggested that a significantly high proportion of transsexual individuals show abnormal electrical patterns of temporal origin when they are tested with the electroencephalograph (Blumer, 1969). Occasional reports have been published of persons suffering from temporal-lobe epilepsy displaying very unusual sexual inclinations. One epileptic with a sexual interest in safety pins was relieved of both his epileptic attacks and his unusual sexual fetish by surgical removal of a part of his left temporal lobe (Mitchell *et al.*, 1964). So far, however, no one has advocated such treatment as a cure for homosexuals generally!

A form of physical treatment which sounds rather drastic, but has some prospect of success, involves direct electrical stimulation of the brain centres to produce pleasurable feelings and euphoric moods. Moan and Heath (1972) reported one such experiment with a suicidally depressed, homosexual patient who was suspected of having an epileptic disturbance in the temporal lobe. Electrodes were surgically inserted into various areas of his brain and the effects of stimulation tried out. Slight stimulation of the septal region was found to produce intensely pleasurable feelings. The patient was provided with apparatus to enable him to stimulate himself in measured doses, by means of which he was able to achieve states of relaxation, confidence, happy mood and sometimes sexual arousal. Unless restrained he would go on stimulating himself to a pitch of wild elation.

At the beginning of the treatment, the patient was made to view a film of heterosexual intercourse. He showed no interest, and in fact became resentful and angry. After experience of septal stimulation, however, he became much more 'cooperative', viewed the film with interest, became sexually excited and masturbated to orgasm. Taking advantage of the increased confidence and receptiveness to women induced by the electrical stimulation, the therapists introduced a young female prostitute who successfully seduced the patient. After that, he formed a sexual relationship with a woman friend of his own, and desisted from the compulsive homosexual relationships which had previously provided his only sexual outlet.

One form of drug treatment for homosexuality has been reported which depends upon pleasurable rather than aversive effects. The hallucinogen LSD has been used for homosexuals, as for alcoholics, to induce an emotional state in which past experiences are vividly relived and reappraised, and psychological conflicts hopefully resolved (Whitaker, 1964). Used as an aid to psychotherapy, LSD has been claimed to give good results with male homosexuals (Martin, 1962). It has also been used in conjunction with an aversive technique, the patient receiving a nausea-inducing drug while discussing homosexuality, followed by LSD to promote a pleasant experience while discussing heterosexual ideas. In the example reported, the treatment terminated with the death of the patient from a heart attack brought on by excessive vomiting (*Medico-Legal Journal*, 1964).

The most dramatic form of physical treatment is surgical reconstruction of the male genitals, to give a female appearance, and to enable a man to pass for a woman and to live in accordance with a homosexual orientation without being branded as a homosexual (Kando, 1973; Hore *et al.*, 1975). The drastic, complicated, painful and irreversible procedures needed to produce a satisactory transformation should never be undertaken lightly. Most homosexuals have no wish to change their gender. Even among feminine identified males who might like to be able to play a woman's role more convincingly, few would contemplate the ordeals involved. Only the extremely determined and compulsive transsexuals, persons whose whole lives revolve around the desire to change their sex, are considered by most psychiatrists and surgeons to be suitable candidates for genital surgery. After all, the vast majority of homosexuals, even those with a considerable degree of cross-sex identification, manage to come to terms with their condition without requiring such drastic physical mutilation. Some transsexuals remain unhappy, lonely dissatisfied people even after having had the sex transformation which they thought would solve all their problems.

The actual techniques of sex-change surgery, which are evolving rapidly, are beyond the scope of this review. Some have been outlined in the book by Green and Money (1969). Transformation of the male genitals requires castration, amputation of the penis, and the construction of an artificial cleft to represent the vagina. After removal of the testes part of the skin of the scrotum is left behind to form flaps to simulate the female labia. The whole of the erectile root of the penis, that attaches deep onto the pelvic bone, can be dissected out from the inside, so as to preserve intact an empty sheath of penile skin. By pushing this skin from the outside, so that it inverts into the hole left behind by the removal of the internal genitals, like the empty finger of a glove being turned inside out, a skin-lined depression is created. By stuffing this with gauze, the penile skin is pressed against and unites with the underlying tissues to produce a permanent 'vagina'. The urethral tube that used to pass through the penis, having been dissected out, has to be brought to the surface and tied off in an appropriately feminine position (Granato, 1974). Periodically dilated, and appropriately lubricated, the artificial vagina can be used for successful copulation including the attainment of orgasm. After all, human orgasm depends to a large extent upon cerebral stimulation, and many persons of either sex can attain orgasm by the insertion of a penis into the anus, an organ no better constructed for the purpose than the artificial vagina.

The surgical transformation of female genitals into a male appearance is considerably more complicated and less satisfactory in outcome. Female transsexuals have often to rest content with breast amputations, hysterectomy and hormone treatment, which promotes hairiness, loss of feminine fat, deeper voice, and a more masculine general appearance. A simulation of a male scrotum can be produced by inserting plastic replicas of testes into the labial folds and suturing them together. Construction of an artificial, 'cosmetic' penis falls short of the creation of a functional organ capable of sensitive feeling or of natural erection during sexual activity. If the pseudo-penis is required to pass urine, the urethra has to be extended by means of an artificial tube which, not being naturally self-cleansing, promotes troublesome infections.

Green (1974) has published vivid accounts, illustrated with actual case histories quoting the patients' own words, of the perils of sex-change operations. Some transsexual males have little appreciation of the limits of medicine and surgery, the impossibility of changing bone structure, the need for uncomfortable and expensive electrolysis for elimination of growth of beard, the possible need for plastic breast implants, the irreversible nature of the thickening of the vocal cords that prevents a grown man acquiring a truly soprano voice. They need to be warned of the unpredictable function of the artificial vagina, which may be very slow to heal internally, or may tend to close up or become constricted, and the possible loss of the capacity for orgasm which follows surgical removal of the sensitive nerve endings concentrated in the penis. Because of the even severer limits of surgery for females 'most female-to-male transsexuals are well advised not to pursue the uncertain procedures required for phalloplasty'.

Transsexuals require long continued post-operative care, to help them to preserve their artificial genitals intact, to regulate hormone maintenance treatment, to assist them in coping with the social and legal problems of an apparent change of sexual identity, and to counsel them in dealing with the emotional difficulties of a complicated and perilous love-life. Some of the men who have become women find that their dreams of captivating a princely male, or having the every day burdens of life miraculously taken away from them, or of developing a charming personality, remain sadly unfulfilled. For this reason, every doctor of experience in this field advocates a trial period of hormone treatment, cross-dressing and living as a member of the opposite sex, before irreversible surgery is attempted. Transsexuals in the United States have the benefit of advice from the Erickson Educational Foundation (1974) which issues explanatory pamphlets on the medical, legal and personal problems of transsexuals, and issues a newsletter giving information about specialist seminars, conferences, clinics, books and legal controversies.

4. *Special techniques for learning sexual behaviour*

Old-fashioned methods of authoritarian instruction and moral persuasion have been supplemented, in modern times, by more sophisticated and hopefully more effective aids to learning approved behaviour in the sexual as well as in other fields. Known as behaviour therapy or behaviour modification, the techniques derive from the theories evolved by experimental psychologists from the study of laboratory animals in artificial learning situations. Some psychologists are justifiably sceptical about applying to the human sexual scene, with all its emotional nuances and symbolic meanings, the principles of animal learning. For present purposes, however, the content and efficacy of behaviour modification techniques deserve consideration independently of the theories which inspired them.

Modern exponents of the art of behaviour modification lay emphasis on accentuating the positive rather than discouraging the negative. In the context of helping homosexuals who want to change, this means fostering heterosexual responses on the assumption that homosexual responses will then fade naturally into the background without the necessity to try to suppress them by artificial means. Unfortunately for the public image of behaviour modification, the earliest developed, and hence the best-known of the techniques, now largely discontinued, consisted of methods of 'aversive' conditioning, intended to block the homosexual outlet. Suppressing unwanted responses was optimistically believed to make way for the learning of more suitable alternatives.

The aversion method was based upon the observation that an animal can be readily discouraged from some habitual pattern of behaviour, for example from eating out of a particular bowl, if, over a period of time, it receives an unpleasant stimulus on each occasion that it tries to approach the bowl. Provided the unpleasant stimulus is repeated sufficiently often, and always in conjunction with or immediately following the action the experimenter wants to suppress, the animal soon learns, that is becomes 'conditioned', to avoid such behaviour. Given the right timing and regularity, a quite mild stimulus suffices to establish a strong and lasting aversion to what was previously an obviously pleasurable activity. For example, Hayward (1957) reported an experiment in which young albino rats received an electric shock each time a female in heat appeared. They soon learned to avoid such females, and this reaction persisted, almost unabated, into their adult life and greatly inhibited their heterosexual activity. These rats did not, however, display compensatory homosexual behaviour. An earlier experiment in which adult male rats were given a shock whenever they tried to mate with a female, had resulted in about half of the animals attempting homosexual approaches instead (Rasmussen, 1955).

Aversion therapy enjoyed a considerable vogue some thirty to forty years ago as a method of turning alcoholics against drink. Later it came into frequent use for the suppression of fetishism, cross-dressing and other unwanted sexual habits. The alcoholic receives a taste of his favourite tipple, or the homosexual is shown a picture of an attractive male nude, but his pleasure is interrupted by some unpleasant, punishing sensation, such as sudden nausea induced by the injection of an emetic, or the pain of an electric shock. After frequent repetitions of this sequence, the patient finds his former attraction replaced by an automatic reaction of disaste or aversion.

The method was fraught with technical difficulties and the effects were often dubious. In theory, the timing of the painful stimulus to coincide with the unwanted erotic response was important, but using an injected emetic with a variable delay before the onset of nausea exact timing was difficult to achieve. Electric shocks are easy to control as to timing, but the severity of the sensation induced varies with the individual. Contrary to theoretical expectations, practitioners found it necessary to employ quite severe punishment, and repeated courses of treatment, to achieve any lasting aversive effect. The protracted and exhausting nature of the treatments, particularly when vomiting was repeatedly induced, carried a definite physical risk, besides being exceedingly unpleasant. Some practitioners coupled the physical punishments with moral condemnation, in the form of tape recordings emphasising the disgusting nature of deviant urges (James, 1962). Others believed that states of hunger or exhaustion facilitated the patient's conversion from former habits. In fact, the trend in aversion therapy came uncomfortably close to the popular notions of brain washing and medical torture. One of the most punitive of aversive techniques has been applied from time to time to homosexual patients under compulsory detention in certain American state hospitals. The method involves injections of succinylcholine, a curare-like drug, which induces complete paralysis, arrests speech and respiration, and gives the patient a vivid impression of utter helplessness and imminent death. The use of aversive methods on sexual offenders in penal establishments or in military settings came to be viewed with particular suspicion. Furthermore, the results of the treatment, as applied to homosexuals, hardly warranted all the pain and trouble involved. The aversive effect often proved slight or temporary, but even when a continuing and pronounced homosexual disgust reaction was successfully established, conversion to heterosexuality did not necessarily follow. The patient might be left confused and miserable, with no heterosexual inclination to replace the feelings he had lost. Freund (1960; 1965b), who treated 67 patients using nauseating stimuli while they were looking at homoerotic pictures, took the unusual step of following them up for five to eight years to see what had happened. Twenty-two established some heterosexual behaviour, but only 12 maintained it, and only 3 broke off all homosexual activity.

Some improvements in aversive techniques have been introduced in recent years. Bancroft (1974, p.40) used a phallometer to measure erectile changes in the penis. When an increase in penile volume, indicative of the beginning of arousal, occurred in response to a homoerotic picture, the man received a shock. If, after fifteen seconds, the erectile response continued, a further burst of three shocks was given.

Two variants of the aversive conditioning method deserve mention. Aversion relief endeavours to associate heterosexual interest with the cessation of a sequence of punishing experiences. Thorpe *et al.* (1964) made their subjects repeat a series of words or phrases with a homosexual connotation to the accompaniment of electric shocks to the feet. At the end of the sequence came a heterosexual word, this time with no accompanying shock. In the second variant, known as anticipatory avoidance, the subject can evade punishment if he makes the right response. Feldman and MacCulloch (1971) gave electric shocks while their subjects watched homoerotic slides. The subjects were instructed to switch off the slide when they found it no longer sexually interesting. On some occasions, if they did this before a given time had elapsed, they did not receive a shock.

Some therapists have avoided the use of physical punishments by encouraging subjects to use their imagination to build up their own aversive fantasies, but the method calls for highly cooperative subjects capable of vivid mental imagery. Gold and Neufield (1965) took the process a stage further. They asked their patient to visualise a sexually unattractive person and then to imagine, in addition, some obviously prohibitive circumstance, such as a watching policeman, which effectively prevented any sexual activity. The patient was told to modify the fantasy by degrees, making the figure gradually more attractive, at the same time reducing the prohibitions, but not enough to make a sexual approach desirable. Ultimately, when the patient could imagine turning away from a beautiful young man with the minimum of prohibitions, he was supposedly ready to reject homosexual temptation in real life.

Turning now from methods of suppression to methods of reinforcement, several behaviour therapists have attempted to induce change by a gradual modification of masturbation fantasies in the direction of greater heterosexual content. Thorpe, Schmidt and Castell (1964) asked their homosexual subjects to masturbate while watching homoerotic pictures, but just before reaching orgasm the subjects were shown a heterosexually stimulating slide. The repeated association of a heterosexual picture with sexual climax was thought to encourage heterosexual fantasy. Bancroft (1974. p. 44), in conjunction with aversive methods, 'has routinely advised and encouraged his patients to masturbate privately with heterosexual fantasies'. At first, the patient may achieve this by imagining himself watching a heterosexual man penetrating a woman, a fantasy which many homosexuals find exciting. Each time he masturbates he imagines the man looking more like himself, until, after sufficient practice, he can picture himself in the active heterosexual role. If certain aspects of the coital scene put him off at first, the patient can modify the fantasy as much as he likes to avoid them, but gradually he approximates the mental picture closer and closer to the real thing until, eventually, heterosexual intercourse becomes a stimulating image for masturbatory purposes. Bancroft also made use of the method of progressive desensitisation, a technique mainly employed in the treatment of phobias. The method applies to homosexuals who experience anxiety or disgust at the thought of heterosexual approaches. Essentially it consists of introducing the subject to the anxiety provoking situation in very easy stages accompanying each step with reassurance and relaxing routines. Given a cooperative sex partner, the technique can be applied to real situations, but it can also be applied to a rehearsal, in imagination, of one tiny step after another, beginning with social greetings, progressing through invitations home, kissing, fondling, undressing and genital caressing to final penetration and orgasm. Only after the subject finds he can contemplate a particular step calmly, without uneasiness, does the therapist direct his imagination to the next stage. The desensitisation technique probably works best when combined with other methods (Hanson and Adesso, 1972).

Stevenson and Wolpe (1960) used an indirect desensitisation method very successfully to treat two male homosexuals. Both men had experienced difficulty in asserting themselves in social situations in an approved masculine manner. One of them, a 32-year-old hairdresser, came from a classical family background of domineering, critical mother and weak, passive father. Always anxious and submissive, he was habitually reduced to tearful helplessness by unjustified complaints from his customers. The other man, a 22-year-old student under the domination of an unsympathetic stepfather, had similar social problems. The patients, both exclusive homosexuals, were encouraged to take small steps in assertive action in everyday matters, so that gradually they learned to find a satisfaction in this way and to lose their inhibiting anxiety. The overcoming of their social inhibitions, by the process of desensitisation, enabled them to overcome their sexual anxieties as well, so that they gained courage to embark upon heterosexual advances. As a result, both men changed their way of life and contracted satisfactory marriages. This unusual success story points to the wisdom of fitting the treatment technique to the needs of the particular patient. Desensitisation may work well when the main problem is anxiety and shyness, but might not be so effective in other cases.

Therapists using methods of direct reinforcement of heterosexual responses have taken advantage of the slight volume changes in the penis which indicate the beginnings of sexual arousal. Quinn *et al.* (1970) gave homosexual patients doses of a diuretic to make them thirsty. The patients were then shown heterosexually suggestive slides. Any sign of incipient arousal registered on the phallometer was rewarded with a refreshing drink. After some twenty sessions of this routine the patients showed significantly increased heterosexual interest, according to their responses on a questionnaire. When heterosexual stimuli initially produce no sexual arousal whatever, it has been found possible to induce one by presenting heterosexual and homosexual stimuli simultaneously. After a sufficient number of paired presentations, the heterosexual stimulus alone acquires the power to induce sexual arousal (Herman *et al.*, 1974). An alternative method of inducing the same effect is to superimpose a faint heterosexual image upon the homoerotic stimulus picture, and gradually to increase the intensity. Eventually the homosexual stimulus fades out altogether and the subject finds himself responding to a heterosexual picture.

In his excellent review of the current state of the art, Bancroft (1974) gives a reasoned account of the results of behaviour modification methods applied to male homosexuals. The level of success claimed for behaviour modification is generally similar to that claimed by optimistic psychotherapists, namely 'improvement' in a third or more cases treated (Birk *et al.*, 1971; Feldman and MacCulloch, 1971; McConaghy, 1969). No one technique or combination of techniques appears superior to others so the therapist does well to choose the method that seems best suited to the individual patient, without bothering too much about theoretical niceties (Sieveking, 1972). By 'improvement', most therapists refer to a significant increase in heterosexual interests, but the change usually falls far short of cure in the layman's sense of a complete and lasting reversal of sexual preference. Permanent eradication of all homosexual inclinations appears to be rather rare. Considering that patients who volunteer for the rigours of behaviour modification must be unsettled in their sexual orientation, or very dissatisfied with their way of life and strongly motivated to change, the results are disappointing. A certain number of patients always drop out when they realise what the treatment involves. Even among the select group who go through with the treatment, only a minority succeed in changing.

The contrasts between the immediate and long-term effects of treatment are discouraging. Aversive shocks administered to deter homoerotic fantasies may effectively suppress them temporarily so that the patient can no longer excite himself by conjuring up his customary erotic fantasies, but the unwanted thoughts are likely to recur after an interval as powerful as ever. Even during the period of suppression, when the patient avoids thinking about certain sexual scenes, homosexual behaviour does not necessarily cease altogether. Bancroft (1974, p. 115) cites the case of a homosexual paedophile who, as a result of aversive treatment, no longer responded with erections to homoerotic pictures, and reported complete loss of interest in homoerotic fantasies, but nevertheless continued to visit public lavatories. In spite of his seemingly favourable response in the treatment setting, he was soon after detected in a homosexual offence. Another difficulty is that for some people aversive shocks have the paradoxical effect of increasing rather than decreasing their sexual arousal.

The likelihood of change following behaviour modification, or for that matter following any other treatment depends upon the degree of exclusiveness of the individual's sexual orientation. Feldman and MacCulloch (1971), who claim a higher proportion of successful treatments than most other behaviour therapists admit that they usually fail with any patient who says that he has never experienced the slightest heterosexual interest in his whole life. The therapist can build upon even a faint capacity for heterosexual arousal more easily than he can call into being a capacity that has never been exercised before. It seems to be an example of those that have being given more, while those that have not remain as they are. If a homosexual pattern becomes more and more fixed with practice, as one might expect on learning principles, long experience as an actively practising homosexual should lessen the prospects of change. Some evidence of this has been reported by Mayerson and Lief (1965). They found that homosexual patients who failed to change following psychotherapy tended to have commenced homosexual behaviour earlier, and continued with it longer, than those who 'improved' with treatment.

Most behaviour therapists find that younger patients change more readily, but a clear association between age and outcome is not invariable (Bancroft, 1974, p. 153). Younger patients have several factors in their favour, including a strong sexual urge with which to experiment, a shorter history of homosexual experience, a less developed commitment to personal relationships in the homosexual world, and a youthful appearance that wins ready favour from members of the opposite sex. On the other hand, until he comes of an age when social pressure to marry and settle down becomes coercive, he may well feel no pressing need to give up the easy access to a variety of rewarding sexual relationships which gay circles offer to the young.

A sincere wish to alter sexual habits at almost any cost, and a willingness to cooperate in any exercises or procedures with that end in view, increase the likelihood of change. Freund (1960) goes so far as to suggest that treatment forced upon a patient by a court order or other external pressure hardly ever results in a satisfactory outcome. The strength of a patient's motivation is very difficult to assess, however, and it is all too easy for a therapist to argue in a circular manner, attributing absence of change to presumed lack of motivation. Some therapists express scepticism when a patient wants to change in order to satisfy social expectations, but the fact is that a person with no experience of heterosexual desire can hardly have any motive for becoming heterosexual other than the fulfilment of some social or ethical ideal.

Cross-sex gender identification in male homosexuals, or a definite disaste for the conventional masculine social role, is generally believed to lessen the prospects of change. Bieber *et al.* (1962) found that homosexual patients undergoing psychoanalysis had less chance of becoming heterosexual if they had developed effeminate mannerisms during childhood. Reasons for this are not difficult to find. A homosexual male who has a clear, masculine self-image may find his sexual tastes somewhat anomalous and incongruous with all his other attitudes and preferences, and may therefore want to change in order to bring his sexual behaviour into line with his masculine ideal. On the other hand, a male homosexual who has no wish to become an assertive, tough, masculine type, and doesn't mind being classed as effeminate, has less reason to try to acquire heterosexual skills. He might also find it rather more difficult to do so, because effeminacy is not likely to appeal to heterosexual women.

5. *Psychotherapy: aims, methods and results*

So far not many psychiatric clinics in England provide the newer behaviour modification treatments. Psychotherapy remains the usual form of help offered to homosexual clients. The duration and method varies greatly according to the aims, theoretical affiliations, practical experience and personal interests of the psychiatrists who carry out treatment, and according to the type of problem or complaint the patient presents (Willis, 1967). Classical psychoanalysis, which involves regular, hour-long sessions several times a week for months or years, can be given only to a select few, usually to those able to pay for extended private treatment. By encouraging the patients to recall and talk about and to an extent relive critical emotional experiences of the past, especially the turmoils of childhood, analysts attempt to lead them through a process of self-revelation to a re-appraisal of their present attitudes and way of life.

Psychoanalysts believe that aversion to heterosexual contact can be traced back to long-forgotten infantile terrors and fantasies. Recalled and brought into the open, these infantile fears lose their power, and the patient becomes free to develop new relationships unhampered by irrational suspicion or anxiety. Psychoanalysts used at one time to avoid giving the patient too many suggestions or interpretations. They might draw attention to important topics, such as the formative influence of relations with parents and other key figures in early life, and they might point out gaps and inconsistencies in the patient's descriptions of his feelings, but as far as possible they let the patient achieve his own insights, work through his own conflicts, and reorientate his life in his own way. Present-day analysts, possessed of greater confidence in their understanding of the origins of psychological problems, or at any rate more dogmatic in their theories, tend to intervene more actively. They not only proffer psychodynamic interpretations with less restraint, but they also feel free to praise or criticise the patient's everyday conduct, especially his sexual conduct (Allen, 1958; Ellis, 1965; Hatterer, 1970).

The sort of material which emerges during psychoanalytic treatment, upon which analysts base both their claims to effect cures and their claims to understand causes, is well illustrated in the lengthy examples quoted by Socarides (1968, ch.12). In one case, an intelligent, personable young man referred to as patient B, who despised 'fairies' and hated the idea of a 'gay life', was tormented by homosexual impulses he could not resist. Usually after drinking he would go to bed with some anonymous stranger, whom he would never meet again. At other times he would feel impelled to visit Turkish baths and have multiple contacts with different men. He had a dominating mother, convinced of her own social and intellectual superiority to his father, whom she eventually deserted. His father, who became disgruntled and alcoholic, looked upon the patient as a mother's boy and called him a 'sissy'. The patient clung to his mother as an infant, and throughout his childhood she kept up an unusually close, intimate relationship with the boy, which included undressing in front of him and allowing him no privacy even in the bathroom.

During treatment B recalled terrifying episodes in childhood when his mother expressed disapproval and threatened to leave him to his father. He recalled fear and disgust coupled with sexual desire when his mother sat on his bed. He was angry with her for treating him as a sexually innocent child, fearful of being engulfed by her; yet at the same time he identified with her womanly ways. Though feeling miserable and crushed at the idea of being an effeminate mama's boy, he interested himself in girls' toys and clothes, and in later years felt impelled to shave off the body hair that made him look too masculine. He had nightmares of physical torture and mutilation, attributed by the analyst to incest guilt and castration fear. Sex jokes disgusted him. He was scared even of kissing a woman, and the idea of any sexual contact with one terrified him. He was also scared of men, and horribly sensitive to any reference to effeminacy. On the other hand, the idea of attracting another man sexually gratified him. In this situation he had for once the upper hand. In his sexual contacts with men he liked to bite and punch and had fantasies of beating his partner.

Before this patient improved, he went through many painful episodes, sobbing and raving about his castrating bitch of a mother, his lost manhood, the treachery of women, and the cruelty and brutality of men. Eventually, after years of analysis, when he had gained insight into the fact that his compulsive homosexual escapades represented a symbolic escape from mother's dominance, an avoidance of incest guilt, and an attempt to disarm men by seducing them, he was ready to try to come to terms with life in a more realistic way. He formed an attachment to a woman who gently coaxed and playfully enticed him to intimacies. He discovered he could enjoy intercourse without the image of his mother obtruding. Although this initial friendship ended in disappointment, and the girl had an abortion, the patient was able thereafter not only to have heterosexual contacts, but also to assert a more realistic independence of his interfering mother.

As currently practised, psychotherapy often consists of a short-term attenuated version of the classic, analytic, probing technique. The therapist has to be somewhat directive to achieve anything in a relatively few sessions. Armed with analytic theories as to the likely reasons for sexual difficulties, the psychotherapist prompts discussion of topics he believes relevant, forcing the patient to describe his feelings and reactions in specified inter-personal situations. For example, a homosexual male who hates his father, has difficulty in standing up to the boss at work, and can't speak up for himself in a group, might be encouraged to open up about his frustration at failing to live up to paternal expectations, his fear of inadequacy and rejection in social situations, and his unbounded admiration for the successfully assertive males he chooses as lovers. Skilled exploration of such themes might reveal, in this case, that the homosexual orientation was the result of a crippling neurotic complex of inferiority. It would take lengthy analysis to expose thoroughly the ramifications and interconnections of the patient's fears, but a realisation in general terms of the nature of his problems, and of the irrationality of his usual attitudes and reactions, suffices sometimes to induce beneficial changes in various aspects of the patient's life, including the sexual.

Psychotherapists belonging to analytic schools of thought other than the Freudian differ relatively little in their method of approach, but tend to emphasise different themes. The Adlerian school of 'individual psychology' lays stress on the drive for self-assertion and social competitiveness, and the use of sex roles for this purpose. On this view, losers in the social battle, imbued with feelings of inferiority, may try to compensate by adopting a deviant role (Frey, 1962). Jung was less inclined than Freud to attribute all psychological ills to sexual conflict, and rather less interested in variant sexual behaviour. However, he did publish one account of the treatment of a young mother-bound male homosexual. Jung felt that the patient's state of mind at the time of treatment was just as important as the nature of past conflicts in determining the prospect of overcoming a neurosis. He noted that in this case conversion to heterosexuality was preceded by two dreams suggesting readiness for change. In one of these the young man saw himself in a lofty cathedral at the healing shrine of Lourdes where he saw a deep well into which he had to descend. This symbolism Jung interpreted as an intimation of aspiration to change and an awareness of the ordeal to be faced before that could happen (Fordham, 1953, ch.5).

The older schools of analysis seek to invalidate the patient's homosexual experience by reducing it to the status of a symptom understandable only in terms of infantile trauma. Existential analysis concerns itself more with things as they are and tries to explore the essential meaning to the patient of his present behaviour, the ways he sees himself and others in sexual situations. Change will follow if the patient finds his current outlook based on faulty assumptions and a distorted view of existence and of relations between the sexes (Benda, 1963; Serban, 1968). The patient's homosexual preoccupations have first to be understood for what they are, namely his way of seeking confirmation of personal identity and the affection of others, before they can be altered (Wolman, 1967).

An ambitious analytical approach, delving into the past, exposing deeply rooted fears, seeking to stimulate radical changes in sexual feelings, does not suit all cases. Experience shows that some persons never develop a working relationship with an analyst, remain untouched by verbal discussion, or lack capacity for psychological insight. Others simply become more miserable or more ruminative about their problems, without being able to do anything constructive about them. Others find that an awareness of the fears that may have been responsible in the distant past for diverting them away from the heterosexual path does little to help them to make a readjustment in the present. Realistic practical difficulties confront anyone hoping to secure a first heterosexual partner at a time of life when most persons are sexually experienced and usually already married.

The psychotherapist has the difficult task to decide, together with the patient, the appropriate aims of treatment. What the patient says he wants to try for is a very important consideration, but not the only one. Some of the factors which reduce the likelihood of a radical change of sexual orientation have already been mentioned. Ambivalent motivation, absence of any heterosexual experience, a long history of homosexual activity, and an emotional commitment to homosexual relationships, make conversion to heterosexuality improbable. In addition to these general rules, many individual characteristics determine the prospects for treatment. The therapist knows that certain individuals would remain troubled whatever their sexual orientation. Like drug abusers who blame their chemical addiction, when their real problems are the difficulties they cannot bear to confront in a sober state, some homosexuals attribute all their troubles to their unconventional sexual orientation. Anxious, withdrawn, socially inadequate individuals, especially the self-absorbed characters who are chronically dissatisfied and unrealistically demanding in all their personal contacts, are hardly likely to find heterosexual relationships any easier than homosexual ones. Discontent with a homosexual orientation is but slight discomfort in comparison with the unhappiness of a precarious heterosexual adjustment leading to failed marriage, broken home and bewildered children.

For many reasons, it often seems the wisest course to try and help a troubled patient accept his homosexuality, and make the most of the friendship and social support available in homosexual society, rather than go through the disturbing and sometimes futile effort to acquire a heterosexual orientation. Given the limited capacity of the treatment facilities, and the vast numbers of persons affected, it is hardly justifiable to expend too much time and effort on trying to reorientate individuals whose prospects of conversion to satisfactory and stable heterosexuality seem remote. Many authorities believe and frankly state that most patients are best helped by an approach aimed at promoting better social adjustment rather than effecting conversion (Rubin, 1961). The patient in agony from guilt and self-loathing, because he cannot bear the label homosexual, needs first and foremost help to attain self-acceptance, and a more reasonable attitude to sexual matters generally. Panic flight from homosexual temptation is not a sound basis for embarking upon heterosexual exercises.

Where conversion seemed unlikely, sublimation used to be the goal advocated by many therapists (English, 1953). The patient was advised to redirect his energies into non-sexual channels. A devotion to work, especially work involving a disinterested concern for others, such as social work or teaching, may bring a measure of personal fulfilment to those denied the possibility of heterosexual love and marriage. Whether such devotion ever provides an adequate substitute for the satisfactions of an active sex life is open to doubt. Cynics look sceptically upon attempts to obtain substitutes for sexual satisfaction. The youth worker whose devotion to duty springs from his homosexual inclinations all too easily becomes a devoted seducer.

Ethical and legal changes have made it easier for the modern psychotherapist to declare frankly, when the need arises, that the appropriate aim of treatment is the reduction of guilt and anxiety so that the patient can enjoy friendship, love and sex to the full, and in a homosexual context, if that is what suits him best. Many psychoanalysts experienced in dealing with sexual problems would agree with this, which is entirely in line with the spirit of Freud's famous advice to a homosexual's mother (see p. 244). Dr. L.H. Rubinstein (1958), for instance, who did not hesitate to attempt conversion treatment where possible, also pointed out that help in attaining a more rational understanding and acceptance of themselves may release patients' creative powers and improve their personal relationships, thus producing a social gain without necessarily bringing about heterosexual conversion. However, many analysts still feel this very much a second-best solution since, in their opinion, even the best adjusted and apparently creative homosexuals are, by the nature of their condition, anxious and despondent personalities who can never attain full self-realisation (Gershman, 1964).

Once a policy of therapeutic acceptance has been decided upon, should the patient want it, an introduction to the nearest available homophile organisation or meeting places serves to emphasise the therapist's full recognition of the validity of a homosexual adjustment. In subsequent sessions, discussion of the patient's developing friendships, and the difficulties that may arise within them, should proceed with as much sympathetic interest and encouragement as if he had taken a turn towards heterosexuality. This policy will inevitably be criticised by some as a capitulation to the patient's neurosis, and by others as a medical license for immorality, but in many cases it is no more than an honest admission of the realities of the situation. At least it involves no irrevocable steps. If the patient finds gay life not to his liking he is free to revert to a celibate existence. The therapist's aim is to alleviate irrational fears, to widen the patient's horizon, but not to dictate the choices he must make.

At one time psychotherapy nearly always meant an individually administered, psychoanalytically oriented approach, but today a bewildering variety of methods and theories are in use. Group psychotherapy, in which some six or more patients discuss their problems with each other, the therapist taking part as commentator and referee, has become increasingly popular. It permits the therapist to choose patients with similar, or perhaps complementary, problems, who may learn from each other and give each other some support. In the nature of things, the members of a therapeutic group must confide in and trust each other, and this can be a useful exercise in itself. Since one person can always see another's blind spots more readily than his own, when one member of the group tries to make excuses for behaviour or attitudes obviously governed by neurotic fears others can point out and interpret what is happening. The patient who receives the interpretation cannot avoid facing up to the fact that something must be wrong when others can see it so plainly. In trying to interpret others' reactions, members of the group can come to a better appreciation of their own. Self-deception becomes more difficult in the presence of other persons with similar experience. Verbal protestations concerning supposed changes in sexual outlook may receive a sceptical reception when the group notices evidence of the patient's continued links with persons or places associated with his previous sexual habits.

In America, group psychotherapy has often been used with serious sexual offenders (Cabeen and Coleman, 1962; Kozol *et al.*, 1966; MacDonald *et al.*, 1971; Marcus and Conway, 1971; Peters *et al.*, 1968; Slater, 1964). In a penal setting the pressure on men to lie during group sessions to secure release, or to preserve face in the presence of other prisoners, presents a serious difficulty, but one which most therapists believe it possible to overcome. The greatest disadvantage experienced in penal groups aimed at changing sexual behaviour is that they usually take place in a one-sexed custodial environment where anything other than homosexual activity can take place only in imagination. Whether the new outlooks attained in group discussion have any practical effect upon behaviour cannot be properly assessed until after release.

In ordinary psychiatric practice, with freedom to select both patients and therapists, there has been continuing discussion about the optimum composition of a therapeutic group dealing with homosexual problems (Hadden, 1968; 1972). Groups have been made up of one sex or both, with homosexuals only or including heterosexuals.

Experience suggests that one or two male homosexuals among a group of heterosexual men fare badly. Their particular problems meet with not much appreciation, and sometimes with positive antagonism. In a mixed group, however, the isolated homosexual member may do better (Litman, 1961). An even balance of heterosexual and homosexual patients assures adequate attention to the homosexuals and their preoccupations, while giving them the helpful experience of being taken seriously by heterosexual people. On the other hand, a group composed exclusively of homosexuals enables them to discuss their sexual and social problems more openly than they might otherwise do, and to recognise more clearly the nature of their dissatisfactions (Smith and Bassin, 1959). So far no generally agreed rule as to the best composition for a group has emerged. The employment of a pair of co-therapists, male and female, has been reported to give good results with a group of male homosexual patients. In addition to supplying experience of heterosexual interaction in a safe setting, the situation stimulated the patients to project on to the therapist feelings, attitudes and ideas derived from their own disturbed relations with their parents. The stormy emotional exchanges which ensued, taking place within the protective therapeutic environment, were both revealing and beneficial to patients wanting to understand and change their outlook (Singer and Fischer, 1967; Birk *et al.*, 1970).

The benefits of psychotherapy are variously attributed to improved insight, emotional catharsis, loving acceptance, the transference of infantile feelings on to the therapist, or social learning experience in the treatment situation. In view of the bewildering variety of techniques and theories, and the difficulty of specifying exactly what happens during sessions, it would be profitless to try to disentangle the factors responsible for psychotherapeutic 'cures' of homosexuality. A more important question is how often a satisfactory and permanent conversion to heterosexuality occurs, regardless of the means by which it comes about. Extreme opinions abound, both optimistic and pessimistic, but the true answer remains curiously elusive. Some authorities contend that conversion treatment is futile because 'genuine' homosexuality is fixed by heredity or irrevocably determined in infancy. Many have been influenced by Magnus Hirschfeld (1936), the great German clinician, who used to argue that homosexual disposition and homoerotic interests emerged in childhood, long before puberty, and remained ineradicable. Stanley-Jones (1947) referred to conversion therapy as a 'moral outrage'. Eustace Chesser (1958) thought 'genuine' homosexuals virtually unchangeable. The authors of the Home Office (Wolfenden) Report (1957) which recommended the relaxation of the English criminal law against adult homosexuality, were equally sceptical about therapeutic conversions, remarking (Para 193): 'We were struck by the fact that none of our witnesses were able, when we saw them, to provide any reference in medical literature to a change of this kind.'

In spite of these expressions of opinion, the possibility of radical change in individual cases appears established by published case reports, for instance by the several examples described by Hadfield (1958, 1966), which he followed up for some years to establish the permanence of the cures. Clifford Allen (1958), in his popular book on treatment, has also given a number of examples. Poe (1952) published one particularly striking example of a man of 40, who liked the passive role in buggery, and had practised homosexuality for 22 years, who was completely converted to heterosexuality in the course of 85 therapeutic sessions over a period of nine months.

Some therapists go to absurd extremes in claiming success, not just with exceptional individuals, but in the generality of cases. Dr. Daniel Cappon (1965), for instance, asserted that in his experience of treating 150 private psychiatric patients for sexual problems, 80 per cent of homosexuals were markedly improved and 50 per cent fully cured. Ninety per cent of the bisexuals who completed treatment were also cured, with no reversion to homosexual desire or behaviour. Albert Ellis (1956) another optimistic therapist, reported on the outcome of psychoanalytically oriented psychotherapy (from five to over two hundred sessions) undertaken by 28 men and 12 women with 'severe' homosexual problems. Eight of the women and 11 of the men were 'considerably improved', that is they began to lose their fears and to enjoy amorous relations with the opposite sex. Among the patients were 20 men with 'little or no heterosexual activity before therapy'. Only 5 of these were 'considerably improved' compared with 6 out of the 8 men with some previous experience of heterosexuality. The women improved more often than the men, in spite of being considered more emotionally disturbed to begin with. The treatment, described in detail in a later publication (Ellis, 1965), was based on the assumption that homosexual behaviour arises out of irrational and self-defeating beliefs which need to be brought to light and challenged. Attention focussed on the accompanying neurotic disturbance, sexual orientation being left to right itself in due course. The goal was removal of heterosexual fears, and a reduction of the obsessive need for homosexual outlets, but not necessarily the eradication of all homosexual interests.

Systematic studies of representative samples of patients assessed before and after treatment, and with an adequate period of follow-up, are scarce. In general, the more careful the assessment the more modest the claims. Curran and Parr (1957) studied 100 documented cases of male homosexual patients seen in private practice. They secured follow-up information about the subsequent sexual orientation of 52. Among the 24 men who had been exclusive homosexuals at the outset, only one changed towards heterosexuality. Among the 28 bisexuals or partial homosexuals, 8 changed towards heterosexuality but 3 became more homosexual than before. Although changes of sexual preference were few in number, and often minimal in degree, half the patients felt improved in their general well-being. A sub-group of 25 patients who had received psychotherapy were matched with a similar number of cases otherwise dealt with, the results being compared after an average follow-up period of over four years. The treated patients more often reported coming to better terms with their problem, but they showed no greater change towards heterosexuality than the control group, and some of them became less inhibited and more overt in their homosexual conduct following psychotherapy.

Qualified success in the treatment of male homosexual patients was reported by Mary Woodward (1958), working at the Portman Clinic, London, a centre specialising in out-patient psychotherapy on analytic lines, for maladjusted delinquents. Out of 133 cases referred, mostly from courts or probation officers, 92 were selected as suitable, but only 48 actually went through with their treatment. Out of this 48, only 6 were exclusively homosexual at the outset, and none of them became heterosexual. On the other hand, 28 out of the remaining 42 bisexuals or partial homosexuals were said to have lost their homosexual impulses at the end of the treatment. The results indicate that exclusive homosexuals are less likely to convert to heterosexuality.

In one unusually conscientious study, Mayerson and Lief (1965) at Tulane University traced 19 former patients (14 men and 5 women) after an average lapse of time of four-and-a-half years following completion of their psychotherapy. Their treatment had varied from 13 to 420 sessions per patient. At the time of the follow-up inquiry, 2 out of the 9 patients originally considered exclusive homosexuals had become substantially heterosexual (in behaviour) and 7 out of the 10 bisexuals or partial homosexuals had also become heterosexual. Substantially similar findings emerged from the larger study of Bieber *et al.* (1962) carried out for the Society of Medical Psychoanalysts in New York. Of 106 male homosexuals who had undergone private treatment, 27 were said to be exclusively heterosexual at the end of their treatment, or when they last reported to their analyst. The duration of treatment varied considerably, and a third of the patients were still attending, after more than 350 sessions, at the time of the check on sexual orientation. Half the initially bisexual cases (15 out of 30), compared with less than a fifth (14 out of 76) of the exclusively homosexual or sexually inactive cases, were heterosexual at the time of the inquiry. Very few of the patients who dropped out of the treatment early, that is in less than 150 hours, became heterosexual. Those who began analysis when they were aged less than 35, those who undertook treatment because they wanted to change into heterosexuals rather than to alleviate anxiety or other symptoms, those with a satisfactory relationship with their fathers, those who did not have too close a tie to their mothers, and those who had not developed effeminate mannerisms in childhood, all had better chances to become heterosexual. In other words, the less exclusive the sexual orientation, and the less ingrained in early development and subsequent conduct, the greater the likelihood of change.

Considering that the analysts included in Bieber's survey dealt with a favoured group of educated and financially secure patients, motivated to expend substantial sums on lengthy treatment voluntarily undertaken, a successful conversion in less than one in five cases of exclusive homosexuality is not a particularly impressive claim. Moreover, even this modest statistic is open to question. In view of the well-known tendency of sexual converts to lapse back into their original orientation, the absence of systematic follow-up is a serious defect. The statistics derived from what the analysts said their patients told them. Understandably, after an expensive and exhaustive course of treatment, patients have a need to convince themselves of benefit, or perhaps to assure the analyst that no more work is required. Change confirmed by the evidence of contented sexual or marriage partners (as in the extended follow-up carried out by Mayerson and Lief) would have been more convincing.

Statistical considerations never solve the problem what to do or what to hope for in a particular individual case. However, the general tenor of the reported results of psychotherapy, like those of behaviour modification, point to a cautious optimism that persons with some heterosexual experience may develop more, but suggest that persons, especially adult male persons, with no heterosexual experience, have relatively slight prospects of change.

If therapists had at their command the facilities to organise training in sexual relations with methods more practical than talk, and more effective than laboratory conditioning, I suspect the statistics might improve. However, unless the social and moral climate in which psychiatry operates changes more than seems probable, this hunch is unlikely to be put to the test.

CHAPTER TEN

Social Controls

1. *Criminal law*

The sexual habits of male homosexuals are more likely to lead them into committing breaches of the criminal law than the analogous pursuits of heterosexual men. In New Zealand, in Australia and South Africa, in the Soviet Union, in most of the United States, and in many other parts of the world, any sexual act between two males contravenes the law. Where the criminal law has been relaxed in modern times, as in England, the restraints applied to homosexual behaviour exceed those applied to heterosexual relations. In matters of public decorum, sexual invitations and acts involving young adults, the statutes single out homosexual behaviour for wider prohibition and heavier penalties.

For one brief period of European history, following the French Revolution of 1789, homosexuality disappeared from the criminal law. Traditionally, homosexual offences had been dealt with by ecclesiastical courts as outrages against the laws of God, punishable by torture and death. As late as the mid-eighteenth century homosexuals were burnt at the stake in Paris. The principle underlying the criminal code introduced by Napoleon, taken from rationalist philosophers like Voltaire, was essentially utilitarian. Demonstrably harmful acts, such as rape and violation of children were punished, moral choices concerning the practice of fornication or homosexuality were left to the private conscience of the individual citizen.

In those European countries, including France, Belgium, Spain and Italy, whose criminal law derives from the Code Napoléon of 1810, homosexuality was traditionally ignored. Abuses such as public indecency, unwanted sexual assaults, and sexual acts with minors, were punished equally without reference to whether the participants were of the same or different sex. Discrimination against homosexuality, where it occurs at all in these countries, developed later, with the introduction of stricter definitions or harsher punishments for homosexual misbehaviour. For example, in France, the age of consent for homosexual relations, but not for heterosexual relations, was raised from 18 to 21 by an Act of 1942 by the wartime Vichy government. The penalty for public indecency involving acts between persons of the same sex was increased by an Act of 25 Nov., 1960.

In Holland, where the Code Napoléon had operated since 1811, the law was modified in 1911, by article 248 bis, proposed by a Roman Catholic Minister of Justice, and carried through Parliament against considerable opposition. It raised the age of consent for homosexual acts to 21, leaving that for heterosexual acts unchanged at 16 (Ramsay *et al.* 1974). The modern Penal Code of Switzerland punishes 'immoral' acts, whether heterosexual or homosexual, with children under 16 (Article 191), but punishes 'immoral' acts with minors aged between 16 and 20 only if committed by persons of the same sex (Article 194).

In Germany, with the formation of the Reich in 1871, homosexual acts between males became an imprisonable offence under the well-known Article 175 of the Penal Code. In spite of a considerable campaign between the two world wars for a repeal of this law, a social atmosphere in Berlin and other large cities notable for its permissiveness towards homosexual night life, and a Parliamentary Penal Commission in favour of the reform, Article 175 was still in force when Hitler came to power. The Nazi regime in fact increased the penalties and extended the law, specifying 'tongue kissing' between men as punishable under Article 175, and introducing a penalty for homosexual prostitution of up to ten years' imprisonment. After the war, attempts were made in the Federal Republic of (West) Germany to have Article 175 declared a violation of Article 8 of the European Convention of Human Rights, which guarantees the sanctity of private life. The attempt foundered because the Convention permits some regulation of family life for the protection of the health and morals of the community as a whole (Fairburn, 1974). However, in 1967, the law was eventually repealed and homosexual acts in private between males over 21 ceased to be a crime. Thereafter, controversy concentrated upon whether the age of consent should be lowered to 18.

After the war the (East) German Democratic Republic introduced various amendments to mitigate the harshness of the Nazi law, which had clearly been used as an instrument of political oppression. In 1967 they produced a new Penal Code under which relations between an adult and a young person under 18 remained punishable, but otherwise homosexual behaviour ceased to be a crime. Other countries in Eastern Europe have had similar developments. On 1 January 1962 punishment of adult homosexuality ceased in Czechoslovakia. According to Paragraph 244 (1) of the Penal Code, anyone over 18 who commits an 'immoral' act with a person under 18 of the same sex is liable to one to five years imprisonment. Paragraph 244 (2) of the Code prohibits the giving or taking of money for homosexual acts, and the commission of homosexual acts in circumstances amounting to public indecency. The law in Poland is almost identical. Article 204 of the Penal Code punishes homosexual acts procured by violence, menace or fraud. The Polish Code also legislates against boys who offer sex for money. In Sweden, Denmark,

Finland, Norway and Austria laws against consenting adult homosexuality were repealed in 1930, 1945, 1970, 1971 and 1971 respectively. Of course, in some countries prosecutions under the old laws had virtually ceased long before the statutes were changed. Sections 278 to 281 of the Criminal Code of the Hungarian Peoples' Republic (Hungary, 1962, p. 104) deal with homosexual acts by force or threat, or with children of either sex under 14, or by older persons with minors of either sex aged under 20, or committed in a manner scandalising others, but make no mention of private acts between adults. The Criminal Code of Yugoslavia (Yugoslavia, 1964, p. 94) prohibits, under Article 186, acts of 'unnatural concupiscence' (i.e. buggery) between males, but makes no mention of 'lewdness'. However, Articles 181 and 183 prohibit both 'lewdness' and 'unnatural concupiscence' with a child under 14, or with a minor over 14 by an instructor, educator, guardian, or foster father into whose care the minor has been entrusted. The comparatively liberal provisions of some of the Eastern European countries do not extend to the Soviet Union. Initially, the Soviet Penal Code included no provisions against homosexuality, but in 1934 a decree was issued instructing the republics to make all sex acts between males a criminal offence, on the grounds that such behaviour is a social crime, on a par with sabotage and counter-revolutionary activity (Mannheim, 1946).

European countries differ considerably in the legal 'age of consent' for homosexual acts. In Turkey, under the Criminal Code of 1926, though penalties for sexual assault and sex with minors are very heavy, private consensual homosexual relations are legal so long as both parties are over fifteen. In Holland, in 1971, following the recommendation of a medical committee, and with little opposition, the legal age of consent to homosexual acts was lowered from 21 to 16, the same as for heterosexual acts (Ramsay *et al.*, 1974). Eighteen is the age of consent for homosexuality in most European countries, but in Italy, Norway and Switzerland it is 16, in Greece 17 and in England 21. The laws vary also in regard to homosexual prostitution, which in itself is no crime in England, but illegal in Denmark, Holland and Sweden. In some countries, the law makes specific provision for protection from exploitation. The Swiss Penal Code, for example, in Article 193, specifies that it is an offence for persons who have care of hospital patients, prisoners or inmates of poor homes to commit any immoral act with their charges. Article 194 punishes any immoral act by a person of the same sex obtained by abuse of an emergency, or an official status, or a situation of dependency arising from employment or some similar relationship. Aiding in the prostitution of any person under 18 is also an imprisonable offence (Article 200).

In the Australian states the criminal law follows the pattern of English law before the 1967 reform. The crime of buggery attracts very heavy maximum penalties, and other forms of indecency between males are also proscribed by statute. In New South Wales, Section 81 of the Crimes Act specifies that whosoever commits an indecent assault upon a male person, of whatever age, with or without the consent of such person, shall be liable to penal servitude for five years. This Section has been held to apply to homosexual acts by consenting adult males.

Various African countries have acquired similar patterns. Under Section 214 of the Nigerian Penal Code 'carnal knowledge of any person against the order of nature' (i.e. buggery) or permitting a male person to have carnal knowledge (i.e. passive buggery) is punishable with imprisonment up to fourteen years. The consent of the partner is no defence. In Ghana, the same crime done with consent ranks as misdemeanour and hence is subject to a maximum of only three years imprisonment. Section 217 of the Nigerian Penal Code prohibits 'gross indecency' between males, whether in public or private, on penalty of up to three years imprisonment. Gross indecency apparently covers any kind of sexual behaviour (Seidman, 1966).

South Africa, not surprisingly perhaps in view of the political climate prevailing, has anti-homosexuality laws both harsh and all-embracing. Sodomy (defined as sexual relations per anum) and 'unnatural offences' (which, in the case of a male couple, have been held to include mutual masturbation, fellatio and friction of the genitals against the other person's body) have long been punished severely under South African common law. More recently, under the Immorality Act 23, 1957, Section 14 (i)b, any male person who commits or attempts to commit an immoral or indecent act with a boy under 19 is liable to imprisonment with compulsory labour for up to six years. The Immorality Amendment Act 57, 1969, prescribes a penalty of up to two years imprisonment for any male person who commits with another male at a party any act calculated to stimulate sexual pleasure or to give sexual gratification. More than two persons present makes a 'party'.

In many parts of the Third World, whatever may happen in actual practice, statutes of extraordinary severity govern sexual misconduct, including homosexuality. In Morocco, for instance, the new Legal Code drawn up in 1956, after the country gained independence from the French, reverted, in Articles 489 and 490, to ancient Muslim religious prohibitions against both homosexuality and extra-marital heterosexual relations (Brongersma, 1964).

The 1957 Penal Code of Ethiopia provides, under Article 600, that whosoever performs with another person of the same sex an act corresponding to the sexual act, or any other indecent act, is punishable with simple imprisonment. Article 601 provides that where such an offender makes a profession of such activity for gain, or where he uses a position of tutor, protector, teacher, employer or the like to cause another to submit to the act, these are aggravating circumstances requiring imprisonment for not less than three months and up to five years in serious cases.

The legal system of Japan is outstanding in that homosexual practice as such is not a criminal offence. However, acts of 'indecent liberty' imposed upon an unwilling male or female by a person of the same or different sex are prohibited under Article 176. If the partner to the act, whether male or female, is less than 13, the perpetrator commits an indecent liberty even if it is done with consent (Koshi, 1970, p. 139).

The historical development of the English criminal law on sexual offences has been reviewed in some detail by Gigeroff (1968). Homosexual offences first became a matter for the secular courts in 1533 when a statute was introduced (25 Henry VIII c6) making 'the detestable and abominable vice of buggery committed with mankind or beast' punishable by death. Except for some short, unimportant intermissions, it remained so until the nineteenth century, when the penalty was reduced to life imprisonment. Early in the seventeenth century Sir Edward Coke, Chief Justice of the King's Bench, wrote an extremely influential treatise on *The Institutes of the Laws of England* (Third Part) which dealt extensively with this crime. He referred to it as 'a detestable and abominable sin, amongst Christians not to be named, committed by carnal knowledge against the ordinance of the Creator, and order of nature, by mankind with mankind, or with brute beast, or by womankind with brute beast'. The conspicuous omission of the category of womankind with womankind underlies the traditional immunity of lesbians from criminal prosecution. Coke also makes clear in his discussion that carnal knowledge means copulation with some degree of penetration. In the case of male offenders this must involve an act of anal intercourse. He does, however, somewhat confuse the issue by citing love of little boys, a vice which he attributes to the influence of foreign immigrants, as a species of buggery.

Another great legal authority, William Blackstone, in his *Commentaries on the Laws of England*, compiled in the mid-eighteenth century, classed 'crimes against nature' with abduction and rape as offences affecting the security of the person. Presumably both penetrator and penetrated were guilty of the spiritual harm sustained. He had no doubt that capital punishment was the proper penalty for these breaches of the law of God. Uncompleted sexual acts, where one 'laid hands on the other with intent to commit, and the other permitted the same with intent to suffer, the commission of the abominable crime ...' were properly punished (as assaults with intent) with fine, imprisonment and pillory rather than death.

In the nineteenth century executions for homosexuality were seldom carried out, and in 1861, by the Offences Against the Person Act (24Vict. c100 S.61), life imprisonment was substituted for capital punishment. A minimum penalty was written into the statute, which read: 'Section 61. Whosoever shall be convicted of the abominable crime of buggery, committed either with mankind, or with any animal, shall be liable, at the discretion of the Court, to be kept in penal servitude for life or for any term not less than 10 years.' Under Section 62 'Whosoever shall attempt to commit the said abominable crime, or shall be guilty ... of any indecent assault upon any male person, shall be ... liable, at the discretion of the court, to be kept in penal servitude for any term not exceeding 10 years and not less than 3 years ...'

The punishments were modified subsequently, and the minimum sentences abolished, but 'buggery with another person' (Sexual Offences Act, 1956, S.12) remained in all circumstances a crime until the passing of the Sexual Offences Act, 1967. Homosexual behaviour, such as mutual masturbation, which could not be classified as an assault (unless committed with a boy under 16) or as an attempted act of buggery, escaped statutory definition as crime until the offence of gross indecency between males was introduced under Section 11 of the Criminal Law Amendment Act, 1885 (48 Vict. c.69). The provision was inserted into the Bill as an amendment, by Henry Labouchere, MP for Northampton. Objection was raised because the amendment had no obvious relevance to the topic of the Bill, which was intended to protect young girls from exploitation as prostitutes. Nevertheless, the Speaker ruled the amendment in order. Labouchere said he thought it unnecessary to discuss the proposal at any length as he understood the government was willing to accept it. The clause, providing imprisonment of up to two years for 'any male person who, in public or in private, commits or is party to the commission of, or procures or attempts to procure the commission by any male person of, any act of gross indecency with another male person ...', was agreed without discussion at a poorly attended session in the small hours of the morning. Before long the new law was being dubbed 'the blackmailer's charter'. With a minor amendment of wording (in the Sexual Offences Act, 1956, Section 13) it remained unchanged till 1967.

Once on the statute book, the clause was interpreted by the courts as strictly as possible. The Act made no attempt to specify what kind of behaviour would amount to 'gross indecency', but it was held that indecency could occur without the offending parties actually touching each other. In one such case Lord Chief Justice Goddard referred to the defendants as having been 'found in a shed in positions which can only be described as constituting filthy exhibition by one to the other ...' (*R. v Hunt* [1950] 2 *All England Reports* 291). With this as precedent, any deliberately lewd exhibition of the genitals for purposes of sexual invitation, such as might occur between men in a public urinal, could be charged as gross indecency.

Under Section 32 of the Sexual Offences Act, 1956, which replaces Section 1 of the Vagrancy Act, 1898, 'it is an offence for a man persistently to solicit or importune in a public place for immoral purposes'. Originally intended to control the activities of men touting the services of female prostitutes, this clause has been used almost exclusively against male homosexuals trying to make contact with other homosexuals in public lavatories or at the notorious picking-up spots in big cities. This provision has also been interpreted most rigorously by the courts. Police observation, without any complaint of annoyance or nuisance, suffices to secure conviction. It has been held that the person solicited does not need to notice the efforts made to attract his attention in order for an offence to occur. Knowing glances suffice (Radzinowicz, 1957, p. 352). Lingering unnecessarily long in a public convenience fulfils the requirement of 'persistence'. The offence carries a maximum sentence of two years imprisonment (or six months on summary conviction).

The movement to reform the English criminal law on homosexuality may be said to have originated as a liberal backlash against police policy in the early fifties. According to Hyde (1970) who was a Member of Parliament at the time, a repressive policy had the enthusiastic support of the then Home Secretary (Sir David Maxwell Fife, later Lord Kilmuir) the Metropolitan Police Commissioner (Sir John Nott-Bower) and the devout Catholic Director of Public Prosecutions (Sir Theobald Matthew). Action against homosexuals in government employ who might become security risks was in full swing in the United States. In England the drive intensified after 1951, following the defection of two British diplomats, Guy Burgess and Donald Maclean, who were known to have been involved in homosexual conduct. The interest shown by their superiors in rooting out homosexuals naturally communicated itself to policemen of all ranks, with the result that their zeal in the pursuit of convictions of homosexuals led to some sordid prosecutions. Gross violations of privacy, the use of compromising letters unearthed in searches of doubtful legality, and dependence upon guilty persons prepared to give evidence against their friends in return for immunity from prosecution, began to alienate public opinion. Two of the prominent persons brought to trial during the period wrote books about their experiences criticising the unethical methods used to secure their convictions (Croft-Cooke, 1955; Wildeblood, 1955). At Wildeblood's trial the main witnesses were two airmen, both homosexuals who had willingly accepted his hospitality. They were shown to have been involved in many affairs with men, but they were prepared to give evidence in the case against Wildeblood, and no charge was brought against them. In Croft-Cooke's case the prosecution witnesses were again two young men to whom he had given hospitality. They were later taken into custody for assaulting a roadmender after trying to steal his bicycle. They mentioned where they had stayed the week-end, whereupon the police started to probe. The men were apparently led to believe that it could help them in their assault case to make a statement about Croft-Cooke.

The notorious trials of 1953 and 1954 provoked strong comment in the national press, much of it critical of the authorities. The exploitation of the tainted evidence of accomplices to convict a few unfortunate scapegoats, when everyone knew of homosexuals at large in society, many of them in positions of eminence or responsibility, had become an obvious hypocrisy. The Church of England Moral Welfare Council brought out a pamphlet recommending decriminalisation of adult homosexuality. The Home Secretary, bowing to popular demand, agreed to set up a Departmental Committee to look into the law and practice relating to both homosexual offences and prostitution. The report of this Committee, universally known as the Wolfenden Report, after its chairman, was published three years later (Home Office, 1957). It argued at length for decriminalisation, both on utilitarian grounds, and as a matter of principle. It cited some of the social evils created by the existing law and pointed to the absence of any reason to believe that homosexual behaviour between males inflicted greater damage on family life than adultery, fornication and lesbian behaviour, none of which were thought to warrant control by means of the criminal law. It argued the principle that sin and crime differ, that a sphere of private moral choice exists which is no business of the criminal law. This contention set off a widely publicised debate between legal luminaries (Devlin, 1965; Hart, 1963) that continues to this day. Professor Hart argued that the criminal law should apply only to acts that cause demonstrable harm to others. Lord Devlin argued that the law should sometimes be used to define the limits of private conduct in the interest of defining and hence helping to preserve the moral standards upon which the continued stability and happiness of the community may depend (Geis, 1972; Davies 1975). This controversy affects many other social issues besides homosexuality (abortion, prostitution, gambling, pornography, divorce, child welfare, drug-taking and smoking for example), but the fact that it came into prominence following the Wolfenden recommendations helped to direct critical attention to the shaky assumptions that lay behind anti-homosexual legislation. In all probability the criminal law influences moral judgments on such issues less than might be supposed. In one experiment, ignorant students were led to believe in the criminality of certain questionable acts, such as attempted suicide, while others were led to think the same acts were not criminal. Much the same moral opinions were expressed regardless of what the individual supposed the law had to say on the question (Walker and Argyle, 1964; Berkowitz and Walker, 1967).

Although favourably reviewed by the more serious press, the Wolfenden proposals had a cool reception from the Conservative government. Three months after publication, Lord Pakenham (later Lord Longford) initiated a debate in the Lords, but more than a year passed before the Commons, in a motion designed to avoid a vote, took note of the Report. The then Home Secretary, Mr. R.A. Butler (later Lord Butler) explained that, in view of the state of public opinion, the government did not feel justified in introducing the reform proposed. Nevertheless, public discussion continued, and a small pressure group, the Homosexual Law Reform Society, was formed under impeccably respectable auspices, to spread the Wolfenden gospel. The various attempts to revive the issue in Parliament over the following nine years are of interest to the historian of social change, and to the collector of vitriolic and emotional pronouncements from prominent personages. In June 1960, a motion by Kenneth Robinson in the Commons to implement the Wolfenden proposals was defeated by a vote of 213 to 99. A Private Member's Bill with the same object was introduced in the Lords in 1965 by the Earl of Arran, swiftly followed by an unsuccessful attempt by Leo Abse to introduce a similar Bill in the Commons. The Arran Bill was duly debated, but the session ended before a conclusion was reached. It was opposed vigorously by Lord Kilmuir on the grounds that the law was needed to preserve minimum standards of decency. Yet another Bill, by Humphrey Berkeley in the Commons, failed because Parliament was dissolved for a general election. After a revival of the Arran Bill in the Lords in 1966, Leo Abse obtained leave at last to present his Bill to the Commons. After amendments by a standing committee, the Bill was finally passed in July 1967.

When it finally emerged, the Sexual Offences Act, 1967, fell far short of equality in law between heterosexuals and homosexuals. Charges of buggery or gross indecency were abolished in relation to acts between two consenting males, but only provided the behaviour took place in private and provided both parties were over 21. The age limit compares unfavourably with the age when heterosexual relations become permissible, which at present is 16, although proposals for a lower limit have recently been made (Robinson, 1972; Beaumont *et al.*, 1974; Card, 1975). The Act lays down that homosexual behaviour will not be treated as being in private 'when more than two persons take part or are present' or 'in a lavatory to which the public are permitted to have access'. The Act also specifically prohibits buggery or gross indecency between male members of the crew on board any United Kingdom merchant ship. It does not repeal the Army, Air Force or Naval Discipline Acts, which prohibit members of the armed services from participation in homosexual acts, however private. The first test case on this point after the new Act took place early in 1969 (Hyde, 1970 p. 269). An RAF flying officer, questioned by a security officer about his friendship with a fellow officer, confessed that he was having a homosexual affair. No suggestion of public indecency or of an adverse effect upon his efficiency was made, but instead of being allowed to resign he was convicted by a court martial and dismissed with ignominy.

The maximum penalties for some homosexual offences became heavier as a result of the 1967 Act. The maximum for buggery with a boy under 16 (or with a woman or an animal) is life, and for any form of indecency with a boy under 16, ten years. It does not lessen the penalty if the boy participates willingly because persons under 16 can give no legal consent, so any sexual activity involving them constitutes an assault. Gross indecency or buggery by a man over 21 with a consenting partner under 21, but over 16, attracts a maximum of five years. The maximum for gross indecency or for buggery, committed outside the permitted circumstances by men over 21 is two years. The contrast in the maximum penalty for an indecent act (assault) with a girl under 16 (two years) and with a boy of the same age (ten years) points to the greater seriousness of homosexual, as opposed to heterosexual, misconduct in the eyes of the law.

It is still an offence to 'procure' the commission of homosexual acts by others. The penalty is up to two years, even if the behaviour 'procured', being in private and between adults, is perfectly legal. Theoretically, counselling services, or advertising agencies, or private citizens who introduce two homosexual males, knowing they are going to have sex together, could be prosecuted. Living on the immoral earnings of a male prostitute is subject to a maximum of seven years imprisonment on indictment, and allowing 'people to resort to [premises] for the purposes of lewd homosexual practices' (Section 6) counts as the offence of keeping a brothel.

A quite sensational example of the use of the charge of homosexual procuring came up in 1969. Together with some guardsmen friends, a wealthy gentleman who liked to entertain soldiers was convicted of conspiring to procure. According to the prosecution some thirty or forty men were involved, soldiers of varying ranks, and rich homosexual gentlemen who enjoyed their favours. One soldier admitted receiving from the accused £180 for his help in introducing other willing soldiers.

The reform introduced by the Sexual Offences Act, 1967, applies only to England and Wales. Homosexual behaviour under any circumstances is still a crime in Scotland and Northern Ireland. In Scotland, the Criminal Law Amendment Act, 1885, Section 11, which deals with 'outrages on decency', still applies. 'Any male person who in public or private commits, or is a party to the commission of, or procures or attempts to procure the commission of by any male person an act of gross indecency with another male person shall be guilty of misdemeanour and being convicted thereof shall be liable at the discretion of the court to be imprisoned for any term not exceeding two years.' In practice, however, this law has never been enforced against acts in private. Prosecutions in Scotland are controlled, not by the local police, but by the Procurator Fiscal in the lower courts and the Lord Advocate in the High Court. These officials have never countenanced the selective intrusions into privacy that in England provoked a public outcry and the Wolfenden inquiry. As Fairburn (1974) puts it, the Scottish Act has fallen into somnolent desuetude which is frequently a better system of reform since it raises no clamour. Of course, not everyone would agree with Fairburn's views about the retention of obsolete laws. So long as persons in authority retain the power to do so, there can be no guarantee that they will not one day decide to revert to a less liberal policy.

Since the passing of the 1967 Act in England, publications have appeared carrying very frank advertisements by homosexuals seeking contacts with others similarly inclined. For example, among a hundred or more similar 'personal' notices in *Gay News* each fortnight, issue No.66 (March 1975) contained the following: 'Handsome guy,

26, interested in leather/denim, wishes to attend young-gay parties at weekends. Brighton/London. Box -.' And another: 'Quiet, slim, lonely Londoner, 28, would like a gentle, hairy friend.' Such advertisements are of doubtful legality. In a case against *Gay News* (see issue No.66, March 1975) under the Obscene Publications Act, which was heard by the Bournemouth Magistrates on 24 February 1975, the prosecution agreed that a large part of the paper was not obscene, but drew the attention of the court to the personal advertisements which might be thought to 'deprave and corrupt'. The charge was dismissed, but the paper was left to pay the legal costs of the defence.

More important in establishing the legal status of homosexual advertisements in England were the successful obscenity prosecutions against *Oz* and *International Times*. The results showed 'that the encouragement or facilitation of homosexual behaviour was seen by the prosecution as being far more anti-social and immoral than promoting heterosexual behaviour' (Grey, 1974). In the *International Times* case the defendants were charged with having 'conspired together and with persons inserting advertisements in issues of a magazine called "It" under the heading of "Males" ... to induce readers thereof to meet these persons inserting such advertisements for the purpose of sexual practices taking place between male persons and to encourage readers to indulge such practices, with intent to debauch and corrupt the morals ...' The Court of Appeal in this case (*R. v Knuller* [1971] 3 *All England Reports* 314-319) confirmed that, notwithstanding the fact that buggery and gross indecency in private between consenting adult males are no longer crimes, an agreement between two or more persons to insert advertisements in a magazine for the purpose of inducing or encouraging such acts to take place in private may constitute the offence of 'conspiracy to corrupt public morals'. This curious offence first came into prominence in 1962 with the successful prosecution on these grounds of a man who produced a *Ladies Directory* listing women prostitutes (*Shaw* v. *DPP* [1962] Appeal Cases 220). Shaw was charged with publishing an obscene article and living on the earnings of prostitution. Apart from some doubt whether the Directory was covered by the Obscene Publications Act (1959), and whether the profits came under the scope of 'earnings of prostitution', the reason for adding the conspiracy charge was to take the offence out of categories in which the maximum penalty was limited to two years imprisonment. The Appeal Court upheld the convictions on all three counts. The Knuller decision was further appealed to the House of Lords, who upheld the conviction for conspiracy to corrupt public morals, thereby indirectly confirming the Shaw decision and reasserting the legitimacy of this type of charge. Lord Diplock argued that the defendants in Knuller might also have been found guilty had they been charged with inviting or procuring acts of gross indecency by male persons under 21 (Section 13, Sexual Offences Act, 1956). Lord Morris thought that some of the advertisements, which amounted to offers of male prostitution analogous to the Shaw case, would have been covered by the Obscene Publications Act (1973, Appeal Court, 435).

Many British lawyers have expressed uneasiness about the use of common law conspiracy charges, especially in relation to ill-defined offences such as corrupting public morals. In a recent working paper the Law Commission (1974) recommends abolishing such common-law offences as corrupting public morals and outraging public decency, obscene libel and conspiracy to debauch. Statute laws already in existence cover adequately most forms of anti-social behaviour in the sexual field. The Law Commission further recommends that conspiracy to corrupt public morals or to outrage public decency should cease to be criminal where the object of the conspiracy falls short of being a crime.

The anomalies and inconsistencies in English criminal law relating to homosexuality have naturally aroused the ire of the Campaign for Homosexual Equality, which has recently produced a tersely argued pamphlet urging statutory reform (Sturgess, 1975). The English legal anomalies, however, pale into insignificance in comparison with the situation in the United States. A minority of the States of the Union (e.g. Illinois, Connecticut, Colorado, Oregon, Hawaii, Delaware and Ohio) have recently reformed their codes so as to legalise private, consenting homosexuality, the minimum age for consent varying from 16 to 18. In Idaho, where the reform was quietly introduced as part of a new Penal Code, public criticism prevented it being put into effect. Elsewhere in the States, homosexual behaviour in private remains an offence, although New York, Minnesota, Kansas and Utah have reduced its status from a felony to a misdemeanour. Since the 1967 Penal Code, the maximum penalty for this offence in New York State has been three months in jail.

Considerable confusion has arisen from the vague, archaic language of many of the American enactments, and the consequent uncertainty as to the range of behaviour covered by such terms as 'infamous crime against nature', 'sodomy', 'unnatural sex act' or 'carnal knowledge against the order of nature'. Different States have arrived at contrary decisions as to the kinds of behaviour prohibited. Some have declared that the sodomy statutes embrace all forms of sexual activity between males, as in a decision in North Carolina in 1965 (*State* v. *Harward* 264. NC 746). In contrast, a decision in New Jersey in 1953 (*State* v. *Morrison* 25 NJ Super 534) held that 'sodomy, or the infamous crime against nature' applied only to anal intercourse. Some States have declined to delve into the disgusting details required to produce more precise definitions. An Oklahoma court in 1955 (*Berryman* v. *State* 283P. Ed.558. 562.Okla.Cr.) declined to do so because the behaviour was, echoing Coke, 'such as should not be described among Christians'. Some States have enacted additional laws to overcome the difficulty that 'sodomy' may not cover all forms of indecency between males. In the California Penal Code, Section 286 refers only to 'the infamous crime against nature', but Section 288(a) specifically prohibits copulation with the mouth. Michigan has a statute prohibiting 'gross indecency' in public or in private, which presumably stretches to any kind of homosexual behaviour. According to Barnett (1973, p.24), who lists the relevant decisions, Arizona, California, Colorado, Kentucky, Louisiana, Michigan, Nebraska, New Jersey, New Mexico, Texas, Utah, and Virginia have held that fellatio is not within the common-law meaning of 'crime against nature', 'sodomy' or 'buggery', whereas the opposite has been held by Alabama, Delaware, Florida, Idaho, Maine, Mississippi, Montana, Nevada, North Carolina, Tennessee and some others.

In addition to their felony laws most of the States also have a multiplicity of misdemeanour statutes against 'outrageous conduct', 'lewd behaviour', 'vagrancy' and the like which they use to suppress homosexual behaviour or homosexual solicitation. Outrageous conduct covers acts in public places liable to provoke a breach of peace. The vagrancy statutes prohibiting 'loitering' or 'disorderly' conduct', even though they do not specifically cite sexual misbehaviour, can be used against homosexuals in bars or elsewhere. Some vagrancy statutes, however, specify indecency as one of the offences covered. The New York Code, Section 887, mentions loitering 'for the purpose of inducing, enticing or procuring another to commit ... any indecent act.' Typical of the sort of misdemeanour provision used against homosexuals is Section 647 of the Californian Penal Code. This defines as guilty of 'disorderly conduct' anyone 'who solicits anyone to engage in or who in any public place or in any place open to the public or exposed to public view engages in lewd or dissolute conduct ...' These misdeameanour provisions are more widely used than the felony statutes directed against sodomy. Paradoxically, therefore, the man caught in a hotel bedroom risks greater punishment than one caught in a public lavatory. In order to prosecute behaviour in private the sodomy statutes must be invoked, and many of these lay down minimum sentences of two years imprisonment, whereas the maximum sentence for public misdemeanours is usually only one year. A similar injustice used to occur in England before the 1967 reform. In his survey of men imprisoned for homosexuality Michael Schofield (1965a) found that some of those serving the longest sentences were men with no previous convictions whose offences were limited to private conduct with other adults. Having unwisely confessed to acts of buggery, they had laid themselves open to prosecution under the older statutes carrying much heavier maximum penalties.

American citizens have the advantage of a written Constitution to protect them from unjust or oppressive laws. Many attempts have been made to get the sodomy statutes declared unconstitutional, but so far without much success (Barnett, 1973). A decision by the United States Supreme Court in 1965 held that 'the right to privacy in marriage' was one of the 'privileges and immunities of citizens', protected by the Fourteenth Amendment, and in consequence a state law prohibiting contraception was declared unconstitutional (*Griswold v. Connecticut* 381 US 479). It seems a small step to extend the protection of privacy to all citizens, but so far the case decisions have interpreted Griswold as applicable only to married couples. Thus, in 1971 (*Dixon v. State* 268 NE 2d. 84) the Supreme Court of Indiana held that the Griswold right of privacy did not extend to an act of cunnilingus between an unmarried man and woman.

The United States Supreme Court has from time to time declared statutes void on the grounds of vagueness, because they fail to give a clear guide to laymen what is meant. The sodomy statutes would appear rather good candidates for excision on these grounds, especially in view of the varied interpretations in force in different States, but judicial decisions or supplementary statutes can generally be cited in support of the contrary view that within each state the offences have been adequately defined. Nevertheless, on 17 December 1971, the Supreme Court of Florida declared its own statute concerning crimes against nature void because the wording of a hundred years ago could not be assumed to be understandable to the average citizen today. Following this decision a bill was passed redefining sodomy in modern language, but providing only misdemeanour penalties in the case of acts between consenting adults (Barnett, 1973, p.39).

Another constitutional argument cited by Professor Barnett derives from the Eighth Amendment which prohibits 'cruel and unusual punishment'. Any punishment whatsoever may be considered cruel and unusual if the offender has committed no definite anti-social act. In *Robinson v. California* (370 US 660, 1962) the Supreme Court held invalid a statute that sought to punish a narcotic addict in the absence of evidence for the sale or possession of drugs. A status or condition was held to be insufficient grounds for punishment in the absence of an overt crime. An alcoholic who drinks in private commits no crime. To punish a homosexual for behaviour in private comes close to punishing him for his condition rather than for anti-social behaviour. Controversy on these matters continues very actively in the United States. The concepts of a right to privacy, and a right to equal protection before the law, are the two which seem the most likely to induce substantive changes in legal practice (Michigan, 1974).

In all the issues raised by Professor Barnett, the difficulty has always been to find suitable test cases. The majority of sodomy prosecutions in the United States involve some factor, such as age or public situation or absence of full consent, which bring the behaviour into the ambit of legal prohibitions that cannot be challenged on constitutional grounds. Even more suspect than the sodomy laws, from the point of view of possible infringement of constitutional rights, is the much criticised legislation against 'sexual psychopaths' (Bowman and Engle, 1965; Lindman and McIntyre, 1961). Many of the States enacted these laws hastily in response to the clamour that follows any widely publicised sexual atrocity. Intended to protect the community against dangerous sexual offenders, these statutes introduce special provisions, over and above ordinary judicial sentence, authorising compulsory detention for indefinite periods of treatment in prison hospitals. As with so many laws dealing with sexual matters, imprecise drafting has led to abuses. In California, a person convicted of any offence, sexual or otherwise, can be dealt with as a 'mentally disordered sex offender' if the court finds sufficient reason to do so. In their well-known text on American criminal law Kadish and Paulsen (1969) cite at length the rejected appeal of a homosexual paedophile named Levy (151 Cal. app. 2d. 460, 311 P. 2d. 897). This man found himself committed indefinitely, possibly for life, to San Quentin Prison, although his offence under Section 647a, namely annoying and molesting a child under the age of 18, rated as no more than a misdemeanour. Ordered psychiatric examinations, he was detained for observation and finally committed to Atascadero State Hospital. After a period of some eighteen months, on medical evidence that he was not recovered and would not benefit from further treatment, he was sent to San Quentin. The Appeal Court held that evidence of lack of control and potential dangerousness had been adequately established, and that Levy's confinement for the protection of society was legitimate. The authors also cite another case, under the Michigan Sexual Psychopath Laws in 1958 (Maddox, 35a Mich. 358, 88 NW 2d 470), in which a man charged with a crime, but never formally convicted, was declared, on psychiatric evidence, a sexual psychopath, and committed to Ionia State Hospital. He proved a recalcitrant patient and was accordingly transferred to the State prison. In this instance, the Supreme Court held the man's detention unconstitutional, because he had never been formally proved guilty, because the chief reason he was sent from hospital to prison was that he declined to admit his alleged sex crimes, and because the imprisonment violated his right to proper treatment.

These cases illustrate the drawbacks of the sexual psychopath procedures. Relatively harmless homosexuals who have on only one occasion been found guilty of indecency with a minor risk far longer detention than the seriousness of their misconduct warrants. Since an offender's sexual reactions in freedom are virtually impossible to predict from his conduct inside an institution, he may languish for very long periods pending a release decision based upon vague and conflicting medical ideas about what to look for as a sign of fitness for discharge. Moreover, the treatment provided for sex offenders in some state institutions has been, to say the least, minimal, and certainly without demonstrable effectiveness (Nasatir *et al.*, 1966). The obvious defects in the system for defining, assessing and treating social dangerousness have been forcefully pointed out by the American Bar Association (1967) and some of the States, such as Ohio, have already repealed their sexual psychopath laws.

Notwithstanding the frightening profusion of anti-homosexual laws and draconian penalties which still prevail in the United States, a nation-wide relaxation may well take place in the foreseeable future. Many respected American psychiatrists have long argued in favour of reform. Thomas Szasz (1965) in a characteristically forthright essay challenged the irrationality of anti-sex laws, the use of the sickness label to enable psychiatrists to control homosexual conduct, and the moral bias that confidently assumes without justification that heterosexual behaviour is right and homosexual behaviour wrong. He criticised psychiatrists for lending their support to coercive measures whereby a tyrannical majority seeks to reduce diversity of opinion and action. As long ago as 1955 the Model Penal Code proposed by the American Law Institute recommended the deletion of all laws concerning consensual sodomy in private. On 8 August 1973 the American Bar Association adopted a resolution calling for the repeal of all state laws which classify as criminal non-commercial sex between consenting adults (42 *U.S. Law Week*, 2098, 14 August 1973). It would appear that American lawyers favour such decriminalisation, but American public opinion and American politicians are not yet ready for it.

2. *Law enforcement and civil liberties*

The letter of the criminal law matters much less to the homosexual in his everyday life than the manner in which the agencies of social control go about their business of suppression. Paradoxically, homophile organisations and publications, gay liberation demonstrations, bars, baths, cinemas, clubs and neighbourhoods catering specially for homosexuals, all flourish particularly strongly in America in spite of the fact that most of the States retain, in theory, more inflexible laws and severer penalties for male homosexual behaviour than most European countries. The ancient sodomy statutes lack the support of large sections of the American public. The authorities, even if they wished to do so, no longer find it practicable or politic to enforce the laws against private sexual conduct, save in exceptional cases.

A similar situation developed in England even before the law reform of 1967. The unpopular witch hunts of the fifties had given way to a go-softly policy on the part of the police. Almost all the cases brought before the courts concerned importuning, sex acts in public, or the involvement of young persons. Since all these categories of behaviour remained crimes, the 1967 Act brought no obvious change in the numbers of men convicted for homosexual offences. The following table, abstracted from the *Criminal Statistics for England and Wales* for the years 1965 to 1973, displays the main categories of prosecution for homosexual offences and the numbers of males convicted.

The figures suffice to give a general impression of trends in prosecution, but they are not complete. They do not include convictions under the Indecency with Children Act, 1960, of which there are about four hundred annually, because the published figures fail to distinguish between indecencies with girls and indecencies with boys. There are probably more of the former. Also omitted from the statistics are convictions under bye-laws or local statutes governing offensive or indecent behaviour in parks or elsewhere. Under the Metropolitan Police Acts, for example, individuals can be prosecuted for public nuisance and indecency without invoking the Sexual Offences Acts. Since prosecutions under these local rules are not classified according to the exact nature of the offence, whether urinating in public, appearing inadequately clad, or committing homosexual acts, the total incidence of prosecutions for homosexuality remains obscure. The transgressors in such cases have every reason to plead guilty without fuss, since they escape the stigma of the sex offender label. The police avoid the necessity to refer to the Director of Public Prosecutions if the offender is under 21, a procedure they must follow in cases brought under the Sexual Offences Act. Occasionally, prosecutions under headings apparently unrelated to sex may conceal a homosexual incident. According to a report in the London *Evening Standard* (27 June 1975) a vicar was convicted of 'insulting behaviour' following an arrest 'after being seen to press up against a man in the crowd'.

Male Persons found guilty of homosexual offences in England and Wales

Offence Category	Year									
	1965	1966	1967	1968	1969	1970	1971	1972	1973	1974
Buggery	219	194	200	201	191	212	164	172	164	19
Attempts to commit buggery. Indecent assault on males, etc.	822	931	953	934	930	887	869	844	889	89
Indecency between males	437	420	444	629	739	840	1,137	1,079	1,627	1,71
Male importuning	820	878	631	619	413	451	520	556	526	54
Total persons convicted	2,298	2,423	2,228	2,383	2,273	2,390	2,690	2,651	3,206	3,34

The table shows that from 1965 to 1970, a period just before and just after the passing of the Sexual Offences Act, 1967, the annual total of convictions remained fairly steady. Certainly the Act brought about no reduction in convictions. In more recent years, particularly in 1973, there has been a quite startling increase in convictions for homosexuality due to prosecutions for indecency between males. Many of these arise from police surveillance of public lavatories. The

Home Office Supplementary Statistics, which give separate returns for each police authority, show that the increase comes about from activity in certain areas and not in others. For example, in the year 1973, much the largest numbers of crimes of indecency between males recorded by the police were reported from Nottingham, Northumberland and the London Metropolitan Police District, with 85, 174 and 553 cases respectively. In all three areas there had been a dramatic increase in the space of a few years. In 1969 the corresponding figures had been 21, 13 and 189 respectively. In contrast, many areas reported a continued low or decreasing incidence. For example, in 1973, the Mid-Anglia, Norwich, Wiltshire, Cheshire and Derby forces recorded 5, 0, 2, 3 and 2 cases respectively. In 1969 these forces had recorded 0, 6, 3, 37 and 12 cases respectively.

One of the points which particularly annoy homophile campaigners is the contrast between the leniency shown by the courts towards men involved sexually with under age girls and the severity of their attitude towards men who have had homosexual relations with youths. It seems to be assumed automatically that the younger party is relatively innocent and the older one a corrupting influence. In 1974 a man of 26, a first offender, was sentenced to eighteen months imprisonment by a Chelmsford court for homosexual offences with a youth of 16 who had been living with him. The youth came to the attention of the police as a result of a minor theft at his place of work. When his living circumstances became known questions began. To many persons the sentence upon the older man might seem well-deserved if in fact he had used his comparative affluence to press unwanted sexual activity upon the youth. Indeed the judge referred to the corrupting influence of the older man in explaining the need for a tough sentence. According to a local representative of the Campaign for Homosexual Equality, the true situation was very different. The youth was notorious among homosexual circles in the neighbourhood, he had had relations with a number of different men, and had allowed photographs to be taken during sexual activity. But of course none of these other men could give evidence for the defendant without incriminating themselves (Jordan, 1975). In spite of letters to the Home Office, who reviewed the case, the convicted man served his full sentence.

Notwithstanding the fact that for most purposes young men of 18 are legally adult, the English judiciary still takes a serious view of cases of homosexuality involving men of this age. In May 1975, the Appeal Court, with the Lord Chief Justice presiding, refused to reduce the sentence on a man aged 27 who had been awarded imprisonment of two-and-a-half years for homosexual activities with two consenting men aged 18 (*Gay News*, June, 1975).

The ambiguity of sexual situations, and the homosexual's understandable desire to avoid publicity, ensure that pleas of guilty are sometimes obtained, and convictions secured, on evidence which would, in other circumstances, be regarded as dubious. In a case which took place in 1970, and was described to me by the offender concerned, a youth aged 19 was given a lift in a car. He took a note of the car number and complained to the police that the driver had misbehaved sexually during the journey. In order to avoid the publicity likely to result from challenging this testimony, the driver pleaded guilty and was convicted of indecent assault upon a male person. The offender admitted privately that he had been guilty of touching the youth's thigh, as if by accident, and of making some suggestive comments. The youth's reaction had been to unfasten his trousers and gesture to the driver to play with his penis, which was erect. As they drew near their destination the youth suggested stopping the activity, because he might be seen and recognised, and the driver did so at once. The reason for the complaint was a mystery. The youth may have experienced a guilt reaction and a need to punish the man responsible for provoking the incident, or he may have expected some material reward and been angry at receiving none, or he may have thought that somebody had seen them and that he must therefore accuse the driver to protect himself. The driver, in touching the young man's thigh, possibly committed a technical assault, and what followed was an offence of gross indecency, so arguably no injustice was done. However, the fact that the driver, despite advice from his lawyer that he was not guilty, felt he must plead guilty to avoid having to give evidence and so provoke publicity, illustrates the difficulty any older man has in contesting an uncorroborated complaint of a sexual nature made by a young man.

The common assumption that the older partner in a homosexual encounter with an under-age male is necessarily the more blameworthy is often not borne out in practice. As Sturgess (1975) remarks in a CHE tract urging a lowering of the age of consent, in many so-called seduction scenes the older man is often more at risk from the blandishments of the younger than the other way round. The younger partner 'for his part, may be quick to extract the maximum advantage from the encounter, and, knowing the law to be on his side, will not hesitate, if caught, to make things easier for himself by claiming that far from inviting sexual attention, he hadn't even known what "homosexuality" meant until he met the defendant'.

Like pot-smoking and other 'victimless' crimes (Schur, 1965) most homosexual offences occur by mutual consent. In the absence of an aggrieved citizen ready to lay a complaint, detection by the police necessarily depends upon clandestine methods of surveillance. These include the employment of 'infiltrators' and informers, the use of plain-clothes decoys, and the exploitation of any compromising letters or address books that fall into the hands of the police accidentally or otherwise. The prosecution of Peter Wildeblood and others (see p. 282) which caused such a scandal in 1954, was achieved by the discovery of some correspondence in an airman's kit bag during a search conducted for a totally unconnected purpose. In another instance known to the author, prosecution of a wealthy paedophile came about as a result of a break-in at his home while he was on holiday abroad. A servant called in the police. While searching the premises they unearthed suggestive photographs and some letters from a schoolboy which interested them far more than any clues the burglar might have left. Prosecutions of young men under 21 sometimes occur when police discover, accidentally, that they have been having homosexual affairs. In one case reported by Tony Parker (1969, p.97ff.) a young man went to the police to recover a lost wallet. To his horror, the police were examining addresses and letters they had found inside. Encouraged to make a statement to avoid the police interviewing all his friends, he quickly incriminated himself and eventually, though a first offender, he received three years imprisonment for buggery, the judge commenting that he was 'the ring leader of a large circle' and 'a most corrupting influence'. He had been having a love affair with another youth and a sexual relationship with an older youth club worker.

In the face of changing and contradictory public attitudes, the control of offences of personal morality presents the police with a difficult and unenviable task. If they spy too ruthlessly and prosecute too often they lose public support. If they turn a blind eye when homosexual cruising grounds become too notorious they suffer criticism for failing to enforce the law. In seeking an acceptable middle course, different police forces not surprisingly develop different standards. The policing of men's lavatories has evoked much comment, both in England and the United States. Some years ago, an influential study by Gallo *et al.* (1966) of the University of California Law School described frankly and critically some of the more doubtful methods of law enforcement in that state. Police decoys dressed up to look like homosexuals, wearing tight pants, and jingling coins in their pockets, would loiter about the conveniences, eye men suggestively while making use of the urinals, and start up conversations. If these tactics resulted in someone making a sexual proposition, the decoy would suggest going elsewhere, and they would then leave the lavatory together. This was the signal for a second police officer to approach and effect an arrest. The police decoys were not supposed to initiate any lewd behaviour themselves, but of course they were often accused of having done so.

The American sociologist Laud Humphreys (1970) who, with the assistance of the police, conducted a protracted investigation of the behaviour of the patrons of a particular men's convenience, cites some of the techniques of detection used by the American police. In Mansfield, Ohio, the police made use of a 16mm. camera concealed behind a two-way mirror in a park lavatory (Kyler, 1963). In the space of two weeks the camera recorded indecencies by sixty-five different men. The cameraman was in radio communication with police waiting outside ready to arrest the culprits as they emerged. Unsuccessful attempts were made to have the evidence from the films declared legally inadmissible (McKee, 1964). The FBI reprinted the description of the technique for distribution to police departments all over the country. The Central Young Men's Christian Association of Philadelphia subsequently prepared a confidential report on 'the use of Closed Circuit TV for the Study and Elimination of Homosexual Activity in the YMCA'.

Less technologically advanced, the police in England have more often been criticised for time spent in lavatories hiding in closets, peeping through spy holes, or lying on the roof looking down at the clients below – time which might, according to some, be better spent catching 'real' criminals. The evidence so acquired does not always go unchallenged. The forensic psychologist Dr. L.R.C. Haward (1963) once managed to secure the acquittal of two men said to have been caught *in flagrante delicto* in a public urinal. He was able to cast doubt on the accuracy of observations made under the conditions prevailing. The police witnesses were in dim light and watching at an awkward angle through a fanlight above the door of a broom cupboard. In recent years, however, except in particular areas, police activity of this kind appears to have decreased. Complaints of incitement and entrapment by plain clothes officers have become fewer, and when they do occur they are liable to attract publicity from homosexual militants. For example in September 1974 *Gay News* (No.55) reported that 'some pretty unsavoury things have been happening in ... Reports have been received of men being approached in the loos by a man who exposed himself to them. When they reciprocated he invited them to go elsewhere. Once outside, he identified himself as a police officer and then arrested them ...'

In most American jurisdictions entrapment is recognised as a legal defense available to an accused who has been induced by a police officer to commit an offence he would not have done without encouragement (Sagarin and MacNamara, 1970). In a leading case from the District of Columbia Circuit, 1956 (*Guarro* v. *US*, 237 F.2d 578) it was ruled that a homosexual touching of an apparently willing and competent person was not an 'assault'. In this case a police officer had first encountered the defendant in the mens' room at a cinema and later saw him standing on the mezzanine balcony. The officer remained leaning against a wall, in what was presumably an inviting posture, and was approached by the defendant. After some conversation the defendant touched the officer indecently and was immediately arrested. The defending attorney argued that officers should not be permitted to tease and torment weak men beyond their powers of resistance in order to bring a case of assault. In England the citizen has no formal defence against arrest by entrapment, but the courts frown upon it, and may take into account the special circumstances of an arrest as a mitigating factor. Furthermore, if a defendant could show that a police decoy initiated an indecent act the officer would be equally guilty and, at least in theory, liable to prosecution (Heydon, 1973). Entrapment by enticement has been expressly forbidden in many American police forces. In 1966 the

Mayor of New York City ruled that charges of soliciting could be brought only on the complaint of a citizen. Nevertheless, in the town where Humphreys carried out his survey the police were still using decoys. They had even enlisted the services of a young delinquent. In return for their silence about his shop-lifting, he worked for the vice squad, visiting picking-up places and enticing men into compromising situations.

If misbehaviour in lavatories were so frequent and so blatant as these controversies suggest, it seems surprising that heterosexual men do not more often complain spontaneously to the police of unwanted solicitation, thereby enabling arrests to be made without the need for any kind of police trap. One reason, of course, is that a complainant lays himself open to counter-accusations from offenders trying to shift the blame. The Humphreys (1970) study brought out another, more important reason. Aware of the hostility of many heterosexuals, and of the dangers of police decoys, homosexuals making use of lavatories have to conduct themselves with some discretion. The situations of the favourite lavatories, and the times for visits, are deliberately chosen to avoid frequent encounters with legitimate users. Initial overtures often consist of no more than a casual glance, which an uninterested heterosexual would hardly notice and certainly not reciprocate. Only after some considerable exchange of increasingly bold and meaningfully reciprocated moves will the homosexual feel safe to commit himself to an unequivocally sexual gesture. Actual physical contact is unlikely to be attempted until the potential sex partner has expressed tacit interest and consent by exhibiting an erection. When masturbation or other sexual acts begin, one man may stand near the entrance to act as look out and warn the others of any unidentified stranger approaching. It was in the assumed role of voyeur and lookout man that Humphreys was able to record his observations. He found that the entry of obviously under-age youths inhibited activity, possibly because they frequently turned out to be prostitutes or 'queer bashers'. The silent and impersonal nature of the sexual exchanges struck him most forcibly. Hardly a word was spoken, just occasionally a whispered 'thanks' in the few seconds between ejaculation and departure from the scene.

The reason for this feature became clear when Humphreys followed up some of the men afterwards. He traced them with the help of the police through their car numbers, having previously kept watch on nearby parking places to see which cars belonged to the regular patrons of the lavatory. He found that many of the men were not at all the kind of person ordinarily thought of as homosexual. Most were married, with no strong sexual preference for other males, and no connections in the gay community. The largest category consisted of ageing married men whose conjugal relations had deteriorated. They were seeking not homosexual contact as such but 'a form of orgasm-producing action that is less lonely than masturbation and less involving than a love relationship'. They needed a quick, free, and completely anonymous outlet that, so long as it remained undiscovered, would have no repercussions on their home life. Another category Humphreys called the 'ambisexuals', men with strong homosexual urges which they dare not express in any other way without risking total disruption of their apparently conventional marriages. The remainder were more completely homosexual. Some of these were 'closet queens' who needed a sexual outlet but did not want to compromise their reputations by frequenting gay meeting places where they would have to reveal their identity. The lavatories were also frequented by some members of the local gay set, especially the older ones, who exploited the lavatories, like the steam baths, as an opportunity for easy and undemanding sexual contact. Having many friends in the homosexual subculture, and knowing the locality and the habits of the police quite well, these less innocent patrons were the ones most skilled in avoiding arrest.

The need to control immorality by public action leads all too often to bribery and extortion. Humphreys found that every man over 30 in his interview sample had at least one story of police 'pay offs'. One travelling salesman gave accounts of eight instances in which he had bought off police decoys for amounts ranging from sixty to three hundred dollars. Few men threatened with a sexual charge, even if they happened to be innocent, would decline the opportunity to buy their way out if they had the means and were given the chance. Where real policemen are known to extort bribes, criminals posing as police have a golden opportunity to do the same. An extensive racket of this sort was exposed in the United States in 1966 after thousands of dollars had been extorted from different businessmen by bogus police threatening arrests for homosexual misconduct. On a smaller scale similar events are by no means unknown in England.

The severe legal restrictions upon homosexuality which still exist in England, even after the 1967 Act, mean that 'the reformed law remains a blackmailer's charter in some respects' (Grey, 1974, p.144). *Gay News* regularly features cases of homosexual blackmail coming before the English courts. In one issue alone (No.66, March 1974) three such cases were described. Two youths were sent for borstal training by Derby Crown Court on 27 February for threatening a man who gave them a lift that they would tell the police he had tried to interfere with them unless he handed over some money. In another recent case at Exeter Crown Court a former prisoner was convicted for homosexual blackmail. He had got the impression that one of the prison visitors was having a sexual relationship with another inmate. After his release he arranged a meeting with the victim, but the police were notified and the conversation, which included a demand for £100, was tape-recorded. In the third case, two young men were convicted at the Old Bailey, London, on 21 February for blackmailing a city businessman. The younger of the pair, aged 20, had acted as the decoy, spending the night with the businessman, then threatening to go to the police unless he was paid £5,000. These reported cases represent the tip of a of a very nasty iceberg. Many homosexuals, if they have compromised themselves with young men who might be under age, or if they dare not risk a possible scandal, would much sooner pay up than call the police.

The decriminalisation of consensual adult homosexuality in England has not produced any apparent decrease in the severity of the punishments meted out to those found guilty of breaches of the laws still remaining. The courts still take a very serious view of offences involving minors. For example, in 1971, a man aged 38 who had no previous convictions appealed against a sentence of four years imprisonment for gross indecency with two boys, one a youth of 16 who had previous homosexual experience, the other a boy of 12 who was the son of a friend (*R.* v. *Sheppard* 22 January 1971). A probation officer reported that he considered the man would benefit from probation and would be unlikely to offend again. It was submitted that a suspended sentence was appropriate, but the Court ruled that the nature of the offences called for immediate imprisonment even though the man was a first offender (*Criminal Law Review,* 1971, 298). Cases of sexual activity in groups have attracted heavy sentences. A youth of 18 who had pleaded guilty to buggery and indecent assault was sentenced to five years imprisonment. It was said that he belonged to a group of youths who habitually behaved indecently with each other. He had no previous convictions. The trial judge felt that despite his age a long sentence was necessary to deter others. The Appeal Court (*R.* v. *Linnett* 11 January 1968) found no reason to vary the sentence (*Criminal Law Review,* 1968, 173). Even where the formal punishment is slight, the consequences of a conviction for homosexuality can be very serious for the person concerned, and from time to time one still reads newspaper reports of suicides in these circumstances. In November 1974, for example, a medical practitioner in Herefordshire took his own life the day following a conviction for gross indecency for which he received a small fine. When he departed to kill himself he left behind for his wife to read a newspaper account of his appearance at court.

3. *The status of the homosexual citizen*

Law and custom sometimes differ. If people treat him decently in everyday life, it does not matter so much to the homosexual if the penal code classes him officially a criminal. From the somewhat niggardly degree of 'decriminalisation' introduced in the 1967 Act it by no means follows that homosexuals in England will henceforth find ready acceptance by workmates, employers, landlords, parents or other individuals upon whom their existence depends, or that their dealings with the legal and welfare systems will run as smoothly as those of the citizen who has no sexual stigma. No amount of civil rights legislation can save the homosexual from social discrimination if his presence in any ordinary community evokes disgust and hostility, and if public opinion holds on to the belief that homosexuals are untrustworthy and unreliable people and a danger to youth. Opinions of this kind have been long entrenched, not only in popular belief, but in the authoritative pronouncements of medical and other self-declared experts who should know better than to lend their names to untested myths. For example, one criminological adviser to a prominent American detective bureau (Matthews, 1957) wrote confidently that both male and female homosexuals suffer from psychotic ills of the mind, and whether they molest people or not they are not stable enough to be friends to normal people. Living with a homosexual can drive a person mad.

A national survey carried out in the United States by the Institute for Sex Research (Levitt and Klassen, 1974) showed that when presented with a list of employments, and asked if homosexual men should be allowed to work in these jobs, the great majority of the population, varying from over two-thirds to over three-quarters, said no to the responsible professions of judge, school teacher, minister, medical doctor and government official. A substantial majority, 71 per cent, agreed, either 'strongly' or 'somewhat', that homosexuals try to play sexually with children if they cannot get an adult partner. The statement that 'all or almost all homosexuals are a high security risk for government jobs' was endorsed by 43 per cent, and the opinion that 'homosexuality is obscene and vulgar' was held 'very much' by 65 per cent. The notion that in the majority of cases homosexuality is a sickness that can be cured was endorsed by 62 per cent, and 40 per cent thought that most homosexuals could stop being homosexuals if they wanted to. The statement 'I won't associate with these people if I can help it' was agreed to be 'very true' by 59 per cent and 'somewhat true' by 22 per cent. A substantial majority, 70 per cent, thought sex acts between members of the same sex 'always wrong', even when the persons involved loved each other.

It is sometimes said that homophobic attitudes are less prevalent in England than in America, but there have been no published opinion surveys to substantiate such a belief. In the course of research into another topic by the present writer, a sample of 389 young working-class males, aged 18 and 19, interviewed in London during 1971 to 1973, were given an attitude questionnaire which included the following item: 'Homosexuals are OK so long as they don't bother other people.' Even this innocuous-sounding statement was too much for some of the youths; 11.8 per cent of the sample endorsed the response 'definitely false' and a further 6.4 per cent considered it 'probably false'. Questioned in some detail about their own sexual lives, more than a quarter said they had had no experience of heterosexual intercourse, but not one volunteered the information that he preferred his own sex. From this evidence it could be seen that the modern generation of males, even in 'swinging' London, retains, to a very considerable extent, the condemnatory and guilt-ridden attitudes towards homosexuality of a pre-permissive age. As recently as 1976, the forced resignation of the leader of the British liberals, following allegations that he had once had a sexual affair with a man, demonstrated the continuing sensitivity of politicians to accusations of homosexuality.

In England, in the absence of systematic opinion polls, the unfavourable tone of most references to the topic in the popular press gives some indication of the abhorrence with which substantial sections of the public still regard homosexuals. Rarely do homosexuals receive any mention except in connection with some discreditable public scandal, such as the conviction of scoutmasters, vicars or hostel wardens for immoral behaviour with youths in their charge. Typical of this style of journalism was the full-page article in the *Sunday People* of 27 April 1975, headed 'Street of Shameless Men', describing 'a new and horrific' problem. Residents of a once respectable street were said to 'watch helpless as the homosexual vice trade moves in'. A picture of three men standing about on the pavement (faces blacked over in the paper to prevent recognition by readers) were said to be 'male prostitutes arrogantly parading for business'. Foreign visitors were said to be picked up by taxis at the airport and taken straight to the Street, where drivers obligingly cruised up and down while the passenger selected a companion for the night. One girl informant said she had seen men in 'Nazi-style jackets, hot pants, ballet tights and jackboots'. One suspects that some of these lurid newspaper descriptions are written with tongue in cheek to pander to the readers' desire to have their prejudices confirmed. The street described in the article, adjoining a gay bar that has been operating for many years, sees a lot of odd characters around closing time, but otherwise hardly merits the wild reputation now attributed to it.

Experts with advanced liberal ideas, and gay militants who think they can overcome traditional antagonism, delude themselves as to the power of intellectual argument and underestimate the sheer weight of anxiety, revulsion and suspicion which the label homosexual continues to evoke in the great silent majority of conventionally minded people. Where officials display inertia or lack of sympathy in the face of gay liberationist demands, they merely reflect the wishes of a substantial section of the public. Arguably, the fact that so much hostility exists provides good reason for applying to the utmost such legal remedies against unfair discrimination as can be discovered and developed. Ideally, the law should be the handmaiden of social justice, and not an instrument for making the lives of unpopular minorities worse than they need be.

The impetus of the civil rights movements for blacks, for women and for homosexuals, came from the United States. The American Civil Liberties Union has called attention to a wide range of unjust or discriminatory practices in relation to homosexuals. In states which still use statutes against consensual sodomy, such as North Carolina and Arkansas, enormously long prison sentences are still sometimes awarded for these questionable offences. Charges of public indecency are brought for homosexual acts in very secluded areas where heterosexual activity would pass unmolested. Once in prison homosexuals are at a disadvantage in obtaining favoured jobs or accommodation and in the granting of parole. US Army regulations list overt homosexuality as a cause for rejection of employment, enlistment or induction and as grounds for premature discharge. The US Civil Service Commission regulations specify homosexuality as a ground for disqualification from employment. Homosexuality is held to be a reason for denying security clearance because of vulnerability to blackmail. Many private employers refuse to hire homosexuals and bonding companies refuse to bond or insure them. Known homosexuals are denied local authority housing because they might use the premises for immoral purposes. Permission to enter the country, even as a temporary visitor, is refused to homosexuals, and aliens already residing in the country can be denied naturalisation. Custody of children and visiting rights are resisted when it becomes known that a parent is homosexual.

Few of these issues have reached the United States Supreme Court. The legality of the deportation of an alien on the grounds of 'psychopathic personality', which was held to include homosexuality, was confirmed in 1967 (*Boutilier* v. *Immigration and Naturalisation Service* 387 US 118). The petitioner had admitted homosexual conduct prior to his admission into the United States, and Congress had the right to make rules to exclude aliens who possess undesirable characteristics.

The legal disability of homosexuals in the US armed forces has been a particular source of grievance to those concerned with civil rights. Most homosexual servicemen, like most homosexuals in other forms of employment, successfully avoid calling the attention of the authorities to their condition. West and Glass (1965) cite a survey by Fry and Rostow who followed the service careers of 132 former students known to be homosexuals. The great majority served successfully, achieving creditable records. A similarly high success rate was found by Saghir and Robins (1973) in their sample of male homosexuals. Although 16 per cent of those called were not drafted because they declared themselves homosexuals, and a further 4 per cent were rejected because of a previous history of arrests, the great majority who entered military service experienced no problems. However, 6 per cent of those inducted received a dishonourable or undesirable discharge because their homosexuality became known to the authorities, either from observation and report, or because the men felt they could no longer control their sexual attractions and therefore confessed.

Although most do in fact prove satisfactory, homosexuals are officially considered unfit to serve. Supposedly, they constitute a threat to morale, their personal characteristics limit their military effectiveness, their presence exposes other young men to the risks of sexual seduction, and their propensity for forming attachment across the barriers of rank disrupts discipline. In known cases, prompt discharge is mandatory, although the rules governing the mode of discharge have been somewhat softened in recent years (Williams and Weinberg, 1971). Those who have committed no actual offence while in the service, but who profess or exhibit homosexual tendencies, or who associate with homosexuals, may receive an honourable or a general discharge. Those discovered in some overt homosexual act receive discharge as 'undesirable', unless they can plead outstanding performance or heroic service over a long period. The military boards that decide these cases have been criticised for not allowing the defendant to confront or cross-examine witnesses and for not providing legally qualified counsel. The witnesses in question are all too often former partners who have turned informers to save themselves.

In practice, men are rarely caught in the act, but their homosexuality comes to the attention of the authorities through the report of another serviceman or civilian, through being named in connection with the investigation of another homosexual, or by a voluntary confession. Protracted interrogation, interviews with the men's friends, requests to undergo lie detector tests, searches for incriminating diaries, letters or magazines, and even questioning of people in the men's home neighbourhood, suffice to induce many of them to waive their right to a board hearing and to accept an undesirable discharge. Undesirable discharges are intended to be punitive, involving reduction to the lowest rank and loss of veteran's benefits. Even those lucky enough to achieve a general, administrative discharge suffer some stigma, since anything less than a completely 'honorable' discharge certificate excludes men from acceptance in many respectable employments. Williams and Weinberg estimated that up to three thousand men receive less than 'honorable' discharges from the United States military services each year for reasons connected with homosexuality. Code numbers on administrative discharge papers, indicative of the precise reason for separation, which employers have learned to decipher, have made it difficult for men to conceal their homosexuality in civilian life. For this reason the Defense Department agreed recently (April 1974) to supply discharge papers on request free of the controversial code numbers.

By means of retrospective inquiries addressed to volunteer homosexuals who had been through military service, Williams and Weinberg compared groups who had received a less than 'honorable' discharge with groups of substantially similar age distribution and educational status who had passed through successfully without discovery and received an 'honorable' discharge. They found that those with a less than 'honorable' discharge encountered much more difficulty in obtaining settled employment after discharge, were more likely to be known as homosexuals to employers and relatives, and were more likely to experience personal difficulties and harbour thoughts of suicide. They concluded that, although the effects of stigmatisation were less dramatic or permanent than might have been expected, the use of less than 'honorable' discharges purely on grounds of sexual orientation was unwise and immoral. Most homosexuals, especially if they pursued their sex life discreetly outside the military camp setting, discharged their duties satisfactorily and never came to the notice of the authorities. Relatively few predominantly heterosexual men became involved in homosexual incidents during their service careers, and they tended to be the younger and less well educated soldiers (Druss, 1967). West *et al.* (1958), as a result of experience in the US Air Force, gave examples of heterosexual servicemen who have reported homosexual advances from other men, usually taking place during drinking bouts, being given the same 'dishonorable' discharge, and experiencing the same social repercussions, as the men about whom they complained. Chiles (1972), described the deleterious effects of regulation 125-2 of the US Air Force Manual, which prescribes 'administrative segregation' for any prisoner designated homosexual. He recounted the example of one unfortunate Air Force detainee, under sentence for an offence unrelated to homosexuality, who was also under investigation by the Army CID for suspected, and later confirmed, homosexual friendships. The man was isolated in a small cell, with the code letter 'H' on the record card on his door, which of course led to much ridicule from other prisoners. He was allowed out among the other prisoners for a time, and behaved well, but the staff were compelled by the regulations to put him back into the cell when the report on his homosexuality was confirmed. He became anxious and frustrated, and at one point 'kicked a hole in the wall of his cell with his bare feet', but in spite of medical recommendations the staff were powerless to alleviate the situation. Chiles used this example to highlight the point that, under existing regulations, an Air Force prisoner found to have had homosexual associations suffers punishment considerably in excess of what his sentence would otherwise have entailed.

The systematic screening of job applicants for possible homosexuality, using questionnaires, personality tests and probing interviews, became common practice in the United States some years ago. A psychiatrist employed by the Missouri police went so far as to publish an article arguing in favour of the polygraph lie detector in preference to straight interviews for detecting evasive responses and thus aiding in the elimination of men with homosexual tendencies from among candidates for entry to the force (Lawrence, 1966). In a chapter entitled 'How to strip a job-seeker naked' the popular writer Vance Packard (1964) cited many examples. Ordinary citizens began to question and to resent these investigations into personal affairs when it became common knowledge that the Civil Service Commission, the Defense Department and other large organisations had records on the private lives of millions of persons, and that the outcome of requests for loans or mortgages might be influenced by the content of confidential data on marital stability and supposed sex habits supplied by private investigation agencies.

In recent years, the legality of exclusion from employment on grounds of homosexual tendency (or moral turpitude as it was often called) has been seriously questioned. In some American states it appears to be legally possible, even in non-governmental, civilian positions, to dismiss an employee found to be homosexual. A leading case was decided in 1970. A man who had been offered a librarian's post at the University of Minnesota attracted some publicity by applying for a licence to marry another male. The University regents found his personal conduct, as represented in the news media, not consistent with the best interests of the University, and withdrew their offer. Their action was at first declared unconstitutional by a federal court, but this decision was later reversed and further appeal denied by the U.S. Supreme Court (40. *U.S. Law Week* 3484, 1972. Cited in Barnett, 1973, p.9). Notwithstanding this decision, the right of government agencies and professional bodies to refuse employment to homosexuals has been repeatedly and sometimes successfully challenged in the courts in various states. For instance, the California Supreme Court in 1967 held that homosexuality was not, in itself, grounds for disqualifying a teacher, so long as his effectiveness in the job was not impaired (*Morrison* v. *State Board of Education* 1 Cal. 3d, 214). In another instance a lawyer who had been disbarred in Florida because of an arrest under a sexual misconduct statute was refused admission by the New York State Appellate Division to the Bar in New York. On appeal, the Court of Appeals reversed the decision, in spite of the man's declaration that he was a practising homosexual, and he was soon after admitted to the Bar (re Kimball, 301 NE 2d 436, 1973).

Over the last few years several American cities (including Ann Arbor, San Francisco and Seattle) have passed local ordinances to forbid discrimination on grounds of sexual orientation in such matters as employment, housing and loans. In May 1974, after several years of agitation and political negotiation, a comparable bill was put to the vote in New York City. Local laws were already in force to forbid employers to reject or dismiss employees, or landlords to refuse tenancies, or hotel keepers to deny accommodation on grounds of 'race, creed, color or national origin'. The new bill proposed the addition of the words 'sex or sexual orientation' into the relevant statutes. The proposal aroused enormous public controversy. The Uniformed Fire Officers Association inserted newspaper advertisements denouncing 'this abominable legislation' which would 'force an employer to hire a pervert ... Expose our children to the influence of sodomites ... Subvert the laws of our nation and negate police enforcement' (*New York Daily News* 26 April 1974). An editorial in the *Catholic News*, the newspaper of the Roman Catholic Archdiocese of New York, supported the police and firemens' unions in their opposition, referred to the proposed bill as 'a menace to family life', and argued that it would 'afford unrestricted opportunities to propagandise deviant forms of sexuality' and 'be interpreted by many as public license to uninhibited manifestations of sexual preference or sexual relationships and the absence of any moral norm in human sexuality'. The bill was defeated by 22 votes to 19.

In spite of such spectacular defeats, the cause of civil liberties for American homosexuals has gained ground bit by bit. In 1969, no less an authority than the National Institute of Mental Health published the final report and recommendations of a Task Force on homosexuality. After two years of deliberation, they came out unequivocally in favour of social and legal reform declaring themselves 'strongly convinced that the extreme opprobrium our society has attached to homosexual behaviour, by way of criminal statues and restrictive employment practices, has done more harm than good and goes beyond what is necessary for the maintenance of public order and human decency'. In May 1975, in contrast to the attitudes taken up by the New York police, the legal office of the city of Los Angeles announced that homosexuals were not automatically eliminated from recruitment to their local police force. In 1970 the state of New York turned down an application for a certificate of incorporation from the Gay Activists Alliance, an organisation dedicated to the repeal of the anti-homosexuality laws and the protection of homosexuals from discrimination. It was held that to grant a certificate would be tantamount to a public sanction of activities that violated public policy and penal statutes. The decision was successfully challenged and reversed by the Appellate Division of the New York Supreme Court, whose ruling was upheld when the secretary of state appealed to the Court of Appeals, the highest court in the State of New York (*Owles* v. *Lomenzo*, 38 App. Div. 2d. 981, 329 NY Supp. 2d. 181. 1972). Today, numerous homophile organisations flourish all over the country, and in many universities, with full legal and practical recognition from the relevant authorities. An assertion of the right of public assembly has enabled such organisations to hold public meetings and protest marches. Similarly, the gay bars in California and New York can now cater openly and legally to homosexual clients. But a series of tedious legal battles and test cases was needed to accomplish each small step.

Recent extensions of the citizen's right of privacy have indirectly benefitted American homosexuals. In the privacy of their homes citizens are protected from police surveillance without a warrant and from unreasonable searches and seizures. A number of state appellate court decisions have ruled unconstitutional police surveillance of the cubicles in public lavatories, since these are also places where citizens have a right to expect privacy. In order to prosecute truly private acts the police must usually depend upon the testimony of one of the participants. Even this will not suffice in the many states which requires corroboration of the evidence of a party to a crime before the testimony becomes legally admissible (Barnett, 1973, p.17).

Legal battles over civil liberties for homosexuals have arisen less frequently in England than in the United States. Differences between the respective legal systems account for this in part, but a more important factor is the relatively low key in which English authorities have dealt with such matters. The British military, for example, have avoided moralistic public pronouncements and have usually rid themselves of self-confessed, or troublesomely obvious homosexuals by quietly discharging them on psychiatric grounds which have no bearing upon service conduct record. The reasons for these discharges are screened from prying employers by the cloak of medical confidentiality. The British government has never taken such an extreme stand against the employment of homosexuals as the Americans did in the McCarthy era. Even in 1962, following the conviction of John Vassall, a homosexual employee in the Admiralty, for giving away secrets to the Russians, official reaction was comparatively calm. While Vassall was serving as a clerk to the Naval Attaché in Moscow, the Russian Secret Service apparently discovered his sexual interests and eventually succeeded in taking compromising photographs of him during sexual activity at a homosexual party. Apparently the threat of blackmail induced Vassall to spy for the Russians, although they also paid him in cash. Dame Rebecca West (1963) suggested that the compromising incidents could have been engineered to provide an excuse for his treachery in the event of detection. The subsequent official inquiry (Home Office 1963) wisely pointed out that homosexuals were not the only ones subject to blackmail. The manufacture of compromising situations was a regular secret service technique 'through involving men with women, women with men, and as in Vassall's case, men with men'. Had Vassall chosen to reveal the blackmail threat to his superiors, they would have known how to deal with it quietly and expeditiously. Years later, on his release from prison, Vassall (1975) published an autobiography in which he alleged that some top ranking civil servants and men still serving in Parliament had been known to him as homosexuals. By that time, however, public attitudes had changed and no one seemed to be bothered.

Unlike their American counterparts, who still suffer the stigma of criminality, English homosexuals are legally free to pursue their private lives according to their own lights. Apart from the major issue of the age of consent, they have no particular need for any special enactments to give them the same rights as other citizens. Consequently, the civil rights campaign for homosexuals in England has not had the courtroom battles over legal principles that feature so prominently in the movement in the United States. Unless any unexpected test cases should establish the contrary, English homosexuals share the protection against wrongful or arbitrary dismissal from employment or eviction from tenancies awarded to all citizens by recent legislation. The activities of the English civil rights campaign have been more concerned with changing public attitude than with arguing points of law. One of the few dramatic steps forward in this respect was the adoption by a large majority at the

1973 annual conference of the National Union of Students of a long resolution in support of equal rights for homosexuals and the abolition of discrimination and prejudice. The resolution noted that 'improvement in the social standing of homosexuals entails positive acceptance rather than condescension. The total integration of homosexuals and other minority groups requires fundamental change in society.'

Much depends upon the discretion of police, employers, official agencies, educationists, parents and others who have the power to make decisions affecting the welfare of individual homosexuals. The Campaign for Homosexual Equality and similar organisations conduct a running battle with education authorities and local government agencies. Now and then they succeed in extracting a pronouncement from one or other official to the effect that teachers, health workers or local authority employees are not disqualified from employment because they happen to be homosexual. How relevant such declarations may be to what happens in practice is hard to say. One young teacher, David Bell, has made several public declarations of homosexuality on television and still been promoted, whereas another was dismissed for refusing to sign a statement promising not to talk about homosexuality in the classroom other than as part of a structured sex education programme approved by the head teacher. From the reports and comments on many such incidents appearing in *Gay News* it seems that, increasingly often, the social services and other agencies are recruiting individuals to responsible posts notwithstanding declarations of homosexuality in their applications. What matters most in determining the work careers of known homosexuals is whether they are acceptable to their workmates, or professional colleages, or, in the case of service professions, to their clients. In the last resort public opinion counts for more than legal rules, and public opinion is still very divided.

In England, pressure from homophile groups has succeeded in producing declarations of good will towards a policy of anti-discrimination by various official bodies. For instance, following declarations from a number of large US companies that they would not discriminate in employment on grounds of homosexual orientation, the United Kingdom branch of the International Business Machines Corporation was induced to make the statement that: 'We do not ask applicants or employees their sexual orientation and it is not a concern of the company unless an individual's behaviour is detrimental to the work or performance expected of any employee' (*Gay News* 69, April 1975). The National Council for Civil Liberties (1975), at their last annual general meeting in London, declared a majority in favour of support for the homosexual law-reform proposals put forward by CHE, the Scottish Minorities Group and the Union for Sexual Freedoms in Ireland. The organisation subsequently published the results of a survey of the attitudes of the education authorities in England to the employment of homosexual teachers. Of the 47 authorities who replied, mostly in very guarded general terms, only one did not object to pupils knowing about a teacher's homosexuality. About a third produced discriminatory replies, some of which were described as 'bigoted'. Many, while not prepared to admit to discrimination, were obviously uneasy, implying by their responses that homosexuality was a threat to children. In May 1975, the National Union of Journalists, at their annual conference, passed a resolution pledging themselves not to originate material designed to encourage discrimination on grounds of race, colour, creed, gender or sexual orientation.

Organisations seeking to help homosexuals, such as the Albany Trust, have recently received small grants of public money from local authorities and from a central fund administered by the Home Office for the purpose of providing financial aid to voluntary social work agencies. This use of money has not passed without critical comment from opponents of the homosexual movement. For example, in March 1975, when Merton Council proposed to allocate £75 to the Wimbledon Area Gay Society, for the provision of a telephone counselling service for homosexuals, Sir Cyril Black, a former MP and an Alderman on the Council, argued strongly against the grant on the grounds that his inquiries had revealed strong opposition to it among ratepayers, who had no sympathy with the purposes it was meant to serve. Nevertheless, the Council went ahead and gave the money. Of course, the trend towards greater legal equality and lessening of social disabilities do not apply to persons found guilty of a homosexual offence. They can be officially black-listed and refused employment in teaching, nursing, medicine and similar professions. If there are children living at home with them, the social service department has a statutory duty to inspect the situation and if necessary to remove the children into the care of the local authority. In several cases known to me, employees of long standing have been dismissed from their jobs following the discovery, by the organisations for which they worked, of a past conviction for a sexual offence. The ways by which employers, with the help of private security agencies, are able to obtain information about criminal records of long ago is a matter which has provoked some criticism from persons concerned to preserve individual freedom (Rule, 1973). Certain public organisations, such as the post office, have a legal right to ask job applicants about past convictions, and to check their answers against criminal records. Those who have secured positions by concealing past offences can be prosecuted for obtaining pecuniary advantage by making false statements.

Although they have become more or less legal, or at any rate temporarily immune from prosecution, self-declared homosexuals often encounter informal, but determined, opposition from outraged citizens who still consider homosexuality reprehensible and immoral. For example, when clients of a Gay Community Centre began to frequent a local bar in Brixton, London, the licensee in charge of the pub complained that kissing and fondling which went on between them was offensive to other customers. Members of the Gay Community were banned forthwith from using the bar. A spokesman for the group, complaining of the injustice of the ban, commented: 'We may kiss or hold hands – but this is no more than heterosexual couples do.' A spokesman for the brewery owners announced: 'This is a matter entirely within the discretion of the licensee.' In England, a licensee of a public bar has a right to ask a customer to leave without giving a reason (*South London Press*, 10 June 1975).

Opposition of a more violent character has been directed against Paedophile Action for Liberation, a self-help and counselling organisation that campaigns for a softening of sex laws and a greater understanding of sexual deviants. Following the publication of a critical article in the *Sunday People*, accusing members of the organisation of being responsible for a 'perverted sex ring' dangerous to children and centred on an address in South Lambeth, bricks were thrown through the windows of the house where the group held its discussion meetings. The police, apparently, took a less serious view. A local Superintendent was reported as saying that there had been no complaints about the house and no action was contemplated (*South London Press*, 30 May 1975). However, it was said that the local authority were taking steps to evict the occupants who had allowed the meetings to take place on the premises.

4. *Religious restraints*

The Christian Churches have always been identified with a conservative, family-based morality inimical to sexual permissiveness in general and to homosexuality in particular. Their attitude follows logically from the historical origins of the religious tradition which were discussed in an earlier chapter. Circumstances have changed, but not the basic principles. That homosexuality is sinful remains the orthodox view of all the major Christian sects. Indeed, it could hardly be otherwise considering the violent language of scriptural denunciations, the severity of ecclesiastical punishments for homosexual transgressions, and the high value placed upon sexual conformity by religious authorities over many centuries. The uncompromising denunciation by the Roman Catholic hierarchy of the proposed law forbidding discrimination against homosexuals in New York, which was cited earlier, is entirely in keeping with orthodox Christian thought. Michael Buckley (1959) sets out the predominant Roman Catholic viewpoint clearly when he commiserates with homosexuals, but totally rejects the idea that Christians would ever tolerate acts which are crimes against natural law.

The effect of this religious condemnation must not be underestimated. Although formal religious affiliations have declined, and attendance at churches has fallen away, the ethical ideas propagated by religion live on in the population. Christian teachings must be held to a considerable extent responsible for the automatic and unthinking revulsion towards homosexuality in any shape or form shown by so many otherwise gentle and tolerant people. The more 'advanced' among Christian writers these days are tending to adopt softer and more fashionable attitudes towards homosexuals, tempering their rejection with expressions of concern and sympathy, but they can hardly reverse a fundamental part of Christian dogma without risking some loss of faith in other parts of the divine revelation. Uncomfortable and inconvenient as it may be, on traditional Christian principles homosexuality is a sin, and to pretend otherwise requires a gross, some might say a hypocritical, distortion of all previous declarations on the subject (Oberholtzer, 1971).

A good example of the sort of line taken by some modern priests, struggling to reconcile their charitable inclinations towards homosexuals with the hostile content of Christian dogma, is the writing of Kimball-Jones (1966), an American Methodist minister. He accepts that (p. 97) 'homosexual acts are contrary to the will of God' and that the homosexual is by his very nature a sinner, but he criticises the policy of outright condemnation as unworthy of Christians. The homosexual who cannot change his orientation should be accepted for what he is and encouraged to remain faithful to one partner. This does not mean that the Church regards a faithful homosexual relationship as a desirable way of life, or as coming up to the standard of a Christian marriage, but it may be the best that an individual can attain. The author suggests that priests should try to persuade their congregations not to exclude a church member who is otherwise useful and of good character just because he is discovered to be homosexual. Unfortunately 'the minister who takes such a stand runs the risk of himself being labelled a homosexual ... and one would have to search far and wide to find a congregation that could be convinced to allow a professed homosexual to maintain a position of responsibility within their church ...' Such well-meaning but grudging tolerance of homosexuality as a third rate and sadly sinful way of life is the most the orthodox Churches can offer without renouncing traditional principles. To the homosexual who sincerely believes in the validity of Christian doctrines this limited acceptance provides rather cold comfort. To the militant homosexual who wants recognition that 'gay is good' it must appear as a red rag to a bull.

An unusually sympathetic view from a Roman Catholic source has appeared in a pamphlet on the pastoral care of homosexuals by Michael Hollings (1972). Nowhere does he deny the sinfulness of homosexuality. He tries to use neutral language, although in doing so he knows he 'may incur the censure of clergy or theologians who would prefer to see an outright statement on sin'. He pleads for an understanding of homosexuals, and a recognition of their human needs. He asks the question whether the Church has any advice to offer other than total abstention. After quoting the view of some moral theologians that 'this is unnatural vice of the worst kind' he gives his own equivocal answer 'think about it'. On the question whether to advise homosexual people to make use of homophile organisations he seems equally uncertain: '... for the pastoral counsellor there must remain a big question mark ...' One cannot but sympathise with these orthodox clerics in the dilemma which forces them to sit on the fence when their humanitarian impulses are obviously urging them to come off it.

A French Catholic authority on sex and morals of unusually liberal views, the doctor and priest Marc Oraison (1952), long ago advanced the opinion that homosexual behaviour is not necessarily a mortal sin. At first, Oraison's book was placed on the Index of writings disapproved by the Church, but Catholic opinion, if not the Catholic principles, have shifted slightly. The Index has been abolished, and, after an interval of twenty years, the book has been republished. In a more recent work, Oraison (1975) has been able to express his views about homosexuality even more frankly. He knows that in practice sexual patterns vary, and that some individuals change their preference over time, but his moral argument starts from the premise that some persons, through no fault of their own, find themselves exclusively and permanently attracted to their own sex. However much they struggle to avoid giving expression to their sexual desires, few people are capable of absolute continence. If one accepts the traditional view that all sexual acts other than marital copulation are sinful, it would seem that the homosexual has no escape from involuntary damnation. He can confess, gain absolution, and hope to die before he sins again, but he cannot ensure this by killing himself, for that also is a mortal sin.

Oraison believes this traditional view at fault. Like some modern Anglican writers, he prefers to judge the morality of a relationship by the quality of love for the other person rather than by the physical nature of the erotic tie. He contends (p. 159) that it is 'rare but not impossible' for a homosexual couple to form a permanent loving relationship, living together and supporting each other in good times and bad. Their condition falls short of ideal Christian marriage, but they should not be condemned, for they have come as close to the ideal as their natures permit. We all have our own crosses to bear, and no human attains perfection. Many heterosexual attachments fall short of the ideal of Christian love.

Oraison thinks that over the past fifteen years an increasing number of priests have been willing to counsel their homosexual penitents in the direction of improving their relationships instead of dismissing all homosexual inclinations as wicked. Needless to say, not all Catholics share these charitable sentiments. Oraison reproduces in his book a violently denunciatory article from *Action française* condemning his ideas as false, subversive and disgusting, and suggesting that he should be driven from the Church.

The official view of the Roman Catholic church was reaffirmed in a

Vatican declaration on sexual ethics issued in January 1976. According to this Christian doctrine 'every genital act must be within the framework of marriage'. Catholic tradition and the moral sense of the faithful 'declare without hesitation that masturbation is an intrinsically and seriously disordered act'. Homosexual practice remains a sin and 'no pastoral method can be employed which would give moral justification to these acts'.

Sects that have a less strict commitment to orthodox dogma have more room to manoeuvre, and in England the Quakers have taken the lead in questioning the axiom that homosexuality is always sinful. But the report of a study group (Heron, 1964) it was argued that homosexual affection could sometimes be as selfless as heterosexual affection, and the authors failed to see why it must always be morally worse. A more recent Quaker pamphlet, written by an avowed homosexual, went even further, in suggesting that homosexual emotions are just as real and good as heterosexual emotions, and in advocating greater honesty, candour and respect for the individual in the matter of sexual orientation (Blamires, 1973).

Norman Pittenger (1970), one of the few Anglican writers who have openly rejected orthodox teachings on the matter, uses the presence or absence of a love relationship to decide whether homosexual contacts are sinful. He has no doubt that selfish sexual activity, which seeks to use others rather than to share with them and to establish a lasting sexual commitment, violates divine will and must be counted as sin. He is equally sure that a genuine love relationship does not become sinful because it happens to involve physical contacts between two persons of the same sex. A logical extension of this viewpoint would be for priests to recognise and bless homosexual unions in much the same way as they solemnise heterosexual marriages.

An equally unorthodox stand has been taken by an English Methodist minister, Dr. Leonard Barnett (1975). In a book addressed primarily to young persons, and to parents and others who deal with the young, he pleads for full acceptance of those who have a homosexual orientation. He quotes two contrasting Christian views, the one opposing all homosexual behaviour as contrary to God's law, the other asserting that homosexual expression within a love relationship conforms with Christian morality. Without making his own theological position altogether explicit, he clearly favours recognition of 'the existence and moral validity' of stable homosexual partnerships (p. 147). He recoils from using the term 'marriage' for homosexual unions, since that concept has such indissoluble links with parenthood and family life, but he sees it as natural that 'responsible and emotionally fulfilled gay couples' should want to proclaim their relationship with a wedding service. Many such services have been carried out in the United States, notably in the Metropolitan Community Church started in California, but elsewhere they have taken place 'typically and understandably not on church premises, where the risk of alienation and distress on the part of uninformed traditional congregations would be considerable'. On one point Barnett is very clear. The same moral regulations should apply to homosexuals as to heterosexuals. Acceptance of homosexuality does not imply a licence to be sexually promiscuous.

In secular law there can be no such thing as a marriage except between a man and a woman. No institutional church in England recognises or solemnises homosexual marriages. In California Troy Perry (1972) pastor of a Pentecostal Church, who was dismissed on account of homosexuality, set up a church of his own where homosexual members would be welcome and where he could celebrate homosexual marriages. According to Altman (1971, p. 104) Troy's Hollywood church 'skilfully combines high camp religion with a muted assertion of gay rights'. The Metropolitan Community Church now has a representation in London, with Reverend Tom Bigelow as pastor, and contributes a column in the paper *Gay News*. Such developments in no way reflect mainstream Christianity. To many Christians the idea of tolerating homosexuals within the church still seems an outrage against the faith. Shortly before he became Archbishop of Canterbury, Dr. Donald Coggan provoked some clergymen to expressions of extreme indigation when he admitted, in answer to a question on a radio phone-in programme, that there were some homosexuals among Anglican priests.

In the early days of the movement for social justice for homosexuals the reformers were glad of any support they could win from the established churches. Backing from the Moral Welfare Council of the Church of England helped in the formulation and eventual implementation of the Wolfenden decriminalisation proposals. In the United States, the tireless efforts of the Rev. Alfred Gross, executive director of the G.W. Henry Foundation (an organisation devoted to counselling homosexuals and educating the public) gave a respectable, religious backing to pleas for law reform and for a better deal for sexual variants. At a later stage, the Council on Religion and the Homosexual, formed in California, continued the attempt to invoke the religious conscience in the interests of the homosexual cause.

An important change in the relations between the homosexual civil rights and law reform movement and established religious organisations came about with the development of radical gay liberation. Homosexuals ceased to present themselves as sinners, begging for tolerance and forgiveness from more virtuous Christians. Standing proud, and asserting their moral right to live as they please, they decisively rejected as stupid and outmoded the so-called natural law that condemned them. Militant homosexuals, instead of providing occasion for a comfortable exercise in Christian forebearance, now presented an uncomfortable challenge to religious dogma. Some religious laymen, guided more by instinct than doctrine, feel that dogma should give way. Monica Furlong, writing in the *Church Times* (8 November 1974), calls homosexuality 'the acid test for Christians', which will determine whether they really believe in the goodness of sex as an expression of love, or whether they are still bound to the notion of sex as a regrettable necessity for procreation which can have no possible justification outside a heterosexual marriage contract. So long as an absurd atmosphere of sin still clings to homosexual inclinations in the eyes of most Christians 'it is not surprising that groups like Gay Lib ... become increasingly aggressive in their insistence that the rest of us overcome our prejudices'. Members of the Anglican Church have formed a small organisation known as *Reach*, under the direction of Reverend Dennis Nadin (1975) for those concerned to reassess the Church's understanding of sexuality in general and homosexuality in particular. As an outsider it would be presumptuous to try to predict whether the churches will eventually come to agree with those dissenting prophets among their own followers, or whether they will close ranks and reassert ever more firmly the authority of divinely revealed natural law. At the time of writing (1975) a working party on homosexuality has been set up by the General Synod of the Church of England's Board for Social Responsibility. In the course of receiving evidence the working party has met representatives of the Campaign for Homosexual Equality. It is evident that a determined effort is being made to secure reliable, up to date information, but whether this will be held to have a bearing on orthodox moral principles remains to be seen.

CHAPTER ELEVEN

Afterthoughts

Throughout this review an effort has been made to present the available information in a fairly neutral style, to avoid preaching and polemics, and to give due attention to all shades of opinion and interpretation, leaving the reader to reach his own conclusions. But personal bias can never be fully concealed, and at this point it seems appropriate for the author to step off the fence and make his current views explicit. Paradoxically, further study of the continually increasing volume of publications concerning homosexuality has led to less firm opinions than before. Increasing awareness of the complexities of the subject brings with it the realisation that on many issues it would be wise to suspend judgment pending further research. Indeed, one conclusion that can be expressed without fear of contradiction is that much more needs to be learned about human sexuality before even quite elementary questions can be answered with any degree of confidence.

Two points deserve emphasis, both because they have emerged more clearly than before, and because they have a bearing upon moral and political issues. The first of these is the ubiquity of homosexual behaviour. It appears in a variety of social guises, but in one form or another it occurs in virtually every culture and period of history. Whatever may be the root causes, it is a common human phenomenon which is never likely to disappear, and as such we must recognise it and come to terms with it as best we can. A second important point is that a homosexual orientation, notwithstanding traditional opinions to the contrary, does not necessarily imply inferiority in other respects. Insuperable difficulties in obtaining fully representative samples, coupled with the inefficiency and subjectivity of conventional tests of personality and social adjustment, stand in the way of exact quantitative comparisons between heterosexuals and homosexuals. All the same, many homosexuals evidently fall well within the normal range in such qualities as social competence, efficiency at work, emotional stability, intelligence, and capacity to form mutually satisfying personal relationships, sexual and otherwise. Nevertheless, a somewhat higher proportion of homosexuals than heterosexuals appear to come to grief in various ways, by falling foul of the law, taking to the bottle, succumbing to depression or social alienation, lapsing into unsatisfying, compulsive sexual promiscuity, or seeking love affairs with persons hopelessly incompatible in age or social background. In many cases these troubles arise as a direct result of the stresses caused by social disapproval, and the absence of any officially recognised place in our culture for homosexual marriages. In other cases the individual homosexual's unhappiness appears to be mainly caused, as the psychoanalysts have always maintained, by his own difficult or neurotic personality development, which in turn derives from a disturbed early upbringing. A considerable amount of evidence has accumulated showing that peculiar and conflict-ridden parent-child relationships, especially evident in attitudes to the child's sexual development, are statistically more frequent in the life histories of homosexuals than in those of heterosexuals. Although by no means invariable, this factor might account for a connection between homosexual orientation and liability to personality problems. Both disturbed upbringing and personal maladjustment appear to be commoner in homosexuals who have some cross-sex identification than in homosexuals who, notwithstanding their unconventional choice of love partner, are otherwise at ease with their gender role.

The fact that a minority of homosexuals suffer from obvious personality problems in no way justifies the writing off of all homosexuals as hopelessly unreliable neurotics. The wholesale labelling of sexual deviants as psychiatrically very sick owed more to the moral prejudices and scientific ignorance of members of the medical profession than to the realities of life. The successful performance of homosexuals in many walks of life, including medicine, teaching, diplomacy, the armed forces, social work and competitive business, demonstrates that automatic exclusion from a profession solely on grounds of sexual orientation has no practical justification. Whether or no such unnecessary and cruel discrimination, or the threat of it, becomes illegal, the climate of official opinion on the matter has so changed in recent years that few organisations are nowadays willing to declare openly a policy of deliberate exclusion of known or suspected homosexuals. Agitation by militant young homosexuals, and the willingness of a few individuals to declare their orientation and put themselves forward as test cases, has undoubtedly hastened this change.

Many people deprecate the tactics of social agitators, because they fear the arousal of smouldering passions and the likely exposure to suspicion or publicity of persons who have always striven to keep quiet about their unorthodox sex lives. It has to be admitted, however, that no liberalisation of social mores, whether it be abolishing racial and religious discrimination, freeing slaves, breaking down class barriers or opening up the priesthood to women, ever takes place without conflict or without some people being hurt. In the context of the present-day campaign for homosexual equality, notions that seem extreme today will probably seem platitudes tomorrow. Under tyrannical political regimes liberal sexual ethics tend to perish along with other liberal ideas and freedoms. Some young radicals, who think the capitalist system oppressive, hope to attain homosexual liberation through Marxist revolution. Apart from their unrealistic optimism, they do a disservice to the cause of sexual freedom. A person's views about sexual controls have no necessary connection with his views about the relative merits of alternative systems of economic controls.

While unhesitatingly urging a tolerant, liberal attitude to homosexual practices, and insisting that our modern, pluralist society should be able to accommodate persons of homosexual orientation without making a fuss, I do not think that the homosexual way of life should be glamourised. Were it possible to choose one's sexual orientation, it would be sensible to choose either bisexuality or heterosexuality. Exclusive homosexuality forces a person into a minority group, cuts off all prospect of fulfilment through a family life with children and hampers participation in mainstream social activities, which are mostly geared to the needs of heterosexual couples. For the many homosexuals whose life interest centres upon short-term sexual liaisons, loneliness and frustration increase with age and loss of sexual attractiveness. Of course, in changing social conditions, the homosexual life-style may become easier and more rewarding, but at the present time it is not a path that one could counsel a young person to take who had a reasonable alternative prospect.

It follows from this value judgment that I am not in favour of policies likely to increase the incidence of exclusive homosexuality, and that I approve of allowing people who are dissatisfied with their homosexual orientation to try methods of treatment to help them to change. Unfortunately, until we have firmer scientific evidence as to the main determinants of an individual's sexual orientation, the methods of translating these general principles into practice remain very much a matter for further research rather than of dogmatic assertion. For example, it is my guess that a social change towards genuine sexual permissiveness would probably lead ultimately to more individual experimentation, to more people becoming at least temporarily bisexual, but to a diminution of permanent exclusive homosexuality, and an increased contentment on the part of the majority, whose heterosexual preference would be freed from elements of fear or coercion.

Unfortunately, research in this field has not got far enough to provide a reliable guide to the formulation of social policies. One of the chief reasons for continued uncertainty on many crucial points is that, in spite of much talk of permissiveness, our society still treats sexual topics with an irrational mixture of fascination and aversion. Instead of being methodically taught what is expected of them in this regard, as they are taught all other social skills, children are deliberately shielded, that is kept in ignorance. Photographs of human sexual activity, which might help clear up childish misunderstandings, are defined as dangerous, pornographic and corrupting, and preserved for adults only. These attitudes make research peculiarly difficult. Until Masters and Johnson broke through the barrier of convention, far more was known about the physiology of copulating mammals than about human intercourse and orgasm.

Information about the early development of human sexual feelings and preference is extremely difficult to elicit. Confidential surveys of adults indicate that the majority have a strong, consistent and lasting erotic preference, which may be either for their own or for the opposite sex. In short, most adults can be categorised fairly readily as either heterosexually or homosexually oriented, but how they arrived at that state is less clear. Judged by their overt erotic responses, males are more often of homosexual orientation than females. A homosexual orientation does not always prevent the individual from having some heterosexual experience, any more than a heterosexual orientation prevents occasional homosexual experience, but contacts with the non-preferred sex tend to be less satisfying, both physically and emotionally. Owing to the extreme difficulty of obtaining fully representative samples from the general population, the prevalence of bisexual adults, that is persons capable of more or less equal satisfaction in contact with either sex, remains uncertain. Still more uncertain is the proportion of the population who experience spontaneous swings of sexual interest, towards or away from homosexuality, during the course of their adult lives.

In the earliest years of life, long before questions about the choice of a partner for sexual activity can arise, small boys and girls manifest differences in attitudes, interests and behaviour, and develop a strong feeling of belonging to either the male or female sex. By the time they reach the age of romantic or erotic attachments, their own self-image, and everything they have learned to associate with masculinity and femininity, dictates that they should choose a partner of the opposite sex. A small minority of boys and girls fail to acquire the attitudes and styles of conduct considered appropriate to members of their sex. Some of these effeminate boys and tomboyish girls realise their peculiarity. They may be very unhappy about it and wish they had been born of different sex, and some of them indulge in fantasies of changing sex, or of being of different sex to what other people think they are. In adopting a homosexual orientation at adolescence, these boys and girls are simply behaving in conformity with their cross-sex identification. A boy who thinks of himself as feminine finds it in keeping to fall in love with a male.

This is one pathway to a homosexual orientation, but not the usual one. In practice much more common, but more difficult to understand, is the phenomenon of the ordinary boy or girl, with an apparently satisfactory identification with his or her gender, who conforms to all expectations in sexual appearance and sexual role-playing, save for a homoerotic preference. Unfortunately, relatively little is known about the earliest manifestations of erotic interest, or how long it takes for distinctive preferences to develop, or to become exclusive, or to become fixed. Does the direction of an adolescent's initial sexual interest represent an inevitable unfolding of tendencies laid down earlier in life, or is it at this stage still fluid and susceptible to modification by practical experience and social expectations? Ethical problems and social inhibitions hamper the investigation of adolescent sexuality, and research into these questions has scarcely got off the ground.

The fact that different human beings acquire different sexual orientations, homosexual, heterosexual and all points intermediate, and the fact that individuals have been known to shift their sexual orientation dramatically even late in life, shows that, compared with many species of lower animals, human sexual behaviour is less rigidly programmed by innate neurophysical mechanisms. The scope for learning, and hence for variation, is very great, as can be seen most clearly in the erotic potentialities of rubber goods and other artificial products that cannot be part of any biological programme, and must therefore represent an environmentally acquired interest. Even so, the possible influence of hereditary predisposition upon the direction of an individual's sexual orientation cannot be discounted. The notion of human behaviour being to some extent fixed in advance by heredity strikes many modern youngsters as repugnant, but research with identical twins strongly suggests that some individuals are born with a definite bias towards the development of a homosexual orientation. The physical processes underlying this predisposition have yet to be discovered. Research has failed to unearth any obvious anatomical or physiological differences between samples of heterosexuals and homosexuals, such as might be expected if they had a distinctive hereditary endowment. Recent work suggests that there may be subtle differences in the functioning of the sex hormones, or subtle changes in brain physiology due to hormone fluctuations before birth, but the findings so far remain inconclusive. But the investigations of twins have established one very important conclusion, namely that hereditary predisposition is not the only factor in producing homosexuality. Identical twins often have divergent sexual orientations. The different life experience and styles of upbringing which appear to be responsible for only one member of a twin pair becoming homosexual provide valuable clues to the causes of homosexuality in general.

Like other aspects of human behaviour, sexual orientation is the outcome of a complex interplay of different factors, some of them physical, some of them hereditary, but most of them environmental. Environmental influences include general cultural habits and expectations, as well as the particular characteristics of the individual's family upbringing and personal circumstances. No single, predominant cause for all cases of homosexual orientation is ever likely to be found. Individuals arrive at the same point on Kinsey's scale of sexual preference by very different routes. In our culture a homosexual adjustment is a recognised and partially tolerated mode of life. It may be taken up by very different types of person reacting to very different sorts of pressure. The crushed, mother-dominated boy who has been taught to doubt his own manhood, and who takes fright at the thought of asserting himself sexually with women, represents one well-known type. He contrasts starkly with the dominating, egocentric man who has no such fears, but who loathes the personal commitment associated with heterosexual affairs, and finds an easier, less demanding and less restricting outlet in homosexuality. Equally striking is the contrast between the manly male who likes men, or the demurely feminine lesbian, and the transsexual characters who are content with nothing less than 'passing' as members of the opposite sex.

Psychological influences, notably those operating early in life through child-rearing experiences, seem to be the most important factors in the genesis of a homosexual orientation. Over-dominating, unsympathetic or rejecting parents, puritanical repression of early sexual curiosity, and discouraging attitudes towards gender assertive behaviour, feature in the backgrounds of many homosexuals. The particular constellation of close, binding, oppressive mother and weak, unsympathetic or absent father has been identified repeatedly in different surveys of male homosexuals. Direct learning of homosexual practices during physical sex play between schoolchildren, or as a result of sexual contacts with older persons of the same sex, does not appear to play an important part in fixing a homosexual orientation, unless the youngster has some prior emotional interest in homosexual relationships, or a fear of heterosexuality. Many developing adolescents and pre-adolescents have frequent homosexual masturbation experiences without this in any way diminishing their enthusiasm for heterosexual relationships. When early sex contacts with persons of the same sex take on a romantic flavour, and the adolescent falls in love with a member of the same sex, then the likelihood of a persisting homosexual orientation is much greater. It would be foolish to underestimate the importance of pleasurable conditioning experiences in favouring the development of sexual behaviour patterns, but some learning theorists place too much emphasis on the physical circumstances in which orgasm occurs, neglecting the importance to human beings of imaginative fantasy and social meaning. An orgasm that represents a satisfying culmination to a complex emotional interaction between two persons, and serves at the same time to confirm the individual's sense of identity and purpose, cannot be compared with a careless masturbatory exercise without emotional involvement. The influence of sexual events in conditioning future behaviour stems more from the emotional context than the physical reality.

Psychiatrists cannot avoid trying to advise the many people who approach them wanting to know about methods of treatment to change sexual orientation. A rule of thumb response has to be resisted. Homosexuals are no less varied in their psychological make-up, personal· histories and sexual development than heterosexuals, and what may be good advice to one need not apply to another. Even in the domain of specifically sexual behaviour, homosexuals vary enormously, some never having been bold enough or interested· enough to seek physical contacts with the opposite sex, others having had considerable experience in heterosexual practices without finding them satisfying or sufficient. Such differences affect the likelihood of becoming happy heterosexuals in response to treatment. Erotic interests that have failed to develop in childhood, or have for some reason been stifled or discouraged, become difficult to arouse in adult life, and even when aroused may be difficult to put into practice owing to the lack of the necessary social skills normally acquired at adolescence. Behaviour therapy that concentrates upon learning sexual skills in easy stages has had relative success, especially among those male homosexuals who would like to approach women but cannot bring themselves to take the required initiatives for fear of humiliating failure. As a method of developing sexual desire, however, engineering sexual experience, even in easy stages, has its limitations. After all a great many lesbians remain unconverted even after extensive sexual experience with men. The only important methods of conversion treatment available, psychotherapy and behaviour therapy, are both in limited supply. It could be argued that they should be limited to the persons in greatest social need, the paedophiles, or to those in acute distress on account of an unwanted sexual orientation. For the most part, psychiatric services, when called upon at all, might be better deployed in helping individuals to accept and adjust to the orientation they already have. Hopefully, the days when psychiatrists were used to diagnose homosexuals so that they could be excluded from employment or otherwise discriminated against have now passed.

A number of homosexual readers of previous editions of this book found it discouraging and calculated to increase feelings of shame. That was never intended and has, I hope, been corrected. Most people discover their sexual inclinations, they do not choose them, and they can be no more blamed for their sexual orientation than for their complexion. Few thinking people any longer believe in the automatic moral, physical and psychological superiority of a heterosexual orientation. Notwithstanding some social disadvantages and deprivation of family satisfactions, millions of homosexuals achieve a workable adjustment to life. It is one of the benefits of civilised living that minorities of different tastes and ways of life can be accommodated by the wider society. While there is still a long way to go before people of different sexual orientations understand and cooperate with each other fully, progress to that end has been remarkable, and the life of the average homosexual is likely to become much easier in the future.

REFERENCES

Aaron, W. (pseudonym) (1972) *Straight: A Heterosexual Talks about his Homosexual Past.* New York: Doubleday

Aaronson, B.S. and Grumpelt, H.R. (1961) Homosexuality and some MMPI measures of masculinity-femininity. *Journal of Clinical Psychiatry, 17,* 245-7

Abbott, S. and Love, Barbara (1972) *Sappho Was a Right-On Woman.* New York: Stein and Day

Abe, K. and Moran, P.A.P. (1969) Parental age of homosexuals. *British Journal of Psychiatry, 115,* 313-18

Abraham, K. (1927) The psychological relationship between sexuality and alcoholism. *Selected Papers on Psycho-Analysis.* London: Hogarth Press

Achilles, Nancy (1967) The development of the homosexual bar as an institution. In Gagnon, J.H. and Simon, W. (eds.), *Sexual Deviance.* New York: Harper and Row

Ackerley, J.R. (1971) *My Father and Myself.* Harmondsworth: Penguin Books

Albany Trust (1966) *The Homosexual and Venereal Disease.* London: 31 Clapham Rd., London SW9 0JD

Aldrich, Ann (1955) *We Walk Alone.* New York: Fawcett Publications

Allen, C. (1958) *Homosexuality: Its Nature, Causation and Treatment.* London: Staples Press

Allen, C. (1961) The aging homosexual. In Rubin, I. (ed.), *The Third Sex.* New York: New Book Co.

Altman, D. (1971) *Homosexual Oppression and Liberation.* New York: Outerbridge and Dienstfrey

American Bar Association (1967) *Project on Minimum Standards for Criminal Justice: Standards Relating to Sentencing Alternatives and Procedures.*

American Library Association (1974) *A Gay Bibliography* (3rd revision) New York: Task Force on Gay Liberation

Apfelberg, B., Sugar, C. and Pfeiffer, A.Z. (1944) A psychiatric study of 250 sex offenders. *American Journal of Psychiatry, 100,* 762-9

Appel, K.E. (1937) Endocrine studies in cases of homosexuality. *Archives of Neurology and Psychiatry, 37,* 1206-7

Apperson, Louise B. and McAdoo, W.G. Jr. (1968) Parental factors in the childhood of homosexuals. *Journal of Abnormal Psychology, 73,* 201-6

'Arcangelo', Angelo d' (1971) *The Homosexual Handbook: For Men and Boys.* London: Olympia Press

Arieti, S. (1967) Sexual conflict in psychotic disorders. In Wahl, C.W. (ed.), *Sexual Problems: Diagnosis and Treatment in Medical Practice.* New York: Free Press

Ariosto, L. (transl. Rose, W.S.) (1907) *Orlando Furioso.* London: Bell

Armon, Virginia (1960) Some personality variables in overt female homosexuality. *Journal of Projective Techniques, 24,* 292-309

Ashton, R. (1969) *James I by his Contemporaries.* London: Hutchinson

Ashworth, A.E. and Walker, W.M. (1972) Social structure and homosexuality: a theoretical appraisal. *British Journal of Sociology, 23,* 146-58

Bacon, Catherine L. (1956) A developmental theory of female homosexuality. In Lorand, S. and Balint, M. (eds.), *Perversions: Psychodynamics and Therapy.* New York: Random House

Bailey, D.S. (1955) *Homosexuality and the Western Christian Tradition*. London: Longmans

Baldwin, J. (1956) *Giovanni's Room*. New York: Dial Press

Bancroft, J. (1972) The relationship between gender identity and sexual behaviour. In Ounsted, C. and Taylor, D.C. (eds.), *Gender Differences*. Edinburgh and, London: Churchill Livingstone

Bancroft, J. (1974) *Deviant Sexual Behaviour: Modification and Assessment*. Oxford: Clarendon Press

Bancroft, J., Tennent, G., Loucas, K. and Cass, J. (1974) The control of deviant sexual behaviour by drugs. *British Journal of Psychiatry, 125*, 310-15

Banis, V.J. (1966) *Men and their Boys: The Homosexual Relationship Between Adult and Adolescent*. Los Angeles: Medco Books

Barahal, H.S. (1939) Constitutional factors in male homosexuals. *Psychiatric Quarterly, 13*, 391-400

Barlow, D.H., Abel, G.G., Blanchard, E.B. and Mavissakalian, M. (1974) Plasma testosterone level and male homosexuality: A failure to replicate. *Archives of Sexual Behaviour, 3*, 571-5

Barlow, D.H., Leitenberg, H. and Agras, W.S. (1969) Experimental control of sexual deviation through manipulation of the noxious scene in covert sensitisation. *Journal of Abnormal Psychology, 74*, 597-601

Barnett, L. (1975) *Homosexuality: Time to Tell the Truth*. London: Gollancz

Barnett, W. (1973) *Sexual Freedom and the Constitution*. Albuquerque: University of New Mexico Press

Barr, R.F. (1973) Responses to erotic stimuli of transsexual and homosexual males. *British Journal of Psychiatry, 123*, 579-85

Barr, R.F. and McConaghy, N. (1971) Penile volume responses to appetitive and aversive stimuli in relation to sexual orientation and conditioning performance. *British Journal of Psychiatry, 119*, 377-83

Barry, H., Bacon, Margaret K. and Child, I.I. (1957) A cross-cultural survey of some sex differences in socialisation. *Journal of Abnormal and Social Psychology, 55*, 327-32

Bartholomew, A.A. (1968) A longacting phenothiazise as a possible agent to control deviant sexual behaviour. *American Journal of Psychiatry, 124*, 917-23

Bass-Hass, Rita (1968) The lesbian dyad. *Journal of Sex Research, 4*, 108-26

Beaumont of Whitley, *et al.* (1974) *Report of the Working Party on the Law in relation to Sexual Behaviour*. London: Sexual Law Reform Society

Beauvoir, Simone de (transl. Parshley, H.M.) (1953) *The Second Sex*. London: Jonathan Cape

Bell, A.P. and Hall, C.S. (1971) *The Personality of a Child Molester*, Chicago: Aldine

Benda, C.E. (1963) Existential psychotherapy of homosexuality. *Review of Existential Psychology and Psychiatry, 3*, 133-52

Bender, Lauretta and Blau, A. (1937) The reactions of children to sexual relations with adults. *American Journal of Orthopsychiatry, 7*, 500-18

Bender, Lauretta and Grugett, A. (1952) A follow-up report on children who had atypical sexual experience. *American Journal of Orthopsychiatry, 22*, 825-37

Bender, Lauretta and Paster, S. (1941) Homosexual trends in children. *American Journal of Orthopsychiatry, 11*, 730-44

Bene, Eva (1965a) On the genesis of female homosexuality. *British Journal of Psychiatry, 111*, 815-21

Bene, Eva (1965b) On the genesis of male homosexuality: An attempt at clarifying the role of the parents. *British Journal of Psychiatry, 111*, 803-13

Benjamin, H. (1966) *The Transsexual Phenomenon*. New York: Julian Press

Benjamin, H. and Masters, R.E.L. (1964) *Prostitution and Morality*. New York: Julian Press

Berdie, R.F. (1959) A femininity adjective check list. *Journal of Applied Psychology, 43*, 327-33

Bergler, E. (1948) The myth of a new national disease: homosexuality and the Kinsey Report. *Psychiatric Quarterly, 22*, 66-88

Bergler, E. (1951) *Neurotic Counterfeit-Sex*. New York: Grune and Stratton

Berkowitz, L. and Walker, N. (1967) Laws and moral judgements. *Sociometry, 30*, 410-22

Bieber, I. *et al.*, (1962) *Homosexuality: A Psychoanalytic Study*. New York: Basic Books

Birk, L., Huddleston, W., Miller, E. and Cohler, B. (1971) Avoidance conditioning for homosexuality. *Archives of General Psychiatry, 25*, 314-23

Birk, L., Miller, Elizabeth and Cohler, B. (1970) Group psychotherapy for homosexual men by male-female cotherapists. *Acta Psychiatrica Scandinavia*, Suppl. 218

Birk, L., Williams, G.H., Chasin, Marcia and Rose, L.I. (1973) Serum testosterone levels in homosexual men. *New England Journal of Medicine, 289*, 1236-8

Blamires, D. (1973) *Homosexuality from the Inside*. London: Society of Friends, Social Responsibility Council

Bluestone, H., O'Malley, E.P. and Connell, S. (1966) Homosexuals in prison. *Corrective Psychiatry and Journal of Social Therapy, 12*, 13-24

Blumer, D. (1969) Transsexualism, sexual dysfunction and temporal lobe disorder. In Green, R. and Money, J.

Botwinick, J. and Machover, S. (1951) A psychometric examination of latent homosexuality in alcoholism. *Quarterly Journal of Studies on Alcohol, 12*, 268-72

Bowlby, J. (1953) *Child Care and the Growth of Love*. Harmondsworth: Penguin Books

Bowman, K.M. and Engle, Bernice (1965) Sexual psychopath laws. In Slovenko, R.

Brady, J.P. and Levitt, E.E. (1965) The relation of sexual preferences to sexual experiences. *Psychological Record, 15*, 377-84

Braff, E.H. (1962) Venereal disease, sex positions and homosexuality. *British Journal of Venereal Diseases, 38*, 165-66

Brantôme, P. de B. de (transl. Allinson, A.R.) (1933) *Lives of Fair and Gallant Ladies*. New York: Liveright

Bremer, J. (1959) *Asexualisation: A Follow-up Study of 244 Cases* New York: Macmillan, and Oslo: Oslo University Press

Brinton, C. (1959) *A History of Western Morals*. New York: Harcourt, Brace and World

Brittain, R.P. (1970) The sadistic murderer. *Medicine Science and the Law, 10*, 198-207

Brodie, H., Gartell, Nanette, Doering, C. and Rhue, T. (1974) Plasma testosterone levels in heterosexual and homosexual men. *American Journal of Psychiatry, 131*, 82-3

Brody, E.B. (1963) From schizophrenic to homosexual: A crisis in role and relating. *American Journal of Psychotherapy, 17*, 579-95

Bro-Jørgensen, Anne and Jensen, T. (1973) Gonococcal pharyngeal infections: Report of 110 cases. *British Journal of Venereal Diseases, 49*, 491-9

Brongersma, E. (1964) Revision of criminal law in Morocco. *Excerpta Criminologica, 4*, 267-72

Brown, D.G. (1963) Homosexuality and family dynamics. *Bulletin of the Menninger Clinic, 27*, 227-32

Brown, J.H. (1963) Homosexuality as an adaptation in handling aggression. *Journal of the Louisiana State Medical Society, 115*, 304-11

Buckley, M.J. (1959) *Morality and the Homosexual: A Catholic Approach to a Moral Problem*. London: Newman Press

Buffum, P.C. (1972) *Homosexuality in Prisons*. Washington, D.C.: U.S. Govt. Printing Office

Burton, Lindy (1968) *Vulnerable Children*. London: Routledge

Burton, R. (1885) *Arabian Nights*. Benares: Kamashastra Soc. (Terminal *Essay*, Section D: Pederasty, reproduced in Reade, B., 1970).

Butts, W.M. (1947) Boy prostitutes of the Metropolis. *Journal of Clinical Psychopathology, 8*, 673-81

Bychowski, G. (1956) Homosexuality and psychosis. In Lorand, S. and Balint, M. (eds.), *Perversions: Psychodynamics and Psychotherapy*. New York: Random House

Cabeen, C.W. and Coleman, J.C. (1962) The selection of sex offender patients for group psychotherapy. *International Journal of Group Psychotherapy, 12*, 326-34

Calleja, M.A. (1967) Homosexual behaviour in older men. *Sexology, 34*, 46-8

Canterbury, Archbishop of (1953) *The Times,* 25 November

Capote, T. (1948) *Other Voices, Other Rooms.* New York: Random House

Cappon, D. (1965) *Towards an Understanding of Homosexuality.* Englewood Cliffs, New Jersey: Prentice-Hall

Caprio, F.S. (1954) *Female Homosexuality: A Psychodynamic Study of Lesbianism.* New York: Citadel Press

Card, R. (1975) Sexual relations with minors. *Criminal Law Review* (July) 370-80

Carpenter, E. (1908) *The Intermediate Sex.* Reprinted in Cory, D.W. (1956)

Carrier, J.M (1971) Participants in urban Mexican male homosexual encounters. *Archives of Sexual Behaviour, 1,* 279-91

Carstairs, G.M. (1956) Hinjra and Jiryan: Two derivatives of Hindu attitudes to sexuality. *British Journal of Medical Psychology, 29,* 128-38

Cattell, R.B. and Morony, J.H. (1962) The use of the 16 PF in distinguishing homosexuals, normals and general criminals. *Journal of Consulting Psychology, 26,* 531-40

Chang, Judy and Block, J. (1960) A study of identification in male homosexuals. *Journal of Consulting Psychology, 24,* 307-10

CHE (1975) *Young Homosexuals.* Manchester: National Campaign for Homosexual Equality

Chesser, E. (1958) *Live and Let Live.* London: Heinemann

Chevalier-Skolnikoff, Susanne (1974) Male-female, female-female, and male-male sexual behaviour in the stumptail monkey. *Archives of Sexual Behaviour, 3,* 95-114

Chiles, J.A. (1972) Homosexuality in the United States Air Force. *Comprehensive Psychiatry, 13,* 529-32

Chodoff, P. (1966) A critique of Freud's theory of infantile sexuality. *American Journal of Psychiatry, 123,* 507-18

Clarke, R.V.G. (1965) The Slater Selective Vocabulary Scale and male homosexuality. *British Journal of Medical Psychology, 38,* 339-40

Cleckley, H. (1957) *The Caricature of Love.* New York: Ronald

Clemmer, D.E. (1958) *The Prison Community.* New York: Rinehart

Coates, S. (1964) Clinical psychology in sexual deviation: A methodological approach. In Rosen, I.

Cochran, W.G., Mosteller, F. and Tukey, J.W. (1954) Statistical problems of the Kinsey Report. *American Statistical Association Journal, 48,* 673-716

Cohen, J.A. (1961) A study of suicide pacts. *Medico-Legal Journal, 29,* 144-51

Comfort, A. (1972) *The Joy of Sex: A Gourmet Guide to Love Making.* New York: Simon and Schuster

Coombs, N.R. (1974) Male prostitution: A psychosocial view of behavior. *American Journal of Orthopsychiatry, 44,* 782-9

Cooper, A.J., Ismail, A.A.A., Phanjoo, A.L., and Love, D.L. (1972) Anti androgen (cyproterone acetate) therapy in deviant hypersexuality. *British Journal of Psychiatry, 120,* 59-63

Coppen, A.J. (1959) Body-build of male homosexuals. *British Medical Journal, (iii),* 1443-5

Cory, D.W. (ed.) (1956) *Homosexuality: A Cross Cultural Approach.* New York: Julian Press

Cory, D.W. (1964) *The Lesbian in America.* New York: Citadel Press

Cory, D.W. and LeRoy, J.P. (1963) *The Homosexual and his Society: A View from Within.* New York: Citadel Press

Cowie, J., Cowie, Valerie and Slater, E. (1968) *Delinquency in Girls.* London: Heinemann

Craft, M. (1966) Boy prostitutes and their fate. *British Journal of Psychiatry, 112,* 1111-14

Croft-Cooke, R. (1955) *The Verdict of You All.* London: Secker and Warburg

Curran, D. and Parr, D. (1957) Homosexuality: an analysis of 100 male cases. *British Medical Journal, (i),* 797-801

Damon, G. and Stuart, L. (1967) *The Lesbian in Literature: A Bibliography.* Reno, Nevada: *The Ladder,* Box 5025, Washington Station

D'Andrade, R.G. (1967) Sex differences and cultural institutions. In Maccoby, Eleanor E.

Dank, B.M. (1971) Coming out in the gay world. *Psychiatry, 34,* 180-95

Daughters of Bilitis (1959) DOB questionnaire reveals some facts about lesbians. *Ladder, 3,* 4-26

Davenport, W. (1965) Sexual patterns in a Southwest Pacific society. In Beach, F.A. (ed.), *Sexual Behaviour.* New York: Wiley

Davids, A., Joelson, M. and McArthur, C. (1956) Rorschach and TAT indices of homosexuality in overt homosexuals, neurotics and normal males. *Journal of Abnormal and Social Pyschology, 53,* 161-72

Davidson, M. (1971) *Some Boys.* London: Bruce and Watson

Davies, C. (1975) *Permissive Britain: Social Change in the Sixties and Seventies.* London: Pitman

Davies, J. (1973) Places: The A and B – story of a friendly boîte. *Lunch, No.22,* 20

Davies, T.S. (1970) Cyproterone acetate in sexual misbehaviour. *Medicine, Science and the Law, 10,* 237

Davis, A.J. (1970) Sexual assaults in the Philadelphia prison system. In Gagnon, J.H. and Simon, W. (eds.), *The Sexual Scene.* Chicago: Aldine

Davis, Katharine, B. (1929) *Factors in the Sex Life of 2,200 Women.* New York: Harper

Davison, G.C. and Wilson, G.T. (1974) Goals and strategies in behavioural treatment of homosexual pedophylia. Journal of Abnormal Psychology, 83, 196-8

Davison, G.C. and Wilson, G.T. (1974) Goals and strategies in behavioral treatment of homosexual pedophylia. *Journal of Abnormal Psychology, 83,* 196-8

Davison, K., Brierley, H. and Smith, C. (1971) A male monozygotic twinship discordant for homosexuality. *British Journal of Psychiatry, 118,* 675-82

Dean, R.B. and Richardson, H. (1964) Analysis of MMPI profiles of 40 college-educated overt male homosexuals. *Journal of Consulting Psychology, 28,* 483-6

Dean, R.B. and Richardson, H. (1966) On MMPI high-point codes of homosexual versus heterosexual males. *Journal of Consulting Psychology, 30,* 558-60

Deisher, R.W., Eisner, V., and Sulzbacher, S.I. (1969) The young male prostitute. *Pediatrics, 43,* 936-41

Delaney, Shelagh (1959) *A Taste of Honey.* New York: Grove Press

De Luca, J.N. (1966) The structure of homosexuality. *Journal of Projective Techniques and Personality Assessment, 30,* 187-91

De Luca, J.N. (1967) Performance of overt male homosexuals on the Blacky test. *Journal of Clinical Psychology, 23,* 497

Denniston, R.H. (1965) Ambisexuality in animals. In Marmor, J. (1965)

Deutsch, Helena (1944) *The Psychology of Women.* New York: Grune and Stratton

Devereux, G. (1937) Institutionalized homosexuality of the Mohave Indians. *Human Biology, 9,* 498-527. Reprinted in Ruitenbeek, H.M. (1963)

Devlin, P. (1965) *The Enforcement of Morals.* London: Oxford University Press

Dewhurst, K. (1969) Sexual activity and urinary steroids. *British Journal of Psychiatry, 115,* 1413-15

Dickey, Brenda A. (1961) Attitudes toward sex roles and feelings of adequacy among homosexual males. *Journal of Consulting Psychology, 25,* 116-22

Diderot, D. (1938) *La Religieuse.* Paris: Editions Cluny

Doerr, P., *et al.* (1973) Plasma testosterone, estradiol, and semen analysis in male homosexuals. *Archives of General Psychiatry, 29,* 829-33

Dörner, G. (1968) Hormonal induction and prevention of female homosexuality. *Journal of Endocrinology, 42,* 163-4

Dörner, G. and Hinz, G. (1968) Induction and prevention of male homosexuality by androgen. *Journal of Endocrinology, 40,* 387-8

Dörner, G. et al. (1975) A neuroendocrine predisposition for homosexuality in men. *Archives of Sexual Behavior, 4,* 1-8

Doshay, L.J. (1943) *The Boy Sex Offender and His Later Career.* New York: Grune and Stratton

Dover, K.J. (1977) *Greek Homosexuality.* London: Duckworth

Drakeford, J. (1971) *Forbidden Love*, Waco, Texas: Word Inc.

Druss, R.G. (1967) Cases of suspected homosexuality seen at an army mental hygiene consultation service. *Psychiatric Quarterly, 41*, 62-70

Duffy, C.T. and Hirschberg, A. (1965) *Sex and Crime.* New York: Doubleday

Dyer, C. (1966) *Staircase.* New York: Grove Press

Edwardes, A. and Masters, R.E.L. (1962) *The Cradle of Erotica.* New York: Julian Press

Edwards, N.B. (1972) Assertive training in a case of homosexual pedophilia. *Journal of Behavior Therapy and Experimental Psychiatry, 3*, 55-63

Eglington, J.Z. (1971) *Greek Love.* London: Neville Spearman

Ellis, A. (1956) The effectiveness of psychotherapy with individuals who have severe homosexual problems. *Journal of Consulting Psychology, 20*, 191-5. Reprinted in Ruitenbeek, H.M. (1963)

Ellis, A. (1965) *Homosexuality: Its Causes and Cure.* New York: Lyle Stuart

Ellis, H. (1915) *Studies in the Psychology of Sex.* (3rd Ed.) Vol.2, *Sexual Inversion.* Philadelphia: F.A. Davis

English, O.S. (1953) A primer on homosexuality. *G.P. (General Practice), 7*, 55-60

Epstein, L. (1948) *Sex Laws and Customs in Judaism.* New York: Ktav

Erickson Education Foundation (1974) *Guidelines for Transsexuals.* 1627 Moreland Av., Baton Rouge, La. 70808

Evans, R.B. (1969) Childhood parental relationships of homosexual men. *Journal of Consulting and Clinical Psychology, 33*, 129-35

Evans, R.B. (1972) Physical and biochemical characteristics of homosexual men. *Journal of Consulting and Clinical Psychology, 39*, 140-7

Fairburn, N.H. (1974) Homosexuality and the Law. In Loraine, J.A.

Feldman, M.P. *et al.* (1966) The Sexual Orientation Method. Behaviour Research and Therapy, 4, 289-300

Feldman, M.P. and MacCulloch, M.J. (1971) *Homosexual Behaviour: Therapy and Assessment.* Oxford: Pergamon Press

Felstein, I. (1973) *Sex in Later Life.* Harmondsworth: Penguin Books

Fenichel, O. (1945) *The Psychoanalytic Theory of Neurosis.* London: Kegan Paul

Ferenczi, S. (1955) *Final Contributions to the Theory and Techniques of Psycho-analysis.* London: Hogarth Press

Fidell, Estelle A. (ed.) (1973) *Play Index 1968-1972.* New York: H.W. Wilson

Field, L.H. (1973) Benperidol in the treatment of sexual offenders. *Medicine, Science and the Law, 13*, 195-6

Field, L.H. and Williams, M. (197) The hormonal treatment for sexual offenders. *Medicine, Science and the Law, 10*, 27-34

Field, L.H. and Williams, M. (1971) A note on the scientific assessment and treatment of the sexual offender. *Medicine, Science and the Law, 11*, 180-1

Firestone, Shulamith (1970) *The Dialectic of Sex: The Case for Feminist Revolution.* New York: William Morrow

Fisher, P. (1972) *The Gay Mystique.* New York: Stein and Day

Fisher, S. (1973) *The Female Orgasm: Psychology, Physiology, Fantasy.* London: Allen Lane. Abridged as *Understanding the Female Orgasm.* Harmondsworth: Penguin Books

Fishman, J.F. (1934) *Sex in Prison: Revealing Sex Conditions in American Prisons.* New York: Padell

Fitch, J.H. (1962) Men convicted of sexual offences against children: A descriptive follow-up study. *British Journal of Criminology, 3*, 18-37

Fitts, D. (transl.) (1956) *Poems from the Greek Anthology.* New York: New Directions

Fiumara, N.J., Wise, J.H.M. and Many, M. (1967) Gonorrhoeal pharyngitis. *New England Journal of Medicine 276*, 1248-50

Flacelière, R. (transl. Cleugh, J.) (1962) *Love in Ancient Greece.* New York: Crown Publishers

Fluker, J.L. (1966) Recent trends in homosexuality in West London. *British Journal of Venereal Diseases, 42*, 48-9

Ford, C.A. (1929) Homosexual practices of institutionalized females. *Journal of Abnormal and Social Psychology, 23*, 442-4

Ford, C.S. and Beach, F.A. (1952) *Patterns of Sexual Behaviour*. London: Eyre and Spottiswoode

Fordham, Frieda (1935) *An Introduction to Jung's Psychology*. Harmondsworth: Penguin Books

Foster, Jeanette H. (1958) *Sex Variant Women in Literature*. London: Muller

Francher, J.S. and Henkin, Janet (1973) The menopausal queen: adjustment to aging and the male homosexual. *American Journal of Orthopsychiatry*, *43*, 670-4

Frank, G.H. (1955) A test of the use of a figure drawing test as an indicator of sexual inversion. *Psychological Reports*, *1*, 137-8

Frazer, J. (1951) *The Golden Bough*. London: Macmillan

Freedman, M.J. (1968) Homosexuality among women and psychological adjustment. *Dissertation Abstracts*, *28*, 42948, *Ladder*, 12, 2-3

Freeman, T. (1955) Clinical and theoretical observations on male homosexuality. *International Journal of Psycho-analysis*, *36*, 335-47

Freud, S. (1905a) Three essays on the theory of sexuality. *Standard Edition of the Complete Psychological Works* (1953) *7*, 125-245. London: Hogarth Press

Freud, S. (1905b) Fragment of an analysis of a case of hysteria. *Standard Edition* (1953) *7*, 3-122

Freud, S. (1908) Character and anal eroticism. *Standard Edition* (1959) *9*, 168-75

Freud, S. (1910) Leonardo da Vinci and a memory of his childhood. *Standard Edition* (1957) *11*, 59-137

Freud, S. (1911) Psycho-analytic notes upon an autobiographical account of a case of paranoia (Dementia Paranoides). *Standard Edition* (1958) *12*, 3-82

Freud, S. (1917) On the transformation of instincts as exemplified in anal eroticism. *Standard Edition* (1955) *17*, 127-133

Freud, S. (1918) From the history of an infantile neurosis. *Standard Edition* (1955) *17*, 3-104

Freud, S. (1919) A child is being beaten, *Standard Edition* (1955) *17*, 175-204

Freud, S. (1920) The psychogenesis of a case of homosexuality in a woman. *Standard Edition* (1955) *18*, 145-72

Freud, S. (1925) Some physical consequences of the anatomical distinction between the sexes. *Standard Edition* (1961) *19*, 248-58

Freud, S. (1931) Female sexuality. *Standard Edition* (1961) *21*, 223-43

Freud, S. (1935) Letter to an American mother. Reprinted in: *American Journal of Psychiatry* (1951), *107*, 252, and in Ruitenbeek, H.M. (1963)

Freund, K. (1960) Some problems in the treatment of homosexuality. In Eysenck, H.J. (ed.), *Behaviour Therapy and the Neuroses*. Oxford: Pergamon Press

Freund, K. (1965a) *Die Homosexualität beim Mann*. Leipzig: S. Hirzel Verlag

Freund, K. (1965b) On the problem of male homosexuality. *Review of Czechoslovak Medicine*, *11*, 11-17

Freund, K. (1967) Erotic preference in pedophilia. *Behaviour Research and Therapy, 5* 339-48

Freund, K. (1974) Male homosexuality: An analysis of the pattern. In Loraine, J.A.

Freund, K., Langevin, R., Cibiri, S. and Zajac, Y. (1973) Heterosexual aversion in homosexual males. *British Journal of Psychiatry*, *122*, 163-70

Freund, K., Langevin, R.L. and Serber, M. (1974) Femininity and preferred age partner in homosexual and heterosexual males. *British Journal of Psychiatry*, *125*, 442-6

Freund, K., Langevin, R., Zajac, Y., Steiner, Betty and Zajac, R. (1974) Parent-child relations in transsexual and non-transsexual homosexual males. (abstract) *British Journal of Psychiatry*, *124*, 22-3

Frey, E.C. (1962) Dreams of male homosexuals and the attitude of society. *Journal of Individual Psychology*, *18*, 26-34

Gadpaille, W.J. (1968) Homosexual experience in adolescence. *Medical Aspects of Human Sexuality*, *2*, 29-38

Gagnon, J.H. and Simon, W. (1968) The social meaning of prison homosexuality. *Federal Probation*, *32*(1), 23-9

Gagnon, J.H. and Simon, W. (1973) *Sexual Conduct: The Social Sources of Human Sexuality*. Chicago: Aldine

Gallo, J.J. *et al.* (1966) Statutory sex provisions. *U.C.L.A. Law Review, 13,* 657-85

Garde, N.I. (1964) *Jonathan to Gide.* New York: Vantage Press

Gebhard, P.H. (1965) Situational factors affecting human sexual behavior. In Beach, F.A. (ed.), *Sexual Behavior.* New York: Wiley

Gebhard, P.H., Gagnon, J.H., Pomeroy, W.B. and Christenson, Cornelia V. (1965) *Sex Offenders: An Analysis of Types.* New York: Harper

Geil, G.A. (1948) The Goodenough Test as applied to adult delinquents. *Journal of Clinical Psychopathology, 9,* 62-82

Geis, G. (1972) *Not the Law's Business?* Rockville, Maryland: National Institute of Mental Health

Genet, Jean (1966) *Querelle de Brest* (transl. Frechtman, B.) New York: Grove Press

Gershman, H. (1964) Homosexuality and some aspects of creativity. *American Journal of Psycho-analysis, 24,* 29-38

Giallombardo, Rose (1966) *Society of Women.* New York: Wiley

Giannell, A.S. (1966) Giannell's criminosynthesis theory applied to female homosexuality. *Journal of Psychology, 64,* 213-22

Gibbens, T.C.N. (1957) The sexual behaviour of young criminals. *Journal of Mental Science, 103,* 527-40

Gibbens, T.C.N. and Prince, Joyce (1963) *Child Victims of Sex Offences.* London: I.S.T.D.

Gibbens, T.C.N. and Silberman, M. (1960) The clients of prostitutes. *British Journal of Venereal Diseases, 36,* 113-17

Gigeroff, A.K. (1968) *Sexual Deviations in the Criminal Law, Homosexual, Exhibitionistic and Pedophilic Offences in Canada.* Toronto: University of Toronto Press

Gigeroff, A.K., Mohr, J.W. and Turner, R.E. (1969) Sex offenders on probation: homosexuality. *Federal Probation, 33(i),* 36-9

Gillespie, W.H. (1964) The psycho-analytic theory of sexual deviation with special reference to fetishism. In Rosen, I.

Gillman, P. (1971) The queer-bash killers. *Sunday Times Magazine Supplement,* 7 Feb.

Ginsburg, K.N. (1967) The 'meat rack': A study of male homosexual prostitution. *American Journal of Psychotherapy, 21,* 170-85

Gioscia, N. (1950) The gag reflex and fellatio. *American Journal of Psychiatry, 107,* 380

Glick, B.S. (1959) Homosexual panic: Clinical and theoretical considerations. *Journal of Nervous and Mental Disease, 129,* 20-8

Glueck, B.C. (1956) Psychodynamic patterns in the homosexual sex offender. *American Journal of Psychiatry, 112,* 584-90

Gold, S. and Neufeld, I.L. (1965) A learning approach to the treatment of homosexuality. *Behaviour Research and Therapy, 3,* 201-4

Goldberg, J. (1964) Studies on granuloma inguinale. *British Journal of Venereal Diseases, 40,* 140-5

Goldberg, P.A. and Milstein, Judith T. (1965) Perceptual investigation of psychoanalytic theory concerning latent homosexuality in women. *Perceptual and Motor Skills, 21,* 645-6

Goldberg, S. and Lewis, M. (1969) Play behavior in the year old infant: early sex differences. *Child Development, 40,* 21-31

Goldman, I. (1963) *The Cubeo Indians of the Northwest Amazon.* Chicago: University of Illinois Press

Gonen, Jay Y. (1971) Negative identity in homosexuals. *Psychoanalytic Review, 58,* 345-52

Goodman, A. (1966) *A Summer on Fire Island.* Washington D.C.: Guild Press

Goy, R.W. (1968) Organizing effects of androgen on the behaviour of Rhesus monkeys. In Michael, B.P. (ed.), *Endocrinology and Human Behaviour.* London: Oxford University Press

Graham, J. (1968) *The Homosexual Kings of England.* London: Tandem

Grams, A. and Rinder, L. (1958) Signs of homosexuality in human-figure drawings. *Journal of Consulting Psychology, 22,* 394

Granato, R.C. (1974) Surgical approach to male transsexualism. *Urology, 3,* 792-6

Grauer, D. (1954) Homosexuality and paranoid schizophrenia as revealed by the Rorschach Test. *Journal of Consulting Psychology, 18,* 459-62

Graves, R. (1955) *Greek Myths.* Harmondsworth: Penguin Books

Greaves, A.B. (1963) The frequency of lymphogranuloma venereum ... with particular reference to the relationship between perirectal abscesses of lymphogranulomatous origin in the male and inversion. *Bulletin of the World Health Organisation, 29,* 797

Green, R. (1972) *Street Boy Swinging London.* London: Silver Publishing Co.

Green, R. (1972) Homosexuality as a mental illness. *International Journal of Psychiatry, 10,* 77-98

Green, R. (1974) *Sexual Identity Conflict in Children and Adults.* London: Duckworth

Green, R. and Money, J. (eds.) (1969) *Transsexualism and Sex Reassignment.* Baltimore: Johns Hopkins University Press

Green, R., Newman, L.E. and Stoller, R.J. (1972) Treatment of boyhood 'transsexualism': An interim report of four years' experience. *Archives of General Psychiatry, 26,* 213-17

Green, R. and Stoller, R.J. (1971) Two monozygotic (identical) twin pairs discordant for gender identity. *Archives of Sexual Behavior, 1,* 321-7

Greenberg, J. (1973) A study of male homosexuals (predominantly college students). *Journal of the American College Health Association, 22,* 56-60

Greenspan, B. (1971) Why homosexual relations don't last. *Journal of Contemporary Psychotherapy, 4,* 34-6

Grey, A. (1974) Homosexuality – some legal aspects. In Loraine, J.A.

Gundlach, R. (1967) Research project report. *The Ladder, 11,* 2-9

Gundlach, R.H. and Riess, B.F. (1968) Self and sexual identity in the female: A study of female homosexuals. In Riess, B.F. (Ed.) *New Directions in Mental Health.* New York: Grune and Stratton

Gundlach, R.H. and Riess, B.F. (1967) Birth order and sex of siblings in a sample of lesbians and non-lesbians. *Psychological Reports, 20,* 61-2

Gunnison, F. (1969) The homophile movement in America. In Weltge, W. (ed.), *The Same Sex.* Philadelphia: Pilgrim Press

Hadden, S.B. (1968) Group psychotherapy for sexual maladjustments. *American Journal of Psychiatry, 125,* 327-32

Hadden, S.B. (1972) Group psychotherapy with homosexual men. In Resnik, H.L. and Wolfgang, M.E. (eds.), *Sexual Behaviors: Social, Clinical and Legal Aspects.* Boston, Mass.: Little, Brown

Hader, M. (1966) Homosexuality as part of our ageing process. *Psychiatric Quarterly, 40,* 515-24

Hadfield, J.A. (1958) The cure of homosexuality. *British Medical Journal, (i),* 1323-6

Hadfield, J.A. (1966) Origins of homosexuality. *British Medical Journal, (i),* 678

Hain, J.D. and Linton, P.H. (1969) Physiological response to visual sexual stimuli. *Journal of Sex Research, 5,* 292-302

Halleck, S.L. (1965) Emotional effects of victimisation. In Slovenko, R.

Halleck, S.L. and Hersko, M. (1962) Homosexual behavior in a correctional institution for adolescent girls. *American Journal of Orthopsychiatry, 32,* 911-17

Hamburger, C. (1953) Desire for sex change as shown by personal letters from 456 men and women. Acta Endocrinologica, 14, 361-75

Hamilton, D.M. (1939) Some aspects of homosexuality in relation to total personality development. *Psychiatric Quarterly, 13,* 229-44

Hampson, J.L. and Hampson, J.G. (1961) The ontogensis of sexual behavior in man. In Young, W.C. (ed.), *Sex and Internal Secretions.* Baltimore: Williams and Wilkins

Hanson, R.W. and Adesso, V.J. (1972) A multiple behavioural approach to male homosexual behaviour: a case study. *Journal of Behaviour Therapy and Experimental Psychiatry, 3,* 323-5

Hare, E.H. (1962) Masturbatory insanity: The history of an idea. *Journal of Mental Science, 108,* 1-25

Harlow, H.F. and Harlow, M.K. (1962) Social deprivation in monkeys. *Scientific American, 207,* 136-46

Harlow, H.F. and Harlow, M.K. (1965) The affectional systems. In Schrier, S.M., Harlow, H.F. and Stollnitz, F. (eds.), *Behavior of Nonhuman Primates*. Vol.2. New York: Academic Press

Harris, M. (1973) *The Dilly Boys*. London: Groom Helm

Hart, H.H. (1958) Fear of homosexuality in college students. In Wedge, B.M (ed.), *Psychosocial Problems of College Men*. New Haven: Yale University Press

Hart, H.L.A. (1963) *Liberty, Law and Morals*. London: Oxford University Press

Hatterer, L.J. (1970) *Changing Homosexuality in the Male: Treatment for Men Troubled with Homosexuality*. New York: McGraw Hill

Hatterer, Myra S. (1974) The problems of women married to homosexual men. *American Journal of Psychiatry, 131*, 275-8

Haward, L.R.C. (1963) The reliability of corroborated police evidence. *Journal of the Forensic Science Society, 3*, 71-8

Hayward, S.C. (1957) Modification of sexual behavior of the male albino rat. *Journal of Comparative and Physiological Psychology, 50*, 70-3

Heckstall-Smith, A. (1954) *Eighteen Months*. London: Alan Wingate

Hedblom, J.H. (1973) Dimensions of lesbian sexual experience. *Archives of Sexual Behavior, 2*, 329-41

Heffernan, Esther (1972) *Making it in Prison*. New York: Wiley-Interscience

Heim, Alice H. (1970) *Intelligence and Personality*. Harmondsworth: Penguin Books

Heller, C.G. and Maddoch, W.O. (1947) The clinical uses of testosterone in the male. In Harries, R.S. and Thimann, K.V. (eds.), *Vitamins and Hormones*. New York: Academic Press

Hemphill, R.E., Leitch, A. and Stuart, A.R. (1958) A factual study of male homosexuality. *British Medical Journal, (i)*, 1317-23

Hendin, H. (1969) *Black Suicide*. New York: Basic Books

Henry, G.W. (1941) *Sex Variants*. New York: Harper

Henry, G.W. (1955) *All the Sexes*. New York and Toronto: Rinehardt

Herbert, J. (1967) *Fortune and Men's Eyes*. New York: Grove Press

Herman, S.H., Barlow, D.H. and Agras, W.S. (1974) An experimental analysis of classical conditioning as a method of increasing heterosexual arousal in homosexuals. *Behavior Therapy, 5*, 33-47

Heron, A. (ed.) (1964) *Towards a Quaker View of Sex*. London: Friends House

Hess, E.H., Seltzer, A.L. and Shlien, J.M. (1965) Pupil response of hetero- and homo-sexual males to pictures of men and women. *Journal of Abnormal and Social Psychology, 70*, 165-8

Heston, L.L. and Shields, J. (1968) Homosexuality in twins: A family study and a registry study. *Archives of General Psychiatry, 18*, 149-60

Hetherington, E.M. (1966) Effects of paternal absence on sex-typed behaviors in negro and white preadolescent males. *Journal of Personality and Social Psychology, 4*, 87-91

Hewitt, C.C. (1961) On the meaning of effeminacy in homosexual men. *American Journal of Psychotherapy, 15*, 592-602

Heydon, J.D. (1973) The problems of entrapment. *Cambridge Law Journal, 32*, 268-86

Highet, G. (1961) *Juvenal the Satirist*. London: Oxford University Press

Hirschfeld, M. (1920) *Die Homosexualität des Mannes und des Weibes*. Berlin: Marcus

Hirschfeld, M. (1936) The homosexual as an intersex. Reprinted in Krich, A.M. (1954)

Hodges, A. and Hutter, D. (1974) *With Downcast Gays*. London: Pomegranate Press

Hoenig, J. and Kenna, J.C. (1974) The prevalence of transsexualism in England and Wales. *British Journal of Psychiatry, 124*, 181-90

Hoffman, M. (1968) *The Gay World*. New York: Basic Books

Holden, H.M. (1965) Psychotherapy of a shared syndrome in identical twins. *British Journal of Psychiatry, 111*, 859-64

Holeman, R.E. and Winokur, G. (1965) Effeminate homosexuality: A disease of childhood. *American Journal of Orthopsychiatry, 35*, 48-56

Hollings, M. (1972) *The Pastoral Care of Homosexuals*. London: Mayhew-McCrimmon

Holloway, R. (1813) *The Phoenix of Sodom*. London: J. Cook

Holroyd, M. (1971) *Lytton Strachey: A Biography* (revised ed.). Harmondsworth: Penguin Books

Home Office (1957) *Report of the Committee on Homosexual Offences and Prostitution* (Wolfenden Report) (Command 247). London: H.M.S.O.

Home Office (1963) (Radcliffe) *Report of the Tribunal appointed to Inquire into the Vassall Case and Related Matters* (Command 2009). London: H.M.S.O.

Homosexual Information Center (1972) *A Selected Bibliography of Homosexuality* (fifth edition). New York: Homosexual Information Center

Hooker, Evelyn (1957) The adjustment of the male overt homosexual. *Journal of Projective Techniques, 21*, 18-31 Reprinted in Ruitenbeek (1963)

Hooker, Evelyn (1958) Male homosexuality in the Rorschach. *Journal of Projective Techniques, 22*, 33-54

Hooker, Evelyn (1961) The case of El: A biography. *Journal of Projective Techniques, 25*, 252-67

Hooker, Evelyn (1965a) Male homosexuals and their worlds. In Marmor, J.

Hooker, Evelyn (1965b) Gender identity in male homosexuals. In Money, J. (ed.), *Sex Research: New Developments*. New York: Holt, Rinehart and Winston

Hooker, Evelyn (1969) Parental relations and male homosexuality in patient and non-patient samples. *Journal of Consulting and Clinical Psychology, 33*, 140-2

Hopkins, June H. (1969) The lesbian personality. *British Journal of Psychiatry, 115*, 1433-6

Hore, B.D., Nicolle, F.V. and Calnan, J.S. (1975) Male transsexualism in England; sixteen cases with surgical intervention. *Archives of Sexual Behavior, 4*, 81-8

Horney, Karen (1954) *Our Inner Conflicts*. New York: Norton

Horowitz, M.J. (1964) The homosexual's image of himself. *Mental Hygiene, 48*, 197-201

Huffman, A.V. (1960) Sex deviation in a prison community. *Journal of Correctional Psychiatry and Social Therapy, 6*, 170-81

Huffman, A.V. (1961) Problems precipitated by homosexual approaches on youthful first offenders. *Journal of Social Therapy, 7*, 216-22

Humphreys, L. (1970) *Tearoom Trade: Impersonal Sex in Public Places*. Chicago: Aldine. London: Duckworth

Humphreys, L. (1972) *Out of the Closets: The Sociology of Homosexual Liberation*. New York: Prentice-Hall

Hungary (1962) *Criminal Code of the Hungarian Peoples' Republic* (translated Pál Lámberg). Budapest: Athenaeum Printing House

Hunt, M. (1959) *The Natural History of Love*. New York: Alfred Knopf

Hunter, J.F. (1972) *The Gay Insider U.S.A.* New York: Stonehill

Hutt, Corinne (1972) Sex differences in human development. *Human Development, 15*, 153-70

Hutton, R. (1958) *Of Those Alone* (an autobiography). London: Sidgwick and Jackson

Hyam, H.H. and Sheatsley, P.B. (1954) The scientific method. In Geddes, D.P. (ed.), *An Analysis of the Kinsey Reports on Sexual Behaviour*. London: F. Muller

Hyde, H.M. (1948) *The Trials of Oscar Wilde*. London: William Hodge

Hyde, H. Montgomery (1970) *The Other Love*. London: Heinemann

Igra, S. (1945) *Germany's National Vice*. London: Quality Press

Isaacs, Susan (1933) *Social Development in Young Children*. London: Routledge

Isherwood, C. (1964) *A Single Man*. New York: Simon and Schuster

James, B. (1962) Case of homosexuality treated by aversion therapy. *British Medical Journal, (i)*, 768-70

James, B. (1967) Learning theory and homosexuality. *New Zealand Medical Journal, 66*, 748-51

James, R.E. (1947) Precipitating factors in acute homosexual panic (Kempf's Disease) with a case presentation. *Quarterly Review of Psychiatry and Neurology, 2*, 530-3

Jefferiss, F.J.G. (1966) Homosexually-acquired venereal disease. *British Journal of Venereal Diseases, 42*, 46-7

Jeffries, D.J. *et al.* (1973) Australia (hepatitis-associated) antigen in patients attending a venereal disease clinic. *British Medical Journal (ii)* 455-6

Jenkins, M. (1928) The effect of segregation on the sex behaviour of the white rat. *Genetic Psychology Monographs, 3,* 461-71

Jersild, J. (1956) *Boy Prostitution.* Copenhagen: G.E.C. Gad

Johnson, L.D. (1970) *The Devil's Front Porch.* Lawrence, Kan.: University Press of Kansas

Johnston, Jill (1973) *Lesbian Nation: The Feminist Solution.* New York: Simon and Schuster

Jonas, C.H. (1944) An objective approach to the personality and environment in homosexuality. *Psychiatric Quarterly, 18,* 626-41

Jones, E. (1927) Early development of female homosexuality. *International Journal of Psychoanalysis, 8,* 459-72

Jordan, P. (1975) Fears behind a minor problem. *Guardian,* 9 Jan. 1975

Kadish, S.H. and Paulsen, M.G. (1969) *Criminal Law and its Processes Cases and Materials.* Boston: Little, Brown. *Supplement,* 1972

Kallmann, F.J. (1952a) Comparative twin study of the genetic aspects of male homosexuality. *Journal of Nervous and Mental Disease, 115,* 283-98

Kallmann, F.J. (1952b) Twin sibships and the study of male homosexuality. *American Journal of Human Genetics, 4,* 136-46

Kallmann, F.J. (1953) *Heredity in Health and Mental Disorder.* New York: Norton

Kallmann, F.J. (1960) Discussion [on a paper by Rainer, *et al.*] *Psychosomatic Medicine, 22,* 258-9

Kando, T. (1973) *Sex Change: The Achievement of Gender Identity among Feminised Transsexuals.* Springfield, Ill.: C.C. Thomas

Karlen, A. (1971) *Sexuality and Homosexuality.* London: MacDonald

Kayy, W.H. (1965) *The Gay Geniuses: Psychiatric and Literary Studies of Famous Homosexuals.* Glendale, California: M. Miller

Kempf, E. (1920) *Psychopathology.* St. Louis: C.V. Mosby

Kendrick, D.C. and Clarke, R.V.G. (1966) Attitudinal differences between heterosexually and homosexually oriented males. *British Journal of Psychiatry, 113,* 95-9

Kenyon, F.E. (1968a) Studies in female homosexuality: Psychological test results. *Journal of Consulting and Clinical Psychology, 32,* 510-13

Kenyon, F.E. (1968b) Studies in female homosexuality. *British Journal of Psychiatry, 114,* 1337-50

Kenyon, F.E. (1970) Homosexuality in the female. *British Journal of Hospital Medicine, 3,* 183-205

Kenyon, F.E. (1974) Female homosexuality: A review. In Loraine, J.A.

Khan, M.M.R. (1964) Infantile sexuality in female homosexuality. In Rosen, I. (ed.), *The Pathology and Treatment of Sexual Deviation.* London: Oxford University Press

Khan, Z. (1971) *The Quran: Arabic Text with a new Translation.* London: Curzon

Kiefer, O. (transl. by Highet, G. and Highet, Helen) (1951) *Sexual Life in Ancient Rome.* New York: Barnes and Noble

Kiel, F.W. (1965) The psychiatric character of the assailant as determined by autopsy observations. *Journal of Forensic Science, 10,* 263-71

Kimball-Jones, H. (1966) *Towards a Christian Understanding of the Homosexual.* New York: Associated Press. London (1967): Student Christian Movement Press

King, A.J. (1974) Homosexuality and venereal disease. In Loraine, J.A.

Kinsey, A.C., Pomeroy, W.B. and Martin, C.E. (1948) *Sexual Behavior in the Human Male.* London and Philadelphia: Saunders

Kinsey, A.C., Pomeroy, W.B., Martin, C.E. and Gebhard, P.H. (1953) *Sexual Behavior in the Human Female.* London and Philadelphia: Saunders

Kirkendall, L.A. (1961) Adolescent homosexual fears. *Sexology, 27,* 818-21

Kirkham, G.L. (1966) The female homosexual. In Esselstyn, T.C. (ed.), *The Female Offender.* San Jose, California: Sparton Bookstore, San Jose State College

Kitsuse, J.I. (1962) Societal reaction to deviant behaviour. *Social Problems, 9,* 247-56

Klaf, F.S. and Davis, C.A. (1960) Homosexuality and paranoid schizophrenia: A survey of 150 cases and controls. *American Journal of Psychiatry, 116,* 1070-6

Klein, Melanie, Heimann, Paula, Isaacs, Susan and Riviere, Joan (1952) *Developments in Psycho-analysis.* London: Hogarth Press

Klimmer, R. (1965) *Die Homosexualität.* Hamburg: Kriminalistik

Kline, P. (1972) *Fact and Fantasy in Freudian Theory.* London: Methuen

Klintworth, G.K. (1962) A pair of male monozygotic twins discordant for homosexuality. *Journal of Nervous and Mental Disease, 135,* 113-25

Knightley, P. and Simpson, C. (1970) *The Secret Lives of Lawrence of Arabia.* New York: McGraw-Hill

Koch, G. (1965) Die Bedeutung genetischer Faktoren für das menschliche Verhalten. *Äryliche Praxis, 17,* 823, 839-46

Koegler, R.R. and Kline, L.Y. (1965) Psychotherapy research: an approach utilizing autonomic response measurements. *American Journal of Psychotherapy, 19,* 268-79

Kohlberg, L. (1967) A cognitive-developmental analysis of children's sex-role concepts and attitudes. In Maccoby, Eleanor E.

Kohlenberg, R.J. (1974) Treatment of a homosexual pedophyliac using in vivo desensitisation. *Journal of Abnormal Psychology, 83,* 192-5

Kolarsky, A., Freund, K., MacKek, J., and Polak, O. (1967) Male sexual deviation. *Archives of General Psychiatry, 17,* 735-43

Kolodny, R.C., Masters, W.H., Hendryx, Julia and Toro, G. (1971) Plasma testosterone and semen analysis in male homosexuals. *New England Journal of Medicine, 285,* 1170-4

Koshi, G.M. (1970) *The Japanese Legal Advisor.* Tokyo: Charles E. Tuttle

Kozol, H.L., *et al.* (1966) The criminally dangerous sex offender. *New England Journal of Medicine, 275,* 79-84

Krafft-Ebing, R. (1934) *Psychopathia Sexualis* (revised ed. translated). New York: Physicians and Surgeons Book Co.

Kremer, Malvina W. and Rifkin, A.H. (1969) The early development of homosexuality: A study of adolescent lesbians. *American Journal of Psychiatry, 126,* 91-6

Krich, A.M. (ed.) (1954) *The Homosexuals: As Seen by Themselves and Thirty Authorities.* New York: Citadel Press

Krippner, S. (1964) The identification of male homosexuality with the MMPI. *Journal of Clinical Psychology, 20,* 159-61

Kubie, L.S. (1948) Psychiatric implications of the Kinsey Report. *Psychosomatic Medicine, 10,* 95-106

Kuethe, J.L. and Weingartner, H. (1964) Male-female schemata of homosexual and non-homosexual penitentiary inmates. *Journal of Personality, 32,* 23-31

Kyler, C.W. (1963) Camera surveillance of sex deviates. *Law and Order, 11(xi),* 16-18

Lambert, K. (1954) Homosexuals. *Medical Press, 232,* 523-6

Lambton, C. (1973) Down at the 'Dilly: A student hustler's view. *Lunch, No.22,* 24-5

Landis, Carney, *et al.* (1940) *Sex in Development.* New York and London: P.B. Hoeber

Landis, J.T. (1956) Experiences of 500 children with adult sexual deviation. *Psychiatric Quarterly Supplement, 30,* 91-109

Landtman, G. (1927) *The Kiwai Papuans of British New Guinea.* London: Macmillan

Lang, T. (1940) Studies in the genetic determination of homosexuality. *Journal of Nervous and Mental Disease, 92,* 55-64

Lang, T. (1941) Untersuchungen an männlichen homosexuellen und deren sippenzwischen homosexualität und Psychose, *Zentralblatt für die gesamte Neurologie und Psychiatrie, 171,* 651-79 (cited by Rosenthal, 1970)

Lange, J. (transl. Haldane, Charlotte) (1931) *Crime as Destiny: A Study of Criminal Twins.* London: Allen and Unwin

Langsley, D.G., Schwartz, M.N. and Fairburn, R.H. (1968) Father-son incest. *Comprehensive Psychiatry, 9,* 218-26

Law Commission (1974) *Conspiracies Relating to Morals and Decency* (Working Paper No.57). London: H.M. Stationery Office

Lawrence, G.H. (1966) The psychiatrist, the polygraph, and police selection. *Security World Magazine, 3,* 23

Lebovitz, P.S. (1972) Feminine behavior in boys: aspects of its outcome. *American Journal of Psychiatry, 128(2),* 1283-9

Legg, W.D. and Underwood, J.M. (1967) *An Annotated Bibliography of Homosexuality.* Los Angeles, California: Institute for the Study of Human Resources

Legman, G. (1966) *The Guilt of the Templars.* New York: Basic Books

Legman, G. (1969) *Oragenitalism: Oral Techniques in Genital Excitation.* New York: Julian Press (English edition: Duckworth 1972)

Levin, S.M., Balistrieri, J. and Schukit, M. (1972) The development of sexual discrimination in children. *Journal of Child Psychology and Psychiatry, 13,* 47-53

Levine, J. (1955) The sexual adjustment of alcoholics: A clinical study of a selected sample. *Quarterly Journal of Studies on Alcohol, 16,* 675-80

Levine, S. (1966) Sex differences in the brain. *Scientific American, 214,* 84-90

Levine, S. and Mullins, R.F. (1968) Hormones in infancy. In Newton, C. and Levine, S. (eds.), *Early Experience and Behavior.* Springfield, Ill.: C.C. Thomas

Levitt, E.E. and Klassen, A.D. (1974) Public attitudes towards homosexuality: Part of the 1970 National Survey by the Institute of Sex Research. *Journal of Homosexuality, 1,* 29-43

Lewinsohn, R. (1958) *A History of Sexual Customs.* New York: Harper

Lewis, S. (1933) *Ann Vickers.* New York: Doubleday

Lewis, V., Ehrhardt, Anke A. and Money, J. (1970) Genital operation in girls with adrenogenital syndrome: Subsequent psychologic development. *Obstetrics and Gynaecology, 36,* 11-15

Leznoff, M. and Westley, W.A. (1956) The homosexual community. *Social Problems, 3,* 257-63. Reprinted in Ruitenbeek, H.M. (1963)

Licht, H. (P. Brand) (1926) *Das Liebesleben der Griechen.* Dresden: P. Aretz

Licht, H. (P. Brand) (1963) *Sexual Life in Ancient Greece* (ed. Dawson, L.J.; transl. Freese. J.H.). New York: Barnes and Noble

Liddicoat, Renée (1961) A study of non-institutionalized homosexuals. *Journal of the National Institute of Personnel Research, 8,* 217-49. Also summarised: (1957) in Correspondence *British Medical Journal, (ii),* 1110-11

Liebman, S. (1944) Homosexuality, transvestism and psychosis: Study of a case treated with electroshock. *Journal of Nervous and Mental Disease, 99,* 945-58

Lindman, F.T. and McIntyre, D.M. (1961) The sexual psychopath and the law. In *The Mentally Disabled and the Law.* Chicago: University Press

Lindner, H. (1953) The Blacky Pictures Test: a study of sexual and non-sexual offenders. *Journal of Projective Techniques, 17,* 79-84

Lindner, R. (1956) *Must You Conform?* New York: Holt, Rinehart and Winston. Extract reprinted in Ruitenbeek, H.M. (1963)

Lindzey, G. (1965) Seer versus sign. *Journal of Experimental Research in Personality, 1,* 17-26

Lindzey, G., Tejessy, Charlotte and Zemansky, H.S. (1958) Thematic Apperception Test: An empirical examination of some indices of homosexuality. *Journal of Abnormal and Social Psychology, 57,* 67-75

Liss, Jay L. and Welner, A. (1973) Change in homosexual orientation. *American Journal of Psychotherapy, 27,* 102-4

Litman, R.E. (1961) Psychotherapy of a homosexual man in a heterosexual group. *International Journal of Group Psychotherapy, 11,* 440-8

London University (1974) *ULU: A Students Guide 1974-5.* London: London University Press

Loney, J. (1972) Background factors, sexual experiences, and attitudes towards treatment in two "normal" homosexual samples. *Journal of Consulting and Clinical Psychology, 38,* 57-65

Loney, J. (1973) Family dynamics in homosexual women. *Archives of Sexual Behavior, 2,* 343-50

Loraine, J.A. (ed.) (1974) *Understanding Homosexuality: Its biological and psychological bases.* Lancaster: Medical and Technical

Loraine, J.A., Ismail, A.A., Adamopoulos, D.A. and Dove, G.A. (1970) Endocrine function in male and female homosexuals. *British Medical Journal, (iv)*, 406-9

Lorand, S. (1951) *Clinical Studies in Psychoanalysis*. New York: Interntional Universities Press

Lorenz, K.Z. (1958) The evolution of behaviour. *Scientific American, 199*, 67-83

McBride, A.F. and Hebb, D.O. (1948) Behaviour of the captive bottle-nose dolphin. *Journal of Comparative and Physiological Psychology, 41*, 111-23

McCaghy, C.H. (1967) Child molesters: A study of their careers as deviants. In Clinard, M.B. and Quinney, R. (eds), *Criminal Behavior Systems: A Typology* (1st ed.). New York: Holt, Rinehart and Winston

McCaghy, C.H. (1968) Drinking and deviance disavowal: The case of child molesters. *Social Problems, 16*, 43-9

McCleary, R.D. (1972) Patterns of homosexuality in boys; observations from Illinois. *International Journal of Offender Therapy and Comparative Criminology, 16*, 139-42

Maccoby, Eleanor E. (ed.) (1967) *The Development of Sex Differences*. London: Tavistock

McConaghy, N. (1969) Subjective and penile plethysmograph responses following aversion-relief and apomorphine aversion therapy for homosexual impulses. *British Journal of Psychiatry, 115*, 723-30

McCord, W. and McCord, Joan (1960) *Origins of Alcoholism*. London: Tavistock

McCord, W., McCord, Joan and Verden, P. (1962a) Family relationship and sexual deviance in lower-class adolescents. *International Journal of Social Psychiatry, 8*, 165-79

McCord, Joan, McCord, W. and Thurber, Emily (1962b) Some effects of parental absence on male children. *Journal of Abnormal and Social Psychology, 64*, 361-9

MacDonald, G.J. *et al.* (1971) A guided self-help approach to the treatment of the habitual sex offender. *Hospital and Community Psychiatry, 22*, 310-13

MacDonald, J.M. (1961) Homosexuality in ex-prisoners. *Journal of the American Medical Association, 175*, 834

MacDonald, Martha W. (1938) Criminally aggressive behavior in passive effeminate boys. *American Journal of Orthopsychiatry, 8*, 70-8

McDougall, Joyce (1970) Homosexuality in women. In Chasseguet-Smirgel, J. (ed.), *Female Sexuality*. Ann Arbor: Michigan University Press

McDougall, Joyce (1972) Primal scene and sexual perversion. *International Journal of Psycho-Analysis, 53*, 371-84

McGeorge, J. (1964) Sexual assault on the children. *Medicine, Science and the Law, 4*, 245-53

McGrew, W.C. (1972) Aspects of social development in nursery school children. In Blurton-Jones, N. (ed.), *Ethological Studies of Child Behaviour*. London: Cambridge University Press

McGuire, R.J., Carlisle, J.M. and Young, B.G. (1965) Sexual deviations as conditioned behaviour: A hypothesis. *Behaviour Research and Therapy, 2*, 185-90

McIntosh, Mary (1968) The homosexual role. *Social Problems, 16*, 182-92

McIntosh, Mary (1973) Gayspeak. *Lunch, No.16*, 7-9

McKee, W.F. (1964) Camera surveillance of sex deviates: Evidentiary problems. *Law and Order, 12(viii)* 72-4

MacKenzie, C. (1956) *Thin Ice*. London: Chatto and Windus

MacNamara, D.E.J. (1965) Male prostitution in American cities: A pathological or socioeconomic phenomenon? *American Journal of Orthopsychiatry, 35*, 204

McNeill, J. and Gamer, Helena (eds.) (1938) *Medieval Handbooks of Penance*. New York: Columbia University Press

Mainord, F.R. (1953) A note on the use of figure drawings in the diagnosis of sexual inversion. *Journal of Clinical Psychology, 9*, 188-9

Malinowski, B. (1929) *The Sexual Life of Savages*. London: Routledge and Kegan Paul

Mann, T. (1965) *Death in Venice* (transl. Burke, K.). New York: Alfred Knopf

Mannheim, H. (1946) *Criminal Justice and Social Reconstruction*. London: Kegan Paul

Manosevitz, M. (1970) Early sexual behaviour in adult homosexual and heterosexual males. *Journal of Abnormal Psychology, 76*, 396-402

Manosevitz, M. (1971) Education and MMPI scores in homosexual and heterosexual males. *Journal of Consulting and Clinical Psychology, 36*, 395-9

Mantegazza, P. (1932) The perversion of love. Reprinted in Cory, D.W. (1956)

Marcus, A.M. and Conway, C. (1971) A Canadian group approach study of dangerous sex offenders. *International Journal of Offender Therapy, 15*, 59-66

Marcus, F. (1965) *The Killing of Sister George.* London: Samuel French

Margolese, M.S. (1970) Homosexuality: a new endocrine correlate. *Hormone and Behaviour, 1*, 151-5

Margolese, M.S. and Janiger, O. (1973) Androsterone/etiocholanolone ratios in male homosexuals. *British Medical Journal, iii*, 207-10

Marlowe, R. (1964) *Mr. Madam: Confessions of a Male Madam.* Los Angeles: Sherbourne Press

Marmor, J. (ed.) (1965) *Sexual Inversion.* New York: Basic Books

Martensen-Larsen, O. (1957) The family constellation of homosexualism. *Acta Genetica et Statistica Medica, 7*, 445-6

Martin, Agnes J. (1962) The Treatment of 12 male homosexuals with LSD. *Acta Psychotherapeutica, 10*, 394-402

Martin, Del and Lyon, Phyllis (1972) *Lesbian/Woman.* San Francisco: Glide Publications

Martins, T. and Valle, J.R. (1948) Hormonal regulation of the micturition behavior of the dog. *Journal of Comparative and Physiological Psychology, 41*, 301-11

Mason, W.A. (1968) Early social deprivation in the nonhuman primates: Implications for human behavior. In Glass, D.C. (ed.), *Environmental Influences.* New York: Rockefeller University Press

Mason, W.A., Davenport, R.K. and Menzel, E.W. (1968) Early experience and the social development of rhesus monkeys and chimpanzees. In Newton, G. and Levine, S. (eds.), *Early Experience and Behavior.* Springfield, Ill.: C.C. Thomas

Masters, W.H. and Johnson, Virginia E. (1966) *Human Sexual Response.* Boston: Little, Brown

Masters, W.H. and Johnson, Virginia E. (1970) *Human Sexual Inadequacy.* Boston: Little, Brown

Mathers, E.P. (ed.) (1930) *Eastern Love.* New York: Liveright

Mathews, A.M., Bancroft, J.H.J. and Slater, P. (1972) The principal components of sexual preference. *British Journal of Social and Clinical Psychology, 11*, 35-43

Matthews, A.G. (1957) *Is Homosexuality a Menace?* New York: McBride

Maugham, R.C.R. (1966) *Somerset and all the Maughams.* London: Longmans

Mavissakalian, M., Blanchard, E.B., Abel, G.C. and Barlow, D.H. (1975) Responses to complex erotic stimuli in homosexual and heterosexual males. *British Journal of Psychiatry, 126*, 252-7

Mavor, Elizabeth (1971) *The Ladies of Llangollen.* London: Michael Joseph. Penguin Books, 1974

Mayerson, P. and Lieff, H.I. (1965) Psychotherapy of homosexuals. In Marmor, J.

Mead, Margaret (1935) *Sex and Temperament.* London: Gollancz

Medico-Legal Journal (1964) Fatal emetine poisoning from aversion treatment. *32*, 95

Melikan, L.H. and Prothro, E.T. (1954) Sexual behavior of university students in the Arab Near East. *Journal of Abnormal and Social Psychology, 49*, 59-64

Mesnikoff, A.M., Rainer, J.D., Kolb, L.C. and Carr, A.C. (1963) Intra-familial determinants of divergent sexual behaviour in twins. *American Journal of Psychiatry, 119*, 732-8

Michigan (1974) The constitutionality of laws forbidding private homosexual conduct. *Michigan Law Review, 72*, 1613-37

Miller, A. (1955) *A View from the Bridge.* New York: Viking

Miller, M.M. (1963) Hypnotic-aversion treatment of homosexuality. *Journal of the National Medical Association, 55*, 411-15

Miller, P.R. (1958) The effeminate passive obligatory homosexual. *A.M.A. Archives of Neurology and Psychiatry, 80*, 612-18

Miller, W.G. and Hannum, T.C. (1963) Characteristics of homosexually involved incarcerated females. *Journal of Consulting Psychology, 27*, 277

Millett, Kate, (1970) *Sexual Politics*. New York: Doubleday

Mitchell, W., Falconer, M. and Hill, D. (1964) Epilepsy with fetishism relieved by temporal lobectomy. *Lancet (ii)*, 626-30

Moan, C.E. and Heath, R.G. (1972) Septal stimulation for the initiation of heterosexual behaviour in a homosexual male. *Journal of Behavior Therapy and Experimental Psychiatry, 3*, 23-30

Mohr, J.W., Turner, R.E. and Jerry, M.B. (1964) *Pedophilia and Exhibitionism*. Toronto: University Press

Moll, A. (1931) *Perversions of the Sex Instinct: A Study of Sexual Inversion based on Clinical Data and Official Documents*. Newark, N.J.: Julian Press

Money, J. (1963) Factors in the genesis of homosexuality. In Winokur, G. (ed.), *Determinants of Human Sexual Behaviour*. Springfield, Ill.: C.C. Thomas

Money, J. and Erhardt, Anke A. (1972) *Man & Woman Boy & Girl*. Baltimore: Johns Hopkins University Press

Moore, R.A. and Selzer, M.L. (1963) Male homosexuality, paranoia, and the schizophrenias. *American Journal of Psychiatry, 119*, 743-7

Moran, P.A.P. (1972) Familial effects in schizophrenia and homosexuality. *Australian and New Zealand Journal of Psychiatry, 6*, 116-19

Morris, Jan (1974) *Conundrum*. London: Faber

Morris, T.P. and Morris, Pauline (1963) *Pentonville: A Sociological Study of an English Prison*. London: Routledge and Kegan Paul

Morrow, J.E., Cupp, Marion E. and Sachs, L.B. (1965) A possible explanation of the excessive brother-to-sister ratios reported in siblings of male homosexuals. *Journal of Nervous and Mental Disease, 140*, 305-6

Mulcock, D. (1954) A study of 100 non-selected cases of sexual assaults on children. *International Journal of Sexology, 7*, 125-8

Murdock, G.P. (1957) World ethnographic sample. *American Anthropology, 59*, 664-87

Murphy, Lois (1957) Psychoanalysis and child development. *Bulletin of the Menninger Clinic, 27*, 177-88

Nadin, D. (1975) *Cause for Concern: The Christian Church and the Homosexual*. Salford: Reach Pamphlet, 27 Blackfriars Road, M3 7AQ

Nasatir, M., Dezzani, D. and Silbert, Mimi (1966) Atascadero: Ramifications of a maximum security treatment institution. *Issues in Criminology, 2*, 29-46

Nash, J. and Hayes, F. (1965) The parental relationships of male homosexuals: Some theoretical issues and a pilot study. *Australian Journal of Psychology, 17*, 35-43

National Council for Civil Liberties (1957) *Homosexuality and the Teaching Profession*. London: 186 King's Cross Road, WC1X 9 DE

Neodoma, K. (1951) Homosexuality in sexological practice. *International Journal of Sexology, 4*, 219-24

Nice, R.W. (1966) The problem of homosexuality in corrections. *American Journal of Corrections, 28*, 30-2

Nicolson, N. (1973) *Portrait of a Marriage*. London: Weidenfeld and Nicolson

Nisbett, R. and Gurwitz, S. (1970) Weight, sex and the eating behavior of human newborns. *Journal of Comparative and Physiological Psychology, 73*, 245-53

Oberholtzer, W.D. (ed.) (1971) *Is Gay Good? Ethics, Theology and Homosexuality*. Philadelphia: Westminster Press

O'Connor, P.J. (1964) Aetiological factors in homosexuality as seen in R.A.F. psychiatric practice. *British Journal of Psychiatry, 110*, 381-91

O'Connor, W.A. (1948) Some notes on suicide. *British Journal of Medical Psychology, 21*, 222-8

O'Day, J. (1964) *Confessions of a Male Prostitute*. Los Angeles: Sherbourne Press

Ohara, K. (1963) Characteristics of suicides in Japan. *American Journal of Psychiatry, 120*, 382-5

Oliver, W.A. and Mosher, D.L. (1968) Psychopathology and guilt in heterosexuals and subgroups of homosexual reformatory inmates. *Journal of Abnormal Psychology, 73*, 323-9

Ollendorff, R. (1966) *The Juvenile Homosexual Experience and its Effect on Adult Sexuality*. New York: Julian Press

Opler, M.K. (1965) Anthropological and cross-cultural aspects of homosexuality. In Marmor, J.

Oraison, M. (1952) *Vie chrétienne et problèmes de la sexualité*. Paris: Lethielleux (Placed on Index, 1953; Reissued Fayard-Lethielleux, 1972).

Oraison, M. (1975) *La Question homosexuelle*. Paris: Seuil

Orwin, A., James, Sheelah R.N. and Turner, R.K. (1974) Sex chromosome abnormalities, homosexuality and psychological treatment. *British Journal of Psychiatry, 124*, 293-5

Ovesey, L. (1969) *Homosexuality and Pseudohomosexuality*. New York: Science House

Owen, R.L. and Hill, J.L. (1972) Rectal and pharyngeal gonorrhoea in homosexual men. *Journal of the American Medical Association, 220*, 1315-18

Packard, V. (1964) *The Naked City*. London: Longmans (Penguin Books 1966)

Palmore, E. (ed.) (1970) *Normal Aging*. Durham, N.C.: Duke University Press

Panton, J.H. (1960) New MMPI scale for the identification of homosexuality. *Journal of Clinical Psychology, 16*, 17-21

Papatheophilou, R., James, Sheelah and Orwin, A. (1975) Electroencephalographic findings in treatment-seeking homosexuals compared with heterosexuals: A controlled study. *British Journal of Psychiatry, 127*, 63-6

Pardes, H., Steinberg, J. and Simons, R.C. (1967) A rare case of overt and mutual homosexuality in female identical twins. *Psychiatric Quarterly, 41*, 108-33

Pare, C.M.B. (1956) Homosexuality and chromosomal sex. *Journal of Psychosomatic Research, 1*, 274-51

Parker, N. (1964) Homosexuality in twins: A report on three discordant pairs. *British Journal of Psychiatry, 40*, 489-95

Parker, T. (1969) *The Twisting Lane*. London: Hutchinson

Parker, W. (1971) *Homosexuality: A Selective Bibliography of over 3,000 Items*. Metuchen, New Jersey: Scarecrow Press

Parker, W. (1972) The homosexual in American society today: the Homophile-Gay Liberation Movement. *Criminal Law Bulletin, 8*, 692-9

Parnell, R.W. (1958) *Behaviour and Physique*. London: Arnold

Pascal, G.R. and Herzberg, F.C. (1952) The detection of deviant sexual practice from performance on the Rorschach Test. *Journal of Projective Techniques, 16*, 366-73

Pastore, N. (1949) The genetics of schizophrenia. *Psychological Bulletin, 46*, 285-302

Pattison, E.M. (1974) Confusing concepts about the concept of homosexuality. *Psychiatry, 37*, 340-9

Paul, D.M. (1975) The medical examination in sexual offences. *Medicine, Science and the Law, 15*, 154-62

Pauly, I.B. (1968) The current status of the change of sex operation. *Journal of Nervous and Mental Disorders, 147*, 460-71

Perloff, W.H. (1965) Hormones and homosexuality. In Marmor, J.

Perry, T.D. (1972) *The Lord is my Shepherd and He Knows I'm Gay*. Los Angeles: Nash

Peters, J.J. *et al.* (1968) Group psychotherapy of the sex offender. *Federal Probation, 32* (ii), 41-5

Petronius (transl. Sullivan, J.P.) (1969) *The Satyricon and the Fragments*. Harmondsworth: Penguin Books

Peyrefitte, R. (transl. Hyams, E.) (1958) *Special Friendships*. London: Secker and Warburg

Pierce, D.M. (1972) MMPI HSX scale differences between active and situational homosexuality. *Journal of Forensic Psychology, 4*, 31-8

Pillard, R.C. and Rose, R.M. (1974) Plasma testosterone levels in homosexual men. *Archives of Sexual Behavior, 5*, 13-26

Pittenger, W.N. (1970) *Time for Consent* (2nd enlarged ed.) London: Student Christian Movement

Pittman, D.J. (1971) The male house of prostitution. *Trans Action, 8*, 21-7

Planansky, K. and Johnston, R. (1962) The incidence and relationship of homosexual and paranoid features in schizophrenia. *Journal of Mental Science, 108*, 604-15

Plaut, P. (1960) *Der Sexualverbrecher und seine Personlichkeit*. Stuttgart: Ferdinand Enke Verlag

Poe, J.S. (1952) The successful treatment of a 40-year-old passive homosexual. *Psychoanalytic Review, 29*, 23-33

Poole, K. (1972) The aetiology of gender identity and the lesbian. *Journal of Social Psychology, 87*, 51-7

Pritchard, M. (1962) Homosexuality and genetic sex. *Journal of Mental Science, 108*, 616-23

Psychiatry, Group for the Advancement of (1955) *Report on Homosexuality, with particular emphasis on this problem in Governmental Agencies*. Report No.30 Topeka, Kansas

Querlin, Marise (1965) *Women Without Men*. London: Mayflower Books

Quinn, J.T., Harbison, J.J.M. and McAllister, H. (1970) An attempt to shape human penile responses. *Behaviour Research and Therapy, 8*, 213-16

Raboch, J. and Nedoma, K. (1958) Sex chromatin and sexual behaviour: A study of 36 men with female nuclear pattern and of 194 homosexuals. *Psychosomatic Medicine, 20*, 55-9

Radzinowicz, L. (ed) (1957) *Sexual Offences*. London: Macmillan

Rainer, J.D., Mesnikoff, A., Kolb, L.C. and Carr, A. (1960) Homosexuality and heterosexuality in identical twins. *Psychosomatic Medicine, 22*, 251-8

Ramsay, R.W., Heringa, P.M. and Boorsma, I. (1974) A case study: Homosexuality in the Netherlands. In Loraine, J.A.

Rasmussen, A. (1943) Die bedeutung sexueller Attentate auf kinder unter 14 Jahren für die Entwicklung von Geisteskrank heiten und characteranomalen. *Acta Psychiatrica et Neurologica, 9*, 351-433

Rasmussen, E.W. (1955) Experimental homosexual behavior in male albino rats. *Acta Psychologica, 11*, 303-34

Ratnatunga, C.S. (1972) Gonococcal pharyngitis. *British Journal of Venereal Diseases, 48*, 184-6

Raven, S. (1959) *The Feathers of Death*. London: Blond

Raven, S. (1960) Boys will be boys. *Encounter, 86*, (November), 19-24. Reprinted in Ruitenbeek, H.M. (1963)

Raybin, J.B. (1969) Homosexual incest: Report of a case involving three generations of a family. *Journal of Nervous and Mental Disease, 148*, 105-9

Reade, B. (1970) *Sexual Heretics: Male Homosexuality in English Literature from 1850 to 1900: An Anthology*. London: Routledge and Kegan Paul

Rechy, J. (1963) *City of Night*. New York: Grove Press

Rechy, J. (1967) *Numbers*. New York: Grove Press

Rechy, J. (1969) *This Day's Death*. New York: Grove Press

Reifen, D. (1972) Protecting the sexually assaulted child in Israeli courts. In David, H.P. (ed.), *Child Mental Health in International Perspective*. New York: Harper

Reiss, A.J. (1961) The social integration of queers and peers. *Social Problems, 9*, 102-20. Reprinted in Ruitenbeek, H.M. (1963)

Resnik, H.L.P. (1972) Erotized repetitive hangings: A form of self-destructive behavior. *American Journal of Psychotherapy, 26*, 4-21

Resnik, H.L.P. and Peters, J. (1967) Out-patient group psychotherapy with convicted paedophiles. *International Journal of Group Psychotherapy, 17*, 151-8

Resnik, H.L.P. and Wolfgang, M.E. (1972) *Offensive Sexual Behaviour and its Treatment*, London: Churchill Livingstone

Riess, B.F., Safer, Jeanne and Yotire, W. (1974) Psychological test data on female homosexuality. *Journal of Homosexuality, 1*, 71-85

River, J.P. de (1958) *Crime and the Sexual Psychopath*. Springfield, Ill.: C.C. Thomas

Robertson, G. (1972) Parent-child relationships and homosexuality. *British Journal of Psychiatry, 121*, 525-8

Robinson, J.A.T. (1972) *The Place of Law in the Field of Sex* (The Beckley Lecture for 1972). Delivered at the Methodist Conference, Nottingham 5 July 1972

Rochester, Bishop of (1954) The Church and sex. *The Practitioner, 172*, 350-4

Rodgers, B. (1972) *The Queens' Vernacular: A Gay Lexicon.* San Francisco: Straight Arrow Books. London: Blond and Briggs

Roeder, F.R. (1966) Stereotaxic lesion of the tuber cinereum in sexual deviation. *Confinia Neurologica, 27,* 162-4

Roeder, F., Müller, D. and Orthner, H. (1971) Weitere Erfahrungen mit der stereotaktischen Behandlung sexueller Perversionen. In Orthner, H. (ed.), *Zentralnervöse Sexualsteuerung, Journal of Neuro-Visceral Relations,* Supplement *10,* 317-24. Wien and New York: Springer-Verlag

Romm, May E. (1965) Sexuality and homosexuality in women. In Marmor, J.

Rooth, F.G. (1971) Indecent exposure and exhibitionism. *British Journal of Hospital Medicine, 5,* 521-33

Roper, P. (1967) The effects of hypnotherapy on homosexuality. *Canadian Medical Association Journal, 96,* 319-27

Rosen, D.H. (1974) *A Study of Female Homosexuality.* Springfield, Ill.: C.C. Thomas

Rosen, I. (ed.) (1964) *The Pathology and Treatment of Sexual Deviation.* London: Oxford University Press

Rosenthal, D. (1970) *Genetic Theory and Abnormal Behavior.* New York: McGraw-Hill

Ross, H.L. (1959) The 'hustler' in Chicago. *Journal of Student Research, 1,* 13-19

Ross, H.L. (1971) Modes of adjustment of married homosexuals. *Social Problems, 18,* 385-93

Rubin, I. (1961) The possibility of cure. In Rubin, I. (ed.), *The Third Sex.* New York: New York Book Club

Rubinstein, L.H. (1958) Psychotherapeutic aspects of male homosexuality. *British Journal of Medical Psychology, 31,* 14-18

Ruitenbeek, H.M. (ed.) (1963) *The Problems of Homosexuality in Modern Society.* New York: Dutton

Ruitenbeek, H.M. (ed.) (1967) *Homosexuality and Creative Genius.* New York: Astor-Honor

Rule, J.B. (1973) *Private Lives and Public Surveillance.* London: Allen Lane

Rupp, J. (1970) Sudden death in the gay world. *Medicine, Science and the Law, 10,* 189-91

Russell, D.H. (1971) On the psychopathology of boy prostitutes. *International Journal of Offender Therapy, 15,* 49-52

Sagarin, E. (1969) *Odd Man In: Societies of Deviants in America.* Chicago: Quadrangle Books

Sagarin, E. and MacNamara, D.E.J. (1970) The problem of entrapment. *Crime and Delinquency, 16,* 363-78

Sagarin, E. and MacNamara, D.E.J. (1973) The homosexual as a crime victim. *First International Symposium on Victimology.* Institute of Criminology, Hebrew University of Jerusalem

Saghir, M.T. and Robins, E. (1969) Homosexuality: sexual behavior of the female homosexual. *Archives of General Psychiatry, 20,* 192-201

Saghir, M.T. and Robins, E. (1971) Male and female homosexuality: Natural history. *Compehensive Psychiatry, 12,* 503-10

Saghir, M.T. and Robins, E. (1973) *Male and Female Homosexuality: A Comprehensive Investigation.* Baltimore: Williams and Wilkins

Sambrooks, Jean E. and MacCulloch, M.J. (1973) A modification of the Sexual Orientation Method and an automated technique for presentation and scoring. *British Journal of Social and Clinical Psychology, 12,* 163-74

Sanders, J. (1934) Homosexucele Tweelingen. *Ned Tijdschr Geunesk, 78,* 3346-52

Santrock, J.W. (1970) Paternal absence, sex-typing, and identification. *Developmental Psychology, 2,* 264-72

Sappho (transl. by Barnstone, W.) (1965) *Lyrics.* New York: Doubleday, Anchor

Saul, L.J. and Beck, A.J. (1961) Psychodynamics of male homosexuality. *International Journal of Psycho-Analysis, 42,* 43-8

Saunders, N. (ed.) (1974) *Alternative London/4.* London: Wildwood House

Sawyer, Ethel (1965) *A study of a public lesbian community.* Master's Thesis, Washington University

Schneck, J.M. (1950) Some aspects of homosexuality in relation to hypnosis. *Psychoanalytic Review*, *37*, 351-7

Schnelle, J.F. *et al.* (1974) Pupillary response as indication of sexual preference in a juvenile correctional institution. *Journal of Clinical Psychology*, *30*, 146-50

Schofield, M. (1964) Social aspects of homosexuality: *British Journal of Venereal Diseases*, *40*, 129-34

Schofield, M. (1965a) *Sociological Aspects of Homosexuality: A Comparative Study of Three Types of Homosexuals*. London: Longmans

Schofield, M. (1965b) *The Sexual Behaviour of Young People*. London: Longmans

Schreber, D.P. (1903) *Memoirs of my Nervous Illness* (transl. and ed. by Macalpine, Ida and Hunter, R.A., 1955). London: Dawson

Schrenck-Notzing, A. von (1895) *Die Suggestions-Therapie bei Krankhaften Erscheinungen des Geschlechtsinnes mit besonderer Berücksichtigung der conträren Sexualempfindung*. Stuttgart: von Ferdinandenke

Schur, E.M. (1965) *Crimes without Victims – Deviant Behavior and Public Policy*. Englewood Cliffs, N.J.: Prentice Hall

Schwartz, B.J. (1956) An empirical test of two Freudian hypotheses concerning castration anxiety. *Journal of Personality*, *24*, 318-27

Scott, P.D. (1964) Definition, classification, prognosis and treatment. In Rosen, I.

Scott, T.R., Wells, W.H., Wood, Dorothy Z. and Morgan, D.I. (1967) Pupillary response and sexual interest reexamined. *Journal of Clinical Psychology*, *23*, 433-8

Sears, R.R. Maccoby, Eleanor E. and Levin, H. (1957) *Patterns of Child Rearing*. New York: Harper

Sechrist, L. and Flores, L. (1969) Homosexuality in the Philippines and in the United States: The handwriting on the wall. *Journal of Social Psychology*, *79*, 3-12

Seidman, R.B. (1966) *Law in Africa* (Number 21). Lagos: African Universities Press. London: Sweet and Maxwell

Selling, L. (1931) The pseudo-family. *American Journal of Sociology*, *37*, 247-53

Serban, G. (1968) The existential therapeutic approach to homosexuality. *American Journal of Psychotherapy*, *22*, 491-501

Serber, M. and Keith, Claudia G. (1974) The Atascadero Project: Model of a sexual retraining program for incarcerated pedophiles. *Journal of Homosexuality*, *1*, 87-97

Sevringhaus, E.L. and Chornyak, J. (1945) A study of homosexual adult males (17 ketosteroid assays). *Psychosomatic Medicine*, *7*, 302-5

S.I.E.C.U.S. (1973) *Homosexuality: Study Guide No.2.* (revised edition) New York: Sex Information and Education Council of the U.S.

Sharma, U.D. and Rudy, W.C. (1970) *Homosexuality: A Select Bibliography*. Waterloo, Ontario: Waterloo Lutheran University

Shearer, M. (1966) Homosexuality and the pediatrician: Early recognition and preventive counselling. *Clinical Pediatrics*, *5*, 514-18

Sheldon, W.H. (1949) *Varieties of Delinquent Youth*. New York: Harper

Shoor, M., Speed, Mary H. and Bartelt, Claudia (1966) Syndrome of the adolescent child molester. *American Journal of Psychiatry*, *122*, 783-9

Sidney, P. (1912) *The Countess of Pembroke's Arcadia*. London: Cambridge University Press

Siegelman, M. (1972a) Adjustment of male homosexuals and heterosexuals. *Archives of Sexual Behaviour*, *2*, 9-25

Siegelman, M. (1972b) Adjustment of homosexual and heterosexual women. *British Journal of Psychiatry*, *120*, 477-81

Siegelman, M. (1973) Birth order and family size of homosexual men and women. *Journal of Consulting and Clinical Psychology*, *41*, 164

Siegelman, M. (1974a) Parental background of male homosexuals and heterosexuals. *Archives of Sexual Behavior*, *3*, 3-18

Siegelman, M. (1974b) Parental background of homosexual and heterosexual women. *British Journal of Psychiatry*, *124*, 14-21

Sieveking, N.A. (1972) Behavioral therapy – Bag of tricks or point of view? Treatment for homosexuality. *Psychotherapy: Theory, Research and Practice*, *9*, 32-5

Silverman, D. and Rosanoff, W.R. (1945) Electroencephalographic and neurological studies of homosexuals. *Journal of Nervous and Mental Disease, 101,* 311-21

Silverman, L.H., Kwawer, J.S., Wolitzky, Carol and Coron, M. (1973) An experimental study of aspects of the psychoanalytic theory of male homosexuality. *Journal of Abnormal Psychology, 82,* 178-88

Simon, R.I. (1967) A case of female transsexualism. *American Journal of Psychiatry, 123,* 1598-601

Singer, M.I. (1970) Comparison of indicators of homosexuality on the MMPI. *Journal of Consulting and Clinical Psychology, 34,* 15-18

Singer, M. and Fischer, Ruth (1967) Group psychotherapy of male homosexuals by a male and female co-therapy team. *International Journal of Group Psychotherapy, 17,* 44-52

Slater, E. (1962) Birth order and maternal age of homosexuals. *Lancet, (i),* 69-71

Slater, M.R. (1964) *Sex Offenders in Group Therapy. As Told to George Bishop.* Los Angeles: Sherbourne Press

Slovenko, R. (ed.) (1965) *Sexual Behaviour and the Law.* Springfield, Ill. C.C. Thomas

Smith, C.E. (1954) The homosexual federal offender: A study of 100 cases. *Journal of Criminal Law, Criminology and Police Science, 44,* 582-92

Smith, A.B. and Bassin, A. (1959) Group psychotherapy with homosexuals. *Journal of Social Therapy, 5,* 225-32

Socarides, C.W. (1968) *The Overt Homosexual.* New York: Grune and Stratton

Soddy, K. (1954) Homosexuality. *Lancet, (ii),* 541-46

Solyom, L. and Beck, P.R. (1967) GSR assessment of aberrant sexual behavior. *International Journal of Neuropsychiatry, 3,* 52-9

Sonenschein, D. (1968) The ethnography of male homosexual relations. *Journal of Sex Research, 4,* 69-83

Sparrow, G. (1966) *Satan's Children.* London: Odham's Books

'Spartacus'(1976) *International Gay Guide.* Amsterdam: Euro-Spartacus

Spencer, S.J.G. (1959) Homosexuality among Oxford undergraduates. *Journal of Mental Science, 105,* 393-405

Stanley-Jones, D. (1947) Royal Society of Medicine symposium on homosexuality. *Medical Press,* September, 213

Stearn, J. (1965) *The Grapevine.* New York: Macfadden-Bartell

Stephan, W.G. (1973) Parental relationships and early social experiences of activist male homosexuals and male heterosexuals. *Journal of Abnormal Psychology, 82,* 506-13

Stephens, W.N. (1963) *The Family in Cross-Cultural Perspective.* New York: Holt, Rinehart and Winston

Stevenson, I. and Wolpe, J. (1960) Recovery from sexual deviations through overcoming non-sexual neurotic responses. *American Journal of Psychiatry, 116,* 737-42

Stoller, R.J. (1968) *Sex and Gender.* New York: Science House

Stoller, R.J. (1969) Parental influences in male transsexualism. In Green, R. and Money, J.

Stoller, R.J. (1972) Etiological factors in female transsexualism: A first approximation. *Archives of Sexual Behavior, 2,* 47-64

Stoller, R.J. *et al.* (1973) A symposium: Should homosexuality be in the APA nomenclature? *American Journal of Psychiatry, 130,* 1207-16

Stone, Rolling (pseudonym) (1973) Places: The Continental Baths. *Lunch, No.22,* 15-16

Storr, A. (1964) *Sexual Deviation.* Harmondsworth: Penguin Books

Strain, F. (1948) *The Normal Sex Interests of Children from Infancy to Adolescence.* New York: Appleton Century

Sturgess, B. (1975) *No Offence: The Case for Homosexual Equality at Law.* Manchester: Campaign for Homosexual Equality

Sturup, G.K. (1968) *Treatment of Sexual Offenders in Herstedvester Denmark* (The Third Isaac Ray Lecture). Copenhagen: Munksgaard

Sturup, G.K. (1972) Castration: The total treatment. *International Psychiatry Clinics, 8,* (No.4) *Treatment of the Sex Offender,* 175-96. Boston: Little, Brown

Suetonius (transl. Graves, R.) (1957) *The Twelve Caesars.* Harmondsworth: Penguin Books

Summers, M. (transl.) (1928) *Malleus Maleficarum.* London: J. Rodker

Swanson, D.W. (1968) Adult sexual abuse of children. *Diseases of the Nervous System, 29,* 677-83

Swanson, D.W., *et al.* (1972) Clinical features of the female homosexual patient: A comparison with the heterosexual patient. *Journal of Nervous and Mental Disease, 155,* 119-24

Swartzburg, M., Schwarty, A.H., Lieb, J. and Slaby, A.E. (1972) Dual suicide in homosexuals. *Journal of Nervous and Mental Disease, 155,* 125-30

Sykes, G.M. (1958) *The Society of Captives.* Princeton, N.J.: Princeton University Press

Symmers, W. St. C. (1968) Carcinoma of breast in trans-sexual individuals after surgical and hormonal interference with the primary and secondary sex characteristics. *British Medical Journal, (ii),* 83-5

Symonds, J.A. (1891) A Problem in Modern Ethics, being an enquiry into the phenomenon of sexual inversion. London: Reprinted in Cory, D.W. (1956)

Szasz, T.S. (1965) Legal and moral aspects of homosexuality. In Marmor, J. (ed.),

Tanner, J.M. (1961) *Education and Physical Growth.* London: London University Press

Tarnowsky, B. (1967) *Anthropological, Legal and Medical Studies on Pederasty in Europe* (translated). North Hollywood, California: Brandon House

Taylor, A.J.W. (1965) The significance of 'Darls' or special relationships for borstal girls. *British Journal of Criminology, 5,* 406-18

Taylor, F. Kräupl (1966) *Psychopathology: its Causes and Symptoms.* London: Butterworth

Taylor, G.R. (1953) *Sex in History.* London: Thames and Hudson

Taylor, G.R. (1958) *The Angel Makers.* London: Heinemann

Taylor, G.R. (1965) Historical and mythological aspects of homosexuality. In Marmor, J.

Teal, D. (1971) *The Gay Militants.* New York: Stein and Day

Tennent, G., Bancroft, J.H.J. and Cass, J. (1974) The control of deviant sexual behaviour by drugs: a double-blind controlled study of benperidol, chlorpromazine and placebo. *Achives of Sexual Behavior, 3,* 261-71

Terman, L.M. and Miles, Catherine C. (1936) *Sex and Personality.* New York: McGraw-Hill

Thompson, Clara (1947) Changing concepts of homosexuality in psycho-analysis. *Psychiatry, 10,* 183-9

Thompson, G.N. (1949) Electroshock and other therapeutic considerations in sexual psychopathy. *Journal of Nervous and Mental Disease, 109,* 531-9

Thompson, N.L., McCandless, B.R. and Strickland, B.R. (1971) Personal adjustment of male and female homosexuals and heterosexuals. *Journal of Abnormal Psychology, 78,* 237-40

Thompson, N.L., Schwartz, D.M., McCandless, B.R. and Edwards, D.A. (1973) Parent-child relationships and sexual identity in male and female homosexuals and heterosexuals. *Journal of Consulting and Clinical Psychiatry, 41,* 120-7

Thomson, R.C. (1928) *The Epic of Gilgamish* (A new translation from a collation of the cuneiform tablets in the British Museum). London: Luzac

Thorpe, J.G., Schmidt, E., Brown, P. and Castell, D. (1964) Aversion relief therapy: a new method for general application. *Behaviour Research and Therapy, 2,* 71-82

Thorpe, J.G., Schmidt, E. and Castell, D. (1964) A comparison of positive and negative (aversive) conditioning in the treatment of homosexuality. *Behaviour Research and Therapy, 1,* 357-62

Tiller, P.O. (1967) Parental role division and the child's personality development. In Dahlstrom, E. (ed.), *The Changing Roles of Men and Women.* London: Duckworth

Timms, N. (1968) *Rootless in the City.* London: National Council of Social Service

Tinbergen, N. (1964) Aggression and fears in the normal sexual behaviour of some animals. In Rosen, I.

Tobin, Kay and Wicker, R. (eds.) (1972) *The Gay Crusaders*. New York: Coronet Paperback Library

Tolsma, F.J. (1957) *De betekenis van de verleiding in homefiele ontwikkelingen*. Amsterdam: Psychiatric-juridical Society

Tong, J.E. (1960) Galvanic skin response studies of sex responsiveness in sex offenders and others. *Journal of Mental Science, 106*, 1475-85

Toobert, S., Bartelme, K. and Jones, E. (1959) Some factors related to pedophilia. *International Journal of Social Psychiatry, 4*, 272-9

Tourney, G. and Hatfield, L.M. (1973) Androgen metabolism in schizophrenics, homosexuals and normal controls. *Biological Psychiatry, 6*, 23-36

Troubridge, Una (1963) *The Life of Radclyffe Hall*. New York: Citadel Press

Turner, R.K., Pielmaier, H., James, S. and Orwin, A. (1974) Personality characteristics of male homosexuals referred for aversion therapy: A comparative study. *British Journal of Psychiatry, 125*, 447-9

Tyler, P. (1973) *Screening the sexes: Homosexuality in the movies*. Garden City, New York: Anchor

Ullerstam, L. (transl. Hollo, A.) (1966) *The Erotic Minorities: A Sexual Bill of Rights*. New York: Grove Press

United States Senate Committee (1950) *Employment of Homosexuals and other Sex Perverts in Government*. Senate Document 241, 81st Congress, 2nd Session

Van den Haag (1963) Notes on homosexuality and its cultural setting. In Ruitenbeek, H.M.

Van Gulik, R.H. (1961) *Sexual Life in Ancient China*. Leiden: E.J. Brill

Van Schumann, H.J. (1965) *Homosexualität und Selbstmord*. Hamburg: Kriminalistik Verlag

Vassall, J. (1975) *Vassall: The Autobiography of a Spy*. London: Sidgwick and Jackson

Vedder, C.P. and King, Patricia G. (1967) *Problems of Homosexuality in Corrections*. Springfield, Ill. C.C. Thomas

Vidal, G. (1960) *The Best Man*. Boston: Little, Brown

Wade, C. (1965) *Male Homosexuality: Case Studies*. New York: LS Publications

Wälinder, J. (1967) *Transsexualism: A Study of Forty-three Cases*. Göteborg: Scandinavian University Books

Wälinder, J. (1971) Incidence and sex ratio of transsexualism in Sweden. *British Journal of Psychiatry, 119*, 195-6

Walker, N. and Argyle, M. (1964) Does the law affect moral judgements? *British Journal of Criminology, 4*, 570-81

Ward, D.A. and Kassebaum, G.G. (1965) *Women's Prison: Sex and Social Structure*. Chicago: Aldine

Ward, Ingeborg (1972) Prenatal stress feminizes and demasculinizes the behavior of males. *Science, 175*, 82-5

Ward, Ingeborg L. and Renz, F.J. (1972) Consequences of perinatal hormone manipulation on the adult sexual behavior of female rats. *Journal of Comparative and Physiological Psychology, 78*, 349-55

Ward, J.L. (1958) Homosexual behavior of the institutionalized delinquent. *Psychiatric Quarterly Supplement, 32*, 301-14

Warren, Carol A.B. (1974) *Identity and Community in the Gay World*. New York: Wiley

Waugh, M.A. (1972) Studies on the recent epidemiology of early syphilis in West London. *British Journal of Venereal Diseases, 48*, 534-51

Weideman, G.H. (1962) Surveys of psychoanalytic literature on overt male homosexuality. *Journal of the American Psychoanalytic Association, 10*, 386-409

Weigall, A. (1933) *Sappho of Lesbos: Her Life and Times*. New York: Stokes

Weinberg, G. (1972) *Society and the Healthy Homosexual*. New York: St. Martin's Press

Weinberg, M.S. and Bell, A.P. (1972) *Homosexuality: An Annotated Bibliography* New York: Harper and Row

Weinberg, M.S. and Williams, C.J. (1974) *Male Homosexuals: their Problems and Adaptations*. London: Oxford University Press

Weisman, A.D. (1967) Self-destruction and sexual perversion. In Shneidman, E.S (ed.), *Essays in Self Destruction*. New York: Science House

Wellman, M. (1956) Overt homosexuality with spontaneous remission. *Canadian Medical Association Journal, 75*, 273-79

West, D.J. (1959) Parental relationships in male homosexuality. *International Journal of Social Psychiatry, 5*, 85-97

West, D.J. (ed.) (1970) *Criminological Implications of Chromosome Abnormalities.* Cambridge: Institute of Criminology

West, L.J., Doidge, W.T. and Williams, R.L. (1958) An approach to the problem of homosexuality in the military service. *American Journal of Psychiatry, 115*, 392-401

West, L.J. and Glass, A.J. (1965) Sexual behaviour and the military law. In Slovenko, R.

West, Rebecca (1963) *The Vassall Affair.* London: Sunday Telegraph

Westermarck, E. (1906) Homosexual love. In Cory, D.W. (1956)

Westermarck, E. (1939) *Christianity and Morals.* London: Kegal Paul

Westwood, G. (1952) *Society and the Homosexual.* London: Gollancz

Westwood, G. (1960) *A Minority.* London: Longmans

Wheeler, W.M. (1949) An analysis of Rorschach indices of male homosexuality. *Journal of Projective Techniques, 13*, 97-126

Which? (1974) *Sex With Health: guide to contraception, abortion and sex-related diseases.* London: Consumers' Association

Whitaker, L.H. (1959) Oestrogen and psychosexual disorders. *Medical Journal of Australia, 46*, 547-9

Whitaker, L. (1961) The use of an extended Draw-a-Person Test to identify homosexual and effeminate men. *Journal of Consulting Psychology, 25*, 482-5

Whitaker, L.H. (1964) Lysergic acid diethylamide in psychotherapy. *Medical Journal of Australia*, (i) 5-8, (ii) 36-41

Whitener, R.W. and Nikelly, A.G. (1964) Sexual deviation in College students. *American Journal of Orthopsychiatry, 34*, 486-92

Wilbur, Cornelia B. (1965) Clinical aspects of female homosexuality. In Marmor, J.

Wildeblood, P. (1955) *Against the Law.* London: Weidenfeld and Nicolson

Willcox, R.R. (1973) Homosexuality and Venereal Disease in the United Kingdom (Compiled for the British Co-operative Clinical Group). *British Journal of Venereal Diseases, 49*, 329-34

Williams, C.J. and Weinberg, M.S. (1971) *Homosexuals and the Military: A Study of Less than Honorable Discharge.* New York: Harper and Row

Williams, E. (1973) *Emlyn: An Early Autobiography.* London: Bodley Head

Williams, T. (1958) *Suddenly Last Summer.* New York: New Directions

Williams, V.L. and Fish, Mary (1974) *Convicts, Codes and Contrabands: The Prison Life of Men and Women.* Cambridge, Mass.: Ballinger

Willis, S.E. (1967) *Understanding and Counselling the Male Homosexual.* Boston: Little, Brown

Wilson, A. (1952) *Hemlock and After.* London: Secker and Warburg

Wilson, M. and Green, R. (1971) Personality characteristics of female homosexuals. *Psychological Reports, 28*, 407-12

Wittman, C. (1974) Gay Liberation Manifesto. In Radical Therapist (eds.), *The Radical Therapist Collective.* Harmondsworth: Penguin Books

Wolff, Charlotte (1971) *Love Between Women.* London: Duckworth

Wolman, B.B. (1967) Interactional treatment of homosexuality. *Psychotherapy and Psychosomatics, 15*, 70 (abstract)

Woodcock, K.R. (1971) Re-appraising the effect on incubating syphilis of treatment for gonorrhoea. *British Journal of Venereal Diseases, 47*, 95-101

Woods, S.W. (1972) Violence: Psychotherapy of pseudohomosexual panic. *Archives of General Psychiatry, 27*, 255-8

Woodward, L.T. (1958) Homosexual panic. Reprinted in Rubin, I. (ed.)

Woodward, Mary (1958) The diagnosis and treatment of homosexual offenders. *British Journal of Delilnquency, 9*, 44-59

Woodward, R. *et al.* (1973) A comparison of two scoring systems for the Sexual Orientation Method. *British Journal of Social and Clinical Psychology, 12*, 411-14

Wortis, J. (1937) A note on the body-build of the male homosexual. *American Journal of Psychiatry, 93*, 1121-5

Wortis, J. (1940) Intersexuality and effeminacy in a male homosexual. *American Journal of Orthopsychiatry, 10*, 567-9

Wyden, P. and Wyden, Barbara (1968) *Growing up Straight: What every thoughtful parent should know about homosexuality.* New York: Stein and Day

Wysor, Bettie (1974) *The Lesbian Myth: Insights and Conversations.* New York: Random House

Wyss, R. (1967) *Unzucht mit Kindern.* Berlin: Heidelberg

Yamamoto, T. (1962) Hormonic factors affecting gonadal differentiation in fish. *General and Comparative Endocrinology, 1,* (Suppl.) 341-5

Yankowski, J.S. and Wolff, H.R. (1965) *The Tortured Sex.* Los Angeles: Holloway House

Yarrow, L.J. (1954) The relationship between nutritive sucking experiences in infancy and non-nutritive sucking in childhood. *Journal of Genetic Psychology, 84*, 149-62

Yugoslavia (1964) *Criminal Code.* Belgrade: Institute of Comparative Law

Zamansky, H.S. (1956) A technique for assessing homosexual tendencies. *Journal of Personality, 24*, 436-48

Zlotlow, M. and Paganini, A.E. (1959) Autoerotic and homoerotic manifestations in hospitalized male postlobotomy patients. *Psychiatric Quarterly, 33*, 490-7

Zuckerman, M. (1971) Physiological measures of sexual arousal in the human. *Psychological Bulletin, 75*, 297-329

Zuger, B. (1970) The role of familial factors in persistent effeminate behavior in boys. *American Journal of Psychiatry, 126*, 1167-70

INDEX